The Zimbabwe African People's Union 1961-87

The Zimbabwe African People's Union 1961-87

A POLITICAL HISTORY OF INSURGENCY IN SOUTHERN RHODESIA

Eliakim M. Sibanda

Africa World Press, Inc.

P.O. Box 1892
Trenton, NJ 08607

P.O. Box 48
Asmara, ERITREA

Africa World Press, Inc.

P.O. Box 1892
Trenton, NJ 08607

P.O. Box 48
Asmara, ERITREA

Copyright © 2005 Eliakim M. Sibanda
First Printing 2005

All rights reserved. No part of this publication may be reproduced, stored in a retrieval system or transmitted in any form or by any means electronic, mechanical, photocopying, recording or otherwise without the prior written permission of the publisher.

Book and Cover design: Sam Saverance

Library of Congress Cataloging-in-Publication Data

Sibanda, Eliakim M.
  The Zimbabwe African People's Union, 1961-87 : a political history of insurgency in Southern Rhodesia / Eliakim M. Sibanda.
    p. cm.
  Includes bibliographical references and index.
  ISBN 1-59221-275-1 -- ISBN 1-59221-276-X (pbk.)
  1. Zimbabwe African People's Union--History. 2. Zimbabwe--Politics and government--1965-1979. 3. Zimbabwe--Politics and government--1980- I. Title.

DT2981.S55 2004
968.91'04--dc22

2004012196

To My People!

Table of Contents

Preface ix

Chapter 1: Introduction 1

Chapter 2: The Land and Its People 9

Chapter 3: Gestation Stage: Zapu Reincarnation – Sranc and Ndp 33

Chapter 4: The Founding of Zapu, Leadership, Split and Struggle, 1961-69 71

Chapter 5: Evaluation, Introspection and Re-organization: Zapu Looks on Its Inside, 1960-71 121

Chapter 6: The Storm and then Spears Turned into Plowshares: Zapu Goes on Military and then Peace Offensive, 1972-79 161

Chapter 7: The Best and The Worst of Times: Zapu Post-Independence to the Time of Its Demise, 1980-87 237

Glossary 305

Appendix 1: The ZANU (PF) and PF ZAPU Agreement 307

Appendix 2: Zimbabwe Declaration of Unity 308

Appendix 3: Declaration of Intention to Negotiate a Settlement 309

Appendix 4: The Agreement 311

Appendix 5: PF Assembly and Rendezvous Points 312

Index 315

Preface

Purpose Of The Book

This book is an exploration of the political history of insurgency in Southern Rhodesia, with particular reference to the Zimbabwe African People's Union (ZAPU). Formed on December 17, 1961, ZAPU became the first revolutionary, national, movement to explicitly call for majority rule on the basis of one-man one vote.

During the early years of its struggle, ZAPU employed non-violent means to try and achieve its goal for majority rule and a non-racial society. Because of the belligerency of the White settler regime, ZAPU added the armed resistance to its strategy of non-violence, and went on to build a formidable army. During the struggle, ZAPU contributed diplomatically and militarily towards the liberation of Zimbabwe. In 1980 it lost elections to its compatriot party, the Zimbabwe African National Union, but joined the government at the invitation of the latter.

The marriage of convenience between the two parties dissolved in less than three years, and what followed was the unconscionable persecution of ZAPU members and the AmaNdebele, the people who formed the core of ZAPU, by ZANU in its drive for a one-party state. The party's resistance of intimidation and violence for more than five years, helped foster a climate of political pluralism in the country, the climate that was further enhanced by the use of theater by some of its members, who dramatized the grievances. Tired of being hunted down, and also seeing its own members butchered, the ZAPU leadership decided to merge its party with the ruling party on December 22, 1987

Organization

The book is organized in seven chapters. The first chapter provides an introduction and a statement of the problem. The second chapter presents the history of the people of Zimbabwe before colonization, specifically addressing the relationship between the two major ethnic groups: the AmaNdebele and AmaShona. The effects of colonization on the indigenous people are also discussed here. Chapter three looks into political activities that occurred before the founding of ZAPU, particularly between 1950 and 1960, and the politics that formed the context of their founding.

The fourth chapter deals with the founding of ZAPU, and its first major split, which resulted in the formation of ZANU. Also discussed in this chapter is the proscription of the party, which was followed by either the incarceration or exile of many of its leaders and supporters. The period covered in this chapter is between 1961-1969.

Chapter five concentrates on the evaluation of ZAPU's activities in the 1960s and the process of its self-examination and reorganization. Basically this chapter looks into the party's life in exile and the activities of its supporters inside Rhodesia with regard to the liberation struggle. Again, in this chapter I intend to explore external factors that influenced the existence of ZAPU. The people's revolution in Zimbabwe had regional and international dimensions. On the regional level, ZAPU received both moral and material support from the Frontline States, while the Smith regime, against which the nationalists were fighting, had South Africa as its patron.

On the international level, there existed a tri-polar situation whereby ZAPU depended on the Soviet Union and Eastern Europe for moral and material support, ZANU on China, and the Smith regime on the Western States. Hopefully this discussion on a tri-polar relationship will provide a model with respect to the role of patrons in conflict resolution situations for other liberation groups, or groups dealing with situations of conflicts. The section will also look into ZAPU's attempts at joint operations with FRELIMO, ZANLA and ANC's *Umkhonto We Sizwe* (The Spear of the Nation).

Chapter six looks into ZAPU's prosecution of war and its pursuit for a peaceful settlement through negations, leading to the Lancaster House Conference, where finally a peaceful settlement was reached between the warring groups. Because not much has been written on the military operations of this party, I concentrated more on ZAPU's military activities than on the time the party spent pursuing peaceful negotiations or talking unity with its nationalist opponents. Thus, this is a chapter on ZAPU's military and peace offensive between 1972 and 1979.

The last chapter deals with ZAPU's role in the post-independence era, until the time it merged with the ruling party, ZANU, in 1987. Here is discussed the darkest period in Zimbabwean history when the ruling party practiced carnage against ZAPU members in an endeavor to force ZAPU to merge with ZANU. Also covered are activities of democratization that ZAPU members performed through theater. The chapter concludes the work with an overall discussion of the findings.

ACKNOWLEDGEMENTS

No work is ever the result of the efforts of an individual and/or his or her committee alone. This study is no exception; it has developed over the years and has benefited from many people. I am indebted to my dissertation advisor, Professor Ralph Mann for his direction, encouragement and understanding, and the rest of the members of dissertation committee for their unreserved

Preface

assistance and guidance. I can never be thankful enough for the hours he spent reading draft after draft of my work, and also being my advocate in a complex University bureaucracy.

I am also grateful to all my people, especially those in the Mtshabezi area. I deeply thank you for nurturing in me an appreciation for the struggle for freedom, and dedication to the spirit and ideals of democracy. My friends and colleagues in the academy also deserve my profound thanks for their encouragement and inspiration. They have always provided the support I needed at very crucial times. Of special mention is Dr Andrew DeRoche, who provided me with a lot of encouragement and invaluable sources for my work.

My parents and extended family deserve the lion's share of my appreciation: I thank you all for teaching me the importance of education, even during the "ugly" years of colonialism. Thank you for instilling in me the spirit of dedication to the ideals of freedom and democracy by both precept and example.

Last but not least, I am grateful to my wife and our children. I can never adequately express my heart-felt gratitude for your unfailing love and support over the years. You have always been my anchor and beacon during stormy times, as well as a source of laughter and joy!

E.M.S.
WINNIPEG, CANADA
AUGUST 2003

Chapter 1
INTRODUCTION

There have been many studies done on 'great' revolutions in such places as England, France, Russia and China.[1] After the World War II a sizeable number of surveys of the post-colonial revolutions and those of twentieth century Latin America appeared.[2] Thus, up until 1970, France, Russia, and China usually formed the basis for the study of revolutions. However, from 1970 and on, these paradigms failed to capture the dynamics of revolutions in such places as the Philippines, Poland, Iran, Nicaragua, South Africa and Palestine. In Zimbabwe and South Africa, the revolution pitted a majority black population against a white minority rule. Thus the revolution had a racial dimension. This racial variable is total absent in the classic situations of revolution that have been used as a basis for studying liberation movements prior to 1970, so that any study of these them should yield new information on revolutionary situations post-1970.

In Zimbabwe, as elsewhere in Africa, the history of black struggle against white minority rule was a long one. Black Zimbabweans locate the beginning of their resistance to white rule in the 1890's when their ancestors rose against the first white settlers to try and stop them from settling on their land.[3] This study, however, is primarily concerned with the modern liberation struggle, which started its radical and militant phase in the early 1960s, and concentrates mostly on one black liberation movement.

Thus, this study is a political history of the Zimbabwe African People's Union (ZAPU), and its contributions towards the liberation of Zimbabwe. (Zimbabwe was known as Zimbabwe-Rhodesia during the last part of 1979, Rhodesia, from 1964 to the early part of 1979, and Southern Rhodesia from the early 1890s). Its thesis is that ZAPU made significant diplomatic and military contributions to the collapse of the colonial government, and thereafter to the ruling party's failure to introduce a de jure one-party rule. To establish my thesis, I narrate the history of ZAPU from its inception in 1961 to the time it merged with the ruling Party, the Zimbabwe African National Union (ZANU) in December 1987.[4]

The Zimbabwe African People's Union 1961-1987

Essentially, this is an account of the liberation struggle in Zimbabwe by the nationalist liberation movements, with a special focus on ZAPU. It should be made clear from the beginning what this study is not. It does not pretend to be a final word on the history of ZAPU, neither is it a comprehensive history of all the nationalist movements of Southern Rhodesia. Since there were two major nationalist groups, ZAPU and ZANU, that waged the war of liberation during the struggle, one would expect this study to deal with both of these movements in an equal way. However, this is not the case. This study does not deal in any substantial way with ZANU. While acknowledging the contributions ZANU made in the fighting for the liberation of Zimbabwe, I do not discuss that aspect in detail. The reason for not discussing ZANU's role in the liberation struggle extensively is because much has already been written on the subject.[5] Thus, ZANU and the other nationalist movements in colonial Southern Rhodesia make their appearance in this study only as they impinge on ZAPU.

I have tried to offer just enough information about these other groups to make sense of ZAPU's political history and its contributions towards the liberation of Zimbabwe. Also, this study deals with the struggles of the AmaNdebele by way of indirection, since it is this people who made up the core of ZAPU.[6] The association of ZAPU with the AmaNdebele became even more pronounced immediately after independence when the government of Prime Minister Robert Mugabe's troops tortured and killed AmaNdebele indiscriminately because they were believed to be ZAPU, and when being ZAPU even became synonymous with being an Ndebele.[7]

One of the arguments that inform this study is that tribalism is destructive to nationalist movements, and ultimately to the nation. This is evident in how tribalism was used as a basis of a split in ZAPU at a crucial time of the struggle in the early 1960's, resulting in the founding of ZANU, and thereby undermining the strength of the nationalist movement, and also how it split ZAPU again in the 1970's. Last but not the least, it explains how tribalism undermined the formation of one Zimbabwean nation as the ruling Party exploited the tribal factor for its benefit. On the bright side we see ZAPU trying to reverse this tide of tribalism throughout its struggle and beyond independence, 1980.

I also posit that ZAPU's Liberation experiences were comparable but not identical to those of other Southern African Liberation movements such as the African National Congress (ANC), Front for the Liberation of Mozambique (FRELIMO), The People's Movement for the Liberation of Angola (MPLA) and ZANU, and that being the case that each experience must be included to arrive at a more comprehensive Southern African liberation historiography. Much has been said about differences in strategy between ZAPU and ZANU, leading readers to believe that the former operated on the Marxist-Leninist ideology and the later, on a Maoist one.

This conceptual distinction between these two parties is false, and supporting it leads to an inadequate rendition of these liberation movements,

Introduction

especially ZAPU, as its ascribed ideology cuts out the history of its relationship to the masses. Existential evidence points to the fact that all these nationalist parties, ZAPU included, were eclectic in their approach in that they borrowed freely from ideologies such as Maoist, Marxist-Leninist and Cuban models.[8]

1.1 Rationale and Contributions

There is a three-fold justification for conducting this study. First, there is a historiographical need for doing a historical narrative of ZAPU's history and its contributions towards the liberation of Zimbabwe. Studies on the liberation struggle in Southern Rhodesia by scholars[9] who sympathized with ZANU have tended to focus on ZAPU's wartime compatriot, ZANU, as the only legitimate expression of the liberation struggle.[10] Robert Mugabe is presented in this literature as a hero spearheading the war against the supremacist regime.

A good example of literature that elevated Mugabe to "messianic levels" is the book by David Martin and Phyllis Johnson's *The Struggle for Zimbabwe*. David Martin and Phyllis Martin, like other biographers of Mugabe, have given undue emphasis to his role in the liberation struggle but have not provided convincing documentation in support of their claims. Mugabe and ZANU are portrayed as having fought the hardest for the liberation of Zimbabwe, by authors who sound testimonial at best. Until solid evidence is provided, one is obliged to believe that his, and his party's alleged inordinate involvement in the fighting for the liberation of Zimbabwe remains unproven. Little wonder Martin and Johnson wrote the way they did because they were among the foreign writers commissioned by ZANU to write the history of the struggle so that it was portrayed as the leading, and perhaps only bona fide liberation movement.[11]

The same literature portrayed ZAPU as a reactionary movement. The end-result of this position was that ZAPU has been effectively excluded as a contributory force by Southern African liberation historiography. Writing in the *Daily News* on 12 July 1999 on the need to write the history of the liberation struggle so that it could be more representative, Nevanji Madanhire observed:

> *So far, the record of liberation struggle has been written very simplistically as follows: Colonization epitomized by Ian Smith was the villain; Robert Mugabe spearheading the war against institutionalized racism was the hero. Like all heroes he had to meet a few nuisances in his struggle for the common good. These nuisances were ZAPU...ZANU led by ... Sithole and UANC.*

Second, the exclusion of ZAPU's insurgency history has, in turn, resulted in a distorted Southern African Liberation Movements Historiography. This situation must be rectified for two crucial reasons:

1) A few scholars, especially after the independence of Zimbabwe, have started to write about the critical role ZAPU played both militarily and in negotiating for peace during the wartime.[12] The literature further indicates that ZAPU's contributions were quite different than that of other liberation Movements in Africa. This was true particularly with regard to

its military strategy and its attitude towards negotiations. The difference in its approach towards liberating Zimbabwe in and of itself is enough reason for one to write a history of this movement, as such a rendition might make a significant contribution to the Southern African Liberation Historiography.

2) ZAPU was the first mass liberation movement in Southern Rhodesia, and also the movement with the most years of existence at the time of independence. To date, no comprehensive work has been done on this party, in part because before independence its history was suppressed by authorities in the country, in part because those who had the inside information did not want to write anything on the party because of fear of compromising its war strategy. Immediately after independence, the government confiscated and destroyed most of ZAPU's documents[13] so that most of its history now is largely in individual possession in document form or people's memories. Because most of this precious information now exists in an easily "perishable state"[14] and because of the importance of publishing the history of ZAPU as the oldest mass political party in the country, there is a need to write the history of this party now.

This need to write a ZAPU history in this respect is necessitated by the fact that there is some information available on the party that could not be accessed before independence. Also, what is new in this area is that the potential of getting fresh information on this movement is great given the fact that those who were involved in one way or another in the war of liberation, can be interviewed on the subject. Thus this study has an advantage over previous work on ZAPU in that it has access to new information through oral sources and documentation that was hitherto unavailable. Otherwise, a history of national liberation in Southern Rhodesia, which excludes ZAPU, and the voices of its hitherto silenced majority, fails to capture crucial historical moments in the development of the liberation movements in Southern Rhodesia. A history of such an organization should also help in understanding how an insurgency group moved from moderation to militancy.

There is also a political benefit to such kind of study. How ZAPU was able to survive during and after the struggle for liberation, when it was under attack from within and without, is an intriguing story, which should provide valuable information on survival mechanisms of liberation movements. It also reveals behaviors, which might help us predict prospects and problems relating to nation building once the goal of independence has been achieved.

Third, there is a sense in which it can be said the history of ZAPU is the history of the AmaNdebele minority group in Zimbabwe. This is largely because the core membership of ZAPU constituted of the AmaNdebele. A preservation of this minority group is a worthy thing to do in and of itself. The history

Introduction

of ZAPU therefore becomes an interpretative narration of the AmaNdebele minority group's history. These reasons for writing the history of ZAPU also serve as the contributions made by this study to the literature on liberation movements and nation-building, particularly in Zimbabwe, and in general, in Africa and other developing countries where liberation wars are occurring.

Although the intention of this study is not to make generalizations about all nationalist movements in Zimbabwe, I believe a study of this nature can contribute to the understanding of the struggle for liberation, in general, by these groups.

It is in this sense that this study, on a broader scope, is about the struggle for liberation by Zimbabwean nationalist movements against a white minority government. Also the study makes a contribution towards an understanding of conflict-resolution and peace-making in areas where armed revolution is about to take place or is already occurring

1.2 METHODOLOGY

My approach has been thematic rather than chronological. As such, repetition has not only been unavoidable but necessary. Because the struggle for Zimbabwe did not involve clear and huge positional military confrontations, which fell into a natural sequential order, but small scale attacks and ambushes that had basically similar patterns, trying to chronicle these chronologically and in detail would virtually bore most of the readers to death.

The study depended for its sources on documentary and oral sources. I interviewed mostly ZAPU former supporters, former members of its military wing as well as its leadership. As one who was an active ZAPU member, I also incorporated my own personal observations of ZAPU, and the general political developments in Zimbabwe. One is immediately faced by a problem of subjectivity as a participating observer since I am writing a history of a party of which I was a member. Also, a majority of my relatives played key roles as leaders of this party, and its soldiers.

In this context is it possible for me to have my research free of influences of personal bias particularly in the selection of interviewees? This is not to say subjectivity is only common in oral interviews where one is a participating observer as it occurs also in the interpretation of documentary evidence. For instance, can a researcher ever really know the mind of an original audience or author? Further complicating this whole hermeneutical question of non-bias is the fact that awareness of any kind of knowledge is a social construct, a reality that is shaped by the social environment and personal interests of the knower. As such, we are able to read into texts from another era our own bias.[15]

How does an historian maintain that critical distance between herself/himself in light of this reality? Beneath this question of objectivity, there lurks a persisting "Cartesian anxiety."[16] Within this realm, the admonitions are: aim at objective knowledge totally free of personal bias or values, and be indifferent to what you are writing about. Knowing what is subjective or objective is the beginning of solving the problem of one being too emotionally involved with their subject. However, one would have to be a prisoner permanently kept behind Rawls' veil of ignorance to fail to notice the dilemma and social condition which calls upon historians to be objective in the same way as a natural scientist.

As a result of these observations, I have tried to be scholarly in my work in the following ways: One, by including various views on this party by outsiders, even those who did not appraise the party in favorable terms. Hopefully, the reader would be able to arrive at her/his own conclusion after being exposed to these various and differing perspectives. Two, one way to consciously and intentionally mitigate the problem of being a participant-observer is to focus on the social scientific ethical guidelines of the research at hand.[17] In addition, I consulted with the scientific community[18] at conferences where I presented in order to ensure the validity and reliability of the data gathered. It is very common in research to make use of the insights of others who have awareness of the problem under study. To that end I have scrutinized and compared my sources.

Three, also as an attempt to be objective, I used neutral terms. During the war of liberation, Africans generally referred to this country as Zimbabwe, and the whites as Southern Rhodesia and Rhodesia respectively. Africans called the white regime soldiers, imperialist, racist soldiers or mercenaries, and they themselves were referred to as terrorists by the latter. I use the names Zimbabwe, Southern Rhodesia, and Rhodesia interchangeably. The white regime soldiers are referred to as the security forces and their opponents, guerrillas or freedom fighters.

ENDNOTES

1. See Crane Brinton, *The Anatomy of Revolution*, Revised Edition (New York: Vintage, 1965); S.N. Eisenstadt, *Revolution and the Transformation of Societies A Comparative Study* (New York: Free Press, 1978);Theda Skocpol, *States and Social Revolutions: A Comparative Historical Analysis of France,Russia, and China* (Cambridge: Cambridge University Press, 1979); Jack Goldstone, "State Breakdown in the English Revolution: A New Synthesis" in the *American Journal of Sociology*, 92 (1986b), pp. 257-322.

2.. Gerard Chaliand, *Revolution in the Third World: Myths and Prospects* (New York: Viking, 1977); John Dunn, *Modern Revolutions: An Introduction to the Analysis of a Political Phenomenon* (Cambridge: CambridgUniversity Press, 1972); Susan Eckstein, "The Impact of Revolution on Social Welfare in Latin America" in *Theory and Society* II (1982), pp. 43-94; John Walton, *Reluctant Rebels: Comparative Studies of Revolution and Underdevelopment* (New York: Columbia University Press, 1984); Eric Wolf, *Peasant Wars of the Twentieth Century* (New York: Harper and Row, 1969).

3. O.T. Ranger, *Revolt in Southern Rhodesia, 1896-7: A Study in African Resistance*(London: Heinemann, 1967).

Introduction

4. Canaan S. Banana, *Turmoil and Tenacity: Zimbabwe 1890-1990* (Harare: The College Press, 1989), p. 288.

5. Blessing D. Maringapasi, "The Development of ZANLA Strategy of Guerrilla Warfare," B.A. thesis, University of Zimbabwe, 1983; Norma J. Kriger, "Rural Conflicts and the Struggle for Independence: The Case of Zimbabwe," Published dissertation, Massachusetts Institute of Technology, 1985; Kriger, *Zimbabwe's Guerrilla War: Peasant Voices* (Cambridge: Cambridge University Press, 1992; Kriger, "The Zimbabwean War of Liberation: Struggles Within the Struggle," in the *The Journal of Southern African Studies* 14, 2 (January 1988): 304-322; David Lan, *Guns and Rain. Guerrillas and Spirit Mediums in Zimbabwe* (Berkeley, University of California Press, 1985; Alec J.C. Pongweni, *Songs that Won the Liberation War* (Harare: CollegePress, 1982); Terence O. Ranger, *Peasant Consciousness and Guerrilla War in Zimbabwe: A Comparative Study* (Berkeley: University of California Press, 1985); David Martin and Phyllis Martin, *The Struggle for Zimbabwe: The Chimurenga War* (Harare: Zimbabwe Publishing House, 1981); Paresh Pandya, *Mao Tse-tung: An Investigation into ZANU's Strategies* (Braamfontein: Skotaville Publishers, 1988). Pandya's book developed out of his 1986 Masters thesis which he wrote for the University of South Africa. William Cyrus Reed, III, "From Liberation Movement to Government: ZANU and the Formation of the Foreign Policy of Zimbabwe," Ph.D. dissertation, Indiana University, 1990; K. Manungo "The Role of Peasants Played in the Zimbabwe War of Liberation: With Special Emphasis on Chiweshe District," Ph.D. dissertation, University of Ohio, 1991; J. McLaughlin, "The Catholic Church and Zimbabwe's War of Liberation," D. Phil. thesis, University of Zimbabwe, 1991; B.D. Maringapasi, "The Development of ZANLA Strategy of Guerrilla Warfare, 1964-1979," BA Honors thesis, University of Zimbabwe, 1983.

6. It is unfortunate but accurate that the core membership of ZAPU and ZANU reflects the ethnic make-up of their leadership. This is reflected mostly by the way they voted during elections. I will deal with elections later in the book.

7. For the division of party membership along language lines see, Masipula Sithole, *Zimbabwe Struggle Within Struggle* (Salisbury: Rujeko, 1979). For atrocities against AmaNdebele post-independence, see William Spring, *The Long Fields: Zimbabwe Since Independence* (London: Anchor Brendon Ltd., 1986); Richard Carver, *Zimbabwe: A Break with the Past? Human Rights and Political Unity, An African Watch Report* (London: Africa Watch Committee, 1989).

8. Just as Colin Stoneman and Lionel Cliffe accurately observed, no party nationalist party in Zimbabwe had Marxism as a prevailing ideology although both ZAPU and ZANU got their arms from Marxist countries (Colin Stoneman and Lionel Cliffe, *Zimbabwe: Politics, Economics and Society* (London: Printer Publishers Limited, 1989), p. 37. In an interview with Tor Sellstrom, Dumiso Dabengwa, former ZAPU's Head of Military Intelligence, said that countries that supported them did not require of them to subscribe to their ideologies, and this gave them the freedom to be whoever they wanted to be. [The same could be said about ZANU] (Tor Sellstrom, *Liberation in Southern Africa-Interviews from Angola, Mozambique, Namibia, South Africa, Zimbabwe, the Frontline and Sweden* (Stockholm: Elanders Gotab, 1999), pp. 209-212.

9. John Day, *International Nationalism: The Extra-Territorial Relations of Southern Rhodesia Nationalists* (London: Routledge and Kegan Paul, 1967); Michael Raeburn, *We Are Everywhere: Narratives from Rhodesian Guerrillas* (New York: Random House, 1979);

David Martin and Phyllis Johnson, *The Struggle for Zimbabwe: The Chimurenga War* (Harare: Zimbabwe Publishing House), 1981; Sithole, *Zimbabwe Struggle Within Struggle* (1979); D. Smith and C. Simpson, *Mugabe* (Salisbury: Sphere, 1981); Nathan Shamuyarira, *Crisis in Rhodesia* (New York: Transatlantic Arts, 1965).

10. ZAPU in a way encouraged this misrepresentation by not publicizing its political activities as extensively as ZANU did. Throughout the war, it seems ZAPU had deliberately imposed an almost black-out on the state in so far as information that could provide intelligence on the part of the regime was concerned. They invariably used code language, which happened to be in their own language and had an advantage of being not understood by their white enemies. They mostly depended on bush telegraph. Kees Maxey points to this paucity of self-generated information meant for the public on the part of ZAPU as contrasted with ZANU and the regime who issued more, and misleading ones for that matter, communiqués than ZAPU, (Kees Maxey, *The Fight for Zimbabwe: The Armed Conflict in Southern Rhodesia Since UDI* (London: Rex Collings Ltd., 1975), p. 141.

11. *The Daily News* (12 July, 1999), p. 12. David Martin and Phyllis Martin in their book *The Struggle for Zimbabwe: The Chimurenga War* (Harare: Zimbabwe Publishing House, 1981).

12. Terence Ranger and Ngwabi Bhebhe, eds, *Soldiers in Zimbabwe's Liberation War* (London: James Curry, 1991), pp. 24-35; 48-72; H. Ellert, *The Rhodesian Front War: Counter-Insurgency and Guerrilla War in Rhodesia 1962-1980* (Gweru: Mambo Press, 1989).

13. Ngwabi Bhebe and Terence Ranger, eds., *Soldiers in Zimbabwe's Liberation War* (London: James Currey, 1991), in the General Introduction, p.3.

14. "Perishable state" here refers to the conditions under which these documents are found and also the state in which it is kept. Most private individuals do not have the best of conditions that are conducive to storing printed materials for too long. Thus the documents that are in the hands of individuals are bound to perish sooner. People's memories have the same problem as well; people forget things the further removed there are from them time-wise. Consequently, collecting information from such sources sooner is always advisable.

15. Terry A. Veling, *Living in the Margins: International Communities and the Art of Interpretation* (New York: The Crossroad Publishing Company, 1996), p. Xiii.

16. Richard J. Bernstein, ed., *Beyond Objectivity and Relativism: Science, Hermeneutics and Praxis* (Philadelphia: Pennsylvania Press, 1983), p. 54.

17. *Ibid.*

18. *Ibid.* Lofland and Lofland recommend constant consultation by the researcher with a scientific community as one way of overcoming the difficulties associated with the insider-outsider syndrome.

Chapter 2
THE LAND AND ITS PEOPLE

For one to better understand the background of the ethnic groups that composed the ZAPU Party it is important to briefly investigate the immediate pre-colonial history of Zimbabwe. Equally important, one must appreciate the physical environment in which ZAPU carried its insurgency against the regime and the socio-economic milieu that formed the background to the formation of the movement. Therefore, a study of the physical features of Zimbabwe and its socio-economic structures is necessary.

It is befitting to ask why a history of the AmaNdebele and AmaShona prior to colonization is important, or linked with ZAPU's struggle. There are two reasons that present themselves as to why this history was connected to ZAPU's liberation struggle.

The first reason has to do with ZAPU's relationship to the Amatshe in Matebeleland. The Amatshe embodied the history, culture, and religion of the people of the land. As such they provided inspiration and direction for ZAPU nationalists and military cadres during the war. Ancestors made the connection between the pre-colonial history of the AmaNdebele and ZAPU. During the liberation struggle, spirit mediums spoke for the African ancestors and expressed their support for the guerrilla war, and hence Nkomo's visit to the *Ilitshe* in Dula during the early stages of the struggle in 1953.

In his autobiography, Joshua Nkomo, the leader of Zapu, wrote bout his visit to *Ilitshe* in Dula in Matebeleland, where he was told by the *uMlimu* that his people would gain power in a big war.[1] Also, Nkomo was promised protection in the forthcoming war.[2]

It was no coincidence therefore that Nkomo went to the *Ilitshe* in Dula to receive his commission from *uMlimu*. According to Zimangele Mpofu, the *Ilitshe* at Dula had a historical connection with war. She told of how in 1896 the spirit of the Dula *Ilitshe* which was known as *Ihloka Elibomvu* (The Red Axe), possessed Mtuwane Dhlodhlo, one of the leading Ndebele commanders. Zimangele said that the *Ihloka Elibomvu* gave Dhlodhlo the power to wage war, which was known in Matebeleland as the war of *Ihloka ELibomvu*, and when it was over, the power to negotiate.[3]

The second reason why it is important to discuss the pre-colonial times, mostly during this time when ZAPU was formed is that some essential issues that led to the armed struggle started unfolding between 1890 and 1961. The colonization of Zimbabwe in the 1890s began after the crushing of the AmaNdebele kingdom by the white settlers. Then began the divide-and-rule tactics, which sowed the seed of ethnic conflict between AmaNdebele and Shona that continued to the post-independence Zimbabwe, and made national unity difficult. The white version of the relationship between AmaNdebele and AmaShona which emerges from this study is that the AmaNdebele used to terrorize the AmaShona, kill their men and carry off with them the latter's women and children to their Kingdom.

Basically, according to this version, the AmaNdebele held the Shona who, were the rightful heirs to Zimbabwe, in slavery until the settlers themselves rescued them. It was shown in this study, however, that the settlers perpetuated this version of the relationship between the two ethnic groups in order to divide-and-rule them. While the facts support the assertion that AmaNdebele fought and defeated Shona people, and that the former used to carry out periodic raids against the latter, most of the atrocities were exaggerated and even multiplied.

By and large, the AmaNdebele kings, using their terrific skills of nation-building forged a nation out of diverse ethnic groups to form what is today known as the AmaNdebele nation. Thus, to understand Nkomo's way of trying to build a nation out of the various Zimbabwean people groups, one has to appreciate workings of King Lobengula on nation building, the second and last King of the AmaNdebele nation whom Nkomo not only resembled structurally, but in nation-building skills as well.

Nkomo also organized his army along the lines of the pillars of the AmaNdebele *ibutho* which were discipline, cohesion and respect for civilian lives. It is therefore against this background that we are to understand the reaching back into the pre-colonial through the colonial times in Zimbabwe.

Thus, many ZAPU supporters saw continuity in the armed struggle from *Impi YoMvukela* of the 1890s and the war of independence led by ZAPU. Nationalists and cadres made this connection known in speeches in rallies. It could also be witnessed in the revival of African history, culture and religion. The *Chronicle* of 23 October 1967 discussed the revival of the traditional Wednesday as a holy day with the support of Nkomo and his followers. With the commencement of the struggle pilgrimages to the *Amatshe* increased around the country.

In the 1970s, ZAPU guerrillas made the *Ilitshe* at Bembe in the Shashe Hills, a particular sacred place of resort. Thus, ZAPU's nationalist ideology incorporated at various levels, the power and discourse of African history, culture and religion. Consequently a study of pre-colonial history is vital in the understanding of ZAPU's ideology.

The Land and Its People

The third reason it is important to understand history of this era, is so that we can understand the main cause/s of the division among the Zimbabwean population, with a view to creating a nation at peace with itself. Zimbabweans are people composed of different ethnic and racial groups with different histories, culture and languages. As has been already shown in this chapter, one of the unfortunate fallout of the wars of the 1890's was the division of the Zimbabwean population along ethnic and racial lines.

The divisions have continued to exist to date making it difficult to create a nation. Definitely, uniting all these ethnic and racial groups in the independent Zimbabwe is a condition *sine qua non* for the success of nation building. Since the fundamental roots of these ethnic and tribal divisions lie in the history of the peoples of the land, a visit to that history is imperative.

Also important for us to possess is a basic knowledge of the taxonomy of the Zimbabwean population before civil war broke out. Aside from appreciating this composition for a better comprehension of the dynamics of the struggle in Zimbabwe, as Ranger points out, ethnicity, and by extension race, continue to be used as "an explanation for every significant political development,"[4] including, in the case of Zimbabwe, one might add, a clamor for One-Partyism.

It is against this background that a narration of ethnic and racial composition of Zimbabwe prior to the crisis that led to its civil war must be understood.

2.1 ZIMBABWE: PHYSICAL FEATURES

The Republic of Zimbabwe is a land-locked state that is situated within the tropics. On the east of it lies the Republic of Mozambique, on the northwest, Zambia, south, South Africa, and southwest, Botswana. The natural demarcation between Zimbabwe and Zambia is the Zambezi River which runs the northern boundary length of Zimbabwe into Mozambique. The Limpopo River marks the short border Zimbabwe has with South Africa. In the East is the Sabi River. The country's long borders are with Botswana, Mozambique and Zambia. This nation, one-third the size of the Republic of South Africa, and half the size of Zambia comprises of an area of about 390,759 sq. kms (150,873 sq. mls).[5]

The center of this state is a plateau largely characterized by a pronounced peneplain that divides the Zambezi river basin and the Sabi-limpopo river basin. Running along the eastern border are high mountains with, sometimes, thick forests lying at their foot. Otherwise, by and large, the Zimbabwean landscape is undulating plateaus and flat grassland dotted with granite and steep hills.

Zimbabwe has a sub-tropical climate, with rains during summer, from November through March, with the exception of the eastern Highlands that have an extended and variable rain period. The dry winter season starts in May and ends in August. Generally, the weather is moderate, however, the winter period is known for a wide diurnal range, with occasional deadly night frosts, especially on the high plateau.[6]

2.2 THE PEOPLE OF ZIMBABWE

The African population early in the rule of the white colonizers was categorized into a fundamental ethnic opposition between AmaShona and AmaNdebele. The AmaShona occupied what later became known as Southern Rhodesia for centuries prior to the arrival of the AmaNdebele, an off-shot of the Zulu people. However, the AmaShona, despite the fact that others collectively knew them by this name, did not share any sense of national unity so that they could be called a nation. Right up to the establishment of a colonial government in the 1890s, AmaShona people lived as decentralized agriculturally based chiefdoms. Beach correctly observes:

> *[T]he Shona people of Zimbabwe have never been united under one ruler at any point in their history...although the Zimbabwe, Torwa and Changamire states undoubtedly brought large numbers of Shona-speakers under their rule.*[7]

In the 1000 years of their existence in Zimbabwe before the arrival of the AmaNdebele in this country, the Shona people established four states, the last of which, the Rozvi State, was the most military conscious as can be evidenced by the fact that the new Changamire state, which begins to emerge in the 1670s, had available to it armies of "2000-4000 men that the ruler could send as far away as Zumbo and Manyika"[8]

Interrelationships amongst the various Shona ethnic groups were relatively peaceful, as they traded amongst themselves, and later, with the Portuguese. However, in the 18th century on, the Shona ethnic groups proved to be like all other ethnic groups and nations in Southern Africa who were caught up in migratory violence, as they fought among themselves and raided for land and cattle. The increase in violence among the VaShona people was well noted by one of the modern AmaShona historians, Beach. On the question of how the AmaShona ethnic groups related among themselves during the seventeenth and eighteenth centuries Beach said:

> *The eighteenth century Shona were beginning to pay more attention to raiding and warfare as a means of making a living. There was a definite increase in the level of violence in society, and the Rozvi of the late seventeenth century were soon to be followed by the Nyai bands of the Mugapa, the bands of Chikunda in the lower Zambezi Valley, the raiding Heya of the 1760s...*[9]

Clearly, Beach's observation on what was going on among the AmaShona ethnic groups contradicts authors such as David Chanaiwa who always tried to depict this group as unwarlike and living in peace with one another.[10] Much of the eighteenth century into the nineteenth century witnessed the rise and reign of the Rozvi Mambos, especially in the southwestern part of the country where they had such ethnic groups as the AmaKalanga and the Karangas under their rule. These are the same peoples that the AmaNdebele would dominate when they took over the region.

The Land and Its People

Besides the BaNgwato people who constantly attacked the Rozvi kingdom, palace revolutions and plots, which became more frequent by the close of the seventeenth century, and continued throughout most of the nineteenth century, helped to significantly weaken the reign of the Rozvi mambos. These internal conflicts, coupled with attacks from the Portuguese and their African allies had, prior to the beginning of the disintegration of the Rozvi Kingdom, undermined the viability of the Mwene-Mutapa Empire. By about 1650 the Mutapa and also the Torwa states were on the verge of extinction, dismantled by civil wars and the Portuguese.

The Changamires, who were the Rozvi leaders, inherited the Mutapa state structures and also incorporated some of its peoples.[11] Simultaneously with their defeating the Mutapa Empire, the Rozvi people overthrew and took over the Torwa State and chased the Portuguese from the Manyika State. On the strength of these victories the Changamire established a very powerful state with a very strong military.[12]

The Umfecane, the driving engine of the 19th century migrations and nation-building,[13] subjected the Changamire people to three major waves of attacks by three groups from what is known today as Natal Province. Soshangane led the first group, and it established itself in the 1820s, after conquering a few chieftaincies in the vicinity, at a place east of the Sabi River in what is today known as Gazaland. Using Gazaland as their base, the Soshangane people collected tributes from chieftaincies under their jurisdiction, which lay, between the Zambezi and the Limpopo Rivers and between the Indian Ocean and the Sabi River. Paramount chiefs who fell under Soshangane oversight were reduced into vassal sub-chiefs.

Because of their small number, and unlike their cousins the AmaNdebele who would occupy the Southwestern part of the country around the middle of the nineteenth century and culturally absorb their subjects, the people they had conquered culturally absorbed the Soshangane people.[14] In the same wave, two more contingents led by Zwangendaba and Nxaba from South Africa came into Zimbabwe and for a while co-existed with Soshangane. In 1831 the three groups fought among themselves.

Fleeing from both Soshangane and Nxaba, Zwangendaba headed westward into the region then under the Changamire dynasty. The Changamire dynasty had wrested this region from the Karanga leaders in the 17th century. Zwangendaba attacked and conquered the Changamire Empire. The extent of the destruction wrought by Zwangendaba on the Rozvi kingdom was such that it was never to recover from its downward trend and it disintegrated.[15] From this region Zwangendaba proceeded, still wreaking havoc among the Rozvi Empire, to where Bulawayo stands today, in the southwestern part of the country.

Once Nxaba tasted defeat from Soshangane, he also ran-off and headed westward, retracing the footprints of Zwanngendaba and his people, and in the process further weakening the Changamire Empire. He too went as far as Bulawayo. After a short while, both Zwangendaba and Nxaba led their respective followers north across the Zambezi River. Zwangendaba left behind the Queen warrior Nyamazana who remained to finish off the already severely disintegrated Rozvi Empire.

It was the UmSwazi Queen Nyamazana who killed Chirisamhuru, the last of the Changamire Mambos, in the 1830s.[16] The Queen warrior Nyamazana would marry Mzilikazi the founder of the AmaNdebele kingdom when the latter arrives and conquers the Rozvi Empire in the southwestern part of the country in about 1847. The marriage between the two powerful leaders meant that the Swazis who were then the followers of Nyamazana became part of the AmaNdebele Kingdom.[17] In about 1840 the second and third wave of immigrants from the south of the Limpopo, the Kololo and the AmaNdebele, invaded Zimbabwe at the same time.

Before leaving Zimbabwe, when they got to the Changamire Mambo land, the Kololo, a Sotho group, under the leadership of the politically astute Sebetwane, unsuccessfully challenged Nyamazana over the possession of the southwestern region. The Kololo people quickly moved through the Southwestern part of Zimbabwe and settled on the Northern side of the Zambezi River, in today's Zambia. However, they continued to harass the Nanzwa people whom they used as a buffer between themselves and the AmaNdebele people.[18] The AmaNdebele came to stay forever in Zimbabwe, and their arrival is often viewed by many an historian as the beginning of the modern Zimbabwean State.

2.3 The AmaNdebele and the Formation of the Modern State

The AmaNdebele nation traces its origins to today's Natal when its leader and founder, Mzilikazi, one of Tshaka's army Generals, led what would become the nucleus of the AmaNdebele Nation, a splinter-group of 300 men accompanied by women and children away from Tshaka. They thereby separated themselves permanently from the Zulu nation in 1822.[19] This was not the first time that Mzilikazi defected from his superior. He had left Zwide, the leader of the Ndwandwe people and his mother's father and joined Tshaka whom he served as a military commander.[20]

The conflict between Tshaka and Mzilikazi arose when the latter was sent to attack the wealthy Sotho group to the northwest, apparently so that King Tshaka could replenish his dwindling cattle stock. Mzilikazi carried out a successful military campaign, and looted his victim's cattle, but only handed part of the spoil over to Tshaka. The general practice was for the invading Commander to give all the spoil to the King, who in turn "usually returned generous rewards to such commanders."[21] As such, the act of returning only part of the spoils by Mzilikazi constituted a crime against the king, who accordingly sent his troops to punish the rebel, who, by that time, had fled and taken refuge on the top of the Ntumbane Hill.

The Land and Its People

Now fleeing under the attack of the formidable Tshaka's commando, Mzilikazi advanced into the trans-Vaal settling first among the Kwena and Kgatla people whom he conquered and subsequently incorporated into his nation. For at least the next fourteen years, 1823-1839, Mzilikazi would spend time building his nation by adding to his original Nguni group refugees from the Zulu nation and the Sotho-Tswana population in the trans-Vaal through voluntary assimilation and forcible incorporation. This two-pronged method would be the main method by which the AmaNdebele[22] nation would be built henceforth. It was while Mzilikazi and his people were still living in the trans-Vaal that their terrified enemies, the Sotho people, gave them the name maTebele.

After warding off a Zulu attack in 1832, Mzilikazi decided to move his people to a more secure place, Marico valley, where he and his people enjoyed relative peace as there was nothing for him to fear from his neighbors, the Tswanas. However, this relative peace did not mean that it was a period free from serious attacks for the AmaNdebele, as they twice had to engage the Zulu army under Dingane, and also the Griquas and "other half-breeds from the South."[23] Apparently, the Griquas and their allies seemed to be having an edge over the AmaNdebele as they had an advantage of using guns and horses. However, because they were disunited and lacked discipline, they were defeated.

For a while it seemed as if the AmaNdebele position was impregnable in the Marico district until the arrival of the Voortrekkers moving away from what they perceived to be unpalatable treatment by the British. Unhappy with restrictions which the British imposed on the use of land and free black labor, which came as a natural result of the abolition of slavery in British colonies in 1832, and perceived British intrusion into their "cherished" life-style, the Voortrekkers[24] decided to trek North from the eastern Cape districts in search for a place where they could preserve these freedoms.[25] The Voortrekkers' journey inland became known as the Great Trek.[26]

The Voortrekkers gave the AmaNdebele their last fight before they crossed the Limpopo River into the southwestern part of Zimbabwe. Their attack on the AmaNdebele followed a successful attack on the same by the Zulu army, which left the AmaNdebele people in a weaker position and also cost them much of their livestock. Apparently Dingane, the Zulu King, still harbored ill feelings against Mzilikazi for having defied, and subsequently split from the formidable Zulu nation.

Sensing serious threat to himself and to the very existence of his newly formed nation Mzilikazi went on the run again, and this time from an allied group of Africans, coloreds, and Afrikaners. Before leaving trans-Vaal the AmaNdebele nation, as a survival strategy, broke-up into two groups and moved in two separate columns that never united until about 1840 when they met in the southwestern part of Zimbabwe.[27]

2.4 THE CREATION OF A STATE: AMANDEBELE SETTLE IN MAMBO'S LAND

When the AmaNdebele moved into the Southwestern part of Zimbabwe in about 1840 the Rozvi Kingdom had already been shattered and the region was mainly under different squabbling chieftaincies. In the immediate region where Mzilikazi settled, to the North of the Matopo Hills the residents were Karanga, Khalanga, Ngwato, Swazi and Sotho people as well as the group that had separated from him in South Africa. The Swazi people immediately merged with Mzilikazi's nation after he married their leader, Warrior Queen Nyamazana.

Using his two-pronged method of nation-building, voluntary assimilation and forcible incorporation, which he had perfected in transvaal, Mzilikazi built a formidable nation out of the residents of his newly found haven in Zimbabwe, and created a new state around a nucleus of Nguni and BaSotho/Batswana, the group that came with him from today's South Africa.[28] The AmaNdebele had created a stable state by 1847, after overrunning the Khalanga people in the northern part of Botswana and the southwestern part of Zimbabwe, and after making allies of some ethnic groups around Bulawayo, and tributaries of others, as well as assimilating some.[29] The area effectively controlled by Mzilikazi was in the shape of a rough circle, and its radius ranged from fifty to eighty miles around the State capital Bulawayo.

Within this area, Mzilikazi succeeded in bringing all of its residents, including the BaSotho and AmaShona, under his cultural, military and political dominance. When the white settlers invaded the Mambo country they named this section of the state Matabeleland, and it is known by that name to this day. Essentially, the area of effective AmaNdebele settlement was co-extensive with the Rhodesia's Matebeleland. This left approximately two-thirds of Zimbabwe under the jurisdiction of the other ethnic groups and one major nation, the Soshangane people in the Southeast part of the country. Exploiting previous ties developed while they were still in Zululand/Natal, Mzilikazi quickly established good relations with the Gaza-Nguni Kingdom, under Soshangane.

To enhance the bonds of relationship, Mzilikazi's son King Lobengula would marry two daughters of the Gaza king, Thikili and Xhwalile. What this amounted to was that during the last part of the nineteenth century Zimbabwe was effectively under the control of two powerful kingdoms both of which were created around a refugee nucleus. Both would be shattered before the end of that century, with the Soshangane state going first.

The AmaNdebele had livestock in abundance but needed herding people and seasonal grazing land for the livestock. Because of this, it was to their interest that they, where possible, courted friendship from surrounding ethnic groups who had grazing land but did not have as many cattle. The AmaNdebele therefore gave these people their cattle to look after. Keeping the King's cattle, for one, assured that group of people protection from, and a peaceful co-existence with, the AmaNdebele state. However, those who either were reluctant or refused to pay tax to the King were subject to his periodic attacks. By and

The Land and Its People

large, the relationship between the AmaNdebele State and the Shona residents in their immediate vicinity were non-hostile.

The economy of the AmaNdebele state revolved around livestock. Cattle were used to settle disputes and also for *Lobola*.[30] In some sense, the payment of *Lobola* could be seen as one way of redistributing wealth, and so was a redress of injustice through cattle compensation. Cattle were also used for plowing fields and providing milk, manure and meat. In times of drought, AmaNdebele traveled long distances to exchange their livestock for grains.[31] Generally the terms of exchange were equal, and that fostered a sense of synergistical relationship between the AmaNdebele and the people in and out of their effective settlement area with whom they traded.

2.5 The AmaNdebele State Loses its Founder and a Crisis Ensues

The nationhood, cultural cohesiveness and national pride of the AmaNdebele state were predicated heavily on their founder king Mzilikazi, a man with a cheerful countenance, soft voice, and even-temper, who was an observant, dignified, politically astute strategist and General. His position as king had been well earned as one who had gone through very trying times. Mzilikazi lived during the most of the violent and turbulent times of African History. During his time, powerful empires, kingdoms and states rose and got shattered within a single generation.

Wars of unprecedented proportions engulfed the whole of Southern Africa. Ethnic groups were defeated and subsequently absorbed by their conquerors. Mzilikazi was one of the few who did not only survive but went on to create a nation that still is in existence today. He was the creator of what is generally referred to as a modern state, built out of a variety of ethnic groups, with ambassadors, borders, external relations and embassies within itself. In 1868, Mzilikazi died. An interregnum of sixteen months elapsed before the installation of the next king, Lobengula, in 1870.[32]

The delay in the installation of Mzilikazi's successor has been variably attributed to the uncertainty of who the legitimate heir was, the presence elsewhere of a claimant to the throne and the traditional view that ceremonies after the death of the family head lasted a year during which time, in the case of the king, a regent presided. Whatever the cause of the delay, installation of Lobengula precipitated a rift within the AmaNdebele State between the Zwangendaba group (who had joined this state after their defeat and the marriage of their Warrior-Queen-Leader, Nyamazana) who did not accept the installation of Lobengula and the rest, the majority, who did.

In time, bitter war broke out between these two factions and those who supported the candidacy of Lobengula won. Hardly had the nation healed from this long and bitter struggle when the white foreigners with various motives started to arrive in great numbers.

2.6 THE ADVENT OF THE WHITE SETTLERS AND THE DEMISE OF THE AMANDEBELE STATE

Efforts at penetration and military subjugation of indigenous subjects by colonial regimes intensified during the second half of the nineteenth century. Zimbabwe was not exempted from that on-rush and onslaught by white powers who paved their way through the use of superior weapons and the principle of divide and conquer. The principle of divide and conquer broke down the traditional social order, fragmented ethnolinguistic groups and set them against each other, while enlisting the co-operation of others to its side.

Whites from various countries, with various motives and representing different social locations, invaded Zimbabwe:

> *The competitive struggle for the north country (Zimbabwe) was waged by subordinate officials and private adventurers. There are Boers, Portuguese, Englishmen, Americans, and Germans, and their occupations and motives were as varied as their nationalities: missionaries, hunters, traders, scientists, explorers, prospectors, and, only lastly, the official agents of governments.*[33]

The first group of white people to travel or live among the indigenous population of Zimbabwe prior to the whites' permanent settlement, were missionaries, traders and hunters. The relationship between these respective white groups and the indigenous population were generally amicable, and trade went on smoothly in the AmaNdebele state under the keen eye of king Lobengula. One way to account for these amicable relations could be that at that point, unlike the settlers of 1890, the new invaders' commercial interests in no way threatened the indigenous people's way of life and their source of livelihood.

Missionaries, starting with the London Missionary Society (LMS) personnel, the first group to secure a residential place within the AmaNdebele state, were interested only in winning souls for Christ, hunters in ivory and gold, and traders in trading beads in exchange for local items. However, missionaries, hunters and traders collaborated in the colonization of Zimbabwe by giving the British South African Company (BSAC) vital information they needed to conquer the territory.[34]

Gold hunters went beyond the provision of mere information about the presence of gold to the starting of a rumor about the presence of famed King Solomon's mines, with gold in abundance, which in turn triggered a gold-rush from the South, finally leading to the colonization of Zimbabwe.[35]

Rumors of the availability of gold, in amounts that would rival that of the Trans-Vaal, were probably the strongest attraction that led the BSAC to colonize Zimbabwe. Henry Hartely and Karl Mauch were personally responsible for exaggerated hopes whey they, on their hunting trip in Mashonaland in 1867, identified gold in specimens taken from several old diggings along the Sebakwe and Umsweswe Rivers. Upon their return to South Africa, Muach told his

The Land and Its People

stories about his massive gold discoveries to the *Transvaal Argus*, which in turn published his account.

The Lieutenant Governor and the Colonial Secretary in Natal were so pleased with Mauch's gold discovery stories that they hosted him upon his arrival in Natal. The two officials also joined print media in spreading stories about the King Solomon's mines in Zimbabwe, thereby contributing to the gold fever which later ensued. In England, the story of gold discoveries was spread through such pamphlets as *To Ophir Direct*.[36]

In 1869, before the BSAC responded to the news, a flurry of international companies flooded Zimbabwe in search of gold. Included among these companies were: the Glasgow and Limpopo Company, the Durban Gold Mining Company, and the Limpopo Mining Company. Subsequently, competitions for mining concessions from King Mzilikazi followed even though a very little gold had been found by one of the companies on the Tati.

2.7 THE BRITISH SOUTH AFRICAN COMPANY: ADVANCE AND CONQUEST

Zimbabwe as Rhodesia began as a historical anachronism in that it was the last colony in history to be established by a private company through the use of a private army. The Company's conquest of Zimbabwe was a partial fulfillment of Cecil Rhodes[37] dream of building a British Empire that would stretch from the Cape to Cairo.

Rhodes was armed with a dubiously acquired concession,[38] which Lobengula rejected before it even got the approval of England. He used his only powerful arm, the BSAC, which in turn engaged as its military instrument the Pioneer Column.[39] Cecil Rhodes took over Mashonaland in 1890 and subsequently laid the foundations of the colonial state, Rhodesia. Before they left South Africa for Zimbabwe, each member of the pioneer column was promised 3000 acres of land and fifteen gold claims.[40]

Land would be promised again to those involved in the expedition when a decision to attack Matabeleland from their base in Mashonaland was made. Since the land issue would become the primary root cause of the war of liberation in Zimbabwe in the late 1960s and 1970s, it is important that we quote extensively the elements of agreement entered into by the men who later served in the attack against Lobengula in 1893. To have land as the main cause of civil war in Zimbabwe is understandable in the light of the fact that land was a portmanteau issue covering various facets and aspects of the indigenous people's lives, as we shall see in our discussion later in this study.

These terms of conditions of service against the AmaNdebele people are also crucial, as they are indicative of the total disregard the settlers had of African interests. Those who participated in the expeditions were promised the following:

1) That each member shall have protection on all claims in Mashonaland until six months after the date of cessation of hostilities.
2) That each member will be entitled to mark out a farm of 3,000 (three thousand) morgen in any part of Matabeleland. No occupation is required, but a quit-rent will be charged on each farm of ten shillings per annum.
3) That no marking of farms and claims will be allowed, or held valid, until such time as the Administrator and the Commanders of the different columns consider the country sufficiently peaceful, and a week's clear notification will be given to that effect.
4) That members be allowed four (4) clear months wherein to mark out and register their farms, and that no such marking or registration will be valid after that time, with the exception of the rights belonging to the members of the force filled, invalidated, or dying on service.
5) The government retain the right at anytime to purchase farms from members at the rate of 3 (three pounds) sterling per morgen, and compensation for all improvements. This does not include the purchase of claims already pegged out on farms.
6) That any member of the Victoria Force is entitled to 15 (fifteen) claims on reef and 5 (five) alluvial claims....
7) The "Loot" shall be divided: one-half the B.S.A. Company, and the remainder to officers and men in equal shares.[41]

The spirit of the Rudd Concession was consonant with the intentions of the first white settlers of Mashonaland, which was to hunt for gold. Within two years of its arrival, the BSAC quickly discovered that the El Dorado, which Rhodes had thought Mashonaland to be, fell miserably short of its expectation. The Company members then turned to the sale of land and agriculture to try and recoup what they had lost from prospecting for minerals. Agriculture proved in time to be unprofitable as well, as the Company was hit by shortage of labor. Africans in Mashonaland were simply not interested in working for the whites. On the other hand, miners and farmers needed African labor at any cost. The settler situation was compounded by two crucial factors:

1) As the stock fell in price gold prospectors in Mashonaland were soon troubled by the fact that they had to give half of their returns to the Company.
2) Because of the shortage of labor, farming failed to produce the quick wealth that had been expected.[42]

Both the settlers and the company began to think that Matebeleland was the only solution to these problems. Rhodes began to surmise that El Dorado was after all in Matebeleland, a mineral location that would rival the Rand in South Africa. Matebeleland promised new possibilities of wealth.[43] Not only was

The Land and Its People

Matebeleland going to provide minerals in abundance, but African labor as well from among the subjects of King Lobengula.

The only stumbling block to these dreams was King Lobengula and his State. Destroy Lobengula's state, both settlers and the company reasoned, then minerals and labor would be abundantly available. However, the BSAC and the white settlers sought the destruction of the AmaNdebele state for different reasons. For the Company the thinking was that they could stem the tide of the falling stock prices and recoup their investment lost in prospecting for minerals by getting access to what they then thought was the King Solomon's mines.

While the settlers to a certain extent needed to find profitable commercial products, their needs went beyond that to the need of food and other sustenance commodities, whose prices had shot-up exorbitantly at this time.

They therefore figured that their participation in conquest over Matebeleland would bring them spoils of victory in terms of cattle, food and labor. Theirs was a concern for their very survival. Settlers also wanted to strengthen their position vis-à-vis the Company, which seemed to have too much power over their community and thwarted their policy of getting labor and land by "any means possible." They knew the Company would depend on them for soldiers to fight this war and they saw that as offering them the opportunity to renegotiate the terms of BSAC authority over them, particularly their payment of returns they got from mining.[44]

2.8 THE WAR THAT BROUGHT THE WHOLE OF ZIMBABWE UNDER WHITE DOMINATION

Since its arrival in Zimbabwe in 1890 to 1893 the British South African Company had exerted its economic and political authority over Mashonaland, an oversight that it claimed was gotten by right of concession. In theory the Company held that Mashonaland fell under the suzerainty of the AmaNdebele State. Now the Company sought firm control of the AmaNdebele State as well. With Mashonaland proving to be not as productive as had been originally thought, the Company was ready to use any pretext to attack the AmaNdebele kingdom.

The pretext by the Company to attach is well summed by the Zimbabwean historian James A. Chamunorwa Mutambirwa:

> *The opportunity to destroy Lobengula's military power came in July 1893, when the Company alleged that some Africans in the Ft. Victoria Area had stolen its telegraph wire. To punish the offenders, the Company impounded the Africans' cattle, which, however, belonged to Lobengula. When Lobengula realized that some of his cattle had disappeared, he sent an impi to punish the Mashonas whom he mistakenly thought had stolen the cattle.*[45]

While disguising their conquest as a pacification process, and using the telegraph incident, which triggered the AmaNdebele attack against the mistakenly suspected MaShona, the Company attacked and defeated Lobengula's state in 1893. The war was ostensibly to protect AmaShona from AmaNdebele raids.[46] After the defeat of the AmaNdebele, the Company imposed its authority over the whole of Zimbabwe, asserting that it had included Matebeleland under its authority by right of conquest as opposed to Mashonaland, which it claimed by right of concession.

Lobengula, upon getting the news that his best regiment had been defeated set his city Bulawayo on fire and headed North. Speculations on his final fate abound, with most historians agreeing on that he died a natural death as opposed to being killed in war. Lobengula's soldiers who had joined him in tactical withdrawal from the city mercilessly killed the company troops, which tried to give hot pursuit.

The 1893 victory over the AmaNdebele by the whites, however, did not completely crush the former's military and administrative structure.[47] In fact, firm control of the whole country by the whites came in three stages: The first stage was in 1890 when the Company hoisted its flag in Mashonaland. The second came with the defeat of the AmaNdebele in 1893, and the third stage was when a general uprising of 1896-1897 by both the AmaNdebele and AmaShona was put down by the Company forces with the help of some converted indigenous people, Africans from South Africa as well as some imperial forces. Africans until after 1960 would carry out no general armed resistance.

The 1893 victory over the AmaNdebele brought out all the greed there was within the white men. They seized land from Africans, reduced them to forced laborers, looted their livestock and stole their freedom. AmaNdebele suffered a lot as settlers poured into their land between 1893-96, and extensively raided their cattle and took much of their land. The extent of the settlers' raiding and its effects on the African population, specifically on the AmaNdebele population, is eloquently expressed by Ruth Weiss who asserts that:

> Prior to 1893, the Ndebele alone possessed more than 200,000 head of cattle. By 1897, following the First Chimurenga, total African cattle holdings were a mere 14,000. African wealth had been decimated by the war, cattle raids by whites, and drought and disease.[48]

2.9 THE 1896-1897 UPRISING: A BRIEF INVESTIGATION OF ITS ENIGMATIC MOTIVATION

Three years after their defeat, which was followed by their extensive dispossession and forced labor, the AmaNdebele, now better armed[49] than in the previous war, went on the offensive against the white settlers, killing several of them, on March 24, 1896. Also killed by the AmaNdebele army were native policemen who had by then joined ranks with the white settlers. This time the Africans were fighting "with accuracy and determination."[50]

> By the evening of March thirteen not a white man was left alive in the outlying districts of Matebeleland.... Between the these two dates many escaped or were brought into the laager (military defensive camp) by relief parties, but a large number, once hundred and forty-five in all, were treacherously murdered.[51]

The Land and Its People

The white population responded with rage and immediately prepared for war. Whites in Mashonaland rushed down to Matebeleland to rescue their holed-up kith and kin, and that created propitious conditions for a MaShona uprising. The settlers, in time, took refuge in a Laager in Bulawayo, and the AmaNdebele hid themselves in the network of caves in the Intaba zikaMambo and the Amatojeni Hills, two of the few strongholds where the rebels made their last stand.

In time, the whole of Zimbabwe was under a general African uprising in both Matebeleland and Mashonaland. The uprising of AmaShona shattered the stereotype by the white settles that the AmaShona were a cowardly people, and also that they viewed whites as their benefactors. War in Matebeleland ended up in an *indaba* after more than 8 months of intensive war.

In retrospect, it came as no surprise that the fighting between the AmaNdebele and the Company was concluded in negotiations rather than in the battlefield. Both sides had come to a point where there could hardly afford the war economically and militarily. Economically, war disrupted the settlers' mining and agricultural industries, and also transportation, thereby frustrating their hopes for profit, as well as hiking up their cost of living.

For the AmaNdebele, the looting and the burning of crops by settler soldiers, coupled with the outbreak of cattle disease and locusts that destroyed their crops, had started to threaten their very existence. Militarily, both of the warring parties had holed themselves in almost impregnable hideouts, the settlers within the laager, and the AmaNdebele in a maze of caves where they could easily pick at their opponents as they approached. The military impasse had further dire political consequences for the Company; it risked the revocation of its Charter to rule over Zimbabwe in the event the Imperial forces became the vanguard of the war against the AmaNdebele.

To forestall the looming possible take over by the British colonial government, Cecil Rhodes, to the chagrin of some of the settler soldiers craving for a military victory, opted for a negotiated settlement. However, the settlement ended up being biased for Company interests. Nonetheless, to pave the way for an effective cease-fire, Rhodes made several concessions to the AmaNdebele negotiators to redress their nation's grievances.

Scholars have advanced several reasons as to why the Impi YoMvukela (uprising) by the AmaNdebele occurred, and all of them seem to be plausible. According to a missionary scholar, Isaac Shimmin, the way in which the Pioneer Company had confiscated AmaNdebele cattle was one of the major causes of the latter's uprising:

> *If the Company regarded all native cattle as a loot, then it would have been better for them to have taken the plunder of war at once, but no one can deny that the Matabele (sic) resented the constant interference of the Government. Generosity on the part of the conquerors concerning the wealth of the native, which is his cattle, would have been a wise policy.*

This feeling of irritation was intensified by some incompetent officials sent to deal with native affairs. Many of the Native Commissioners were men of justice and principle, but a few of them were utterly incompetent.[52]

Ranger cites the same cause as Shimmin and even goes further to say the rough manner in which the Company recruited labor from the AmaNdebele as one of the causes.[53] Other causes involved such grievances as first, the introduction of forced labor and horrible working conditions by the Company after the defeat of the AmaNdebele in the 1893 war, second the outbreak of natural disasters in the form of rinderpest, and finally locusts and drought shortly before the uprising, which the AmaNdebele associated with the arrival of the whites, and the expropriation of land for white use.[54]

What ended up being a general uprising involving the whole black population in Southern Rhodesia (AmaNdebele and AmaShona), was started by the AmaNdebele in March 1896, and the AmaShona joined them after almost three months, in June.

In Mashonaland, the goal of the settlers and the Company was unanimous; they wanted a complete military victory over the AmaShona and made their goal clear to the latter. The AmaShona put up a ferocious fight, prosecuting the war under respective chiefs in an uncoordinated fashion, way beyond the AmaNdebele *indaba*. Unlike the AmaNdebele war, which ended in negotiations, the struggle in Mashonaland ended when Company soldiers brutally dynamited the AmaShona out of their caves that served as foxholes and bunkers.

In Matebeleland the 1896-97 war was known as *Impi Yomvukela* and in Mashonaland *Chimurega*. Among historians, a heated debate has arisen as to the motivations and as to who gave direction to what appears prima facie, a coordinated general uprising by Africans in Zimbabwe. The importance of this uprising is seen in the fact that it laid a foundational basis for the mid-twentieth century Zimbabwean African Nationalism.

This debate on the first general uprisings in Zimbabwe centered around two questions:

1) Who actually hatched the uprising against the settlers, and who directed it? And

2) Was the uprising a coordinated one or was the situation one of many uprisings with the protagonists taking advantage of a chaotic situation, however, in an uncoordinated fashion.

In his persuasive 1967 study, Ranger argued that the 1896-1897 confrontation was fomented and directed by the Mwari priesthood in collaboration with the AmaNdebele indunas (chiefs). Ranger's position was reminiscent of the one espoused by the company authorities and settlers who maintained that Africans who were involved in the rebellion were incited and directed by the oracular priest of Mwari, who in turn acted out of superstitions involving magic, prophecy, spells and witchcraft.

The Land and Its People

However, unlike the Company authorities and settlers who saw this African uprising as misguided efforts by superstitious people, Ranger valorized them as a pro-national liberation movement.[55] For many years this view about an African cult-led resistance revolt enjoyed a hegemonic influence among historians who wrote on the revolutionary history of Zimbabwe. Modern history scholars, however, are becoming increasingly skeptical of this thesis of the dominant-role of the Mwari priests and its attendant position that the rebellion was a well-coordinated national effort by Africans.

Jullian Cobbing, for instance, cogently argues that the AmaNdebele *impi yomvukela* was planned and directed by the AmaNdebele *induna* with no collaboration from the Mwari priests. Cobbing, therefore, dismisses the cult-led movement theory as "essentially the story of myth," calculated at catching the "imagination of the British press."[56] Cobbing further points out that this coordination by the *induna* was possible because the AmaNdebele civic, political, administrative and military structures survived the 1893 defeat by the Company troops. He also observes that, the Mwari oracular priests-led rising was exaggerated by Ranger to try and make a link between the 1896-97 African resistance and modern, African revolutionary nationalism.[57]

Likewise, David Beach, an Shona historian, refutes Ranger's position that the Mwari priests fomented and directed the AmaNdebele and AmaShona Risings. Beach asserts that AmaShona chiefs engaged in the risings independent of one another, although it is true that they may have taken advantage of the already chaotic situation. Further, he argues that small incidents of resistance started as early as 1894 among the AmaShona people, and culminated in a general revolt, however, an uncoordinated one.[58]

One common position emerges out of this debate despite the different views by respective historians, and it is that towards the close of the nineteenth century, Africans in Zimbabwe, both AmaNdebele and AmaShona, pressured by the institutionalized authority of the Company, whose economy was based on the former's oppression and dispossession, attacked the white settlers to try and regain their freedom. A similar struggle would be repeated in the twentieth century.

2.10 Ethnic and Racial Polarization from Colonization

From the day the Company established its authority over the African population it worked at dividing the major ethnic groups, and sometimes even creating new ones in order to keep itself in power. The settlers immediately opposed the AmaNdebele to AmaShona, and this was later followed by the emergence of macro-AmaShona dialect groupings that were created by missionaries[59] with the support of the settler governments who saw these further divisions as helping to establish their favored principle of divide and rule.

The breakdown of ethnolinguistic groups and the adversarial positioning of the AmaNdebele and AmaShona ensured the settlers that all cohesive forces among the African population were rendered inoperative. Skillfully exploiting the hostilities of their own creation among the African population, the white settlers were able to conquer and subsequently rule Zimbabwe for eighty years.[60] By 1969 this is what the African ethnic taxonomy looked like:

Ethnic Group % of the Population:

Korekore	6%
Zezuru	22%
Manyika	12%
Ndau	5%
Rozvi	2%
Kalanga	5%
Karanga	25%
Ndebele	18%
Other small ethnic groups	5% [61]

The expropriation of land continued, from this point, at an accelerated rate. In fact, the expropriation of African lands by the settlers in Mashonaland increased in pace after the purchase of the Lippert Concession in 1891, a document which was thought to have compensated for the weakness of the Rudd Concession that was understood to have given the Company mining rights only. With the purchase of the Lippert Concession, the Company felt that the legal basis for land possession had been met. The rush for the grabbing of land was so extensive and so fast that "by the middle of 1892, virtually all the farms around Salisbury had been pegged out."[62] After 1896, the expropriation of land covered the whole country.

Forced labor, taxation, population relocations to squalid land and discrimination on the basis of their color became the daily lot of the African population thereafter. The settlers thought little of the African population. They saw them as 'permanently' unintelligent and therefore inferior, and as such, people that needed to be treated like children, with harsh discipline. The settler's denigratory attitude towards the black population had been shaped very much by nineteenth century Social Darwinism, an ideology that shaped the British policy of imperialism of that century. It was this same ideology that made the Crown feel comfortable with white dominance over other people of a different color.

By 1900, the BSAP had gained total power over the indigenous African population with full blessings from the British Crown. In 1923, beset by serious financial problems, the British South African Company surrendered the colony to Britain, who in turn gave the electorate, mostly white, a choice between joining the Union of South Africa or assuming self-determination under a property weighted franchise. The franchise would favor whites since it was they who monopolized property ownership. The electorate chose self-determination in preference to incorporation with South Africa as an extra province.

The Land and Its People

In 1953, Southern Rhodesia joined the Central African Federation with Northern Rhodesia (Zambia) and Nyasaland (Malawi). In 1961, Britain came up with a constitution basically to keep whites in Power. In 1963 Britain ended the Federation under pressure from African nationalists movements from the three counties that constituted it. When Northern Rhodesia and Nyasaland were granted independence the Southern Rhodesian white population under the Rhodesian Front (RF) demanded that it be granted independence which excluded the black population.

When Britain refused, the white settler community led by Ian Douglas Smith, leader of the RF, the party that was in government at the time, issued a Unilateral Declaration of independence (UDI) from Britain on the 11 November, 1965. With the declaration of independence, Britain, again under pressure from the national liberation movements in the country, imposed sanctions against the Smith regime, with the United Nations on her side.[63] Again, with the Smith's UDI, the stage was set for the African liberation struggle, which ended with independence and the ascension into power of the first majority black government in 1980.

ENDNOTES

1. Joshua Nkomo, *The Story of My Life* (London: Methuen, 1984), p. 14.
2. Zimangele Mpofu, An Interview by Author, August 25, 1995. Zimangele Mpofu was a daughter of *iwosana*, who was connected to *Ilitshe* in Dula and Njelele.
3. *Ibid.*
4. Terence Ranger, *Invention of Tribalism in Zimbabwe*, Gwelo: Mambo Press, 1985, p.3.
5. For some helpful information on the physical location and features of Zimbabwe see Colin Stoneman, ed., *Zimbabwe's Prospects: Issues of Race, Class, State, and Capital in Southern Africa*, London: Macmillan Publishers, 1988, pp.63-67; Christine Sylvester, *Zimbabwe: The Terrain of Contradictory Development*, Boulder and San Francisco: West View Press, 1991, p. 2.
6. *Ibid.*
7. Cited in Herbert Chimhundu, "Early Missionaries and the Ethnolinguistic Factor During the 'Invention of Tribalism' in Zimbabwe," in *Journal of African History*, 33, 1992:89.
8. D.N. Beach, *Zimbabwe Before 1900*, Gweru: Mambo Press, 1984, p. 46.
9. D.N. Beach, *The Shona & Zimbabwe 900-1850: An Outline of Shona History*, New York: Africana Publishing Company, 1980, p. 320.
10. David Chanaiwa, "The Army and Politics in Pre-Industrial Africa: The Ndebele Nation, 1822-1893," in *African Studies Review*, Vol.XIX, No. 2, September, 1976:53.
11. Beach, *Zimbabwe Before 1900*, pp. 6, 24.
12. *Ibid.*, p. 46.

13. J.D. Omer-Cooper, *The Zulu Aftermath: A Nineteenth-Century Revolution in Bantu Africa*, Evanston: Northwestern University Press, 1969, p. 168. The term *Umfecane* (the word is a Zulu term) portrays the African societies as not static and unchanging, and also as capable of creating nations on their own internal initiatives. Cooper's observation accurately summarizes what the implications of Ufecane for the Central and Southern African societies when he observes that *Umfecane* "was essentially a process of social, political and military change internal to African society and taking place with explosive rapidity." This "revolution," he further observes, "left a profound imprint on the demographic pattern of Southern and Central Africa. It also brought into existence peoples who still define their identity by reference to the leaders and the wars of the Mfecane."

14. So did the Zwangendaba people get culturally absorbed by their AmaShona subjects, see J.A. Barnes, *Politics In A Changing Society: A Political History of the Fort Jameson Ngoni*, Manchester: University Press, 1967.

15. *Ibid.*, p. 65. For the impact of the 1831 Zwangendaba attacks on the Changamire empire see also Beach, *Zimbabwe Before 1900*, p. 53.

16. Julian Raymond Dennis Cobbing, "The Ndebele Under the Khumalos, 1820-1896," Ph.D. dissertation, University of Lancaster, 1976, p. 119.

17. For detailed information on the exploits of the Nyamazana people and their incorporation of her people after she married the King Mzilikazi see N. Jones (Mhlangazenhlansi), *My Friend Khumalo*, Salisbury, 1945.

18. Jullian, "The Ndebele Under the Khumalos," pp. 136-137.

19. Ngwabi Bhebhe, *Lobengula*, Harare: Zimbabwe Educational Books, 1977, p. 9. For a fuller composite picture of the formation and the migration of the AmaNdebele nation to Zimbabwe as well as for the reasons Mzilikazi, the nation's founder decided to split from Tshaka see also Jullian Cobbing, "The Ndebele Under the Khumalos, 1820-1896," Ph.D. dissertation, University of Lancaster, 1976; Omer-Cooper, *The Zulu Aftermath: A nineteenth Century Revolution in Bantu Africa*, Evanston: Northwestern University Press, 1969; R.K. Rasmussen, *Mzilikazi's Ndebele in South Africa*, London, 1978 & ___, *Mzilikazi*, Harare: Zimbabwe Educational Books, 1977.

20. Rasmussen, *Mzilikazi*, 1977, pp. 10-12.

21. *Ibid.*, p. 13.

22. The term MaTebele has been variously defined to mean "wanderer," "plunder," or "those who hide behind their long shields." The second definition is generally espoused by those who saw the AmaNdebele people as having a predatory, militaristic nature, the position legitimately corrected among modern scholars, such as Julian Cobbing as exaggerated. For detailed discussion on this topic see Cobbing, "The Ndebele Under the Khumalos, 1820-1896." The Zulus rendered their designation AmaNdebele.

23. Arthur Keppel-Jones, *Rhodes and Rhodesia: The White Conquest of Zimbabwe 1884-1902*, Kingston and Montreal: McGill-Queen University Press, 1983, p. 3.

24. The Voortrekkers were Afrikaners representing different social classes. They included slave-owners, farmers, the well propertied and others were debtors. They all came from one region, the eastern Cape, however from different districts such

The Land and Its People

      as Albany, Cradock, Graaff-Reinet, Somerset East and Uitenhage, with a sprinkling from Beaufort West and Swellendam.

25. T.R.H. Davenport, *South Africa, A Modern History*, 3rd ed., Toronto and Buffalo: University of Toronto Press, 1987, pp. 76-96.

26. Tradition in Afrikaner historiography has it that the Great Trek represented the beginning of the development of Afrikaner Nationalism, which became celebrated frequently after the take over of power in South Africa by the National Party in 1948, a Party that was predominately Afrikaner in membership.

27. For a detailed account on the migration of the AmaNdebele between 1821 and 1839 see R. Kent Rasmussen, "Ndebele Wars and Migrations c.1821-1839," Ph.D. dissertation, University of California, Los Angeles, 1975. For detailed information on Nguni traditions and also the account of Mzilikazi's life in Zululand, notwithstanding its inaccuracies on some instances, it still stands as an important collection of Nguni traditions, see A.T. Bryant, *Old Times in Zululand and Natal*. London, 1929 (reprinted, Cape Town 1965).

28. See Julian Cobbing for a detailed account of methods used by Mzilikazi for building a new state on the Nguni and Sotho/Tswana nucleus and also the respective ethnic groups that came to be part of his nation.

29. Mzilikazi successfully built a strong, mixed nation by employing a three-pronged Strategy. He attacked and involuntarily incorporated the defeated, accepted those groups who chose on their own to join his kingdom, and took in refugees fleeing persecution by their own people. Last but not the least, Mzilikazi awarded citizenship to those who asked for it and met the set standards. See Gwabi Bhebe, *Christianity and Traditional Religion in Western Zimbabwe* (London: Longman, 1979), ___, *Lobengula* (Harare: Zimbabwe Educational Books, 1977); Julian Raymond Cobbing, "The Ndebele Under the Khumalos, 1890-1896," Ph.D. dissertation, University of Lancaster, 1976; Callistus Ndlovu, "Missionaries and Traders in the Ndebele Kingdom: An African Response to Colonialism: A Case Study 1859-1890," Ph.D. dissertation, State University of New York, 1973.

30. *Lobola* understood within the AmaNdebele concept is a very complex relational concept that is often mistakenly referred to as bride-price. Lobola, which was paid in cattle to the bride's parents, was meant to redeem the name of the husband so that the offsprings born would have called after their father's surname. Grandchildren or children of grandchildren could redeem their father's name by giving cattle to their maternal side. Traditionally, the initiative to pay *Lobola* lay with the bridegroom and his parents or posterity. Technically where *Lobola* had not been given the children were to be called by their mother's surname. In time, with the coming of capitalism this concept got commercialized and therefore corrupted by some.

31. Bhebhe, *Lobengula*, 1977, p. 11.

32. Thomas Morgan Thomas, *Eleven Years in Central South Africa*, London: John Snow and Co., 1873, pp. 227-240; F.T. Posselt, *Fact and Fiction*, Rev. ed, Bulawayo: Rhodesian Printing and Publishing Co., 1942, p. 39; J.P.R. Wallis, ed., *The Matabeleland Journals of Robert Moffat, 1829-1860*, Vol. 1, Oppenheimer Series, No. 1. London: Chatto and Windus, 1945, p. 265.

33. Arthur Keppel-Jones, *Rhodes and Rhodesia: White Conquest of Zimbabwe 1884-1902*, Kingston and Montreal, 1983, p. 9.

34. The BSAC suffered from a lack of ideology that was capable of tying together the divergent images of local realities, and also an ideology that could help justify its incursion and occupation of Zimbabwe to its respective constituencies of imperialism: the British government and humanitarian groups back in Britain. By providing information that depicted the indigenous African population as despicable, ignorant, prone to violence and always at each others' neck, missionaries, hunters and traders contributed to the Company's propaganda to its constituencies which made it easier for the latter to support their conquest, which they viewed as pacification.

35. B. Vulindlela Mtshali, *Rhodesia: Background to Conflict*, New York: Hawthorn Books, Inc., 1967, p. 32. Most of the explorers came to the Region of Mashonaland in hope of discovering gold. Their hopes were based on what turned out to be very misleading information by gold-hunters who talked of Mashonaland as the region of the famed king Solomon's mines. Hugh Marshall Hole in his book *The Making of Rhodesia* (London: Macmillan, 1926, pp. 2-4), graphically describes the impact these explorers' stories about the abundance of minerals in Zimbabwe affected the settlers.

36. E. Mager, *Karl Mauch, Lebensbild eines Afrikareisenden*, Stuttgart: W. Kohlhammer, 1895: 94-98. This source presents a very favorable image of Mauch that is further enhanced by doctored portions of the Mauch's writings himself. However, a completed text of his journals revealed an antithesis of this view. Mauch was pictured by F.O. Bernhard as "a man plagued by emotionalism always willing to accept, seldom giving and utterly incapable of getting along with anyone for long," and to this he added "his aptitude for self-pity ... and his capacity for hate, be it for an individual or for a foreign nation as a whole." Quoted from Keppel-Jones, *Rhodes and Rhodesia*.

37. Cecil John Rhodes, a son of a religious minister was a self-made millionaire who went to South Africa as a very poor young man but in time built himself a lucrative mining empire. After the Company conquered Zimbabwe in the 1890s they named it Rhodesia which can be seen as a mnemonic and metonymic mechanism attaching the person of their founder to the newly found state.

38. By the Rudd Concession Lobengula had authorized mining by the whites in Zimbabwe but not the taking of Land. In fact, some historians believe Rhodes never asked for control over land because he knew very well Lobengula would refuse. But this did not deter the Rhodes from taking land for mining and settlement.

39. The Pioneer Column was composed of military men and settlers whose objective was to open Zimbabwe for white settlement.

40. Philip Mason, *The Birth of a Dilemma*, London: Oxford University Press, 1958, p. 143.

41. Quoted from John H. Harris, *Slavery or Sacred Trust*, London: Williams and Norgate Ltd., 1926, pp. 76-77.

42. John S. Galbraith, *Crown and Charter: The Early Years of the British South Africa Company*, Berkeley: University of California Press, 1974, pp. 282-289; W.H. Brown, *On the South African Frontier*, London, 1899, reprint, New York: Negro University Press, 1970, pp. 162-163.

43. Galbraith, *Crown and Charter*, 1974, pp. 287-291.

44. Brown, *South African Frontier*, 1970, p. 270.

The Land and Its People

45. James A. Chamunorwa Mutambirwa, *The Rise of Settler Power in Southern Rhodesia (Zimbabwe), 1898-1923*, London and Toronto: Associated University Press, 1980, p. 38.

46. One of the major reasons offered by the Company to their heterogeneous sponsors for attacking the AmaNdebele kingdom was that they were defending the peaceful Shonas from the predatory AmaNdebele people. The Company in so saying tried to paint its uncalled for attack as a humanitarian act, in protection of the AmaShona. This divisive language by the whites marked the institutionalization of the divide and rule principle on their part; the principle which would help them conquer and control Zimbabwe for more than 80-years.

47. Cobbing, "Ndebele Under the Khumalos," 1976, p. 366. The 1893 Company military campaign had very minimal effects on the rest of the AmaShona who got cushioned from its impact by distance. The AmaNdebele outside of Bulawayo retained their military and state structure as the BSAC "were in reality unable to control beyond Bulawayo and the main roads," Cobbing, "The Absent Priesthood: Another Look at the Rhodesian Risings of 1896-1897," in the *Journal of African History*, 18, 1977: 72. After King Lobengula vanished, the AmaNdebele nation installed Nyamanda as their new king. The civil structure official structure, chieftaincies, sub-chieftaincies, and ward heads remained intact, and so did the military units and command.

48. Ruth Weiss, *Zimbabwe and the New Elite*, London and New York: British Academic Press, 1994, pp. 32-33.

49. After their defeat in 1893, the AmaNdebele refused to surrender their weapons to the Company authority, instead they decided to cache them. This was especially true of those regiments that were not touched by this first confrontation, and these were a majority given the fact that only one of Lobengula's regiments were involved in this battle.

50. Quoted from Reed in Summers, *From Civilization to Segregation*, 1994, p. 50.

51. This was a narration of the actual account on the war and its impact on the white community as perceived by a settler who latter told it to Terence Ranger which the later included in Terence Ranger, *Revolt in Southern Rhodesia 1896-1897*, Evanston: Northwestern University Press, 1967, p. 127.

52. Wesleyan Method. Mission. Soc. Arch., Corresp., Mashonaland, 1891-9, I. Shimmin, The Mashona Rebellion, 1896.

53. Ranger, *Revolt in Southern Rhodesia, 1896-7* (1967), pp. 105-114; 118-120.

54. *Ibid.*; "History of the Zambesi Mission," Zambesi Mission Rec., III, xxxvi (1906-9): 234-6. This is a Jesuit publication.

55. For a detailed account on Ranger's views of the 1896-1897 uprising see Ranger, *Revolt in Southern Rhodesia, 1896-1897*, 1967.

56. Cobbing, "The Absent Priesthood: Another Look at the Rhodesian Risings of 1896-1897," in *Journal of African History*, 15, 1974:81.

57. Ibid., p. 83.

58. D[avid] N. Beach, *War and Politics in Zimbabwe, 1840-1900*, Gweru: Mambo Press, 1986, pp. 119-147. See also Beach, "Ndebele Raiders and Shona Power," in *Journal of African History*, 15, 1974: 651.

59. Terence O. Ranger, "Missionaries, Migrants and the Manyika: The Invention of Ethnicity in Zimbabwe," in L. Vail, ed., *Studies in the Political Economy of an Ideology*, Berkeley, Los Angeles, and London, 1989, pp. 121-122.

60. Although the AmaNdebele and AmaShona did have adversarial relationships, at no time were their interrelationships as bad and conflictual as during the time of colonization. As soon as they settled in Zimbabwe, Europeans started spreading divisive, and largely exaggerated information about militant, despotic AmaNdebele who were always victimizing the AmaShona by stealing their cattle, butchering their wives and children and reducing some of them to slaves. They then tried to pose as humanitarians who defended the interests of the 'weak and peaceful' AmaShona. The end result of such emphasis on real and imagined, if not exaggerated or false differences between the major two groups, in time was believed by some members of the African population, and that made unity between the same very difficult.

61. Missionaries invented the word AmaShona as an all-encompassing designation in the 1930s. It included Korekore, Zezuru, Manyika, Ndau, Rozvi Karanga all of whom were thought to be speaking languages with common roots. Sometimes the Kalanga are included among the AmaShona on the basis of language as well but this is problematic. Also problematic is the inclusion of Karanga. Since an argument to prove these designations is outside the scope of this work, I will not pursue it.

62. Richard Hodder-Williams, *White Farmers in Rhodesia, 1890-1965, A History of the Marandellas District*, London and Basingstoke: Macmillan Press Ltd., p. 14.

63. For a general introduction to white settlement in Southern Rhodesia, see L. H. Gann, *A History of Southern Rhodesia: Early Days to 1934* (London: Chatto and Windus, 1964); James A. Mutambirwa, *The Rise of Settler Power in Southern Rhodesia (Zimbabwe)*, 1898-1923 (Cranbury: Associated University Presses, Inc., 1980); Phillip Mason, *The Birth of a Dilemma: The Conquest and Settlement of Rhodesia* (London: Oxford University Press, 1958). For the history of white settlers until independence, see P. Mosley, *The Settler Economies: Studies in the Economic History of Kenya and Southern Rhodesia, 1900-1963* (New York: Cambridge University Press, 1983); I. Phimister, *An Economic and Social History of Zimbabwe, 1890-1948: Capital Accumulation and Class Struggle* (London and New York: Longman, 1988); H. Nelson, ed., *Zimbabwe, A Country Study, Area Handbook Series*, United States government as represented by the Secretary of the Army (1983). Martin Meredith, *The Past is Another Country: Rhodesia's U.D.I. to Zimbabwe* (London: Pan Books Ltd., 1980); Elaine Windrich, *Britain and the Politics of Rhodesian Independence* (London: Croom Helm, 1978).

Chapter 3
GESTATION STAGE: ZAPU REINCARNATION - SRANC AND NDP

This chapter covers the period of the founding of ZAPU in 1961 through the time of its initial military activities to the time the onset of lull in its armed efforts against the Rhodesian regime sometime in mid-1970.[1] Also covered are the objectives of the Party, its mobilization strategies, the first split within ZAPU and the events leading to its banning. To help us appreciate the evolution of its Party's ideology I discuss first the mass national movements that preceded it between 1957 and 1961.

Such a discussion should also help us in comprehending the circumstances that led to the founding of ZAPU. Between the two organizations that preceded ZAPU the National Democratic Party (NDP) will receive more attention essentially because, as Temba Moyo correctly noted:

> ZAPU was simply a continuation of the NDP. The structure and most of the officials including the President Joshua, Joshua Nkomo, who was outside the country at the time-were the same. Only the name was different.[2]

In fact an argument could be made that ZAPU was actually an ideologically metamorphosed entity of, first, the Southern Rhodesia African National Congress, and second, the National Democratic Party.[3]

In the 1950's, subsequent to, and as a result of the Second World War, a popular movement for democracy and decolonization was born with the launching of the struggle for independence across the face of the African Continent. The Second World War saw the participation of Africans in the War alongside their white leaders. For the first time Africans saw the whites dying in combat and that made them realize that their bosses were human after all and not superhuman. Melwa Ntini who went first as a supporting staffer but latter was forced to fight against the Germans made this comment on what he gleaned from his participation in the War:

> In the War against Hitler we discovered that the white race, which up to that time represented our masters who we considered superhuman, was human. They too like us had a normal birth; fell ill, felt pain, cried and died from the same causes as we Africans did. They died from bullets and of hunger as well. If they were like us, so most of us thought, they could be defeated in war, and they were

no different from us. Discovering that somebody is human is a leveling experience to say the least.[4]

Those who did not go to War read and saw pictures of whites who had died in the war. The realization that whites were human brought about intensification in the Africans' struggle for the independence of their own countries and some audacity in demanding that they be considered as equal with whites. Thus the push for self-determination and equality was further understood within Articles 1 and 2 of Universal Declaration of Human Rights of 1948. This was, indeed, a great national rekindling and awakening of the spirit of nationalism with people from across economic, religious and status lines joining unions, ethnic political movements, and national groups to fight for self-determination and a materially secure life.

In Southern Rhodesia these radical currents were represented first by the Southern Rhodesia African National Congress (SRANC), and later, the National Democratic Party and then ZAPU, *inter alia*.

3.1 THE SOUTHERN RHODESIA AFRICAN NATIONAL CONGRESS, 1957-59

Inspired and spurred in struggle and demands by the example of nationalists in Nyasaland (Malawi) and Northern Rhodesia, as well as by the rising tide of independence throughout Africa, Southern African nationalists gathered to form a more representative organization in 1957. The SRANC was formed in 1934 but did not become a dynamic organization until 1957 when the one-time trade unionist Joshua Nkomo took over the leadership and breathed life into the otherwise moribund movement.

In that year, on September 12, a date that was also significant to the white settlers for it was their 67th Anniversary of Occupation Day, the Southern Rhodesia African National Congress was formed. Its formation on this date was clearly in defiance of what the minority regime celebrated as settler Occupation Day. The new SRANC was an amalgam of two organizations: the resuscitated and multi-ethnic SRANC and the vibrant but largely single-ethnic City Youth League (CYL).

The City Youth League was founded in 1955. It later changed its name to the African Youth League. Instrumental in the founding of the CYL were four men: Dundizye Chisiza, a Malawian who had worked in South Africa before coming to Southern Rhodesia, James Chikerema, George Nyandoro, and Edson Sithole. James Chikerema became **its** first President with George Nyandoro serving as its Vice-President. The City Youth league was predominantly based in Harare and this made its outreach limited almost exclusively to one main ethnic group, the Shona. Its biggest accomplishment was the organization of a bus boycott of 1956, resulting in the reduction of bus fares.

The boycott overtly challenged the authority of the Southern Rhodesian Government. The CYL was restricted in its operation and goals in that it primarily concerned itself with the grievances of urban—mostly Salisbury

Gestation Stage

workers. In other words, people in rural areas did not feature prominently in their agenda at all. The organization made no efforts at all to call for political independence. However, when the CYL began. it had radical intentions seeking confrontation with the settler regime rather than cooperation.

In that direction, it challenged the authority of Native Commissioners in the rural areas by encouraging the rural people to stand against the Native Land Husbandry Act (NLHA), and opposed multi-racialism and the Federation. Like many other resistant political pressure groups of its day, it called for the reform of the colonial system and piece meal integration based on the concept of racial partnership. The CYL was also concerned with African gradual racial integration into the economic and political system. Its participation in the elections of 1956, in which it swept the elections for the African Advisory Board of Salisbury's Harare Township, is evidence to its softening stance and change of approach in favor of gradual change.

By and large, the bus boycott did not challenge the racial structure of the white regime, and hence it can be correctly argued that the SRANC was the first organization to offer significant challenge to some of the pillars on which this racial structure was founded.

The pre-1957 SRANC had, by 1955, lost most of its membership so that it had only one branch in Bulawayo with Joshua Nkomo as its leader. Despite its depleted membership, the SRANC still boasted of a strong membership of mostly Bulawayo based unionists with a longer history of organization and who had vast experience of working with organizations. Among these were Joshua Nkomo, its President, who in 1954 was elected the President of the Southern Rhodesia Trade Union Congress, Knight T.T. Maripe, Jason Ziyapapa Moyo, Edward Ndlovu and Francis Nehwati.

Before its resuscitation under the leadership of Nkomo, 1952, an educated urban petit bourgeoisie patronized the party. Its program was essentially non-political but rather social to the extent that it could be accurately characterized as a social organization. Richard Gibson succinctly characterized the program of the SRANC before Nkomo took over as its President:

> *Under various leaders, the ANC of Rhodesia was probably even more reformist than its namesake in South Africa. Its action, based on black elites, centered on ceaseless appeals to the white authorities in Salisbury and elsewhere for some measure of justice for the African majority.*[5]

Thus, the SRANC received rejuvenation and better organization when the organizationally experienced Joshua Nkomo, was elected its leader in 1952. In fact, when Joshua Nkomo was elected the leader of the SRANC, the SRANC did not have an active membership.[6] Using his skills as an organizer, and taking advantage of his own experienced union members whom he immediately enlisted to the cause of the movement, Nkomo started building up an organization with an active membership.

In fact, by the time he became President of the SRANC, he had been chosen the leader of a nation-wide trade union organization, the Southern Rhodesia Trade Union Congress (generally known as TUC)[7]. Like other political movements of the day in Southern Rhodesia though, the pre-1957 SRANC was confined primarily to black townships and therefore did not have a mass base. However, under the leadership of Nkomo, it became vibrant and militant contrary to the assertion that when it merged with CYL it was moribund.[8]

These two organizations, the SRANC and the CYL were by no means the only groups agitating for the rights of the African people in Southern Rhodesia. Prior to the founding of the SRANC and the CYL there had been several localized and comparatively much smaller organizations involved in the struggle for the voiceless black population. Such groups included, inter alia, the Matebeleland Home Society under the leadership of Charles C. Ngcebetsha and the African Voice Association of Benjamin Burombo. In the early part of 1957, the proliferation of African resistant movements began to concern African nationalists, who saw it as a source of division among the people and a debilitating factor in their struggle against the oppressive settler government.

With such a welter of organizations, African nationalists felt that they could not, as Ngwabi Bhebe aptly pointed out, "effectively mobilize the African people to forcefully extract whatever concessions out of the white rulers."[9] It was essentially this concern, which pushed African leaders to seek unity under the reconstituted SRANC of 1957, with Joshua Nkomo as its President. The formation of the SRANC therefore heralded the introduction of a truly united, national political movement in Southern Rhodesia with a new and radicalized clarion call: universal suffrage.

At the organization's inauguration at the Mai Musodzi[10] Recreation Hall in Harare Township, today known as Mbare, in Salisbury, on September 12, 1957, participants carried placards, which succinctly summarized the principal objectives of the party for the first time for the public.

Some of these placards read: "We want Universal Adult Suffrage Here and Now," "Down with Police Rule," "Down with Todd's Franchise Proposal," and "End All Forms of Racial Discrimination."[11] Thus, the new Party stated as its goals: the raising of African people's standards of living; eradication of all forms of racism; an expanded and non-racial educational system, and the inauguration of democratic institutions through the introduction of universal suffrage.[12]

The business of the day included the election of the movement's Executive members. Joshua Nkomo was chosen President of the reconstituted SRANC. His lieutenants included: James Chikerema, Vice-President, George Nyandoro, Secretary, Jason Ziyapapa Moyo, Vice-Secretary, Joseph Msika, Treasurer and Paul Mushonga, Vice-Treasurer. The Committee members were Francis Nehwati, Peter Mtandwa Moses J. Ayema and M. Mokwani.[13] As an expression of a strong desire to produce a national resistance movement, the executive members were chosen from all over the country.

Gestation Stage

By choosing leadership from all over the country, the founders of the SRANC rightly surmised that the act would lay down an enduring Unity among those fighting for a fair and just dispensation. The following day, September 13, 1957, the SRANC adopted its constitution.[14] Thus, was born the first political, national mass resistant movement in Southern Rhodesia.

The choice of a leader proved to be a very harrowing experience for the non-ethnic centered delegates. James Chikerema canvassed for the leadership of the Party but most people favored Nkomo not only because of his physical maturity but also, and more importantly, for his wide experience in negotiating with the white man as a unionist as well an African representative in the London discussions about the introduction of the Central African Federation, which he vehemently opposed.[15]

Nkomo also was a skilful and experienced organizer as witnessed in his leadership as the first black trade union leader in the country of the powerful Southern Rhodesia Railways African Employees' Association. Thus many Africans viewed Nkomo as a skilful and experienced organizer who they could trust with the leadership of the mass movement. Also, he was considered by many Africans in the movement as a moderate whose choice as leader would attract other educated Africans to the movement. Thus, his advantageous position as a national leader was not lost sight of by his fellow nationalists in the new political movement. By choosing him as its first president they correctly surmised that it would attract already organized followers from the trade union of which he was leader.

Salient in this arduous task of choosing a leader was the nefarious factor of ethnicity, the variable that would dog the Southern Rhodesia African Resistant Movements for forty years. According to Joshua Nkomo, largely those in potential leadership as compared to the general masses raised the question of tribalism. Nkomo observed:

My friends from the then Salisbury, in their endeavor to win the leadership of the party used every possible means the lowest of which was the weapon of tribalism. While they too felt the need for all of us to transcend our tribal and regional affinities, for officiousness, they, for a while disregarded this awareness and tried to put Chikerema as leader on the rationale that the general population of Zimbabwe would not support a Ndebele leader, which turned out to be a wrong prediction.[16]

Much sometimes is made of the ideological differences between the two contestants for the SRANC. Invariably, these scholars depict Chikerema as a militant who wanted to wrest power from the whites, while Nkomo simply wanted to share power with them. However, a cursory look into the activities of even the CYL would reveal that Chikerema too, at the formation of the reconstituted SRANC, was reformist in his approach to social change.

In other words, the CYL used the constitutionally acceptable means of showing political discontent, just like the Civil Rights Movement of the United

States of America of the late 1950's into the early 1960's. The similarities between the CYL and the US Civil Rights Movement was not lost to the great friend of the Southern African National Liberation Movements, George Houser, who aptly observed:

> *Its [CYL] program was reminiscent of the non-violent civil rights movement in the United States. I was fascinated by the incidents of civil disobedience Chikerema and Nyandoro described to me....*[17]

In many ways Nkomo reflected the shifting of the SRANC's attention from individual problems of discrimination to agitation for "the fullest participation of African people in government [and] Universal Suffrage Now," when he stated:

> *What we are asking for immediately is a direct participation in the...government. And we ask... as people who know their rights cannot indefinitely be withheld from them.*

From the white standpoint this was a very radical message, especially in light of the fact that the Southern Rhodesia white cultural ethos was predicated exclusively on assumed racial superiority. This was, in fact, true since all of the white regimes which ruled after 1890 whose commitment to racial, political and other forms of inequality were very overt. The least the white Rhodesians believed about equality of races was eschatological and contingent on factors almost out of the control of Africans given the way the society was structured at that time. Herein lay the rationale for the founding of the SRANC.

To fully appreciate this Party's goals and the constraints under which it operated one has to understand the contextual antecedents within which it was born, and also within that context we can find reasons why black Zimbabweans felt angry and dissatisfied with the successive white ruling regimes.

3.2 Contextual Factors Surrounding the Founding of the SRANC

A majority of whites were strongly adverse to Nkomo's call for African inclusion in government because they felt it threatened their privileged positions in the society. Since 1945, subsequent to the Second World War, many whites had left war-devastated Britain en masse and immigrated to Southern Rhodesia where they lived socio-economically much better lives. They secured more paying jobs than they could ever dream to earn at home, they could even afford servants because the latter's wages were so low.

Taxes were much lower in Southern Rhodesia than they were in Britain. African labor was cheap and it was this black labor that supported the entire Southern Rhodesian economy. Consequently, Southern Rhodesia's two main exports, cotton and tobacco, could compete in world markets because their production cost was incomparatively low. African urban workers also keenly felt the problem of low wages, and this was coupled with the problem of

Gestation Stage

unemployment, which began to rear its head from 1957 and increased as the years went by.

The 1956 census showed that there were 609,953 employed in the whole of Southern Rhodesia. Of this group 300,178 were indigenous, 42,253 from Northern Rhodesia, 132,643 from Nyasaland, 125,218 from Portuguese Territories and 9,661 from other territories. The demographical breakdown of this employed population comprised of 512,042 adult men, 52,920 juveniles and 44,991 females.[18] The Black population, employment and proportion employment two years later (1958) was as in Table 3.1:

Table 3.1: The Black Population, Employment and Proportion Employed

Year	Population on June 30 (1000's)	Employed Population (1000's)	Proportion Employed (%)
1946	2300	374	16.3
1951	2800	510	18.2
1956	3200	602	18.8
1960	3600	640	17.8
1964	4100	618	15.1[19]

This table roughly demonstrates the relationship between the growth of the African population and the paucity of job opportunities for Africans. Consequently, in 1958 the government introduced the Foreign Labor Act to keep Mozambicans and other African, non-Southern Rhodesians out of towns in that country. Despite this unprecedented measure of alien-control by government, unemployment and the falling wages increased to the extent that even the security agents themselves predicted political unrest. A security report in June stated:

The rising cost of living and growing unemployment among the African people is not likely to impress the security situation in either of the Rhodesias.[20]

Compounding the issue of low wages were unreasonably restrictive conditions under which the African Trade Unions operated. As Bhebe noted:

What was, perhaps, ridiculous was that African Trade Unions were required to notify the Registrar of their existence within three months of their coming into being and were subject to the same restrictions as applied to recognized trade unions. But they were accorded no legal status and could not give evidence before industrial boards.[21]

The downside of being unable to present labor grievances on the part of Africans was that it denied them the opportunity of expressing their concern about low wages and unemployment. Thus, unemployment, stringent laws that governed the existence of African Trade Unions and ballooning unemployment contributed to the rise of the African resistant movement in the form of SRANC.

Second, racial discrimination also had a part in stimulation of African resistance. Largely because the fruits of the Southern Rhodesian economy were shared on the basis of color, so that it favored the whites over and against the blacks, Africans strongly opposed discrimination. As Melwa Ntini, himself a member of the SRANC until its proscription, justly noted:

Whites in Southern Rhodesia saw themselves as gods. To protect themselves from being desecrated by Africans so they thought, they put in place rigid separatism in hospitals, hotels, schools, swimming pools, restaurants, toilets and buses. Africans were always served in stores after whites. At Post Offices, entrances and counters were separate and we were not allowed to partake of European alcoholic drinks or beer, even wine for that matter.[22]

The land Apportionment Act of 1930 legitimized this rigid separation. The only way an African could travel was through the use of certificates and passes as was accurately noted by Anthony Verrier. Verrier wrote:

[Africans] were governed a rigid system of certificates and passes. An African had to have a Certificate of Registration which allocated to some area under the Land Apportionment Act even if he had been born an urban location. Armed with this he could travel, but as soon as he entered an urban area he had to secure..., either a Current Visiting Pass or a Town Pass to Seek Work.

If and when he had got some sort of job he had to procure either a Certificate of Service or have a Certificate of Self-Employment. The head of the family had to have a Certificate of Occupation. A woman, unless employed, was required to have a Certificate of Recognition of an Approved Wife.[23]

The SRANC wanted free travel for everybody irrespective of racial identity within the borders of their country. It wanted the cumbersome system of passes and certificates totally obliterated. To try and curb African sensitivity to racial discrimination of the 1950's Southern Rhodesian whites promoted a paternalistic policy of "partnership" and "parallel development."[24] This move was a step away from rigid white ethnocentrisms in recognition of the fact that Africans were capable of different levels of "African Civilization."

The solution to African progress under these conditions was, so the whites figured, under a policy of partnership and parallel development in which "civilized Africans" could be permitted to advance but under European control. The net effect of this policy was that it created two Southern Rhodesian nations with handsome economic conditions for the white population.[25]

However, the African's stereotype as backwards and politically puerile continued while racial policy stressed the need for control and protection of town labor. Africans, on the other hand, wanted a greater level of participation in the political process and increased sensitivity to matters of discrimination. The SRANC supporters, to test the whites' seriousness with their policy of

Gestation Stage

partnership demanded services at hotels and eating-places as well as on public transport.

In more ways than one the situation in Southern Rhodesia during the 1950's, especially during the Federation, resembled that of the American South during the same period of time into the early 1960's. Of note here are Welensky's reactions to the struggle by Africans for social and political equality, which resembled those of the Southern US governors, Orval Faubus, 1957 and George Wallace in the 1960's. The resemblance was well captured by Martin Luther King Jr. who wrote about it to the editors of the *Dissent* magazine in June of 1959. King wrote:

Although we are separated by miles we are closer together in mutual struggle for freedom and human brotherhood.[26]

Along the same vein, at a dinner with Tom Mboya, a Kenyan nationalist, King made the remark:

[that] there [was] no basic difference between colonialism and segregation ... our struggles are not only similar; they are in a real sense one.[27]

Nkomo, the leader of the SRANC, while visiting United States in 1959 experienced what he termed the "pinpricks" of US racism when he was denied service at a barbershop in Manhattan because of the color of his skin.[28] The importance of showing such a similarity helps in our understanding of the way the various US governments dealt with the African resistant movements in Southern Rhodesia.

Another of the egregious grievance on the part of Africans arose from unfair education the government afforded them. The government paid very little attention to African education. In fact, education was almost completely left in the hands of missionaries for many years. For instance, the government opened its first primary school built specifically for Africans in 1944. By 1950 the government had constructed only twelve schools for Africans as compared to 2,232 parochial (mission and independent schools). Because of a disproportionate amount allocated to white schools to the disadvantage of blacks, the latter by end of 1950 experienced serious shortage of schools, and in the rural areas teachers were, more often than not, either poorly trained or downright unqualified.

The African educational crisis was so bad that in January, 1958, Nkomo, the leader of the SRANC, was calling for a Conference to be attended by representatives from the government, the missionary groups and SRANC, to address what he characterized, "the present crisis in African education." Nkomo wanted for such a conference to focus on education policy and the difficulties with which African students were encountered in schools.

Nkomo stated:

We [in congress] have a pile of letters of complaints from all over Southern Rhodesia regarding lack of government policy in African Education.[29]

The paucity of educational opportunities on the part of youths therefore made them very ready to accept the gospel of the SRANC which promised better educational opportunities.

The most outstanding grievances of the African people generated from two legislative pieces: the Land Apportionment Act and the Land Husbandry Act. The question of land was at the forefront during the first *Impi YoMvukela* of 1890.[30] The SRANC was able to broaden its base of support around these grievances. Day clearly made this connection between the SRANC and the notorious two government legislative acts:

> *ANC attacked on a wide front. It had particular success in mobilizing discontent against the Native Land Husbandry Act which the Government was trying to implement at this time. The aim of this Act was to improve African farming practices, but it was carried out without taking account of African resentment at two of its principal parts, the destocking of cattle and the transference of communally held land into farms for individuals. Africans regarded these measures as fundamental attacks on their livelihood and traditional ways of life.*[31]

The whole scheme in no time backfired. The African areas were so crowded that new allocated pieces of land were much smaller than the regime had promised. This did not escape the notice of the SRANC President who pointed out:

> *Pastoralists found themselves continually destocking their cattle instead of increasing their herds. That being the case they could not compete for markets with their commercial, white counterparts. The two Acts had serious implications for Africans as Nkomo noted at the time of forcing thousands of Africans off the land [and thereby] providing a useful float of labor for European enterprises.*[32]

The Land Tenure Act of 1930 divided land into two parts, one for Africans and the other for whites. It assigned to the minority whites 49.1 million acres of land and to the Majority blacks, 21.1 million acres. Land allocated to Africans had poor soil, sometimes dry and with very few sources of water. Excepting the mostly tsetse fly infested land, 7.5 million acres was put aside for sale to Africans Under the Native Purchase Area Scheme. The distribution of land was basically unfair to the blacks and they felt robbed of their very livelihood. Because about one third of the black population lived in what was considered white land in the 1930's, these 85,000 families, they were resettled following the Second World War when this Act was rigorously enforced by government. Mostly, the blacks were resettled on land with bad soil, areas infested by tsetse flies and malaria.

The land Apportionment Act and the Land Husbandry Act affected the whole African population irrespective of where they lived given that every African was considered as having his permanent residence in the reserves. Thus, most blacks who lived in towns and cities remained tied to the structure and security of the rural tenure.

Gestation Stage

In the reserves the government tried to increase black agricultural products by emphasizing soil conservation methods, destocking and granting of individual farm rights, and these measures, as has already been pointed out, met with strong black opposition. Destocking for instance meant to the Africans the elimination of their wealth and therefore their status. *Izinduna* [African Chiefs] felt insulted and their power undermined when their right to allocate land was taken away by the Land Husbandry Act.

The last problem to be mentioned here was the exclusion of the black population from the political process. For more than fifty years from the inception of white rule in Southern Rhodesia, the African population passively accepted white domination, displaying little signs of resistance against the discriminatory system upon which that hegemony was predicated. To the majority of the African population, the invincibility of the white man seemed to be the order of the day.

However, an inconsiderable number of African petite bourgeoisie emerged after the Second World War, mainly graduates of mission schools, and these limited their political activities to struggling for economic and political rights for themselves. Little challenge if any was directed against the system itself.

However, as has been pointed out elsewhere in this chapter, by the early 1950's Africans had started agitating for the widening of the electorate so that more Africans were included. The whites of the country were too beginning to move towards accepting a limited role of Africans in the political life of the country, but not before they proved to them that they were capable of making what they considered to be prudent political judgments.

The experiment of involving Africans in parliament came with the introduction of the Federation in 1953, which included three countries: Northern Rhodesia, Nyasaland and Southern Rhodesia. Under the federal constitution of 1953, the federal parliament consisted of six Africans, two from each country, in an assembly of 35 members.[33] In the federal civil service few Africans were appointed to senior positions and one African became a junior minister.

The inclusion of Africans in the federal parliament became possible because of the officially professed policy of the Federation Government, which was racial partnership. However, its implementation for all time remained inadequate to stem the tide of opposition from African nationalists. The white minority electorate, which had a virtual monopoly of political power, remained unwilling to offer political concessions to Africans sufficient enough to placate them. African Nationalists in both Rhodesias, Joshua Nkomo, Leader of the SRANC and his Northern Rhodesia counterpart Harry Nkumbula, respectively, regarded the federation "as a failure because in their opinions; it had increased political discrimination."[34]

The idea of racial partnership was at the outset acceptable to the black elite who considered it better than segregation and through their link with Nyasaland

and Northern Rhodesia they hoped to influence Southern Rhodesia to adopt more progressive racial policy. However, two basic behaviors by the white regime proved to the black nationalists that partnership was a vacuous notion. These behaviors were the implementation of a partnership which derived from the way it was interpreted by the white rulers and the stringent voting qualifications.

While the black nationalists thought racial partnership would usher in equality of all races, the whites had a different meaning to it whereby blacks were seen as juniors in this multiracial endeavor. For instance, Godfrey Huggins, who became the first Federal Prime Minister, characterized the partnership between blacks and whites as one between junior and senior partners. More specifically, he characterized that partnership as one between the horse and its rider and the African nationalists were under no illusion as who was the horse and who was the rider. At a rally in Harare Township on March 2, 1958, Joshua Nkomo reminded his restive African audience what the implications of this relationship meant. Uppermost in Nkomo's mind were Huggins specific words when he said of the partnership,

It is the same that exists between the rider and his horse. They don't eat or sleep together but there is a working understanding between them.[35]

Nkomo remarked: "When evening comes, the rider goes into his comfortable house, while the horse is sent to stay in the stables."Nkomo went on to sharply criticize the attempt by whites at widening the franchise for the Southern Rhodesian blacks whereby the regime set educational, income and property qualifications so that an insignificant number of blacks qualified to vote:

The qualifications which Godfrey Huggins' government put as requirements for African voters were ridiculous, especially coming from a man who professed liberalism. He put two requirements to the common roll for Africans: one, demanded an annual income of one two hundred 240 pounds and a satisfactory grade on a literacy test, and another two, which was in place of literacy test and annual income, required a grammar school education.

What was preposterous about the whole scheme was that very few Africans had that money or education, and to make things worse, property that Africans owned in the rural areas did not count towards this income. This made it virtually impossible for the majority of the African population to qualify as voters.[36]

Thus, the whites extended franchise to the black population while demanding "the best means of ensuring that the government remain for all time in responsible and civilized men."[37] They totally repudiated the notion of universal suffrage for the reason that it

[W]ould place the European minority entirely in the hands of a black African majority, a majority for the most part uneducated and backward.[38]

Gestation Stage

Nkomo, however, speaking on behalf of his organization at his first presidential address at the first and last SRANC Congress, made it clear that his party wanted nothing short of majority rule and strongly decried discrimination as the basis of African disenfranchisement.

Nkomo declared:

The monopoly of the settlers for making laws that govern this country has corrupted the democratic parliamentary institution renowned the world over. And not only has it done that, it has also destroyed the human values of the settlers themselves, in that it has made them believe that they alone as a race are capable of ruling this country. What Congress wants is self-government for all the inhabitants.[39]

It is important to note that the majority of the educated African population initially thought kindly of the concept of racial partnership. Consequently, some of them who later became radicalized politically joined different multiracial associations. Largely these Africans were attracted to the African Capricorn Society and the Interracial Association, and some to the Federal Party. A good example is that of Nkomo and Stanlake Samkange who joined Godfrey Huggins' Federal Party, Leopold Takawira became the executive secretary of Capricorn Africa Society and Edson Sithole and George Nyandoro played a prominent role in Interracial Association.[40]

Nkomo, however was first critical of the federation, but later, he changed his mind when he thought the pre-reconstituted SRANC had lost sight of better strategies to achieve opportunities for the blacks to participate in the political life of the country and joined the United Rhodesia Party, formed by Huggins in 1934. Nkomo at that point was so much sold to the idea of partnership that he, in 1956, attended Huggins' Party congress as an experiment in breaking discriminatory political barriers. However, as a result of cynical half-hearted measures on the implementation of the concept of partnership by whites, Africans became increasingly militant and engaged in waves of demonstrations and protests.

Demonstrations and international campaigns by black nationalists became the order of the day, more prominently during the years 1958 and 1959, the year SRANC was proscribed. Houser well captured this change by Africans from a position of avid support of the notion of racial partnership to a position where they stringently decried the concept as well as the factors leading to their newly discovered position.

Houser wrote:

Any hope that partnership in the federation might have worked was dashed by the declaration of a state of emergency, the banning of the congress, and the arrest of the leaders in early 1959.[41]

Once again the exclusion of the majority of blacks as voters created room for easier recruitment by the nationalists. Towards the end of 1960 black nationalists were literally deriding the notion of multi-racialism as espoused by the minority government. Open hostility to this multi-racialism was shown after the nationalist movement repudiated the proposed constitution of 1961.Instead, black nationalists called for the burial of this concept of multiracialism. Nkomo, the president of the party felt "the nonsense of creating a multi-racial society in the country should stop."[42]

The last but not the least source of discontent on the part of Africans which made them more inclined to accept the message of black nationalists and also for the elite black to debunk the notion of partnership was the ouster of Garfield Todd as Prime Minister in February of 1958. Despite a strong African resentment of the Federation, and despite the ruthlessness with which Todd dealt with the 1954 Railway and the Railway strike of 1956, many blacks had confidence in him and his efforts to increase the amount of African representation in parliament.

In Todd, most blacks saw a leader who had their interests at heart and "believed his government was in some sense theirs."[43] Todd was also popular with workers because of his support for what blacks viewed as a reasonable minimum wage of six pounds and ten shillings.[44] It can be justifiably argued that with the expulsion of Todd as Prime Minister, many Africans lost any hope of ever achieving racial equality by espousing the federal notion of partnership.

Thus, poverty and revulsion toward the system in towns, overcrowding in the reserves, the exclusion of Africans from political participation through the introduction of very stringent voters' qualifications, the undermining of African economic and social security through the implementation of the Land Apportionment, and Land Husbandry Acts and the suppression of African unions, all created a context conducive to the growth of the SRANC membership towards the close of the 1950's.

Much of the extant literature on Zimbabwe, in fact, addresses these questions, often stressing the fact that it was some of these fore-mentioned issues which eventually generated political anger on the part of black Zimbabweans.[45] Within a year, the SRANC had established 22 branches throughout Southern Africa and its membership was reported at 6,000 by May 1958.[46]

3.3 SRANC Membership and Recruiting Methods

The fact that the SRANC voiced grievances and also championed some of the basic causes and aspirations of the peasants and workers as well as the rural folk was critical. But this alone could not have guaranteed it the massive following the SRANC received within almost two years of its existence. More than its relevant agenda, it was its leadership's ability to organize, which proved decisive.

The SRANC's organizational strategy ranged from house to house recruiting, village-to-village organization, addressing people at grassroots bodies such as churches, community based organizations such as Burial Societies, and continental conferences such as the All African People's Conference. Its leaders

Gestation Stage

also addressed rallies and engaged in direct confrontation with the regime in terms of demonstrations. The SRANC also canvassed for the support of the international governments and non-governmental organizations.

The SRANC main membership came from the peasantry, workers, the African elites, as well as from the European sector. From the African population the party drew its main following from the rural, mostly uneducated blacks. In acting as a national organization for the blacks the SRANC had an automatic constituency in the urban areas consisting of educated black leaders but mostly workers and members of moribund organizations. Commenting on the nature of the SRANC Nathan Shamuyarira accurately observed:

> *The peasantry and workers overwhelmed the few intellectuals of the country. This was even reflected in the leadership. The ANC was both urban and rural based. The masses shared in the leadership particularly in the rural branches.*[47]

Thus, the SRANC presented a break-through in African organizational activity. Subsequent to its formation most Black organizations with the exception of the Rhodesian Industrial and Commercial Workers Union (RICO)[48] were elitist and therefore by their nature permitted of very little participation on the part of the rural, mostly uneducated Africans.[49] The SRANC was therefore unique in that it extensively recruited the rural folk for its membership. Cognizant of this fact, and essentially agreeing with Shamiyarira, Day wrote:

> *In the history of African political organizations in Southern Rhodesia the revitalized ANC was unique, for it succeeded, as no other had done, in creating by vigorously proselytizing a countrywide, mass movement with perpetual momentum. It united the new proletariat of the African townships with the traditional peasantry of the African Reserves in radical protest at political, economic and social discrimination practiced by the European minority against the Africans.*[50]

The recruitment of people in the rural areas was done largely by the party's faithful, most of whom initially came from the urban areas. They visited people in their villages conscientizing them on the dire political situation. Mzila Moyo was one of the first group of people to recruit membership for this organization. Reminiscing on the initial days of recruitment at the inception of the SRANC in 1957 Moyo commented:

> *It was easy to recruit people for a party that championed their grievances because people were already angry with the government, the Izinduna, [chiefs] and Uzulu, [general black population]. We visited people in their fields, villages and often took advantage of people's gatherings organized by chiefs who sympathized with our causes. We also spoke to people at dip-tanks.*[51]

Thus, as accurately observed by Moyo, black people's anger borne of their frustration with the minority government of the day was the primary organizational factor that made it easier for the party to recruit for membership. The SRANC succeeded in prosecuting a campaign which linked rural and urban problems on the part of the black population. Rural grievances came mainly from the effects of the Land Apportionment Act. Thus low wages, bad housing conditions and inadequate educational funding mainly caused the urban black problems.

The nationalist movement also enlisted membership by appealing to blacks' primordial sensibilities. This marked the onset of the African cultural renaissance. The nationalists draw attention to their adherents of how their "simple and generous" tradition stood in contradistinction to that of the whites which they characterized as selfish and oppressive. To dramatize their convictions they asked people to put on their traditional attire and mostly their skin hats:

> *I am aware some people think that the appeal for people to put on traditional cloths (lion-cloth) was a phenomenon of the 1960's. Nothing can be farther from the truth. The appeal to put on our skin cloths, especially hats, was started and popularized when SRANC was founded in 1957. This approach had a galvanizing effect in that it brought so many of our people into our party which was seen as identifying with their way of traditional life-style and their suffering.*[52]

The method of appealing to the primordial sensibilities of Africans as a way of bringing solidarity among them was so effective that the contemporary Federal Prime Minister, Sir Godfrey Huggins refused to accept Federal African representatives who appeared in their traditional clothes. According to his uncritical supporter, Wood, Huggins, fearing that Dauti (David) Yamba, one of Northern Rhodesia Federal African representative, might attend parliament in traditional cloths and thereby draw publicity to essentially African way of life, Huggins sanctimoniously declared: "Western Parliament required European dress," as this uncritical supporter put it this way:

> *Fearing that he [David Yamba] might appear in a toga, topped by a fantastic headdress, and therefore secure inordinate publicity, Huggins testily ruled that, as Parliament was based on a Western tradition, only Western dress was appropriate.*[53]

This incident might seem inconsequential, but it went a long way in showing that the administration feared the galvanizing effect the appeal to a traditional way of life expressed by putting on traditional cloths had on the African population. Huggins went on to make a law against African traditional cloths. Huggins thought that African traditional dress was dirty and uncouth, a badge of inferiority.

To Higgins, allowing Africans to pass on their own traditional attire would not only be promoting their political identity, but essentially, would have an effect of accepting the notion of the equality of all races, a concept that was totally repugnant to him and his kith and kin. Although Huggins, in theory, subscribed to the notion of equality as Africans' economic lot improved in the long run he proved to be a white supremacist, who was full of mindless

Gestation Stage

prejudice. After five months of passing the law on dress, Huggins, once again, indulging in his undiplomatic lapses, during a debate on African dress and the notion of equality, remarked:

> *You cannot expect the European to form up in a queue with dirty people, possibly an old umfazi [African Woman] with an infant on her back.*[54]

The SRANC also used the phraseology of the white regime, advocating partnership. Because of its non-racial policy, the SRANC attracted membership from the white population. Its membership included, according to Houser, about a hundred European members.[55] Thus, the party extended its recruitment to the liberal white population. Its racial inclusiveness was essentially in keeping with its non-racial policy as outlined in its statement of principles and policies:

> *Its aim is the national unity of all the inhabitants of the country in true partnership, regardless of race, color or creed. It stands for a complete integrated society; equality of opportunity in every sphere; and social, economic and political advancement of all. It regards these objectives as the essential foundation of that partnership between people of all races, without which there can be no peaceful progress in this country.*[56]

To try and gain the sympathy of Britain, the SRANC adopted a pro-Crown policy by affirming, as Shamuyarira points out, "complete loyalty to the crown as the symbol of national unity" sincerely believing that Britain could help in the decolonization of Southern Rhodesia.[57] Britain had already shown that it no longer was interested in preserving formal colonial rule by starting a process of decolonization in Ghana. This was true of Britain particularly after the Second World War.

To the extent that the nationalists wanted Southern Rhodesia decolonized by demanding participation in the country's political process their goal ultimately was the same as that of Britain: decolonization.[58] As such, the SRANC's trust in that Britain was going to help them was not without foundation, and this also explains the organization's unflinching support of the Crown.

The SRANC did not confine its recruitment to only locals. In 1958 Nkomo traveled to Accra to attend the All African People's Conference (AAPC) hosted by Kwame Nkrumah. More than 300 delegates from 65 parties or groups attended to discuss the struggle for independence in the continent. At this meeting there were also organizations from overseas. The American Committee on Africa (ACOA), which was led by George Houser, sent a representative from the United States.

There were also around 25 representatives of American non-governmental organizations in attendance. Apart from the ACOA these groups included the American Federation of Labor-Congress of Industrial Organizations (AFL-CIO), African-American Institute, American Society of African Culture, Harlem-based United African Nationalist Movement, American Service Committee, Associated Negro Press, and African academic specialists. Charles Diggs, a first-term black congressman attended as an observer.

The Soviet Union and China also sent representatives.[59] With this heavy representation, Nkomo did not lose time in galvanizing support for his nationalist party in its efforts to decolonize Southern Rhodesia. Nkomo's active participation in the deliberation of the conference was evidenced by the fact that he was chosen as the Federal member of the Conference's Steering Committee, and undoubtedly, his involvement made him and his cause for his country very visible to the delegates. It was at this conference that Nkomo made friends of George Houser of the ACOA, a man whose organization would support his successive parties to the day of independence in 1980.[60]

It was also after the Accra Conference that independent African and Asian states started to financially and materially support nationalist parties in Southern Rhodesia.[61] On the continent, the SRANC, because of its Pan-African approach, cultivated a close working relationship with its ANC counterparts in Northern Rhodesia and Nyasaland, especially in its fight against the federation.

The following year, 1959, Nkomo left for the United States where he traveled across the country speaking about the struggle for independence in Southern Africa. ACOA and students in some US universities showed tremendous support for his campaign for the decolonization of Southern Rhodesia. Nkomo also quickly appreciated that while some Americans were racists like the leaders who were at the helm of the Federation, many others such as George Houser and the university students who warmly received him were not, and were also helpful. Thus, the SRANC canvassed for support locally, regionally and internationally.

However, it should be pointed out that although the party reached out to all and sundry among the African population, the educated elite and a majority of business people were not initially attracted to the organization. They were still beholden to the notion of the federation and **multiracialism** and "not the sort of struggle the SRANC proposed."[62]

Some scholars viewed the SRANC as a moderate organization, which was only interested in gaining a place in a multiracial government through peaceful and constitutional means. For instance, Terence Ranger points out that SRANC remained, "by comparison with other African movements elsewhere, a moderate and painstakingly non-racial organization." True, the SRANC was non-racial, however, it could not be totally characterized as moderate as one security intelligence report observed:

> There has been nothing constructive in their [SRANC leaders] criticism and distortions of the truth which have formed the greater part of congress propaganda have clearly been designed to cause unrest. The attack on Governments Departments have had as their object the undermining of the prestige of the Native Commissioners and the loyalty of African police.
>
> The inevitable consequences of this trend will be the creation of a situation in which African masses will be induced to take unconstitutional action over

Gestation Stage

some imaginary grievance and the peace and tranquility of the territory will be unnecessarily disrupted.

Also, such a demand as one which Nkomo made on behalf of the SRANC, when he demanded for an immediate inclusion of African in government and went further to tell the white regime that the African people were making the demand not as "supplicants," but as people who knew their rights,[63] could not be interpreted as moderate in any way, shape or form.

Towards the end of 1958, into 1959, it became clear to the nationalists, and even to some African elites who were hitherto uninterested in the cause of the black nationalists, that the Federal government was only interested in cynical half-measures of racial partnership. Otherwise, the whites' main objective was the retention of unmitigated economic and social privilege, as well as political supremacy. This position was well articulated by Sir Roy Welensky, the second Federal Prime Minister, when he explained:

> *We believe that the African should be given more say in the running of the country, as and when he shows his ability to contribute more to the general good, but we must make it clear that even when that day comes, in a hundred or two hundred year's time, he can never hope to dominate the partnership. He can achieve equal standing but not go beyond it.*[64]

The African nationalists responded to the whites' entrenched position by demanding majority rule. Whites were alarmed and blamed Garfield Todd for what they alleged was his moderate stance towards the blacks, and his condemnation of discriminatory electoral practices in the federation, although in reality Todd introduced more stringent qualifications for casting votes on the part of Africans. Meanwhile conditions inside Southern Rhodesia had become tense.

Todd had been defeated because the whites found him to be too moderate. He was consequently forced to resign and Edgar Whitehead, who adopted a stronger position against the demands of African nationalists, although he continued sponsoring the problematic, racial partnership concept, became the Prime Minister of Southern Rhodesia.

For instance, Whitehead rapidly moved to repeal Southern Rhodesia's petty pass laws and opened public service to blacks; he integrated cinemas, eradicated black and white queues at banks and post offices, permitted blacks to attend private multiracial schools and introduced racially integrated sports.[65]

During February, 1959, a wave of protest against the Federation by the SRANC-led blacks swept across the country to which the Federal Government responded by declaring a state of emergency. On February 25, 1959, the SRANC was proscribed throughout the Federation. Nationalists leaders in Northern Rhodesia and Nyasaland were apprehended and thrown into prison.

Although there were no open disturbances in Southern Rhodesia at the time the state of emergency was declared throughout the Federation, Whitehead banned the SRANC on February 26, 1959, and more than 500 of its members were detained at various prisons around the country: Khami, Marandellas and

Selukwe. The government further confiscated the SRANC's property under the infamous Unlawful Organization Act. It was reported that the Whitehead regime confiscated the SRANC's property to the tune of 15,000 pounds.

Nkomo, its leader, escaped the dragnet because he was out of the country. Three months prior to the banning of his party, Nkomo had left Southern Rhodesia to attend a conference in Accra, and instead of returning home at the end of the conference traveled to London via Egypt. He was in Egypt when SRANC was banned. Subsequently, he continued to London where he established a base and did not return home until October 1, 1960.[66] Whitehead justified his banning of the SRANC by alleging that black nationalists incited the black population to violence, ridiculed legal authorities and defied the law of the land. To effect the proscription of the SRANC, Whitehead rushed through parliament the Unlawful Organization Act.

To this Act the regime quickly added the Preventative Detention Act, which gave power to the government to imprison any person who had been involved in the 1959 violence as well as indefinitely detain people without trial, and the Native Affairs Amendment Act,[67] which put the holding of rallies by black nationalists at the mercy of the grudging local commissioners. Thus, Whitehead responded to African nationalism with a mixture of repression and liberalism. The two-pronged approach was calculated at eliminating Black Nationalism by arresting and destroying the property of its leaders and supporters, as well as co-opting the African elite by offering very limited reforms.

The banning of the SRANC had very debilitating implications for Black Nationalism in Southern Rhodesia. The leadership's political activities were severely circumscribed and their access to the rural areas, although possible, was very limited. The party's basic structure was significantly shaken with most of its leadership, among whom were Chikerema and Nyandoro, behind bars, and they would remain imprisoned for four years.[68] This persuaded most of the black leadership to believe that the only way out was by enlisting the assistance of Britain, which still had residual power over Southern Rhodesia, and debunking the notion of partnership.

Thus, the focus of marshalling support against the repressive regime shifted from inside Southern Rhodesia, mainly because of the internal hostile and repressive environment, to the international arena.[69]

At this point the SRANC had come to realize that trying to work for a one-man-one vote within constitutional strictures brought them very little results if any at all, as such reforms did very little to change the structure of white society which concentrated power exclusively in white hands.

3.4 THE FOUNDING OF THE NATIONAL DEMOCRATIC PARTY AND THE INTRODUCTION OF THE CONSTITUTIONAL STRUGGLE

With almost all the Black Nationalist leaders either in prison or in self-exile, there was no organized African organization for nearly a year from the banning

Gestation Stage

of the SRANC. In part, the absence of an organized nationalist party was because of either the restricted or self-exiled leadership, and in part, because of the series of draconian laws promulgated by the government to control political activity.[70] Nevertheless, in January 1, 1960, the NDP was formed to replace the SRANC, and Michael Mawema, a moderate black nationalist who also was abroad when the SRANC got banned, was elected the interim leader.[71]

Chikerema and Nyandoro, although in prison at that time, had a hand in the formation of the NDP. Because of Mawema's failing health, Leopold Takawira was elected interim Leader when he stepped down in September, 1960. When the first NDP's Congress was convened on November 28, 1960, Joshua Nkomo, who until November, 1960 was based in London,[72] was elected President of the NDP in absentia.[73]

The long goal of the NDP was, as has been pointed out, to enlist the British support for majority rule, and its more immediate one was to be included in the Constitutional Conference, which was to be convened by Britain the following year, 1961. Gone and buried was the support of racial partnership as a viable notion by which to attain equality in so far as African nationalists and their supporters were concerned.

However, Whitehead had not given up on the ambivalent partnership notion. The Supreme Court, under his government, in October 1961, opened swimming pools to all races. Reflecting the same disdain for this idea of racial partnership as most of the blacks engaged in resisting the Whitehead regime, Nkomo scornfully remarked about the ruling: "We don't want to swim in your swimming-pools. We want to swim with you in parliament."[74]

This was, evidently, a new emphasis in the black nationalists body politics. More than the SRANC did, the NDP concentrated on trying to bring about constitutional change by demanding outright self-rule. Enock Dumbutshena was more explicit about this new demand for black self-rule and increasing aversion to half-measure reforms in his letter to Shamuyarira who was a journalist at that time. Dumbutshena wrote:

Our people surprise me by continually harping on things like amendments to the State Lotteries, the Liquor Act and so on. These things are useless. What about a majority in the Legislative Council? ... This is the thing that matters.[75]

The NDP inherited the membership of the old SRANC, similar goals and organizational structure, as well as leadership. However, the NDP went a step beyond the SRANC by making the clearest enunciation of the call for black self-rule based on a one man, one vote. The NDP was openly radically political. Its radical nature was seen during the 1960 demonstration in support of its arrested leaders which started out as a peaceful one, but soon turned out violent when the police provoked the peaceful demonstrators.

Because this was a first demonstration in which some demonstrators were killed, and as well as its effect in further radicalizing African nationalism it is worth describing briefly the events of this first black violence leading to the first death of blacks in the hands of whites since the *Impi YoMvukela* of 1890's. In fact, it can be correctly argued that in 1960, Southern Rhodesia was engulfed by a wave of rural and urban violence and destruction of property, which was unprecedented in this country's history since the risings of the 1890's.

The protests were triggered by the arrest of more NDP leaders in July 1960. The organization first engaged in passive resistance. Sketchy Samkange, one of its leaders, who later was joined by wives of detainees, fasted outside Sir Edgar Whitehead's office for three days in protest against the continued detention of black nationalists.[76] The fourteen detainees' wives also staged their own sit-in protest outside Whitehead's office with the support of Sketchy Samkange and other NDP officials. They were arrested, fined, and released. The NDP followed a non-violent path in its quest for justice, which it later converted into a principled philosophy. Sketchy Samkange, one of its founder members articulated this approach in his article that appeared in <u>Dissent</u> in March 1960:

> *The NDP has taken pains to explain to the people that nothing can be achieved by violence.... Less than a month after this was declared to people, `civilized man' demonstrates [in the killing of 72 `African passive resisters' by the South African Police] by means of violence the way to rule in a no more dark Africa.*[77]

In July, things escalated into violence. On the evening of 19 July 1960, 4,000 people attended the protests. Enos Nkala and George Silundika led the protesters. Among the leaders who addressed the protesters was George Silundika who delivered a rousing speech to the crowd, telling them that since Whitehead considered NDP unlawful, they should all turn themselves to the police. Melwa Ntini recounted what happened next:

> *Demonstrators walked to the Highfields police station and told the police to put them under arrest. You should have seen the police force literally begging us to leave. That was a small victory for us there, and yet a significant one. When the police refused to take us into prison we proceeded to the city to see Whitehead.*[78]

By noon of July 20, the following day, the crowd had swelled up to more than 30,000 people. The scene was profoundly disconcerting to Whitehead who immediately sent out police and soldiers to stop the demonstrators at the outskirts of the Harare Township. Before long, police and armed soldiers were charging on the crowd firing tear gas and roughing up the peaceful demonstrators.

The government, by reacting in this manner, as Samkange accurately observed, showed people that peaceful demonstrations would not achieve anything.[79] The demonstrators soon responded in kind destroying property such as churches, schools, beer halls, and stores.

In Bulawayo in particular, black violent response to police brutality was widespread. There the riots spread over two days, July 24 and 25. The show of force in Bulawayo was comparatively more formidable than it was in Salisbury (today's Harare). In a very dramatic fashion, the US Consulate at Salisbury, in

Gestation Stage

an incoming telegram, described the militarily charged situation in Bulawayo as follows:

> *Disturbances [in] Bulawayo continue [to] reach more reported using serious proportions. Four thousand troops and police established [a] six-mile cordon between the city and [the] African townships. Security forces gunfire one morning; 26th bring unofficial death toll [to] seven with several score others treated for injuries. Arrests totaled over one hundred by late 25th.*[80]

Despite the heavy use of physical force by the troops and the police, demonstrators overturned cars, burned buildings, as well as fired rocks into a line of mounted police and troops in armored vehicles.[81] The second day, industry went dead, and blacks boycotted buses, in fact, they attacked anything that belonged to the central government,[82] and public transportation was one such possession.

By the end of the riots, twelve Africans had been killed by government forces and several hundreds injured, by a conservative count.[83] Eleven of this number was killed in Bulawayo. To try and thwart any future demonstrations by nationalist movements, the government promulgated The Law and Order Maintenance Amendment Act, one of the most draconian laws that violated all freedoms known to man.

As I have already observed, the government's violent response to what was a peaceful demonstration forced black nationalists to think peaceful means as the only way of agitating for justice would achieve them nothing. From that point on, blacks used purposive violence each time the government attacked them.

The NDP also became more aggressive in its pursuit of Pan-Africanism as compared to the SRANC. Undoubtedly, Ghana's recently won independence had increased the importance of pan-Africanism ideals in the eyes of black nationalists. This could be deduced from its initial statement of principles. The NDP declared that it was fighting for:

> *The attainment of freedom for the African people of Southern Rhodesia ... the granting of one man, one vote for all inhabitants of Southern Rhodesia [and finally it aimed at] working in Africa for the establishment and maintenance of full democracy in Africa and the achievement of pan-Africanism.*[84]

Evidently, the NDP had repudiated the idea of power sharing, and now wanted all power in the hands of the blacks. Paralleling Black Nationalism was white nationalism, which at this time was approaching a pitch level. The whites wanted independence under white minority rule, and they wanted it before the advent of black majority rule.

Consequently, the first immediate task of the NDP was to try and persuade the British Government not to make any constitutional concessions to the white minority rule, which precluded black self-rule. Black nationalists wanted Britain to waken to its 1921 responsibility over Southern Rhodesia, and intervene to grant black majority rule. For some reason, black nationalists saw Britain as a benevolent imperialist.

Thus, imperialism for once was thought of as a force that could be harnessed to good purposes. To further show their resolve for attaining majority rule, and thereby preempting any imposition of white minority rule, the nationalist boycotted the Monckton Commission, which was holding hearings in Southern Rhodesia on race relations and the future of the Federation.[85]

Black nationalists suspected the Commission was going to side with the white minority government and recommend the elimination of Britain's historical prerogative (reserved powers).[86] Instead, the nationalists sent a delegation to London to present the organization's case to Lord Home.[87] Edgar Whitehead, the Prime Minister of Southern Rhodesia was already in London, trying to persuade the British government to grant his government a larger measure of self-determination by removing its reserved powers. Britain would grant neither party its wishes, but instead would settle for a constitutional conference to promote racial partnership in government.

However, the NDP delegation won a small victory when the British government promised it that no changes would be made to the constitution until the future of the Federation was known.[88]

Along the same vein, the NDP wrote its first ever Memorandum demanding a Constitutional Conference to transfer power to the majority blacks and presented it to Lord Home,[89] the British Secretary for Commonwealth Relations. In this memorandum the NDP also called for the restriction of the constitution so that it included the Bill of Rights. The party also sought to present its views to the British Prime Minister, Harold Wilson, on the Federation and the future of Southern Rhodesia when he visited the colony in mid-January, 1960.

The NDP essentially followed the SRANC strategy of working for a "one man, one vote," within constitutional structures. The major difference was that the NDP party concentrated more on gaining external support than on organizing people eternally, and it was more radical than its predecessor, the SRANC. Clearly, the arrest of some of the SRANC leadership and some of its membership had an effect of radicalizing members of its successor, the NDP.

There was also, understandably, a practical reason for the organization's concentration more on marshalling external support than it did on the internal one. In fact, as was accurately observed by Day, "the NDP was adopted the policy, untried by SRANC, of pressing the British Government to intervene in Southern Rhodesia politics."[90] This reason also accounts for why the NDP essentially was an urban-based organization. As has been alluded to elsewhere in this chapter, at the proscription of the SRANC, the government tried its best to eliminate black political activity in the rural areas by passing the Native Affairs Amendment Act,[91] whose effect virtually proscribed political activities by African nationalists in the rural areas.

Gestation Stage

To this Act was added the notorious and draconian Law and Order Maintenance Act of 1960, which gave power to the police to break-up political meetings and rallies, also to arrest and detain at whim, among other things.[92] Despite all these efforts at stopping political activity in the rural areas, contact between the urban-based leadership and the rural folk remained very effective. Thus, the link in problems that the SRANC established between the urban and rural black population, was continued under the NDP.

Its leader led the campaign for international support for the black people's struggle in Southern Rhodesia. During his self-exile, subsequent to the banning of the SRANC, Nkomo traveled widely explaining the political plight of the Southern Rhodesian blacks, and the need for international action against the white regime. Thus, more than any other person in Southern Rhodesia, Nkomo helped to internationalize the Southern Rhodesian black struggle.

3.5 Membership Recruitment and Strategies of Struggle

I have already alluded to some ways the NDP recruited its membership. Besides inheriting most of its members from the proscribed SRANC, it recruited new members, largely from the black population in the rural and urban areas. Thus, like the SRANC, NDP was a mass movement. Most of the newly recruited members, as well as those who continued with the resistance movement, were either moved to join or to remain in the black movement because of the continued economic deprivations, political repression and land shortage they suffered. In the rural areas, mostly because of the Land Husbandry Act, families suffered as a result of reduced amounts of land made available to them, and cattle destocking.[93]

Taking advantage of these grievances, black nationalists held rallies, knocked on doors, held meetings in churches, funerals and during weddings and many other African social gatherings to recruit membership for their party.[94] The party also continued the strategy encouraging the blacks to repudiate material manifestations of Europeanism. They started using wooden plates, spoons and taking off their shoes and ties at rallies and meetings with more regularity than ever before.[95] Rallies had begun with singing, playing of drums and ancestral veneration.

A call to embrace symbols that were seen as typical African was made so as to instill pride in Africans and also to create a sense of solidarity among nationalists and their followers. NDP became the first black mass-based nationalist movement in Southern Rhodesia to attract, en masse, blacks of distinction.[96]

To extract some concessions from the government of the day, NDP wrote petitions, negotiated, and engaged in demonstrations and protests. They petitioned mostly the British government for representation at the constitutional conference once it became obvious to them that such a conference was inevitable. Whitehead's government strongly opposed NDP's participation because it believed it would interfere with the whites' move toward their own independence from Britain.

Despite Whitehead's regime's opposition, NDP secured representation at the constitutional conference that lasted from the end of 1960 into the early part of 1961. By this time both blacks and whites had given up on the notion of the Federation. The white population had supported the Federation for economic reasons, and the notion of partnership because it was on this concept that the Federation was predicated.

When the Monckton Commission informed the white community that the Federation could succeed only if racial partnership was fully implemented, they went ballistic as they saw the implementation of such a recommendation as synonymous with the elimination of white privilege. I have already pointed out the reason Africans came to oppose the notion of racial partnership so that it is unnecessary to repeat it.

The NDP delegation to the constitutional conference included its President, its National Chairman, Ndabaningi Sithole, who were advised by Herbert Chitepo and George Silundika. At the conference NDP demanded one man, one vote and a Bill of Rights that would protect them from being treated as second class citizens. The delegation initially accepted the constitution, which granted 15 seats to Africans in a house of 65, a franchise that would have postponed African majority rule for decades.

In return, the black nationalists were granted their demand for constitutional provision of a justiciable Bill of Rights, which, however, was not applicable retroactively. This then meant that this Bill of Rights had no effect on the notorious discriminatory Acts which were already in effect. Also, according to these constitutional provisions, a multi-racial constitutional council was established to monitor violations of the declaration of rights provided for by the constitution.

To entice the whites to accept this constitution, Britain indicated she would suspend her residual power clauses regarding Africans. However, the choicest thing which the whites wanted was complete independence from Britain, independence for themselves, to the exclusion of the blacks.

On February 8, the NDP leadership issued a press statement explaining why it accepted the constitution and also taking credit for its final reading. The press statement read:

> *We feel that the new provisions have given us a certain amount of assurance that the country will not pursue policies, which mean that Africans would be perpetually unable to control their country.... Above all we have a new constitution which is an achievement resulting from the pressure of the NDP, a thing never before thought of in this country.*[97]

Robert Mugabe, the party's Publicity Secretary, on February 7, 1960 also echoed the same optimism when he said:

Gestation Stage

Several major features proposed in the Constitution have fallen into line with the demands that have been made by the N.D.P. since its inception. These have been the enshrinement of a declaration of rights, the outlawing of discrimination and the protection of the rights by the Courts.[98]

To this statement Nkomo on his return to Southern Rhodesia added:" *We have moved the mountain an inch. Independence is around the corner."*[99] *Sincerely believing that the compromise on the constitution was the best thing they could make at the time, the delegates celebrated what they initially saw as a political break through on the part of the African population and a great milestone on the road to attaining power.*

In fact, four days after the end of the Conference, the NDP held a special congress at which it did not repudiate the proposed constitution but instead laid down conditions upon which the whole national electorate could participate in the constitutional referendum. The NDP demanded that for it to participate in the referendum, the land question should be settled in a way that met the needs of the black population; all nationalists starting from the SRANC era to date held in prison were to be released; the NDP should be allowed to hold political meetings in the rural areas; and that the Federal government should not meddle in the constitutional deliberations of Northern Rhodesia.

Disturbed by the NDP's reactions to the constitution, Sandys hurried back to Southern Rhodesia. The purpose of his unexpected trip back to Southern Africa was to "discuss points of interests" with participants who had attended the constitutional conference. The NDP met and told him they were more concerned with the discussion of the land issue, and that they wanted a conference on that issue alone.[100] Sandy repudiated their request, and that refusal prompted a second special conference of the NDP. The conference was convened on June 17-18, 1961 in Bulawayo.

The purpose of this meeting was to discuss the constitution in light of the new developments, spurred by Sandys' refusal to discuss the land question. Holding such a meeting in Bulawayo was very symbolic. This was a city known for its violent resistance and also for harder attitudes.[101] True to the resistant character of its residents, the conference rejected the entire constitution and also voted to conduct its own referendum as well as to cast a vote of confidence for Nkomo as the party's president.[102]

Following this second special congress was a very historic retreat for the party leadership that was held in the Matopo Hills. Again the choice of this location for a retreat was both historic and symbolic. Matopo Hills served as an AmaNdebele laager during the *Impi Yomvukela* (the risings of 1896-97). To this day it is known as a place of defiance and fierce resistance. At that retreat the leadership decided not to contest the fifteen seats. This decision was endorsed by the October 1961 congress that was held, again in Bulawayo, at the MacDonald Hall, in Mzilikazi Township.[103]

However, in time, the delegation was immediately met with a storm of protest from some leaders of the NDP particularly, Takawira and Mawema. Mawema took his protest so seriously to the extent that he broke away from the NDP and formed his own party, the Zimbabwe Nationalist Party (ZNP). Although the ZNP was short-lived, it served as a fitting dress rehearsal for a split that would occur in 1963, two years later.

It is important to note that despite its protests against the compromise made by the NDP delegation, the ZNP essentially followed the same political path as the NDP. Like the NDP it considered the British government as a force that could help in the bringing about of black majority rule, and worked for this goal within acceptable constitutional strictures. The President got much of the blame for the compromise, much of which came from Takawira and Mawema, and was based, according to Nkomo himself, on grudges against him for winning the presidency of the NDP.

According to Nkomo, Takawira and Mawema were using the results of the negotiations as a pretext to create negative feelings against his leadership. However, through his skillful management of the crisis, Nkomo was able to avoid a damaging split of his party.

Sensing a clear and present danger to his leadership, Nkomo turned around and strongly repudiated the agreement.[104] The rest of the NDP leadership went on an offensive, vehemently denouncing the constitution and campaigning for the boycotting of the upcoming Government referendum on the constitutional proposals. The NDP also held its own referendum among the blacks, who too rejected the proposals.[105] From that time on, until the day that the people of Southern Rhodesia voted on the new constitution, the NDP repeatedly attacked the proposed constitution, and urged its voting supporters not to participate in the constitutional referendum, or any elections. Instead, blacks held their own unofficial referendum. In this unofficial referendum, the blacks repudiated the constitutional proposals by an overwhelming count of 467,189 to 584. The whites, on the other hand, approved it by a nearly two-to-one margin.[106] Despite the strong opposition from the NDP, the 1961 constitution became law in December, 1961, and three days later NDP was banned.

Events leading to the proscription of the NDP were very telling of the direction that African nationalism would follow from that time on. When the NDP members learnt that Britain was not going to stop the 1961 constitution from becoming the law of the land they erupted into violent riots, which involved the destruction of property owned by whites, schools and churches. As the campaign against the constitution intensified, riots also broke out in the rural areas.

In such places as Wenlock, Esigodini, Enkayi, Kezi, Enkledon, Tsholotsho, Lower Gwelo, indeed all over Southern Rhodesia, deep tanks were put to disuse, rail-lines and farm fencing belonging to the whites cut. In the cities, the black population exploded with retaliatory violence as well. In Bulawayo, on

Gestation Stage

December 8, women demonstrated at the Magistrate Court and 75 of them were arrested. In Salisbury, violent demonstrators gathered in Harare and Highfields Townships, and attacked police with a variety of missiles and projectiles (stones, sticks, etc.). One man was shot dead by the police, fourteen injured by gunshots from police, and nine badly bitten by police dogs.

This time the regime was harsh on women who were increasingly becoming very militant. Consequently, 503 women were arrested.[107] At midnight, December 8, 1961, the Whitehead government banned the NDP at a time when it had numerically grown enormously, with a paid-up membership, according to Nkomo, of 250,000. Its life was only 1-year 11-months 9-days.[108] Prior to its proscription, by refusing to participate in a government referendum constructed on the 1961 constitution, NDP effectively put itself outside the legal framework.

This meant that NDP could now struggle for social change through extra-constitutional means, such as riots and violent demonstrations. Thus, the banning of the NDP coincided with the ending of an era, where Black Nationalists worked for political change within a legal framework. However, before it was banned, the NDP made one great achievement, which was the internationalization of the political plight of the Southern Rhodesian blacks. Nkomo, its leader, almost single-handedly was responsible for internationalizing the grievances of his fellow blacks.

Although the black nationalists, by virtue of refusing to accept the 1961 constitution excluded themselves from any constitutional means of achieving their goal of one-man, one vote for more than a decade, they, however, held strongly to their belief in the impartiality of the courts until the Unilateral Declaration of Independence by Ian Smith on November 11, 1965.

Their excitement over the acceptance of the Bill of Rights as well as the enforcing council goes a long way to show how great a faith the black nationalists had in the courts. It would have benefited the black nationalists if they had remembered the words of Lobengula and the context within which these words were said. When the settler government alleged that King Lobengula had signed the Rudd Concession, and thereby giving away his land to them he exclaimed, "the white man is the father of lies." That way, they would have known that the credibility of the courts of the day was as good as the character of the people who manned them.

In fact, the black nationalists' faith that imperial Britain could be persuaded to help achieve universal suffrage blinded them to the fact that Britain was a silent and yet active partner with the Southern Rhodesian white government, and that the struggle to separate the two would require radical action. Ibbo Mandaza expressed in clearer terms this black nationalists' blind faith on the imperial Britain's benevolence when he wrote:

[The nationalists concentration on reform made it difficult] to recognize the umbilical relationship between imperialism and white settler colonial imperialism.[109]

As the curtain was drawn on the NDP, it had established itself extensively among the black population. Nationalism was rampant and black people's political awareness and militancy had heightened. The party had penetrated into every city and town in Southern Rhodesia, the rural, purchase and reserve areas, as well as into farms where the population was mostly composed of immigrants from the neighboring states, Northern Rhodesia and Malawi.

This time it would not take too long before a new party would be formed to replace the NDP. In ten days the black nationalists founded a new party, the Zimbabwe African People's Union (ZAPU).

3.6 Summary

This chapter showed Nkomo as an experienced politician who led the first mass movement in Southern Rhodesia. The first nationalist mass movement in Southern Rhodesia was founded in the early 1950s, and this was the SRANC. Throughout the 1950s, black nationalists, inspired by their united pre-colonial history, threw their support behind Nkomo as he led the struggle against the settler, racist regime. Blacks presented a united front, irrespective of their ethnic background.

In the meantime the white electorate flirted with the politics of moderation, largely in response to black nationalists' peaceful agitation for change. As blacks became more and more insistent on their demand for majority rule, the white regime inched towards the right. Finally, the SRANC was banned and the NDP founded. Continued activism made the NDP as dangerous to the white regime as the SRANC, consequently it too was banned in 1961.

As the years wore on, it seems the black population lost faith in the colonial institution, and became more and more militant. There is a real sense it could be said the SRANC and NDP foreshadowed ZAPU. However, before it was banned, NDP's political activism had gained new momentum and intensity, forcing the British government to order a comprehensive inquiry into the Southern Rhodesian affairs. Led by Lord Moncton, the commission concluded that black's opposition to the Federation, basically to the white rule, was too strong for the Federation to survive unless steps were taken towards majority rule.

Upon the recommendation of the Moncton Commission, Britain proposed a new constitution for Southern Rhodesia. The proposed constitution implied the principle of majority rule, but the white minority undermined its attainment. NDP, and later ZAPU, saw the constitution for what it was, a confirmation of continued white racist minority domination, a reality much more difficult to accept when a wave of independence was sweeping across the face of the African continent.

Gestation Stage

Under the wise leadership of Nkomo, NDP, and later ZAPU, strongly opposed the constitution not only by denouncing it, but also by traveling inside and outside Southern Rhodesia, galvanizing opposition to it and also bringing the grievances of the Zimbabwean people to the world. Responding to the strongly voiced opposition to the 1961 proposed constitution, the United Nations' General Assembly called upon Britain to suspend it, and begin negotiations leading to majority rule.

With this flurry of diplomacy, internal struggles over the proposed constitution, and increased militancy on the part of blacks, the African liberation movement in Southern Rhodesia was pushed into the limelight as it unleashed its main apostle, Nkomo himself, on the international scene with a message of liberation for his oppressed Zimbabweans. His message was "let those with ears hear," and hear the world did!

ENDNOTES

1. Ole Gjerstad, *George Silundika, Zimbabwe, ZAPU*, Richmond, B.C.: LSM Information Center, 1974, p. 7.
2. Ole Gjerstad, *The Organizer: Story of Temba Moyo*, Richmond, B.C.: LSM Information Center, 1974, p. 71.
3. *Ibid.*
4. Melwe Ntini, An Interview with the Author, Mtshabezi, 1996.
5. Richard Gibson, *African Liberation Movement: Contemporary Struggles Against White Minority Rule*, London: Oxford University Press, 1972, p. 154.
6. Saul Gwakuba Ndlovu, *Zimbabwe: Some Facts About its Liberation Struggle*, n.a. 1973 p. 19. Saul Ndlovu was the Director of the Information and Publicity Department (ZAPU) and Editor-in-Chief of the *Zimbabwe Review*, official organ of ZAPU.
7. The Southern Rhodesia Trade Union was formed in January 1954 as a national trade union body by various trade unions from around the country (Bulawayo, Gwelo, Salisbury and Gwelo). Joshua Nkomo was chosen as its President, Reuben Jamela, Vice-President and G. Bango, General Secretary. TUC was dominated by Bulawayo members who had a wide organizational experience and also in working across ethnic lines. The Bulawayo people's ability to work across ethnic lines helped reduce the element of "tribalism" when the first national political movement (SRANC) was founded.
8. Among the scholars who argued that the SRANC was moribund when it amalgamated with the CYL are: Nathan Shamiyarira, John Day, *International Nationalism*, London: Routledge & Kegan Paul, 1967, p. 14. These scholars and those of like mind, characterize the CYL as militant and the SRANC as moribund. The problem with this approach is that it creates a false dichotomy, which posits the CYL as radical and action-prone and the SRANC as weak and eternally begging to be given a little portion of the white man's heaven (Southern Rhodesia). Facts, however, show that both groups were to a certain extent regionally based, confined only to the city and interested in workers' grievances in the cities in which they operated. If anything, SRANC under the chairmanship of Nkomo

and his experienced unionists lieutenants, seemed to have enjoyed the strength of organization and multi-ethnic representation as contrasted with the CYL. Radical rhetoric aside, both parties had a moderate action-program.

9. Canaan S. Banana, ed., *Turmoil and Tenacity*, Harare: The College Press, 1989, p. 52.
10. Joshua Nkomo, *The Story of My Life*, London: Methuen, 1984, p. 71.
11. *African Daily News*, September 12, 1957.
12. N.A.Z., F163/78/31, *Federal Intelligence and Security Bureau (FISB) Monthly Review of the Current Security Intelligence within the Federation of Rhodesia and Nyasaland No. 19*, July 1957; No. 20, August 1957.
13. *Ibid.*
14. Interview with Joshua Nkomo by author, July 26, 1995.
15. George M. Houser, *No One Can Stop the Rain: Glimpses of Africa's Liberation Struggle*, New York: Pilgrim Press, 1989, p. 222.
16. Joshua Nkomo, "President of the SRANC" Bulawayo, June 18, 1994.
17. Houser, *No One Can Stop the Rain*, 1989, p. 222.
18. Southern Rhodesia, Report of the Secretary of Labor and Social Welfare, Salisbury, 1958.
19. F163/78/31, Federal Intelligence and Security Review (FIBS), No. 26, February 1958.
20. Banana, *Turmoil and Tenacity*, 1989, p. 63.
21. *Economic Survey of Rhodesia*, 1965.
22. Melwa Ntini, interview by the author, Mnhlanhlandlela, August 7, 1994. Ntini was a teacher by profession and a trained theologian as well. He remained faithful to the national movements at a grassroots level, serving in various offices in the SRANC, NDP and ZAPU.
23. Anthony Verrier, *The Road to Zimbabwe, 1890-1980*, London: Jonathan Cape, 1986, p. 84.
24. From the perspective of the only two Federal Prime Ministers, Huggins and Welensky, the only kind of partnership they and their white kith and kin accepted was one in which "Europeans were the seniors and the Africans very much the Juniors," J.R.T. Wood, *The Welensky Papers*, Durban: Graham Publishing, 1983, p.23; Joshua Nkomo defines the notion of partnership as was sponsored by the Federal government of Huggins in his *Story of My Life*, 1984, p. 59.
25. Day, *International Nationalism*, 1967, p. 15.
26. Stephen B. Oates, *Let the Trumpet Sound: The Life of Martin Luther King, Jr.*, New York: Harper and Row, 1982, p. 114.
27. David J. Garrow, *Bearing the Cross: Martin Luther King, Jr., and the Southern Christian Leadership Conference*, New York: Vintage, 1986, p. 118.
28. Houser, *No One can Stop the Rain*, 1989, pp. 104-105.
29. *The African Daily News*, January 31, 1958.

Gestation Stage

30. In 1890, the AmaNdebele fought a fierce war for their land against the white settlers. They again fought against the settlers to try and reclaim land they had lost to the whites after the 1890 war between AmaNdebele and Whites.

31. 152 John Day, *International Nationalism*, 1967, p. 15.

32. Joshua Nkomo, "Statement," *Africa South*, July-September, 1959.

33. Jane Symonds, *Southern Rhodesia: Background to Crisis*, Oxford: Oxford University Press, 1965, p. 20.

34. Ishmael Mlambo, *Rhodesia: The Struggle for a Birthright*, London: Hurst, 1972, pp. 119.

35. Cited from Fergus MacPherson, *Kenneth Kaunda of Zambia*, New York, Oxford University Press, 1974, p. 52. The emphases are mine.

36. Joshua Nkomo, An interview with the author, Harare, June 4, 1994.

37. Hardwick Holdeerness, *Lost Chance, Southern Rhodesia 1945-1958*, Harare: Zimbabwe Publishing House, 1985, p. 176. Citing from the manifesto of the United Rhodesia Party, 1954.

38. *Ibid*. Holderness quoted from the Commission of Inquiry commissioned to advise the government on the franchise question, 1957.

39. Saul Ndlovu, *The Voice of Joshua Nkomo*, published by the World Federation of Democratic Youth, 1978, pp. 13-14.

40. Nathan Shamuyarira, *Crisis in Rhodesia*, New York: Transantic Arts, 1965, pp. 18-19.

41. Houser, *No One Can Stop the Rain*, 1989, p. 102.

42. John P. Meagher, First Secretary of Embassy, "Foreign Service Dispatch to The Department of State, Washington," No. 119, Embassy, Accra, Ghana, August 19, 1960.

43. Lawrence Vambe, *From Rhodesia to Zimbabwe*, London, Heinemann, 1976, p. 255.

44. Interviews with Nkomo, Mzila Moyo, Melwa Ntini and Voti Moyo all pointed to the fact that many Africans had confidence in Todd's ability to work for the betterment of African advancement more than any other white leadership of his day. This in no way meant that they were oblivious of his viciousness with strikers during his tenure of service and his raising of the property qualifications, and thereby, in Nkomo's words, "pushing even the comparatively prosperous Africans back to the bottom of the pile." Nkomo, *The Story of My Life*, 1984, p. 66.

45. Reginald Austin, *Racism and Apartheid in Southern Africa: Rhodesia*, Paris: UNESCO Press, 1965; Eshmael Mlambo, *Rhodesia: The Struggle for a Birthright*, London: C. Hurst, 1972; Montangue Yudelman, *Africans on Land*, Cambridge: Harvard University Press, 1964.

46. Banana, Canaan, ed., *Turmoil and Tenacity*, 1989, pp. 66-67.

47. Zimbabwe Students Union in Europe, *Zimbabwe National War of Liberation: United Front, A Historical Background*, London: Africa/Europe Project, 1971, p. 7.

48. Like many African organizations before the 1950's, Rico founded by South African political activists, and by 1929 it had created branches in Bulawayo and Salisbury. Rico tried to create an economically based non-ethnic organization and its significance lay in that it was the first black organization to canvas for mass support.

49. J. van Velsen, "Trends in African Nationalism in Southern Rhodesia," in *Kroniek van Afrika*, 4, June 1964:141 correctly points out that these organizations, including the pre-1957 SRANC, had no interest in the mass of black Zimbabweans who could not vote because these groups tended to be run by and appeal to the new African elite who were greatly concerned to gain from the whites' social recognition as "advanced natives" in contrast to the "uneducated masses."
50. Day, *International Nationalism*, 1967, p. 14.
51. Joshua Mzila Moyo, interview by author, tape recording, Enhlanhandlela, June 16, 1994. Moyo held several positions in the SRANC in the rural areas and also in the NDP and ZAPU. He also spent several years in prison for his political involvement in the resistant movements and lost his eyesight as a result of torture in prison in the 1970's.
52. Joshua Nkomo, interview by author, 18 June 1998.
53. Quoted from J.T. Wood, *The Welensky Papers: A History of the Federation of Rhodesia and Nyasaland* (Durban: Graham Publishing, 1983), pp. 405, 419.
54. Quoted in Wood, *The Welensky Papers* (1983), p. 419.
55. *Ibid.*
56. Nathan Shamuyarira, *Crisis in Rhodesia* (1965), p. 46.
57. *Ibid.*
58. M. Tamarkin, *The Making of Zimbabwe: Decolonization in Regional and International Politics* (London: Frank Cass & Co. Ltd., 1990), p. 1.
59. Houser, *No One Can Stop the Rain* (1989), pp. 69-72.
60. *East Africa and Rhodesia*, 15 January 1959, p. 588.
61. Shamuyarira, *Crisis in Rhodesia* (1965), p. 53; and Nkomo, *The Story of My Life* (1984).
62. George Houser, *No One Can Stop the Rain* (1989), p. 222.
63. Shamuyarira, *Crisis in Rhodesia* (1965), p. 50.
64. Quoted from Martin Meredith, *The Past is Another Country: Rhodesia U.D.I To Zimbabwe* (London: Pan Books Ltd, 1980), p. 24.
65. Christine Sylvester, *Zimbabwe: The Terrain of Contradictory Development* (Boulder: Westview Press, 1991), p. 43.
66. Nkomo, *The Story of My Life* (1984), pp. 75-91. Nkomo was in self-exile for 22 months. Although he arrived in Lagos, Nigeria to participate in the celebration of Nigeria's independence, he went back to Southern Rhodesia in November after leaving Lagos via Rome.
67. Zimbabwe African People's Union (ZAPU), *Zimbabwe History of A Struggle* (Cairo: The Permanent Secretariat of The Afro-Asian People's Solidarity Organization, March, 1972), p. 21.
68. For the impact of the Native Affairs Amendment Act see Philip Mason, *Year of Decision* (London: Oxford University Press, 1960), pp. 218-223.
69. John Day, *International Nationalism* (1967), pp. 14-16.
70. Shamiyarira, *Crisis in Rhodesia* (1965), p. 57.

Gestation Stage

71. It is interesting to note that a number of elites, who continually were a thorn in the flesh of Joshua Nkomo by severely criticizing him as being a spineless leader, were themselves reluctant if not to say afraid to come forward and announce themselves as leaders of a party to be formed. People who were asked by James Chikerema, then in prison, to form a new party to replace the SRANC were Herbert Chitepo, Leopold Takawira, then organizer for the Capricorn Africa Society, and Nathan Shamuyarira, then editor of African Newspapers and Stanlake Samkange. All of them declined, and Chitepo gave a reason that a new African Party would be instantly banned. Besides being afraid to lead a resistance movement it is possible that these elites represented a group of their kind which still clung unto the concept of multi-racialism, just as much as Stanlake Samkange was according to Maurice Nyagumbo, *With the People* (London: Alison and Busby, 1980), p. 134). Because all these big names refused to lead a new party, the founding of the NDP was therefore left to the unknowns: D. P. Mlianga who became the Vice-President; N.K. Marondera, who became the Publicity Secretary; Esau Nyandoro [George Nyandoro's brother] who became the Organizing Secretary, and Sketchley Samkange, who became Secretary-Treasurer. The President was chosen later, according to Marondera, when the NDP was already in its advanced stage. Michael Mawema, then Provincial Organizing Secretary of the Railway African Workers Union, was chosen as interim President, *Daily News* (February 20, 1961).

72. Joshua Nkomo served the organization as Director of External Affairs. In that capacity he had the responsibility to open party offices in Britain and other parts of the world. In fact, it can be said that this was the most splendid job that Nkomo did so well in his endeavor to bring the plight of the Southern African blacks before the eyes of the international world. Nkomo was frequently criticized by his colleagues for remaining out of the country for protracted periods of time, but a plausible argument can be put forward that until he started his awareness campaign, few people outside of Africa were cognizant of the special circumstances surrounding the argument on the independence of Southern Rhodesia. An overwhelming majority thought that Britain would deal with this issue the same way as it dealt with Ghana and Nigeria, colonies that fell under the orbit of Administrative colonies as opposed to settler colonies, of which Southern Rhodesia was one.

73. The inaugural NDP Congress at which the presidential elections were held took place in Salisbury on 28 November 1960. Again, in these elections for a president as happened at the SRANC of the same nature, candidates vehemently vied for leadership. These included Michael Mawema, Ndabaningi Sithole, Moton Malianga and Leopald Takawira, a man who, almost eleven months ago, had refused the offer from the detainees to lead a new party. The fact that Nkomo was chosen in absentia shows how much the general black population involved in the struggle trusted him.

74. Shamuyarira, *Crisis in Rhodesia* (1965), p. 77.

75. Quoted in Shamiyarira, *Crisis in Rhodesia* (1965), p. 59.

76. *Daily News* (February 29, 1960).

77. *Dissent*, 17, 24 (March, 1960).

78. Melwa Ntini, interview by author, 15 August 1987.

79. *Samkange Newsletter* (July 27, 1960).

80. Palmer in an *Incoming Telegram* to the Secretary of State, Salisbury, US Consulate, No: 173 (July 27, 1960).

81. The Bulawayo riots have been covered by many authors and the following sources taken together give a composite picture of what occurred over those two days: Ole Gjerstad, ed., *The Organizer. Story of Temba Moyo. Life Histories from the Revolution. ZAPU. I* (Richmond: LSM Press, 1974), pp. 54-84. [Gjerstad carried out an interview with Dumiso Dabengwa who passed under the pseudo-identity Temba Moyo. Dabengwa was one of the organizers of this demonstration in Bulawayo]; M. Dodds, "Upheaval and Urban Moral Economy: the Case of Bulawayo," a BA Honors thesis, University of Manchester, 1986; F. Nehwati, "The Social and Communal Background to `Zhii.' The African Riots in Bulawayo, Southern Rhodesia, in 1960," in *African Affairs*, 69, 276 (July 1970): 251-252.

82. F. Nehwati, "The Social and Communal Background to Zhii," *African Affairs*, Vol. 69, No. 276 (July 1970):251-252.

83. *Ibid.* pp. 252-253; also see Shamuyarira, *Crisis in Rhodesia* (1965), p. 64.

84. *Ibid.*

85. L.H. Gann & M. Gelfand, *Huggins of Rhodesia* (London: George Allen and Unwin Ltd., 1964), p. 265. This Commission was organized by the Tories and headed by Viscount Moncktom and it main concern was to investigate the future of the Federation.

86. In 1923, a new constitution that gave Southern Rhodesia a wider measure of self-autonomy on internal matters under the British Crown was introduced. Britain, on her part, reserved for herself the right to veto any legislation that discriminated against Africans, a right Britain never exercised.

87. The NDP delegation included Morton Malianga, Michael Mawema, George Silundika, Leopold Takawira who were joined in London by Bernard Chidzero, Enock Dumbutshena and Joshua Nkomo.

88. N.A.Z., F120/L343/2 Internal Security Weekly Reports 1960-6. Secret Memo (April 26th, 1960).

89. Zimbabwe African Peoples' Union (ZAPU), *Zimbabwe: A History*, 2nd edition (Cairo: The Permanent Secretariat of the Afro-Asia People's Solidarity Organization, March, 1972), p. 22.

90. Day, *International Nationalism* (1967), p. 16.

91. The Native Affairs Amendment Act specified that black political activities in the rural areas could only take place with the permission of the local commissioner, who, for that matter was always a white man with invested interests in white privilege, indeed, white settler ideology.

92. Shamuyarira, *Crisis in Rhodesia* (1965), p. 65.

93. Banana, *Turmoil and Tenacity* (1989), p. 70.

94. Mtshumayeli Sibanda, Letter to the author (January 10, 1994). Mtshumayeli Sibanda joined the NDP in 1960 and served the party as a Secretary at the Gwakwe Branch. He would remain in the black resistant movement from then on, serving in different posts in ZAPU, PCC, ANC, Patriotic Front and ZAPU again.

Gestation Stage

95. Material manifestations of Europeanism such as shoes, ties and jackets, were considered, by black nationalists and their followers, as symbols of white domination. These symbolic acts were important in that they had an efficacy of uniting Africans across ethnic and social divide. They also served to disprove the prevailing hypothesis that everything that was African was inherently inferior to that, which was European.

96. The party attracted the membership of such educated people as: George Silundika, a researcher at the University College of Rhodesia, Bernard Chidzero, scholar and U.N. staffer stationed in Ethiopia; Leopold Takawira, school teacher; Herbert Chitepo, first black advocate, Lot Sitshebo Senda, Schools Superintendent and advocate, and Ndabaningi Sithole, educationist and minister of religion, as well as prolific writer.

97. Quoted in R. Cary and D. Mitchell, *African Nationalist Leaders in Rhodesia: Who's Who* (Bulawayo: Africana Book Society, 1977), p. 22.

98. *Daily News*, February 8, 1961; *Rhodesia Herald* (February 8, 1961).

99. Quoted from Andre Astrow, *Zimbabwe: A Revolution that Lost Its Way?* (London: Zed Books Ltd, 1983), p. 35.

100. Joshua Nkomo, interview by author, 1994. Some authors, especially those who want to condemn Nkomo for having betrayed the blacks in Southern Rhodesia by accepting the 1961 constitution, do not mention this and the subsequent special NDP congresses where decisions on the constitution were made. They are afraid to mention that the congress of the NDP in fact initially did not reject the constitution but instead laid conditions upon which the blacks were going to participate in the upcoming referendum. Their omission of these crucial congresses can only be understood as indicative of the obsessive and sometimes senseless hatred of Nkomo.

101. The fiercest wars of resistance were fought in and around this city in 1890, 1896-7 and the 1960 riots. Again, it was in Bulawayo that resistance against the 1961 constitution started, and that was even before Nkomo received a telegram protesting his alleged acceptance of the constitution from Leopold Takawira and his colleagues in London (*The Daily News*, 9 February, 1961).

102. Thenjiwe Lesabe, interview by author, 1998. See also Eshmael Mlambo, *Rhodesia: A struggle for a Birthright* (London: C. Hurst & Company, 1972), pp. 158-159.

103. The MacDonald Hall congress was also important because it was the last Congress that the black nationalists held until 1963, which they held at Cold Comfort Farm after the split.

104. Nkomo in his book, *The Story of My Life* (1984), p. 93, strongly denies that he and his delegation accepted the final document because "the British proposed a small increase in African representation, but not enough to make any difference to the dominance of the white electorate." He blames the British representative, Duncan Sandy for having lied about his delegation's acceptance of the final document. In a veiled manner he implies that his delegation's advisors were responsible for making Sandy believe the delegation was convinced that, despite the fact that they rejected the proposed constitution, they still believed it might work (pp. 93-94). However, Houser, one of Nkomo's trusted friends, wrote that when he met him at the AAPC in Cairo, Egypt, Nkomo told him that his delegation had to

accept the final constitutional document just because they thought it was the best compromise that could be obtained at that time. Later, people who did not like Nkomo as a person concluded it was Nkomo who made the compromise as if he was the only delegate to this conference. The author believes Nkomo himself was opposed to the constitutional terms, and so were the other delegates serving as advisors, Chitepo, a lawyer, and Silundika, the party theoretician. From a realistic standpoint compromise was more appealing than total rejection of the proposed constitution. According to Shamuyarira, *Crisis in Rhodesia* (1965), pp. 158-160), Edgar Whitehead, the Prime Minister of Southern Rhodesia was strongly opposed the increase of black representation to beyond 15 seats, and even threatened to call off the conference on that issue. It was also reported that if the conference were called off, any talk of land reform, Bill of Rights and Constitutional Council would die with the conference. Shamuyarira further intimates how strongly Chitepo, the lawyer advisor to the NDP delegation felt about seeing the constitution work because it included a Bill of Rights. Within this context, Nkomo's denial that he, himself, did not accept the proposed constitution does not contradict the fact that the delegation as a whole did. It is possible that Nkomo had misgivings. The fact that Sandy could not produce a signed document indicating that Nkomo accepted the final document is further support to Nkomo's denial. Even those who accuse him of having personally accepted the final product of the constitutional proposal of 1961 have not produced any document Nkomo signed to prove their case.

105. Day, *International Nationalism* (1967), pp. 18-19.

106. Nathan Shamuyarira, "The Coming Showdown in Central Africa," in *Foreign Affairs*, 39, no. 2 (1961):297.

107. N.A.Z., F120/725/L343/2 Internal Security Weekly Reports, December 8-13, 1961.

108. Eshmael Mlambo, *Rhodesia: The Struggle for a Birthright* (1972), p. 161.

109. Ibbo Mandaza, "The Post-White Settler Colonial Situation," in *Zimbabwe: The Political Economy of Transition, 1980-86*, Ibbo Mandaza, ed. (Dakar: Codesria), 1986, p. 23.

Chapter 4
THE FOUNDING OF ZAPU, LEADERSHIP, SPLIT AND STRUGGLE, 1961-69

This chapter examines the beginnings of ZAPU, the life of its only President Joshua Nkomo, the first critical split the party suffered, and its initial attempts at prosecuting an armed struggle. I look into these aspects of ZAPU with a view to identifying the evolvement of the party's ideology, tactics, organizational skills and ability to survive defections, among other things. Periodization here is based on the way the struggle was prosecuted. From 1961 to 1969, the nationalist parties engaged actively in agitating against the government, either by direct confrontation or armed struggle or in some cases through both means.

In 1970-1971, there was a lull which even made the regime think that African political agitation was over. The lull was, however, based on other reasons other than black disinterest in politics as I shall demonstrate in the subsequent chapters.

4.1 THE FOUNDING OF ZAPU

Within ten days of the banning of the NDP, ZAPU was founded on December 17, 1961. By and large, ZAPU promoted policies of the banned NDP and abode by its constitution.[1] ZAPU was formed at a very tough political time for any black resistant party. At the time of its inception, 356 leaders of its proscribed predecessor, the NDP (men and women, some of whom were trade union leaders) had been banned from entering or remaining in any African reserve, including their homes. Political rallies and meetings were still banned in the reserves as well.[2] Thus, ZAPU was immediately confronted with an almost insurmountable task of organizing in a hostile environment, with threats of arrest from the police. It, however, lasted nine months before it was banned.

Despite the difficult conditions of organizing under which the party was founded, it was able to establish its interim executive which included:

1) Joshua N. Nkomo: President;
2) Samuel Parirenyatwa: Vice President;
3) Jason Z. Moyo: Treasurer;
4) George Nyandoro: Financial Secretary;
5) Ndabaningi Sithole: National Chairman;
6) Morton Malianga: National Secretary;
7) Agrippa Mukahlera: Deputy National Secretary;
8) Clement Muchachi: National Organizing Secretary;
9) Robert Mugabe: Publicity and Information Secretary;
10) Dan Ncube: Deputy Publicity Secretary;
11) James Chikerema: Secretary for Public Relations;
12) Joseph Msika: Secretary for Youth Affairs;
13) Leopold Takawira: Secretary for External Affairs and Pan-African Affairs; and
14) Jane Ngwenya: Secretary for Women's Affairs.[3]

As an expression of defiance, Chikerema and Nyandoro were elected to the executive, although they were still in detention, and a man who will later be a leader of a rival party, ZANU, Rev. Ndabaningi Sithole became chairman. Conspicuous by their absence on the executive list were George Silundika, former Secretary General of NDP, Herbert Chitepo, one of the NDP advisors to the 1961 constitutional conference, Morton Malianga, former Vice-President of NDP, and former Secretary General, Enos Nkala. Melwe Ntini, a former schoolteacher and ZAPU member gave plausible reasons as to why these powerful people were excluded from the composition of the newly formed party. Ntini explained:

> *I am convinced that Chitepo and Silundika were left out because Nkomo was very unhappy with them for their poor decision and also their underhand work during the Constitutional Conference when they wrote Sandy a letter implying that the proposed constitution was acceptable en bloc to the NDP. Nkomo was not happy about this business which was done behind his back. The eight NDP executive members knew about it too.*
>
> *As for Nkala and Malianga, their problem was that they were too officious, they showed this by being disrespectful and abusive to the NDP President, and hence when ZAPU was formed they were excluded from the executive. After all these two were not even popular with the masses. Both Nkala and Malianga never forgave Nkomo for keeping them out of the ZAPU executive to this day.*[4]

At its founding, Nkomo, its leader, made it clear that ZAPU would concentrate on taking the case of the black majority in Southern African to the United Nations as well as on political agitation within the country. At this point,

The Founding of Zapu, Leadership, Split And Struggle, 1961-69

Black Nationalism shifted its emphasis to trying to organize world opinion in the form of the UN so that the latter could put pressure on Britain so that it (Britain), in turn would use its reserve powers to force the settler regime to concede to black majority rule. Otherwise, like its predecessor the NDP, it was committed to one man, one vote, elimination of colonialism, respect for human rights, Pan-Africanism, and cooperation with organizations sharing its aspirations.

Early in their existence, SRANC and NDP had maintained close contact with other nationalists' organizations but it was under ZAPU that the black leaders specifically turned to the UN and to the newly independent African states rather than to Britain for support. However, more emphasis was put on the goal to support African culture and Pan-Africanism. These goals were clearly enunciated in its objectives, which were by comparison, more explicit, and far reaching in that they reached out to international organizations such as the UN, than those of its forerunner, the NDP. The objectives were spelt out as follows:

1) To fight for the immediate and total liquidation of imperialism and colonialism, direct and indirect; and to co-operate with any intentional forces as are engaged in this struggle;

2) To establish a democratic state with a government based on one man, one vote;

3) To foster the Spirit of Pan-Africanism in Zimbabwe and the maintenance of firm links with Pan-African movements all over Africa;

4) To maintain peaceful and friendly relations with such nations as are friendly and peaceful towards us;

5) To eliminate the economic exploitation of our people; and

6) To foster the best values in African culture and thereby develop the basis of desirable social order.[5]

Because of its deliberate goal to organize the UN and the like, to its favor, ZAPU spent the first half of 1962 concentrating its activities on canvassing international support, especially that of the British government, which it believed had colonial power over Southern Rhodesia, and therefore was the only country capable of decolonizing it. In accordance with its emphasis on winning international support, ZAPU in February 1962, sent its President to New York where he made his position, and that of his party, at the United Nations very clear in a very powerful speech.

Nkomo's speech before the UN spoke to two dominant questions:

1) Was the 1961 proposed constitution for Southern Rhodesia acceptable to blacks? And

2) Should the United Nations examine the rule and domestic policies of Southern Rhodesia to see whether it qualified for a "self-governing" status?

Prior to Nkomo's coming to New York, he and his party ZAPU had made it clear they wanted Britain to suspend the implementation of the new Constitution, and convene fresh constitutional talks. It was little wonder, therefore, that Nkomo strongly denounced the new constitution, and urged the UN to investigate whether Southern Rhodesia was deserving of a self-governing status. Britain accepted the fact that Southern Rhodesia was not independent but posited that it was self-governing, an argument Nkomo found preposterous.

Nkomo's understanding of Britain's argument for Southern Rhodesia's self-government status and his logic for disputing it were cogent and logical. He aptly summarized it in his autobiographical book, *The Story of My Life*. He wrote:

> *In late February the scene moved to the United Nations in New York. The trusteeship committee of the UN decided formally 'to consider whether the territory of Southern Rhodesia has attained a full measure of self-government.' The British objections to this were very absurd. They agreed that the territory was not independent-indeed they could not claim it was, since they as an imperial power spoke for it on foreign policy. But they also claimed that it was self-governing-although they were responsible in law for the new constitution that would deny Africans the prospect of rapid political advancement.*[6]

When Nkomo returned to Southern Rhodesia in July 1962, ZAPU could boast success of some sorts at having attained international support from the Afro-Asian nations. However, its efforts at influencing Britain had thus far made no headway.[7]

In the country, in addition to telling its voters not to participate in the pending elections, ZAPU dissuaded the black population and its sympathizers of other races against Whitehead's program meant to encourage eligible voters to vote. In addition to persuading people to support its cause, ZAPU engaged in violence, hoping that Britain would intervene and force a favorable solution. Its members disrupted railroads, launched petrol bomb attacks, and set on fire a forest that belonged to a white concern in the eastern part of Southern Rhodesia.[8]

On account of Nkomo's eloquent presentations at the UN, and subsequent ZAPU petitions to the same, as well as his, and that of his lieutenants, visits to African independent countries canvassing their support, the UN General Assembly passed resolution 1747 (XVI) on June 12, 1962, which stated that Southern Rhodesia was a non-governing territory within the meaning of Chapter XI of the UN Charter. Nkomo, who, because of the hardships inflicted on the black nationalist movements presented by the regime's draconian laws, was ever conscious of the fact that if his party was to succeed in attaining universal suffrage, external support was necessary, had sought Pan-African support first before proceeding to the UN.

The Founding of Zapu, Leadership, Split And Struggle, 1961-69

In that direction he, in February 1962, attended in Addis Ababa, Ethiopia, the Pan-African Freedom Movement for East, Central and Southern Africa. The conference included all independent African countries and most of the liberation movements around the world. By the close of the conference, Nkomo had gotten, not only political support for his party but financial backing as well. ZAPU was desperately in need of financial support at this time, especially in light of the fact that its predecessor, the NDP, had its property confiscated by the government when it got banned. In fact, it could be argued that Nkomo's appearances before the Afro-Asian countries before the UN session helped ZAPU secure the vote they so desperately needed from this international organization.

In a concerted endeavor to overcome the opposition black nationalists were mounting against the impending constitutional referendum and elections, Whitehead promised to repeal the Land Apportionment Act, the cornerstone of racial discrimination, and other petty discriminatory practices as well. He told the African population that he would appoint a black cabinet minister should his party win elections. He also unsuccessfully tried to recruit qualified blacks to participate in the up-coming elections through his `Build a Nation' campaign.[9]

ZAPU's unrelenting efforts at stopping the new Constitution from being implemented by organizing internal and international support as well as Pan-African solidarity eventually paid off when Britain refused to grant Southern Rhodesia independence. However, the constitution was implemented, and the whites scored their own small victory by succeeding in having Britain's "reserved powers" removed. Undoubtedly, the prospects of unimpeded power in internal affairs made the acceptance of the proposed constitution palatable to the white electorate. Thus, an argument can be made that when the white electorate accepted the 1961 proposed constitution, they voted not so much to make political concessions to the blacks, but for the removal by Britain of her "reserved powers."

In March 1963 as the breaking up of the Federation approached, the future of Southern Rhodesia in terms of self-determination was uncertain. The other two countries that constituted the Federation, Northern Rhodesia and Nyasaland had a guarantee of their independence at the demise of the Federation but Southern Rhodesia did not.[10] This was antithetical to the interests of the whites in Southern Rhodesia who wanted independence from Britain no later than it was granted to Northern Rhodesia and Nyasaland.

The new constitution, to the happiness of the whites, had, however, dropped Britain's 1923 residual powers, which served to protect the rights of the blacks. Replacing it was a Declaration of Rights with a significantly circumscribed force.[11] In an interview Nkomo told the author that his party, ZAPU, told the British in no unclear terms that it would not consent to independence before majority rule, and that the implementation of the constitution depended on the goodwill of the whites.[12] In March 1963, however, the Southern Rhodesia regime formally asked for independence from Britain on the basis of the 1961 constitution at the dissolution of the Federation. The British government refused the Field government's requests asserting that its franchise was too restricted as it excluded the majority of blacks in the country.

The crucial question at this point is why did ZAPU leaders continue to persuade Britain to support their cause when in actuality it was she who colonized their country? Nkomo offered a plausible explanation to this question when he said:

> *When we asked Britain to grant us our independence, we did it because we were aware she had sovereign power over Southern Rhodesia. She was the colonizing power and not the Whitehead, Winston and later Smith government. And this was the only way other nations could understand our argument better; when we presented a logical, legal argument. This line of thinking helped us win the Support of the UN. However, when Britain's intransigence increased we, under ZAPU, for the first time specifically turned to the newly independent African states and the United Nations, and not Britain for support. So this [appeal to Britain] was a tactic more than anything else.*[13]

Nkomo's hope in the intervention of Britain on the part of blacks in Southern Rhodesia was not totally misplaced. Signs of independence around him raised his hope, and that of other nationalists in the country who had adopted the same position. Ghana had gained independence in 1957, Nigeria in 1960, Northern Rhodesia and Nyasaland were in the process of getting their independence, which came in 1963 at the dissolution of the Federation. The same was the situation with East African countries. The Belgians had withdrawn from the Congo, and the French from equatorial and West Africa.[14]

The colonial countries seemed to be awarding self-determination to countries whose blacks asked for it through constitutional means. What many non-Rhodesians, black or white, could not grasp was that because of its special status, Britain's capability to intervene on behalf of blacks was very limited, and the 1961 constitution further diminished its ability to intervene.[15] Thus, if ZAPU wanted independence, it would have to negotiate with the local white population. Besides at this time, Britons were beginning to be sympathetic towards their kith and kin in the already independent African countries, such as Ghana, the Congo and East African countries. Apocalyptic tales of death and destruction coming out of the Congo, and disseminated by fleeing whites, certainly helped in changing attitudes in Britain in favor of the white population in these countries.

As a result of ZAPU's refusal to participate in the elections and government under the new constitution, and its agitation against the implementation thereof, Britain set five principles as conditions whose fulfillment would earn Southern Rhodesia independence. This package of five-principles was also meant to forestall a Unilateral Declaration of Independence by the white settlers.

The Founding of Zapu, Leadership, Split And Struggle, 1961-69

The five principles were as follows:

1) The principles and intentions of unimpeded progress to majority rule, at least as outlined in the 1961 Constitution, would be maintained and guaranteed;

2) There would also have to be guarantees against retrogressive amendment of the Constitution;

3) There would have to be immediate improvement in the political status of the African population;

4) There would have to be progress toward ending racial discrimination; and

5) The British Government would need to be satisfied that any basis for independence was acceptable to the people of Southern Africa as a whole.[16]

In the meantime, in December 1962, there had been elections at which Edgar Whitehead's United Federal Party was defeated by the supremacist party, the Rhodesian Front (RF). The RF formed in March 1962 under the leadership of Winston Field, only about nine months before elections.[17] Early on September 20 1962 Whitehead had banned ZAPU in hopes of winning over to his side the disenchanted whites. However, the RF members, who were opposed even to the theoretical promise of majority rule, were not the least impressed by Whitehead's move.

Thus, the ascension of the RF into power served as an index to the whites' hardening attitudes against black participation in the governance of the country, and the intensification of white nationalism. This is truer in light of the platform on which the RF ran. The clarion call for the RF was immediate independence from Britain, independence that excluded the blacks and rejection of the 1961 Constitution.

The RF also stood for the retention of the Land Apportionment Act of 1930, the cornerstone of racial segregation. However, conviction by some black nationalists that by rejecting the 1961 constitution change in their favor would soon be forthcoming soon proved misplaced. Instead, they were excluded from working for their self-determination within the constitutional system. The constitution was implemented anyway, and the white population continued with their push for independence. Attitudes towards effective black participation in government were increasingly hardening and the divided white population was beginning to close ranks against ZAPU, especially on issues of political privilege and economic advantage.

Thus the development of ZAPU and its prosecution of the struggle from thence on depended largely on the attitude of the white population, and hence a brief account of the nature of the white population would help in the understanding of how the whites saw ZAPU, and the advancement of its people.

The Zimbabwe African People's Union 1961-1987

The question of black advancement in Southern Rhodesia divided the white population into three groups, which, from the Second World War until the Unilateral Declaration of Independence (UDI), were roughly equal in number. The first camp consisted of the avowed racists who were strongly opposed to any extension of political rights to Africans, and therefore were strongly opposed to any modification of any racial laws.

To this group of whites, majority rule, and one man, one vote, was synonymous with 'Black Power' under which whites would serve under the mercy of the blacks. Whites who belonged in this group believed in a rigid racial caste system of the Southern Rhodesian society under the rule of their kith and kin. I label this group the white supremacists.

Second, was the camp composed of the white population, which believed that a rigid racial system of society was impracticable, and were willing to make cosmetic reforms of the discriminatory laws, only as long as the changes did not inconvenience them, and promoted the economy (middle-of-the roaders).

However, they, like the supremacists in the first group, believed that the governance of the country must remain in white hands. Last, was the camp of open-minded whites (radicals) who supported the aspirations of blacks for political participation and hoped to see the dawning of an era when a non-racial society where equality among races was the order of the day.[18]

Group two and three, the moderates and the radicals, dominated the Southern Rhodesian political scene from the inauguration of the Federation in 1953 until 1963 when the Federation was dissolved and the RF ascended into power. During this phase, a majority of whites supported the Federation for the economic advantages it provided them. Since the Federation was based on the notion of racial partnership, whites supported this notion for the sake of keeping the Federation intact. It was during this period that Garfield Todd, who was leader of the United Federal Party, and Prime Minister until 1958, proposed substantial changes of the country's Industrial laws and argued for an increase in the number of black representation in parliament.

After him, Whitehead, his immediate successor, also tried to make reforms and even secured an approval of the 1961 constitution which, although it accorded blacks little representation, opened up the possibility of full independence, however under continued white rule. Whitehead even went further to propose the repeal of the Land Apportionment Act, an act that cost him an election. He also openly talked about black rule in twenty years down the road.

The second phase overlapped with the first and the third, and it was the time when the moderates joined hands with the supremacists to defeat, first in 1958, Garfield Todd and second, to oust Whitehead from power in December, 1962. This phase stretched to the UDI in 1965 when there was total repression of black, nationalist organizations. The third phase lay between 1966-1971 and this period witnessed the grand coalition to protect white governance against freedom fighters and sanctions. It was also during this time that the extreme supremacists split from the RF over Ian Smith's willingness to enter negotiations with Britain between 1966 and 1971, and also because he tampered with discriminatory laws. The white radicals continued to oppose the Smith regime up until the time of independence.

Practically, this opposition against the Smith regime from both the ultra-supremacists and the white radicals was of no significant effect in the late 1970's so that it can be correctly argued that the only party that functioned to the time of change to black majority rule was that of the supremacists led by Ian Smith.[19]

It was the group of the white supremacists, represented by the RF that Britain ended up negotiating with when the UN stated that Southern Rhodesia was not self-governing. This party, in all intents and purposes, killed any effective discussions, which were already underway on the subject of a non-racial meritocracy, and eventually plunged the country into a blood bath. The man caught in the middle of all these sometimes moderately hostile to extremely hostile attitudes against Black Nationalism was Joshua Nkomo, leader of ZAPU. Nkomo's life trajectory is in many ways the life of ZAPU. For one to understand not only the life of ZAPU but the nature of African nationalism in Southern Rhodesia herself, basic knowledge about who Nkomo was is crucial.

While we always conveniently speak about organizations engaging in actions, it must be remembered that organizations never act, it is people who do, so that an individual's coordinated actions can be construed as those of a party or organization.[20] It is in light of this observation, therefore, that Nkomo's actions as ZAPU leader become important for the understanding of not only his party but the nature of modern Southern Rhodesia politics and its conduct.

4.2 Joshua Mqabuko Nyongolo Nkomo: The Man, the Myth and the Legend

Joshua Nkomo[21] has loomed large both mythically[22] and politically for almost half-a-century. First, during the struggle for majority rule in Southern Africa, and then in the post-independent Zimbabwean politics. Born in Semokwe communal land to Thomas Nyongolo Nkomo and Mlingo Hadebe on 7th June, 1917, Nkomo grew up like any African child, heading cattle in Semokwe in Southern Rhodesia. He was the third-born, after an elder sister who was born in 1910, and an older brother in 1913. Nkomo never forgot his rural experiences, and he would later remark: "I am the son of the soil"[23] The fact that he grew up in the countryside certainly shaped Nkomo's ideas. Memories of the settlers' conquest in the 1890s were still fresh and bitter in the minds of many AmaNdebele people.

It was while he was in the rural area that Nkomo learnt that his forefathers denied self-government, fought tenaciously and well. Nkomo then concluded that the historic struggle had to be continued, and saw it as his mission to carry on with it (struggle). Nkomo went on to become the leader of one of the major liberation movements in Southern Rhodesia, and finally was appointed Vice-President of independent Zimbabwe. He passed away on 1st July, 1999, at the Pararinyatwa hospital in Harare, after a long battle with prostate cancer.

Nkomo's parents were relatively prosperous, with his father working as a teacher-evangelist for the British London Missionary Society in the Semokwe reserve, about ninety miles South of Bulawayo. Thus, in a way, Nkomo was a product of mission entrepreneurism. A Christian culture, as he stated it himself, reinforced his sense of dedication, self-sacrifice and volunteerism. Nkomo, in fact, went on to become a lay-pastor in the British Methodist Church of Southern Rhodesia.[24]

Nkomo's family was also very traditional, respecting and practicing the mores and folkways of its people. Consequently, Nkomo was comfortable with both the Christian and African culture, and that quality of his made it easier for him to be accepted by both Christian and traditionalists alike.[25] In fact, ZAPU became acceptable to both traditionalists and Christian because these two currents were linked in its leadership. By the time ZAPU matured, it can be argued that both Christian and traditional apologists were at work defending its cause.

Nkomo was educated in both mission and government primary schools, in Tsholotsho, before leaving for South Africa where he met with other regional black nationalists. Subsequently, Nkomo worked for five years doing odd jobs before he saved enough money to put himself through Secondary school and College, both of which he did in South Africa. In one of his jobs he was a delivery boy for Osborn's Bakery in Bulawayo, which was owned by Sir Donald MacIntyre. Later Nkomo worked as a carpenter in his home area, Kezi, and at Tsholotsho. In 1942, he left for Durban, South Africa, where he enrolled for a three-year High School Diploma at Adams College. In his autobiography, he describes how at 25 years of age, far more advanced in age than his classmates, he had to squeeze his large frame into desks made for children.[26]

In 1945, Nkomo entered Jan Hofmeyr School of Social Science in Johannesburg where Mrs. Julia Hoskin[27] paid for his three-year diploma course. While at Hofmeyer, Nkomo met political activists among whom were the late Sir Seretse Khama, who was then the prime mover for Botswana's independence, and later became the President of Botswana, Lubede, the Africanist, and Dr. Zuma, both of whom were leaders of the African National Congress in South Africa, as well as the legendary Nelson Mandela, who was to become South Africa's first black President.

Nkomo developed a life-long friendship with Khama and definitely developed respect for Mr. Mandela's political views.[28] He admitted being politically influenced by all of these leaders.[29] Nkomo also first met figures who would play a very pivotal role in Zimbabwean nationalism, Dr. Enock Dumbutshena, who would become the first black Chief Justice of an

The Founding of Zapu, Leadership, Split And Struggle, 1961-69

independent Zimbabwe, and Herbert Chitepo, who would become the first black advocate in Southern Rhodesia.

Nkomo returned to Southern Rhodesia in 1947 and began his career as a social welfare officer in his home city Bulawayo at the beginning of 1948. He was the first African to be given such a position. In 1949, Nkomo married his childhood sweetheart, Johanna Fuyane, from his own birthplace, Semokwe. Together they had four children, Thandiwe, Tuthani, Sibangilizwe, and Sehlule.

In time, Nkomo began his political career as a trade unionist before becoming a leader of successive political organizations. He worked with the Welfare Department of the Rhodesia Railways from 1948-1952. In keeping with his determined nature, Nkomo continued to study even after landing a full time job. For two years he read for an external B.A. degree in economics and sociology with the University of South Africa (Unisa). He completed the degree in 1951, and thereby became one of the few black members of the African elite. For that matter, his educational achievement was even superior to a majority of the white population in the country.

During that era, for an African to go beyond elementary education, he had to have superb determination and fortitude, mixed with a large dosage of luck. Because of his promise of organizational skills, and amicable interaction with his African co-workers in the railways, the African staff elected him, in 1951, as secretary of the Railway Workers' Association, later known as the Railway African Workers' Union (RAWU). In just under a year, Nkomo built its membership to a new record level.

In 1952, his old friend Enock Dumbutshena persuaded Nkomo to assume the leadership of the SRANC. That same year, in recognition of his popularity among the blacks, Sir Godfrey Huggins, then prime minister of Southern Rhodesia, invited Nkomo to represent African opinion at the London Conference on the proposed federation of Southern Rhodesia, Northern Rhodesia (Zambia) and Nyasaland (Malawi). His opponents during the 1960s ZAPU split would cite this incident as one of the many they claimed showed Nkomo as a sell-out to the white regime.[30]

Nkomo, however, vehemently opposed the proposed federation, but all the same, because the white electorate overwhelmingly supported the notion of a federation, the federation was introduced in 1953. When his party turned him down as a candidate for a parliamentary seat in the January 1953 first Federal elections, he stood as an independent candidate for the African seat of Matebeleland, but was defeated by Mike Hove, the United Federal Party candidate.

During that same year, Nkomo resigned from the Rhodesia Railways and started his own business in his home city, Bulawayo, as an auctioneer and insurance agent. Nkomo's participation in the Federal Elections, which he first opposed, would earn him bitter criticism from leaders of a splinter group, Zimbabwe African National Union (ZANU), in the early 1960's. In his defense, Nkomo said he was persuaded by his colleagues in the SRANC to run for a Federal seat so that he could be the "voice of the blacks and reason" in a dominantly white parliament. In his autobiography, he wrote that he lost because the electorate was overwhelmingly white. He complained that the qualifications for voting had "brought only about 400 Africans onto the register with tens of thousands of whites," which Nkomo condemned as "ridiculous."[31]

For a man who spent so many years in prison, Nkomo was remarkable in that there were so many things said about him in a manner that clearly clothed him with divine qualities. These myths were in one way or another stories of a people in the process of formulating ideological strategies of resistance. What must be pointed out right at the outset is that myths about Nkomo were part of the ethnic identity of the blacks in Southern Rhodesia. According to Mrs. Thenjiwe Lesabe, both Joshua's father and he, himself, were born only at the intervention of the Ilitshe[32] at Njelele.

In the account of Nyongolo, his parents, Joshua's grandparents, visited Njelele to inquire on their infertility problem and to ask for a child. The Ilitshe granted them their request and further told them that one of their descendants "would be a grinding stone to lead my children." Subsequently, Joshua's father, Nyongolo was born. When Nyongolo got married he bore two children and could not have any more. He, like his father, went to consult with the *Ilitshe* at Njelele and was told the *Ilitshe* closed his wife's womb because *Mlimu* wanted him and his wife to accept responsibility of giving birth to the savior of the her people.[33] Lesabe recounted:

I want you to give me a grandson who is going to lead my people that small grinding stone I told you about is going to come from you. Then MaHadebe got pregnant and Joshua was born with the anointing of Ilitshe.[34]

Thus, according to this account, the birth of Nkomo was divinely ordained, and so was his leadership of his people in a struggle against imperialism. Nkomo's alleged divine birth began to gain national currency in the 1950's during which time his nickname *Chibwe chitedza*, the slippery rock, received common usage. This account of Nkomo's birth is important in understanding how ZAPU's nationalist ideology incorporated in various levels the discourse and power of African religion. For instance, at the grassroots, the populist nationalists observed Wednesday as a day of rest. Wednesday was a day set aside by the *Ilitshe* as a day of rest from any kind of heavy work in the exception of mending fences and houses. But Nkomo also practiced Christianity. Thus, the espousal of these seemingly antithetical religions helped in a long way to arm the liberation movement with symbols of empowerment and hope in the face of a heavily armed regime.

It can arguably be said it was this image of Nkomo as an *Ilitshe* anointed leader, coupled with his charm and grace as well as his leadership skills which endeared him to his followers, and which became inspirational to them as they fought for majority rule.[35]

The Founding of Zapu, Leadership, Split And Struggle, 1961-69

If there was anything that reinforced Nkomo's image as a liberator of his own people, it was when he himself, in person, received a commission to lead a struggle of liberation against the white regime. In 1953, Nkomo paid a visit to the *Ilitshe* at Dula, in the Matopo Reserve. The trip was kept secret for many years, however once it was known it became legendary in the ZAPU circles, and also among the black majority of Southern Rhodesia.

In 1984, Nkomo himself disclosed the details of this trip in his autobiography. Nkomo recounts that he, Grey Bango and William Sivako were well received by the *Ilitshe* when they went to ask to be given the land back. He says the voice came from *Umlimu* and intimated that "the people of this land" would regain their land in "a big war in which many will die," but only "after thirty years." Nkomo adds that he kept the secret of this event for thirty years.[36]

However, the event was soon known among people around Southern Rhodesia, and more widely known among the ZAPU adherents. What is of historical significance in this event is that the *Umlimu* not only predicted the future, but also more importantly revealed the secret of the AmaNdebele history and the secrets of the transition of governments in the past and future in Southern Rhodesia.

In 1952, Nkomo was elected President of the Bulawayo based SRANC. The 1950's were harsh years for blacks in Matebeleland, as well as an era of change in its rural areas. The effects of the Land Apportionment Act were wreaking havoc as blacks were evicted, made to perform forced labor, new agricultural rules implemented and as destocking widely effected. Up to the early 1950's, rural population grievances were articulated by a local, Christian, progressive leadership.

Thus, traditional religion did not play any significant role as an instrument with which the local black population fought against their oppression at this time. Instead, the progressive black population applied Christian principles to engage the oppressive regime on behalf, mostly, of the rural population. This leadership was a product of mission schools. In the Wenlock area for instance, a protest association, *Sofasihamba*, whose leadership was mainly composed of members or former members of the Brethren In Christ Mission at Mtshabezi, was very active.

Opposition in the National Park, in the Matopo area, was lead by Nqabe Tshuma, a London Missionary Society activist who used his local church and school at Whitewaters to organize resistance against the oppression of the black rural population. The active Association in this area was known as *Sofasonke*. Demonstrations in the Matopo Reserve were led by the black Christian elite of the Brethren In Christ Church Matopo Mission.[37] These protest associations, and similar ones around the country, appealed to the moral consciences of the colonial powers and also the promises tacit in the colonial moral economy.[38]

By and large, these organizations put more emphasis on universal African proletarianism in contradistinction to cultural nationalism. The elite black leadership had nothing to do with their own culture. Although some of them had left the church or had been excommunicated by their mission organization, they still lived out mission values that were antithetical to black traditional life.

When the efforts of *Sofasihamba* and *Sofasonke* failed to stop destocking in the Wenlock area, evictions and relocations in the Matopos, and enforced agricultural laws in the Matopo Reserve, there was an immediate change from making moral appeals to the white regime based on Christian values to an immediate embrace of what I would call Christio-Cultural Nationalism by black nationalists. This marked the onset of the switch from Christian progressivism to secular modernist nationalism.

With this change in approach, African culture became a vital tool of resistance and organizing solidarity against oppression. Cultural nationalism rose in the late 1940's and 1950's. It emphasized culture, history, language and religion. Nationalists begun to emphasize the importance of Wednesday as a day designated for worship by the African priests. Not wanting to be outfoxed by some, black teacher/pastors changed mid-week Christian services to Wednesday.[39] The Wednesday Movement was very strong in the Semokwe Reserve, Nkomo's home area. Organizing around this movement, Nkomo opened a SRANC branch in February, 1958. Here the SRANC unsparingly attacked land shortage, destocking, inadequate schooling and the abandonment of African Cultural values.[40]

A central figure in the cultural revival movement was Joshua Nkomo, who paradoxically, because he was a product of mission entrepreneurism, embraced Christian values. Among other incidents that revived Nkomo's strong passion for African culture was his visit to England where he had been struck by the way the Britons respected their past. Immediately after returning from England in 1952, Nkomo began a society "to preserve all the African culture and heroes of Africa."

He pointed out to his people that in England, people drew strength from their past, and spoke at length about respect due to African leaders of the past such as Mambo, Chaminuka and Mzilikazi. A strategist that he was, he took these ideas to the rural areas. Basically, his speeches were the same as one he gave to teachers in Matobo, who he admonished to preserve "customs, language and the tilling of the land, and to "remember African heroes of long ago."

Nkomo even went on a pilgrimage to Inyati to the royal *imbongi* (praise-singer), Ginyilitshe, to ask him about "various matters of Ndebele national interests. He also accompanied Matebeleland Home Society delegations to the *Izinduna* where he argued that Entumbane should be set aside as a burial place for all who acquitted themselves as good citizens in the black community.[41]

Why was culture so important to Nkomo? Nkomo viewed culture or tradition as a teaching tool as well as a form of protest against a regime that

The Founding of Zapu, Leadership, Split And Struggle, 1961-69

demanded conformity in dress on the part of Africans. Asked what message traditional headgear and utensil carried, Nkomo's response was long and worth quoting for its explanatory power.

Nkomo said:

> *Culture for me was a device for encouraging a greater self-awareness, a deeper consciousness of my roots and also of my situation. Treated as less than human, as a mere unit of labor, my culture treated as inherently inferior by whites, I as a black person had to constantly remind myself that I had value and that my culture had value too so that I felt the need that we as a people be proud of being black and of our culture. I felt that conformity to the lifestyle, norms and standards of the white society served only to weaken my sense of self-identity and did not secure me acceptance and respect from that community. So dressing in our on cultural attire and using our traditional utensils was a form of symbolic confrontation. The message was, accept us for who we are; Africans with a culture that is equally important and valuable of which we have been and continue to be denied.*

Nkomo's accessibility to the grassroots, despite the fact that his education and financial comfort put him among the emerging Southern African elites, endeared him to their hearts. Richard Sibanda, one of ZAPU's stalwart supporters, who after independence became a councilor in his district said this of Nkomo:

> *Nkomo, a man who joined the politics of the grassroots when it was still very unpopular for the educated to be identified with the poor and the uneducated rural folk, is modest and courteous when dealing with ordinary people, a quality that has since he joined politics endeared him to their hearts. He could easily communicate with the educated, as an educated man, and the rural folk as one who was an avid student and practitioner of African culture. When he started out his political career in the 1950's, he pointed out to the peasants the importance of culture as a tool of liberation, culturally, politically and economically, hinting mostly on the importance of land.*

> *This hit a nerve with the rural folk who had been deprived of their lands and livestock. In the city, Nkomo would draw the attentions of his people to their problems of unemployment, underemployment and the chronic shortage of accommodation. This was a man of powerful words whose message undermined the racial values of the Colonial status quo, which to a significant extent had gripped many of our people to submission. Nkomo challenged what they viewed as white mini-gods.*[42]

Despite the fact that Richard Sibanda can be said to be a confessional critic of Nkomo's personality, there is a lot of truth in his evaluation, which is collaborated by non-Nkomo stalwart supporters. George Houser of the American Committee on Africa, described him as a "jovial" personality. Perhaps more comprehensive and true to who Nkomo was, was Patricia Cheney's characterization when she wrote:

> Unlike [President Robert] Mugabe, Nkomo is a leader who inspires love and respect from his people. He has the quality desired by all politicians, "the common touch." He can talk to all types of people in words they can understand. As such, he has always posed a threat to the less charismatic Mugabe, and the two have a long history of antagonism.[43]

Melwa Ntini described Nkomo as a remarkable man, "a man strong willed, humorous and tender all at once whose relationship with his supporters was electric."[44] An enigmatic character at best, as aptly described by Mlambo.[45] Some described Nkomo as a great consultative leader who had a hemless passion for justice. The late John Mpofu, a school-teacher, well represented this group of people in an interview with the author when he commented:

> Umdala [old wise man] is a pragmatic leader with a life long passion and commitment to social justice. Because he hated tribalism, racialism and regionalism, Nkomo as a leader stamped his trademark discipline upon his ethnically and sometimes ideologically diverse African resistant movement. Although he was consultative in his approach it did not mean he was wishy-washy, as some have suggested, especially those who were easily deceived by his smile in the heat of a crisis. This is because he is an even-tempered and extremely intelligent politician, a survivor, if you please. Nkomo is a man with steel in his spine. However, despite the fact that some people expected him to make unilateral decisions, he would always take an inordinate amount of time building consensus.[46]

In fact, Nkomo's consensus-building and consultative style lost him support from people who thought of leadership as characterized by making decisions for people, and was interpreted as a weakness by people who entered negotiations with him. What is more important about Nkomo's personality during the 1950's is that he represented a link between the urban, cultural, secular, nationalism, and that of the rural grassroots. Put differently, Nkomo's political career was an incarnation of modern, secular populist nationalism, and hence he has been correctly referred to as Father Zimbabwe.

Not everybody loved Nkomo as leader. There were some people even among his lieutenants who did not like him at all. One of the major reasons they gave was that Nkomo accepted the 1961 constitution that gave Africans 15 out of a parliament of 65 seats, an accusation that Nkomo denies. We have already briefly described the role played by Nkomo at the Constitutional Conference and here we will elaborate on what Nkomo's position was. Nkomo's role in the constitutional talks is critical because it defines the position ZAPU as a party adopted. Nkomo's position towards the 1961 proposed constitution was well captured by Ishmael Mlambo when he wrote:

> Nkomo appeared to believe that his followers would attack him for his failure to achieve the acceptance of `one man, one vote,' and he sought to demonstrate that

The Founding of Zapu, Leadership, Split And Struggle, 1961-69

> *the N.D.P. should not be blamed for not gaining the franchise. He insisted, as did Mugabe, that `the operative word is "considered;"' his party had considered the franchise, but not `agreed' on it. Nkomo wanted his followers to make a distinction between the Constitution itself, the franchise and representation. He rejected the last two while accepting the first. He accepted the constitution because with the bill of rights private citizens were protected from arbitrary arrests and against discrimination....*

If anything, at this conference Nkomo proved himself to be a skillful negotiator who understood very well the implications of every stricture in the proposed constitution. What he and his colleagues failed to grasp, however, was that the courts on which they had pinned their hopes for meting out justice were, in fact, instruments of oppression in the service of white interests. When he realized this, after consulting with his executive committee, he rejected the constitution.

Internationally, Nkomo was gaining respect as an analytic politician. He understood the nature of NATO and the United Nations as inimical to the interest of Afro-Asian peoples. Speaking at an All African People's Conference at Tunis in 1960,

> *[Joshua] Nkomo ... criticized NATO members who helped France in Algeria ... then said: "we have to consider our relationships with countries that profess friendship with the Africans while at the same time investing large sums of money in countries such as Central and South Africa. Is such investment not to be regarded by us as a direct act of unfriendliness...entrenching the minority-privileged groups.*

Nkomo went on to point out the UN as an organization, at least up to 1960, was dominated by western powers. Various speakers had looked with great hope toward the UN to help them in their liberation. Nkomo contended further," correctly, "that the UN's new African and Asian members should scrutinize the provisions of the United Nations Charter," inasmuch as the organization from its founding was dominated "by colonial and imperialists powers with interests to preserve" rather than a desire to transform the status quo.

Thus, Nkomo was and still is regarded as the father of Zimbabwean Politics. Not only did he join and lead Africa resistance when it was unpopular for an educated person to do so, but in significant ways he also shaped the politics of Zimbabwe, its strategies and organization.

Between 1964-1974 Nkomo was both restricted and imprisoned by the Rhodesian government. After his release, Nkomo went to exile in Zambia where he led ZAPU and its military wing, the Zimbabwe People's Revolutionary Army (ZIPRA). With the cessation of hostilities, and at the first elections, 1980, he lost to his former Secretary-General, Robert Mugabe, then leading the Zimbabwe African People's Union. Mugabe, for the stability of the country, however, included Nkomo in his cabinet. However, in 1982 Mugabe fired him amid allegations that ZAPU had hidden weapons for a suspected coup attempt.

It was in this context that Nkomo became the most loved and hated African leader by far in the country. To his admirers he was almost a demi-god, and to his haters he was an imperialist agent extraordinaire. Indeed, in the person of Nkomo, the elements of culture and myth were given a metaphoric spin. To those who supported Nkomo, Mugabe was a despotic extraordinaire, with a despotic style of leadership, ruthless, and thoroughly effective. Thus, views about Nkomo ranged from the highest praise for almost a semi-god-like figure, to the lowest, damning him as a demon.

4.3 The Banning of ZAPU

Towards the end of its life span as a legal Party in Southern Rhodesia, ZAPU's popularity had ballooned to proportions that troubled the Whitehead administration. Particularly troubled was the far right white electorate, which was absolutely adverse to blacks participating in government. After all, ZAPU continued the campaign against the 1961 proposed constitution, and participation by the qualified inconsiderable number of blacks in the up-coming elections, started by its predecessor, the NDP. By acting this way, ZAPU went against the Whitehead government, which considered itself liberal, and even against some of its white liberal supporters. The Whitehead administration was not only troubled by the internal popularity of ZAPU among the populous blacks, but also by the fact that ZAPU at this point had secured firmer international support from the Afro-Asian Nations and the United Nations.

With pressure from the white far right electorate, and even from some white liberals, as well as non-cooperation from black nationalists under ZAPU, the Whitehead government went on a fishing expedition for reasons to ban the movement. It then decided that the best way to do it was by investigating the activities of ZAPU within the country. The prevalence of violence within the country in 1962 provided an understandable basis to even some liberals for the government-sponsored investigation. The regime compiled its findings in a report which apportioned blame on ZAPU for all of the violence prevailing in Southern Rhodesia in 1962.

The report, in addition to providing a basis for the banning of ZAPU was also meant to provide the United Nations with reasons for its (ZAPU's) proscription. However, this White paper report was not published until ZAPU had been banned. It detailed instances of political violence the government alleged were carried out by ZAPU between January and September 1962, which included thirty-three petrol bombings, the burning of eighteen schools and ten churches, as well as twenty-seven attacks on communications.[47]

Although the attribution of all the violence on ZAPU was dubious, for lack of hard evidence, some of it was correctly apportioned to the party. As early as mid-1962, before ZAPU was banned, according to one prominent party official, it had already made a resolution to procure weapons from outside the country and to send young men for sabotage training.[48] To add to the government's

The Founding of Zapu, Leadership, Split And Struggle, 1961-69

fury, before the end of September, 1962, an organization named the Zimbabwe Liberation Army, started publicizing its operations by distributing leaflets. Scrabbling for its very existence, ZAPU repudiated any official connection with the group.

However, as was later confirmed by Nkomo himself in an interview with the author, the organization was part of ZAPU and was headed by General Chedu, a triumvirate of two ZAPU executive members and a Youth leader. The group, whose main purpose was to plan and carry out sabotage around the country, had a membership of about one hundred. In September 1962, barely nine months old, ZAPU was banned.[49]

ZAPU supporters responded to the ban in a countrywide wave of violence, burning government buildings, schools and forests owned by the infamous British South Africa Company. Violent riots erupted at such places a Bulawayo, Darwendale, Concession, Bindura, Hot Springs, Marandellas, Nkai, Melseter, Gwanda, Silobela, Karoi, Gwelo, Salisbury, Matopo, Wenlock, Tsholotsho and Esigodini, just to mention a few.[50] By the time the white regime banned ZAPU its leadership had been banned from addressing rallies, or holding any kind of political meetings. Consequently, when the party was proscribed, its leadership could not respond to the accusations leveled at it by the government.

Undoubtedly, ZAPU leaders had a lot to say given the increasing repression by government and harassment by police with which they and their supporters were faced. Police responded by arresting a total of 1,600 ZAPU leaders and supporters.[51] Before the leadership was arrested, and despite the ban on its addressing public political meetings, it continued to address political rallies in churches under the guise of religious meetings.

Thus, churches became the only free space where ZAPU could hold mass meetings with minimum harassment from the government. What is interesting to note is that the Whitehead government was not interested in knowing the causes for the violence but only the question of who did it. Although ZAPU did engage in some violence within the country, it was not responsible for most of the violence for which it was blamed. However, it did make plans for the use of formal violence in the form of a liberation army in 1962.

This time the white regime made sure no other party with similar goals was formed under a different name. Prior to this, the government did not have laws debarring the black nationalist movements from merely giving changing the name of a banned organization. With the proscription of ZAPU, the Whitehead government amended its Unlawful Organization Act,[52] not only to broaden its purview, but also to increase the severity of its punitive application.

Among these punitive measures was a mandatory death sentence for setting fire to a residential building, aircraft or car, irrespective of whether it was occupied. Because of the prohibition by the amended Unlawful Organization Act against banned parties to reconstitute themselves, ZAPU decided to retain its name but go underground. Nkomo was in Zambia when it was banned. He immediately made arrangements for the party to relocate its headquarters to Tanzania where it was to form a government-in-exile.

To Nkomo's dismay, Julius Nyerere, the Tanzania's President, ill-advisedly refused his endeavor to set up a government-in-exile, asserting that the struggle against the white regime would be effectively fought with the leadership within its country.[53] Nkomo went back to Southern Rhodesia to lead his party in formulating a new approach. It was between the banning of ZAPU and the formation of Peoples Caretaker Council (PCC), on 10th August, 1963, that a split occurred.

4.4 THE MOTHER OF ALL DIVISIONS: ZAPU SPLITS AND ZANU IS BORN[54]

Zimbabweans have a long history of bitter and sometimes violent disagreements based on mostly non-ideological, ethnic, and very often personal differences among the members of various liberation parties. It is possible that wisdom and tact were not always utilized by the new liberation groups that emerged over time in the politically charged Southern Rhodesian's landscape. At times personalities clashed, at times new types of practices were claimed to be the basis of divisions, and most of the time barriers against reconciliation were built.

Such was the ZAPU split, which resulted in the founding of ZANU on August 8, 1963. What made this the mother of all splits among the black nationalists in Southern Rhodesia was that it was responsible for planting seeds of disunity which served as a ready made background of the post-liberation conflicts between ZAPU and ZANU. The cleavages among the Zimbabwean black nationalists have, indeed, been given a melange of conventionally accepted explanations ranging from tribalism to personality clashes. The division among the nationalists first occurred in 1961 over the allegation that Nkomo accepted a British sponsored constitution for Southern Rhodesia that accorded Africans 15 out of a parliament of 65 seats. Despite the fact that general dissatisfaction with the proposed constitution had already been expressed by the Makokoba, Bulawayo N.D.P branch, and that Nkomo had personally and openly strongly spoken against the distribution of seats in the proposed parliament, which he said left power in white hands, a handful of the nationalist movement led by Leopold Takawira, Nkomo's chief contestant for the party presidency accused him of having sold out to the whites.[55] Handful though these dissidents were, their protests against the leadership of Nkomo in particular was sufficient enough to pose a threat to his leadership and to split the party.

However, because of the large support Nkomo enjoyed among the party members and his skilful leadership, both of these possibilities were averted. After all, many people among the followers did not think Nkomo and his team sold to the British imperialists and the Southern Rhodesian settlers. Some even went to an extent of branding the dissidents "a bunch of officious people who joined the party only when there was promise of African participation in the

The Founding of Zapu, Leadership, Split And Struggle, 1961-69

leadership of the country." Melwa Ntini, who described himself as Nkomo's critical supporter when interviewed on the 1961 split, had this to say:

> *The major leaders of the opposition to what I saw as Nkomo's leadership, and not the constitution as such for this was used as a pretext of a personal attack on the president of the party, were power-hungry folk whose main interest was the leadership of the party. In the exception of the sorry Enos Nkala who had his personal vendetta against Nkomo, Sithole, Mugabe, Takawira, were all latecomers to the party who only joined the party after Bottomely announced there was going to be a constitutional conference on Zimbabwe. That is why their motives of raising arguments over the constitutional proposals, making a fuss over what they claimed was Nkomo's selling out even after he had repeatedly said in private and in public that his group rejected distribution of seats, are very questionable, and can only be dismissed as the work of agitators who were bent on securing leadership even at the risk of dividing the party.*[56]

When Takawira and his supporters failed to wrest away the leadership of the party they grudgingly stayed with the party awaiting any slight slip in Nkomo's leadership. However, at that time, Mugabe went so far as to suggest the inauguration of a new party as the only way of ridding the party of Nkomo as leader,[57] the position that gave credence to Ntini's insightful allegation that the dissidents were after power. Twenty years after independence, a senior commander in ZANU's military wing would say this about Mugabe's quest for power:

> *Gradually of course, we realized that we had made a terrible mistake [by choosing Mugabe as leader of ZANU]. I now regret it, as do other members... He was arrogant, paranoid, secretive and only interested in power. Mugabe is only interested in power, it's not even true that he is a racist.*[58]

Such was the tenuous unity of the Nationalist party during the balance of NDP's life. The banning precipitated the second, and real split in 1963. Indeed, when the split actually happened in July/August of 1963, it was perfectly clear that the main cause of dissatisfaction so far as the dissidents were concerned was discontent with Nkomo as a leader.

The road to the split and the formation of ZANU was littered with a battery of accusations and political ploys on the part of the dissidents. Initially the dissidents tried to convene a meeting on the farm of a liberal white sympathizer of liberation movements Sir Stuart Gore-Brown. The group tried to invite Nkomo to attend but when James Chikerema tipped him on the plot to either capture or assassinate him, he declined.[59] During that same time, this group of rebels sent their supporters into Southern Rhodesia to nichodimusly recruit for a new party they had decided to form.

After extracting a confession from one of the dissidents, Edison Zvobgo, that he and his comrades no longer considered Nkomo as their leader, Nkomo, using that confession as a basis, suspended Robert Mugabe, Ndabaningi Sithole, Moton Malianga, and Leopald Takawira from the party as a way of disciplining them pending the holding of a General Congress at which the leadership of the party was going to be decided.

Having failed to lure Nkomo to a death trap, the dissidents decided to convene a meeting of seven executive members in Tanganyika with a view to eliminating Nkomo as leader of the movement. The meeting was attended by the dissidents, Mugabe, Sithole, Moton Malianga and Takawira,[60] as well as Nkomo's loyalists, J.Z. Moyo, Joseph Msika and C.M. Muchachi who boycotted the meeting once they learnt of its purpose. The three loyalists declared the meeting unconstitutional, which indeed it was given that the presidency was chosen by the National Congress. The four dissidents went ahead and deposed Nkomo as leader and put Ndabaningi Sithole in his place.

Before they made their final break, once they concluded they could not wrest the leadership from Nkomo, who was the people's favorite at that time, the dissidents started psychologically preparing people for the formation of a new party. They repeatedly attacked Nkomo's leadership, citing his failures as the main reason for their discontent with the party. Enos Nkala, one of the dissidents, on July 8, 1963, together with ten of his co-rebels, issued a signed statement, alleging ironically that Nkomo had lost the confidence of the people, and therefore the control of the party.

Undoubtedly, the dissidents were misreading the mood of most of the ZAPU supporters, which was staunchly in support of Nkomo. They revealingly went further to contrast Nkomo's leadership with the impending "new, dynamic, fearless nationalist leadership." They also denounced Nkomo as "bankrupt of ideas, without plan for the attainment of freedom and independence," and further alleged that his only strategy then was to "do nothing, avoid jail and keep talking and flying." Thus, much of the criticism became focused on Nkomo's leadership style and personality. He was accused of being a weak leader, an accusation that seems to be inconsistent with his accusers' allegation that he was a dictator.

Nkomo responded to these allegations by calling a rally in the capital city in August, 1963, where he, in public, rebuked the ZAPU dissidents (Morton Malianga, Robert Mugabe, Enos Nkala, Ndabaningi Sithole, Leopard Takawira, Nathan Shamuyarira and Herbert Chitepo). To Nkomo, these dissidents had no legitimate reason to leave the party other than just a pure quest for power and self-aggrandizement. He felt people like Nkala, Mugabe, Ndabaningi and Takawira were nursing a grudge against him for being the people's favorite. Nkomo was evidently still hurting from that split which he thought created a basis for ethnic rivalry in the country at the time of the interview in 1994. In that interview with the author he spoke of the progenitors of the split in very bitter words:

> *The allegations, which Ndabaningi and his colleagues made against me preceding the 1963 split, were nothing but a mortuary of pathological lies, a malicious vendetta of vilification and character assassination. This was proven*

The Founding of Zapu, Leadership, Split And Struggle, 1961-69

by the fact that they did not have any differences with ZAPU. ZANU went about plagiarizing our tactics, strategies and goals. The difference was only in personalities. By coming up with a plethora of false accusations they thought they could influence people with a fleeting knowledge of the liberation struggle by spawning a smear campaign against the leadership using half-truths and crude generalizations. However, the opinion of the majority of our supporters had been galvanized against the troublemakers who hoped to be recognized as the latter-day apostles of the liberation struggle in Zimbabwe.[61]

Two days after ZANU was formed, the underground ZAPU convened a meeting at Comfort Farm on August 10, 1963 leading to the founding of the PCC.

4.5 The Inauguration of the Peoples Caretaker Council

Nkomo's forced return to Southern Rhodesia after President Julius Nyerere kicked him out of his country became a blessing in disguise, for it ultimately gave him a tactical political advantage over those who later split to form ZANU. Once Nkomo returned to Salisbury, he started isolating the dissidents whom he subsequently suspended from ZAPU. This he did by taking control of the party machinery after mustering support from party membership.

Although one of the major criticisms was that Nkomo was running away from a direct confrontation with the settlers, and hence, he spent most of his time out of the country, at that point it was they, Malianga, Mugabe, Takawira and Sithole, who were in exile. Several of these dissidents faced imprisonment in Zimbabwe for jumping bail; consequently, they decided to remain in Dar es Salaam. Their protracted stay in exile undoubtedly gave Nkomo the opportunity to undermine his opponents' argument that he was avoiding imprisonment, and to consolidate his own position.[62]

To make matters worse for his opponents, and to add to Nkomo's tactical advantage, the dissidents suggested that the entire ZAPU executive meet in Zambia, at Sir Stewart Gore-Bowne's estate. Nkomo turned the suggestion down and, instead, called for People's Conference at Cold Comfort Farm for August 10, 1963, near his mostly Shona stronghold, Salisbury, and five-thousand delegates attended, a tremendous show of ZAPU support. Nkomo invited the dissidents but they refused, and instead formed their own party, the Zimbabwe African National Union, (ZANU) on 8 August 1963, two days before the conference at Cold Comfort Farm was convened.

The Cold Farm Conference was, in no way, a constitutional meeting. It was called to resolve the problem of leadership, and also to make practical arrangements regarding the operation of ZAPU as an underground organization since it had already been banned in the country. The conferences made three major decisions:

1) It declared Nkomo "Life President" of the party, conferring upon him "powers of appointing, reshuffling and appointing his cabinet, a decision which ZANU would later use against uniting with ZAPU;"

2) It confirmed the suspension of Messrs. Sithole, Mugabe, Malianga, and Takawira by the President, Nkomo; and

3) It resolved to keep its pledge of not forming a new party by, instead, creating a "caretaker machinery," the People's Caretaker Council.[63]

Subsequently, Nkomo announced a new Executive, also known as "the People's Cabinet", which included:

1) Life President:	Joshua Nkomo
2) Deputy President:	James D. Chikerema
3) Secretary to the President:	William J. Makarati
4) Secretary-General:	George B. Nyandoro
5) Deputy Secretary-General:	Edward S. Ndlovu
6) National Chairman:	Samuel Munodawafa
7) Treasurer-General:	Jason Z. Moyo
8) Financial Secretary:	George Marange
9) Secretary for External Affairs:	Joseph Msika
10) Secretary for Youth and Cultural Affairs:	Clement Muchachi
11) Deputy Secretary for Youth and Cultural Affairs:	Mhariwa B. Gumbo
12) Secretary for Information and Publicity:	T. George Silundika
13) Deputy Secretary for Information and Publicity:	Alois Z. Wingwiri
14) Secretary for Women's affairs:	Jane Ngwenya
15) Secretary for Public Relations:	Willie D. Musarurwa
16) Secretary for Organization:	Lazarus Nkala[64]

The birth of ZANU introduced a new element in the political history of Southern Rhodesia. For the first time, blacks fought each other. In 1964, ZAPU/PCC engaged in serious widespread political violence. The vast majority of its victims, however, were blacks. Most of these blacks were seen as Tshobies[65] or Capricons, and as such, either severely punished or killed. Such was the situation with a sub-chief in the Rusape district who was shot by PCC members on 10 October after they set huts under his jurisdiction on fire.[66] Thus, blacks that were correctly or incorrectly suspected of siding with the white regime were the targets of this violence. Also targeted were blacks that were members of ZANU. In fact, these two parties fought against each other to the extent that the regime left them to self-destruct.

Thus, ZAPU/PCC and ZANU squandered much energy on an intramural struggle that played straight into the hands of the white regime. It is possible that the radicals of the two parties fought against each other more than

The Founding of Zapu, Leadership, Split And Struggle, 1961-69

they did against the white supremacist government. In the course of time, animosity between the two groups escalated, rapidly driving up the number of violent clashes and killings, again, a majority of which involved black on black violence. Smith took advantage of this black nationalists internecine fighting, and withdrew a considerable number of black township patrols at night. This allowed the rival black parties to intensify their street battles against each other, and ultimately weakened their struggle against the white regime.

In fact, very little attention was focused on the causes of the nationalist struggle, and the supremacist government, both of which were ostensibly the concern of black nationalism. The inter-party conflicts disillusioned ZAPU's international sympathizers, and, as it became increasingly out of hand, provided the Rhodesian government with a pretext to ultimately crack down on ZAPU/PCC and its rival ZANU. The regime tightened its sweeping draconian laws meant to further cripple black nationalism in Southern Rhodesia.[67]

4.6 Decision to Use Force: the Stage of Rocks, Induku Umkhonto, Fire and Gun: War in the Making 1960-1968

The decision to use force came when ZAPU concluded that whites would never hand over political power to Africans on a silver platter, and that only by overthrowing the government could the blacks' goal of majority rule be achieved. The adoption of what Black Moses termed the "Fanonian Apocalypse" was not easy for ZAPU mostly because its leadership, Nkomo, regarded the possibility of violent revolution with apprehension. Nkomo's reluctance to use force can be understood within the context of his deep religious experience as well as his Christian liberal realism. On the other hand, he like the rest of his party folk, realized that violence at this stage was inevitable.

The use of violence was progressive, and started with ZAPU's predecessor, the NDP. The introduction of purposive violence into ZAPU's struggle against the white regime marked a transition in the party's ideology from that of partnership-multiracialism and gradual change to radical and violent action calculated at eradicating the white supremacist ideology. I divide this preparatory period into two: 1960-1965 and 1966-1969. The determining factor is the Unilateral Declaration of Independence by the Smith Regime, which in turn determined the change of approach in the prosecution of the struggle by ZAPU.

4.7 Preparatory Stage: The War of Stones, Ukhonto, Fire and Bombs

Between 1960 and 1963 a wave of urban and rural unrest swept across Southern Rhodesia, and dramatically turned the attention of the international world to it. In 1960, the first shots were fired on civilians. In response to this unprovoked violence, blacks set government buildings and vehicles on fire and pelted police with stones and bottles. This mode of retaliatory violence became part and parcel of ZAPU's strategy. Despite the fact that ZAPU dissociated itself with violent activities carried out mostly by its youths, it was not only cognizant of these activities, but also intimately connected with the groups that carried out these violent acts and sabotage around the city.

According to Chikerema, violent resistance was preached and practiced by ZAPU from 1960, and had a significant effect on the party's course and outcome. Since it was banned, the government had confiscated NDP's property during this preparatory period; therefore ZAPU became primarily concerned with the collection of money, arms and men.

4.8 THE COLLECTION OF MONEY

Organizations are costly to maintain. Arms, explosives, cadre training, and travel are expensive too. And so is the printing of propaganda. ZAPU needed money not only for its survival but also to finance its expanded program, which now included the use of force in addition to the employment of non-violent direct means. To raise funds the party engaged its youth wing, which hosted concerts and parties for that purpose. People in rural areas donated chicken, goats, sheep and cattle to be sold for the purpose of supporting the party through their branches.

Mzila observed in an interview with the author that the confiscation of NDP's property encouraged more people than before to donate toward the funding of ZAPU, so that in its short period of existence as a legal party in the country it became the richest among all black, nationalist movements that ever existed in Southern Rhodesia.[68] Its wealth was seen in the many cars it possessed, the ability to rent offices and finance travel by its officers. Money was used instrumentally by ZAPU to further its goals, which involved the use of manpower among other things.

4.9 RECRUITMENT OF MEN

ZAPU also engaged in direct recruitment of young men, not only to collect money, but to join the armed struggle against the white regime as well. In that direction, ZAPU organized the youth, and thereby providing them with an outlet for their newly found political excitement by sending the enlisted to such countries as Russia and China for training as guerrillas. Among the first people to be sent out by ZAPU for training in 1963 were Akim Ndlovu and Dumiso Dabengwa. The sending of men for expert prosecution of war, however, followed a period of time when unorthodox and absolutely amateurish means had been tried, involving the smuggling of the first guerilla weapons into the country.

China accepted both ZAPU and ZANU trainees. However, Algeria, Cuba, Bulgaria, the Soviet Union, and North Korea took only ZAPU cadres for training at least until 1966, while Ghana restricted their training camps only to

The Founding of Zapu, Leadership, Split And Struggle, 1961-69

ZANU trainees.[69] Undoubtedly the Sino-Soviet conflict contributed to keeping ZAPU and ZANU apart and made reconciliation of the two parties difficult.

Training for the ZAPU cadres who went to Russia was very comprehensive, although it emphasized more esoteric sciences than military training. Early information on the kind of training ZAPU forces received was first disclosed to the public by one of their guerrillas on trial before the High Court on 13 August 1968. The cadre told of how he and his eleven comrades were flown to Moscow via Tanzania for training.

For the first four months a Russian who spoke very fluent English grilled them in Political Science. Additionally, they were offered sophisticated military training which involved armed and unarmed combat, revolutionary strategizing, sabotage methods, guerrilla warfare and radio communication. Those selected for intelligence training were schooled in codes and ciphers, surveillance and counter-surveillance, use of dead letter boxes, opening of letters using steam, secret writing, photography, document copying subject photography and Foreign Intelligence Services (American, British and French).[70]

4.10 THE GATHERING STORM: ZAPU COLLECTS WEAPONS, 1962-64

For the most part of 1962, ZAPU used stones, spears and knobkerries for fighting its enemies. Its members stoned government property, schools, offices, and buses and also set fire to them. Its members also used spears and knobkerries to either maim or kill the 'Tshombes'. The main goal for this type of violence by ZAPU was to disrupt the economy and intimidate black sell-outs so that they could not spy on its members' activities, and perhaps join the party.

By the time ZAPU was formed Africans had been banned from carrying spears and knobkerries in cities and towns, and spears in the rural areas. As a show of great resourcefulness, ZAPU argued that people kept knobkerries, axes and *imikhonto* (spears) for the purpose of traditional dances. The same argument was maintained by its members in the rural areas. By incorporating the use of knobkerries, axes and *imikhonto* in their rituals, ZAPU ritualized law breaking. Although it was true that blacks in their traditional dances use knobkerries, axes and *imkhonto*, its wide usage by ZAPU members went beyond ritual purposes.[71]

Towards the close of the year, ZAPU had turned a corner, and at this point was smuggling into the country modern weapons. It started collecting firearms from sympathizing countries, mostly Egypt. In fact, the party used two principal ways to obtain weapons: (a) use of illegal channels; and (b) through the use of illegal home industry.

In September, 1962, police stopped a car between Shabani and Filabuso. The car had two alleged ZAPU trained cadres, led by Bobylock Manyonga, who was one of the two occupants.[72] When the police searched the car, they found in the boot, two 1940 vintage British Lanchester Submachine guns. According to Peter Stiff, these weapons became the first guerrilla arms to be captured by Police.[73] According to Joshua Nkomo, the leader of ZAPU, in his autobiography, he had personally brought these weapons as well as ammunition and grenades from Egypt.

Nkomo further wrote that another ZAPU official, Joseph Msika, ultimately smuggled these weapons into the country. He thus becomes the first person to bring in weapons into the country. This was no light task by any sense of imagination. Southern Rhodesia at that time had a very good intelligence network, so that bringing in illegal weapons was very risky. In a sense, it can be said that transporting weapons into the country became a practical rite of passage, allowing recruits to demonstrate their manliness. By securing the first weapons for the organization, Nkomo added to his popularity among his followers.

ZAPU obviously became interested in explosives as well, and these had a very profound effect on the white regime's psyche. For the first half of the 20th century, nothing could generate wider publicity, catching headlines than a successful bombing.

On the home front, some ZAPU members produced their own guns in their own homes. This kind of gun was known, in the Mtshabezi area by the euphemism *indombi* (the picker, one that chooses the target). One of these creative members was Kumile Moyo, who has a hand missing three fingers to show for his participation as a craftier. These guns were also used for hunting wild animals in farms belonging to whites as a way of passive-aggression against the regime.[74]

During this preparatory period, however, ZAPU did not use the guns it procured against even a single white soul, the perceived enemies. Neither did they use explosives against the same. Explosives were used against property, and, for that matter, especially in the earlier period, by the untrained. However, despite the fact that they were not immediately used against the enemy, guns were very important to ZAPU. Their importance to this party was more than symbolic. ZAPU needed these weapons for future military revolutions against the supremacist regime. At that time, however, ZAPU was not ready to militarily engage the minority government as it was still recruiting young people to train as fighters.

With the breakdown of constitutional talks in London under the Smith regime in 1963, ZAPU decided the time to fight the minority government had come. Thus, it started recruiting the majority of the young people who were already in leadership within ZAPU to leave the country for training. The task lay on the shoulders of James Chikerema, who had been appointed to lead the department of Special Affairs, a department formed in 1963 principally for dealing with issues of the armed struggle.

The group went via Zambia and Tanzania destined for countries in the Eastern Bloc. Zambia and Tanzania, both of which were independent then, and staunch supporters of the liberation forces in Southern Rhodesia, gave an added advantage to ZAPU. Now it could prepare for military insurgency in a safe environment, away from home.

The Founding of Zapu, Leadership, Split And Struggle, 1961-69

Training lasted until the end of 1964 to the beginning of 1965. No question the party was learning on the job. The cadres returned from their training before any planning of executing the war had been mapped-out. According to Dumiso Dabengwa, who was among the first group of trainees, it was when they got back that discussions were held with Chikerema on the program of military operations. The discussions resulted in these three recommendations that Dabengwa articulated as:

1) That we needed to operate as a force and not just a department hence we formed an "Armed Wing" of the Party with a small command structure, confined to a Commander, assisted by logistic head and military Intelligence head.

2) That we needed to create a base for an army.

3) That we needed to deploy inside Rhodesia small units of 2 to 3 men and have them infiltrate different parts of the country with the assignment of: (i) carrying out further recruitment; and (ii) attacking reconnoiter targets such as small economic targets and carrying out sabotage for example post offices, communication, and electricity, etc.[75]

The following year, 1964, ZAPU fine-tuned its war machinery by creating what it called its Armed Wing with a small command structure consisting of a commander, heads of operations and personnel, intelligence and reconnaissance, as well as logistics. The plan by ZAPU at this point was, however, not to engage in a direct armed confrontation with the enemy, but to infiltrate small units of cadres into various parts of the country. Once these units got into the country they were further divided into small groups of between three and four people with an assignment to, and contrary to what some scholars have alleged, recruit fresh cadres, sabotage economic and industrial infrastructure. At this point, constitutional ways of achieving liberation had been closed.

The option had disappeared in the early 1960's. By the time PCC was formed ZAPU had already taken itself out of any constitutional means of negotiating for majority rule. Britain felt that nationalists were not interested in reform. As I have elsewhere in this chapter pointed out, even some liberals who had supported this party saw its rejection of participating in parliament on the basis of the 1961 constitution as an absolute rejection of engagement in reform ways that would have eventually led to majority rule.

One of the strongest advocate of this position is Barber who argued that if Africans had gone to the legislative Assembly, "the African Leaders could have revealed the strength of their support and have exerted on the Government of the day." Thus, Barber considered the 1961 Constitution a step forward in the direction of African advancement. He saw the constitution as introducing a dispensation whereby Africans could, in a piece-meal fashion, however, an effective one, assume higher posts in armed forces and civil service, and also acquire ministerial as well as parliamentary experience.[76]

Robert C. Good was another of the liberals who said that Nkomo was foolish to have denied himself privileges that would have come with accepting the 1961 constitution. Good enumerated these privileges as:

A substantial tactical advantage, a platform of national and even international prominence, a degree of leverage on Whitehead, and the possibility of legitimatizing his claim for further African advances which, at worst, would have placed the onus for failure on a recalcitrant white establishment rather than the rebellious nationalists.[77]

To his credit though, Good, however, conceded the fact that this would have only postponed rather that averted the crisis given the polarization of the Southern Rhodesian community on racial lines and also black frustration and white fear.

In an ideal situation, this could have been the case, but the history of Southern Rhodesia does not support both Good's and Barber's logic. For many years, blacks in Southern Rhodesia had worked and cooperated with white leadership in multiracial organizations, especially during the Federation Era, but their involvement with these organizations did not bring them even close to meeting their own goals.[78]

It seems to me by expecting the whites to write their own political obituary by voluntarily working themselves out of political power and privilege, Barber was expecting too much of them. This then means that if ZAPU had accepted the 1961 Constitution as it was, it would have gratuitously given the whites in Southern Rhodesia their independence. This position is borne by the results of the 1962 election, which were based on this constitution but put a supremacist government in power. By their own choice, whites indicated that they were not interested in liberal reforms, let alone majority rule. So the path that ZAPU had elected to use, extra-constitutional means, was justifiable in light of these developments within the country.

In the meantime, the Smith regime was pushing on with its quest for independence. To make sure there was no effective opposition to what appeared to be an inexorable push to an illegal declaration of independence, the regime, threatened by one claiming indisputable leadership of the majority black people, started to harass Nkomo and further severely restrict ZAPU's political activities. At this point Nkomo had become a serious political threat to both the white settlers and their government. Especially alarming to the settler community was the ZAPU/PCC's program of the Book of life, which was meant to officially enroll PCC supporters.

In February 1964, ZAPU/PCC announced that it had made 500,000 cards to sell to its members. Enrolling members was contrary to ZAPU/PCC founding policy of not registering its supporters as it was said to be "a people's movement in which all people who were born or lived in Zimbabwe could be members without registering or paying subscription."[79] It can be surmised

The Founding of Zapu, Leadership, Split And Struggle, 1961-69

that ZAPU/PCC decided to convert into a party because of its struggle and competition with the newly founded ZANU.[80] Nkomo was personally involved in organizing the party into cells of every fortieth house in townships. To avoid being arrested since he had been banned from addressing any political meetings, Nkomo met the leaders of these cells in ones and twos.

Figure 4.1: ZAPU Organizational Structure in the 1960s

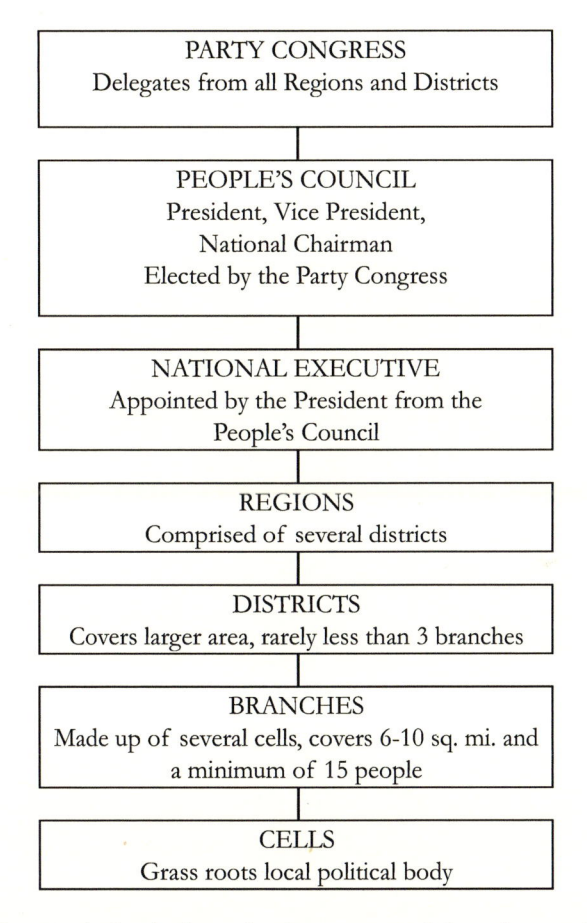

```
PARTY CONGRESS
Delegates from all Regions and Districts
         |
PEOPLE'S COUNCIL
President, Vice President,
National Chairman
Elected by the Party Congress
         |
NATIONAL EXECUTIVE
Appointed by the President from the
People's Council
         |
REGIONS
Comprised of several districts
         |
DISTRICTS
Covers larger area, rarely less than 3 branches
         |
BRANCHES
Made up of several cells, covers 6-10 sq. mi. and
a minimum of 15 people
         |
CELLS
Grass roots local political body
```

Sources: The organizational scheme has been structured from the material gathered from Ole Gjerstad, ZAPU '2': Zimbabwe African People's Union / George Silundika (Richmond, B.C.: LSM Press, 1974) Page 3

By February 1964, the ZAPU/PCC was already talking of declaring its internal wing, PCC, a party, after an anticipated sale of 500,000 membership cards. To the settlers, the program, the Book of Life, was particularly an affront because they deemed the designation of the program sacrilegious as the term, the Book of Life, was taken from the Bible.[81]

Consequently, the government banned the Book of Life and confiscated all the cards. Besides, Nkomo had not denounced the use of violence the way ZANU had, and this was too much for the government to handle. To that extent ZAPU/PCC had engaged in a confrontational path against the government, boycotting schools as a protest against paying fees and stores and shops that were discriminatory.

To allay the fears of the white population immediately after Smith replaced Field on 13 April, 1964, the government cracked down on ZAPU/PCC leaders, arresting and restricting Nkomo three days after Smith took the reins of the country. He was sentenced to ten years and six months in prison.[82] Soon after more ZAPU officials were arrested and restricted with Nkomo in Gonakudzingwa, 141 other PCC supporters were detained.[83]

In response to Nkomo and his colleagues' arrest, thousands of ZAPU supporters took to the streets in protest. "Women carrying their babies on their backs, boys and girls in their thousands, staged yet the fiercest demonstration," observed *Zimbabwe Review*.[84] Many business operations were brought to a standstill as ZAPU supporters stayed away from work. Police vehicles were stoned, government property set on fire and other police cars overturned.[85]

The thinking behind the arrest of ZAPU officials was that once the leaders were removed from public resistance against government, they would be eliminated. Undoubtedly the regime had misread the situation. ZAPU/PCC continued to gain support. Again, threatened by the flourishing of ZAPU/PCC, and despite the fact that its leadership was in detention, the Smith regime banned the PCC on 26 August, 1964, after one year of its legal existence in the country. The PCC, however, emerged as the Zimbabwe Church of Orphans (ZCO), *Ibandla LeZintandane*.[86] The ZCO remained a secret replacement of ZAPU/PCC though, so that following the banning of both ZAPU/PCC and ZANU in 1964, virtually no political effective challenge in form of African movements existed in the country.

4.11 HEEDING HEAVEN'S COMMAND AND TAKING HEAVEN BY STORM: ZAPU ATTACKS

The second phase of ZAPU's resistance during the 1960's was ushered in by the declaration of independence by Smith. Smith, rather than accept British grounds for independence, set up an illegal government based on white supremacy after declaring Unilateral Independence on 11 November 1965. Smith's declaration of independence was so dramatic, and was crafted in such a way as to attract and appeal to both United States and Britain.

The declaration was couched in the language of the American declaration, and it was planned such that it coincided with Armistice Day to emphasize the white Rhodesians' contributions to British wars. Smith also made sure

The Founding of Zapu, Leadership, Split And Struggle, 1961-69

he appealed to the Christian world in general. On that eleventh hour of the eleventh month of 1965, he concluded his declaration thus:

> *We have struck a blow for the preservation of justice, civilization and Christianity and in the spirit of this belief we have this day assumed our Sovereign independence. God bless you all.*[87]

Nkomo and some of his ZAPU members had been in prison for a year when Smith declared independence. Nkomo, however, continued to direct resistance against the government from detention through people who visited him, and sometimes through the media. Sensing the inevitability of the UDI. Nkomo informed a visitor that there would be no compromise on the question of majority rule.

He insisted: "Power must be handed over to us, who represent the majority of the people." Nkomo was no less demanding of majority rule when Wilson visited him during his trip to Southern Rhodesia.[88] Because most ZAPU leaders were either in prison or exile at this time, coupled with the draconian laws that governed political activity within the country Smith's declaration of independence was met with very little resistance from the African population.

Smith had made it clear that he would not tolerate any opposition from Africans, especially the nationalist leaders whom he considered a small band of gullible nationalists used by communists.[89] Government officials found it convenient portraying nationalists and freedom fighters as part of a great international plot. Undoubtedly, nationalists of different countries collaborated, but reports of international links often seem to have been exaggerated. The cry of "foreign hand" was for Smith a convenient way of discrediting the claims of ZAPU. Thus, Smith characterized ZAPU as part of an international anarchist movement, and not part of a genuine movement of national liberation.

Although ZAPU admitted to being inspired by Afro-Asian revolutionary movements, it, however, believed its acts were a national and necessary response of a subjugated people against an oppressive regime.[90] The argument had as its basis a gut-level conviction that the minority government had no right to be ruling them.

To disprove the Smith's assertion that it was only the nationalist leaders who were a problem, the general population staged strikes and demonstrations against the UDI. Because the regime had already deployed troops before the declaration, they were quickly and handily put down.[91] The response by Britain was very feeble. Its Prime Minister Harold Wilson tried to seize the initiative by imposing `symbolic' sanctions against Smith. He, however, made it clear that he was not going to use armed forces to bring Smith back to the fold,[92] and that correctly made nationalists believe he encouraged the supremacist government to declare independence.[93]

Confronted with internal repression by the white regime, and diplomatic indifference by the British government, ZAPU initiated a second phase of its struggle that involved clandestine attacks on persons rather than on property only. After the UDI, the first guerrillas to strike against the white regime, according to some scholars,[94] were those belonging to ZANU (ZANLA). Propelled by a desire to prove to the Organization for African Unity (O.A.U.) ZANLA clashed with government security forces near Sinoia on 28 April 1966.[95]

ZANLA insurgents infiltrated from Zambia into Rhodesia before splitting into three groups. It was the group of seven that clashed with government forces near Sinoia suffering a huge military defeat as all were killed, with no loss to the regime forces.[96] The military defeat of ZANLA did not escape one of its political leaders, Simbi Mubako, Zimbabwe's first Minister of Justice who made the following sobering observation:

> *In purely military terms it [Sinoia] must be seen for what it was a defeat. We do not have to accept the figures of those killed or captured given by the Salisbury regime to come to that conclusion, fortune has shown that gallant effort displayed by the pioneer band of freedom fighters was not and could not be sustained.*[97]

However, the Zimbabwe government under ZANU apotheosized this military debacle as the central event of the liberation war at which the first shots were fired, an assertion ZAPU denies.[98] It is doubtful that the Sinoia ZANLA attack was the first one involving guerrillas after the UDI. In fact, in March of that year, ZAPU sent commandos who engaged the Smith Regime in fierce fighting at the Nkayi Reserve in western Rhodesia. According to ZAPU, Smith retaliated to this March attack by destroying peasants' livestock and property. Although the regime denied that this battle ever occurred, [99] some residents confirm the incident.[100]

Despite claims by ZAPU that it was the first to militarily engage the enemy forces, ZANU stood by its claim that its forces were the first to battle the enemy and set aside that day for commemoration. The date is commemorated as the Chimurenga Day.[101] To further tarnish ZANU's celebrated day, it was later learned that the seven ZANU cadres were not only fed by police special branch, but were also allegedly led by an agent of the Rhodesian Central Intelligence Organization (CIO).[102] Despite ZANU's military failure, its attacks had favorable implications for the party's cadres.

The battle contributed to the Zambian leader's, Kenneth Kaunda, change of heart to supporting the armed struggle as the only way of liberating Rhodesia. As a disciple of Gandhi, Kaunda believed in non-violence. Consequently, prior to the ZANU battle, he would not allow ZAPU to use the Zambian soil as a launching pad for its military incursions. Praising the bravery of ZANLA, Kaunda asserted at a Press Conference on 12 May 1966: "Blood I am afraid has got to be spilled. It is the foundation of any freedom movement that leads to success."[103] With this change of heart on the part of the head of government, Zambia was ready to not only provide holding camps but training camps as well.

The Founding of Zapu, Leadership, Split And Struggle, 1961-69

Thus, it was willing to support the nationalists in their military efforts against the settler government.

ZAPU took advantage of Kaunda's change of heart, and in July, 1966, its forces infiltrated Rhodesia from Zambia, and clashed with government forces in the Zambezi Valley.[104] In September, another group battled with the Smith forces in Lupane, and then in Karoi.[105] The October battle was significant in that the Smith regime lost four warrant officers, and a Chinese "guerrilla expert," a mercenary from Chiang kai-Shek's Formosa (Taiwan), China.[106] By the sheer use of mercenaries, the Smith regime was tacitly acknowledging that it was experiencing the kind of fighting with which it was not familiar. This also indicates an earlier involvement of foreign troops fighting on the side of the Smith regime earlier than is speculated by some historians of the liberation war in Rhodesia.[107]

From March, 1966, to the end of the year, ZAPU forces engaged the settler forces in several skirmishes with losses on both sides, depending on whose story one reads. The theater of operation spread from the western part of Matebeleland, Plumtree, Tsholotsho, Nkayi reserve, to the northern part of the country, Chinoi, Kariba, Karoi, and Mana Pools inter alia. According to the regime sources, most ZAPU insurgents were either killed or arrested, with very minimal losses on their part.[108] However, this is contrary to what ZAPU supporters report. They tell of scores of regime soldiers killed. Given that each side is prone to exaggerate its victories here, it is best to believe that the exact number of those killed from both sides is smaller than what is reported by each side.

The aim of these infiltrations by ZAPU was to organize people's resistance groups throughout the country and, also possibly to incite people to revolt against government, with an ultimate goal of expelling the minority government. The forces were to fight only in self-defense. Thus what was crucial during this period was winning the hearts of the population, gathering information on targets and bringing in weapons to be cached for future use. In that direction, the cadres continued the goals of the intelligence officers who had entered the country earlier in 1965. They visited/set-up new reception networks, identified targets, organized people into cells, this time with a military orientation, all the time liaising with Lusaka.[109]

The locals were also organized in to a courier system upon which guerrillas on the operational theater would depend for information and co-ordination of contacts. According to Dengilizwe Dewa, more than twenty local villagers received military training from the insurgents, and others left for Zambia to receive training. The "more than twenty" local trainees did not leave the country, but continued to fight from inside and some trainees like Mhlanhlandlela Mpofu developed into finished soldiers on the job.[110]

Ellert observes that the cadres' "general efficiency, discipline and esprit de corps was of high standard."[111] Given the good quality of the regime's intelligence, this observation cannot be doubted when we note that some of the cadres were able to evade the security forces for four months. The fighters mostly relied on the local population for sanctuary, intelligence and food. They were also armed with a variety of weapons, which included PPSH sub-machine guns, automatic Tokarev pistols, grenades, AK-47 rifles, explosives and Soviet two-way short-range radios.[112]

In mid-1967, ZAPU entered an agreement with the South African National Congress to carry-out joint operations. According to Dumiso Dabengwa, ZAPU was approached by the ANC with a proposal for joint operations. ANC had tried to infiltrate its forces through Botswana, but because of the military co-operation between South Africa and Botswana, the Botswana Security forces disarmed most of its men. In search for a new entry country ANC concluded using Rhodesia with the help of ZIPRA was the only reasonable option. Because of the ZIPRA forces' knowledge of the terrain, according to this plan, they would accompany ANC forces to the Limpopo River.

Another advantage of ANC using Rhodesia for infiltrating South Africa was that most of their cadres spoke Zulu, a language well understood by the locals of Matebeleland, since there was some historical affinity between Zulus and AmaNdebele. Dumiso concludes by stressing that ANC/ZAPU joint operations occurred, contrary to the belief of some scholars today, after Rhodesia had entered military co-operation with South Africa.[113] George Silundika made the same remarks earlier, and so did Philemon T. Makonese.

Against this background, the first joint ANC/ZAPU commando crossed the Zambezi River at the Gwaai Gorge, between Victoria Falls and Kazungula towards the end of July. According to the Rhodesian sources the men numbered 80. On 13 August 1967, the first major battle occurred between one section of the ANC/ZAPU commando and the Rhodesia African Rifles supported by a police anti-terrorist unit (PATU) in the Wankie Game Reserve. On 27 August, the Rhodesian forces ran into an ambush of twenty-two guerrillas.

The guerrillas were well dug in, and the Rhodesian forces met with stiff resistance. The battle lasted for several hours leaving, according to the Rhodesian sources, five guerrillas dead, two regime soldiers dead, and two policemen wounded.[114] Because the ground forces had totally failed to rout out the guerrillas who seemed to be scoring some victory of some sorts, Rhodesian Air Hunters were sent in to join the war for the first time, and rocketed guerrilla positions, initially with very little effect.

The clashes between ANC/ZAPU Commandos and Rhodesian forces, which started towards the end of July, finally wound down by the end of September 1967. Rhodesia had incurred its heaviest loss to date with seven dead and several wounded and firearms, ammunition and radio equipment captured. Thirty-one ANC/ZAPU commandos were either killed or captured.[115] Some of the ANC men punched holes through the Rhodesian forces' cordon, and with the help of the locals, some went into Botswana and others into South Africa.

The Founding of Zapu, Leadership, Split And Struggle, 1961-69

ZAPU and ANC did not officially announce their forces' joint venture until after the first incursion of their eighty insurgents. This was perhaps done to maintain the surprise element, one of war's critical ingredients. On 19th August, 1967, James Chikerema representing ZAPU and Oliver Tambo of the ANC, announced that their soldiers were already engaged in a joint military campaign in Rhodesia.

In response to this announcement, South Africa and Rhodesia announced their military co-operation as well. They used the ANC/ZAPU joint operations as a justification for their entering a military co-operation. Silundika was very clear that co-operation between South Africa and Southern Rhodesia started before ANC and ZAPU formed their joint operations. Already by the late 1960s a tripartite defense agreement existed involving Rhodesia, South Africa and Portugal.

Overwhelming and convincing evidence now exists, which proved that South African and Rhodesia's Alliance existed before the ANC/ZAPU.

On the 19th and 23rd March, 1967, South Africa first dispatched soldiers to assist the Rhodesian soldiers that numbered 525 men. In July, in keeping with the tripartite defense agreement, South Africa dispatched another 320 soldiers. South Africa had a two-fold reason for helping Zimbabwe. First, they wanted to use Rhodesia as a buffer against ANC attacks and, second, they wanted to gain experience in fighting a bush war. The performance of the first group of South African soldiers was mediocre at best.

In addition to being shot by guerrillas, they were attacked by mosquitoes and tsetse flies and strange sounds after dark turned their nights into nightmares. Consequently, some suffered from psychological problems and were sent home. The involvement of the South African soldiers, which by 1968 had bases along the Zambezi River, along the border with Zambia would end in 1980 after independence.

The worst was yet to come for the Rhodesian troops. During the month of December into January of 1968, more than 200 ANC/ZAPU insurgents infiltrated Rhodesia and camped in Chewore, a controlled hunting area in the northeastern part of the country. For several months they trekked back and forth from Zambia using inflatable rubbers to ferry weapons that they stored in their base. The guerrillas lived in Vietcong type of bunkers dug in the forest. The bases were built in a sophisticated manner, with networks of underground bunkers forming a long line of 30 to 50 kilometers apart.

The place was well watered and covered by a thick forest. The guerrillas built six camps underground and kept constant communication with Lusaka utilizing a single side Band and very High Frequency radio transmitter. Thus the bases had been skillfully situated and camouflaged to make them hard to see from the air. By this time the Rhodesian government had already shown its limitation in containing the intelligence of ZAPU insurgence. Consequently, it enlisted Chinese and as ex-Nazi officers supplied by West Germany.[116]

Smith's soldiers discovered their hideout, after the guerrillas had built their fort to a point where it was almost impregnable. This time the regime was not going to rush into war without serious preparation. The previous engagement had shown them that ZIPRA was no easy pushover. The battle in the Wankie Game Reserve on 27 August, 1967, was the toughest ever fought by the Rhodesians and their mercenaries.

Smith immediately responded by requiring the formation of a Joint Operations Command (JOC) code-named Op Cauldron with Headquarters as Karoi Police Station to contain the large presence of guerrillas. Leaves of both police and army personnel were immediately canceled, and announcements to that effect were made over radios and flashed in cinema screens across the country. Fear haunted the white population in isolated farms. This was the largest mobilization of forces of its kind in Rhodesian history.

The Rhodesian army launched an offensive on an unprecedented scale. The war was fierce. Rhodesia involved the Rhodesia Light Infantry and the Rhodesia African Rifles. The two units futilely tried to break through and winkle out the guerrillas from their strongholds. The guerrillas clearly had both a superior position, and firepower. According to Sigawugawu, the guerrillas moved their military equipment out of the bunkers to the cliffs and rocks nearby.[117]

Taking advantage of their superior position they were able to pin down their adversaries with withering firepower. To balance off the odds, Rhodesia called in the Air force that dropped napalm, phosphorus bombs and defoliants into the guerrilla hideouts. Again this these running battles spread over several months, ending with ANC/ZAPU insurgents either withdrawing, being killed or captured. Another combined operation occurred in 1969 after which the ANC and ZAPU did not carry out any notable combined operations. However, co-operation continued until the ZAPU crises of 1970/1971.

In the heart of Salisbury, the capital, bombs erupted at various places laid by liberal whites[118] who belonged to ZAPU and by individual guerrillas who went after soft targets.[119] Even ministers of religion participated in this struggle as ZAPU members. As the least suspected group, leaders of the Zimbabwe Church of Orphans were used to ferry and cache weapons.[120] The participation of clergy was not limited to the ZOC leaders only. The mainline black leaders participated too, and these had an advantage of being the least suspects.[121]

Throughout this phase of fighting, guerrillas suffered a lot of limitations ranging from lack of food, poor maps, logistics, and invariably being sold out by their own members and the community members. Some villagers had no choice but to disclose the movement of the guerrillas because of the torture they suffered from the Smith regime. Although some scholars assert that guerrilla endeavors during this time were futile, it is difficult to determine the truth of those assertions.

For one, as we have pointed out elsewhere in this chapter, all of these scholars depended on almost exclusively on Rhodesian sources which were

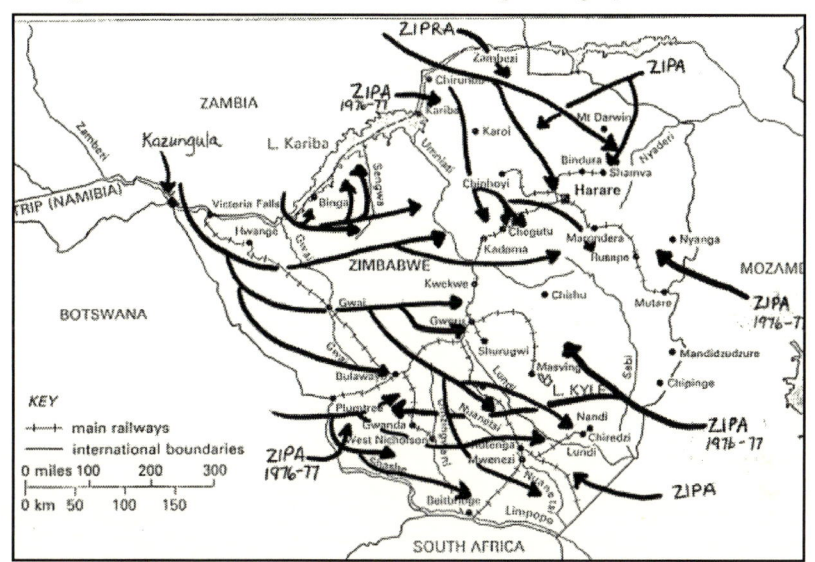

The Founding of Zapu, Leadership, Split And Struggle, 1961-69

Figure 4.2: Areas in which ZIPRA was Operating by End of 1970

prone to stretch the truth. Also, they did not judged the actions of ZAPU according to the organization's stated goals. ZAPU made it clear that between in the 1960s it deployed its forces for reasons short of an all out war against the regime, and yet these scholars judged ZAPU's success based on this element.

While it is clear that victory did not fall into the hands of ZAPU like proverbial over ripe plums, it is equally indisputable that the Rhodesian forces did not have the same fortune either. That they engaged mercenaries attest to this fact. Undoubtedly both sides lost more of their men than they cared to admit. More evidence, given the protracted running battles between the two forces, supports the position that ZAPU was finally the winner. This is truer when we consider their main goal, which was to organize people against the government and recruit soldiers. Undoubtedly, they won the battle of hearts and minds of the black population, and also scored a psychological scare victory against the white population.

4.12 Summary and Conclusion

The mother of all splits occurred hardly months after ZAPU's founding, leading to the inauguration of ZANU in 1963, and with its birth, tribalism on a larger scale was injected into Southern Rhodesian black politics for the first time. The practice of tribalism as a political tool specifically by ZANU, brings the white man's version of the pre-colonial relationships between the two major ethnic groups in Southern Rhodesia into currency.

During the colonial period, settlers used tribalism to divide the blacks so that they could rule over them. Mugabe did the same, and his party ran for power on a tribal basis. This then led to the introduction of internecine fighting at an unprecedented scale between the black movements for the first time in Southern Rhodesia. Before the split, ZAPU brought the first bunch of weapons from Egypt. Nkomo himself becomes the first person to go and secure arms and training bases, in addition to increasingly bringing the Zimbabwe Question to the UN and OAU.

Although these weapons were never used against the white settler regime until the time they were discovered by police, the symbolical significance of their acquisition cannot be overemphasized. With their discovery came the awareness to the white government that blacks were serious about their demand for majority rule, and even ready to die for it. However, with the institution of unprecedented factional fighting between the major liberation movements, Smith responded by exploiting the division, and thereby weakening the struggle for majority rule. He did this by encouraging factional fighting which Smith did by implanting pseudo-groups within the movements whose purpose was to stir-up trouble.

In the meantime, Malawi and Zambia became independent, and both countries got black leaders. The white regime moved to the far right, and under the direction of Ian Smith declared UDI, disregarding the on-going discussions on majority rule. Before Smith declared UDI, he arrested most of the leading ZAPU leaders including its leader Nkomo, along with those of ZANU who, ironically, were charged as ZAPU members, and drove more out of the country to join already burgeoning numbers of their compatriots already based in the neighboring states, most of them in Zambia.

The 1960s also witnessed ZAPU's fight for majority rule move from constitutional approach to a painful birth of armed confrontation as negotiations failed to secure blacks' demands and the banning of ZAPU banned. By the UDI, ZAPU and its counterpart ZANU, the only effective voices for those seeking majority rule had been banned, and its leadership was either in prison or exile. ZAPU members in exile concentrated on publicizing the plight of blacks inside Rhodesia to the world. In fact, during this period, ZAPU managed to internationalize the need for blacks for economic and political rights. Also the party concerned itself with building military bases in Zambia, from which it launched trained commandos into Rhodesia.

This period was characterized by the politicization and organization of the Rhodesian masses. Insurgents spent most of their time organizing, caching weapons inside the country, reconnoitering paths for crossing the Zambian border with Rhodesia, gauging the preparedness of the masses, establishing an a courier system for information and co-ordination of contacts. Winning the hearts and minds of the masses became their major goal as a preparation for launching a major offensive against the regime forces.

The insurgents only fought in self-defense. Thus, the ZAPU cadres spent most of this time essentially making contact with ZAPU underground structures and constructing some others where they did not exist, in preparation

The Founding of Zapu, Leadership, Split And Struggle, 1961-69

for the upcoming war of which mostly the rural people at inception were to form a critical part.

The last five years of the 1960s see ZAPU adopting an explicit armed struggle approach, which with no chances of negotiations, served as the only way to communicate with the Rhodesia government. This period also witnessed fruitful joint operations between ZAPU and ANC forces, and briefly with FRELIMO, which continued to the end of 1969. By 1969, ZAPU had either bombed or fired shots or both, in six of the eight regions, Matebeleland North and South, Midlands, Mashonaland North and Central, and Mashonaland East (see figure 4.2).

Smith responded to ZAPU's infiltration by inviting mercenaries from abroad and the neighboring South Africa. Alarm and despondency was already awash among the white population, although the exodus was not felt immediately since Italian and Nazi Germany prisoners were brought in to boost the white population, and these could not leave, and therefore formed a constant white population mainstay.[122]

ZAPU closed the 1960s victorious in two ways despite its losses in the battle. One, the presence of insurgents inside the country and their activities mobilized the masses, and for the first time the settlers admitted that there was an unwinnable war going on in Rhodesia.

Second, ZAPU scored a psychological victory over a military priding itself in its vast expertise. With all the help from mercenaries with knowledge on the operations of guerrillas, Rhodesian troops could not keep the insurgents off. Guerrillas punched holes into their cordon as it were. Such incidents as instances where ZAPU forces ably eluded the security forces after violating what Smith considered sacred borders, evidently undermined the notion of the invincibility of the Rhodesian forces. However, ZIPRA still faced the formidable challenge of the Air Force, which disadvantaged them greatly.

Thus, by the close of this period, ZAPU had scored both a symbolic as well as a strategic victory over the white regime.

Endnotes

1. Zimbabwe African People's Union, ed., *Zimbabwe: History of a Struggle* (Cairo: The Afro-Asian People's Solidarity, March, 1972) p.24; see also Joshua Nkomo, *The Story of My Life* (1984), p. 97.
2. Mtshumayeli Sibanda, interview by author, 10 January 1994. Between December 7 and 9, when the party was banned, a total of 503 women were arrested, Canaan S. Banana, ed., *Turmoil and Tenacity: Zimbabwe 1890-1990* (Harare: College Press, 1989), p. 102.
3. N.A.Z., F120/725/L343/3, Internal Security Weekly Reports, December 17-19, 1961; *African Daily News* (December 19, 1961); *Bantu Mirror*, December 23, 1961.
4. Melwa Ntini, interview by author, 25 August 1987.

5. *Bantu Mirror* (December 23, 1961); see also for the same objective, however, in a different order, Shamuyarira, *Crisis in Rhodesia* (1965), p. 71.

6. Nkomo, *The Story of My Life* (1984), p. 99.

7. Day, *International Nationalism* (1967), pp. 25-43.

8. Anthony R. Wilkinson, "From Rhodesia to Zimbabwe" in Basil Davidson, Joe Slovo and Anthony R. Wilkinson, *Southern Africa: The New Politics of Revolution* (New York: Penguin Books, 1976), p. 227.

9. The purpose of Whitehead's 'Build a Nation' campaign was to persuade Africans to register to vote under the new constitution. African massively boycotted it. The campaign was meant, specifically, to enroll qualified Africans for both 'A' and 'B' electoral rolls. It was estimated that about 5,000 Africans qualified for the 'A' roll, and 50,000 for the 'B.' At the end of the campaign, a little less than 2,000 had enrolled on the 'A' roll, and a little less than 10,000 on the 'B.'

10. Ian Douglas Smith, *The Great Betrayal: Memoirs of Ian Douglas Smith* (London: Blake Publishing Ltd., 1997), p. 41.

11. Anthony Lake, *The "Tar Baby" Option: American Policy Toward Southern Rhodesia*, (New York: Columbia University Press, 1976), p. 19.

12. Joshua Nkomo, interview by author, 26 July 1995.

13. *Ibid.*

14. Frank Clements, *Rhodesia: A Study of the Deterioration of a White Society* (New York: Frederick A. Praeger, 1969), p. 160.

15. *Ibid.*

16. A sixth principle was added in 1966 which read thus: It would be necessary to ensure that, regardless of race, there was no oppression of majority by minority, or of minority by majority.

17. The gurus of the Rhodesian Front at its inception were Winston Field, Ian Douglas Smith and D. W. Lardner-Burke.

18. Ian Hancock, *White Liberals, Moderates and Radicals in Rhodesia 1953-1980* (New York: St Martin's Press, 1984), pp. 79-104. In fact, Hancock provides a detailed description of the three types of whites from the introduction of the Federation to the time Ian Smith surrendered power. Most of my discussion on the three types of whites during this period is based on this work of his.

19. In 1977, the RF led by Ian Smith took all the white seats in parliament.

20. David G. Bromley and Philip E. Hammond, eds., *The Future of New Religious Movements*, CMacon Georgia: Mercer University Press, 1987), p. 16.

21. For straight-from-the-shoulder style writing on his life in which he recounts his conflicts with President Robert Mugabe, and essentially gives insight into his life and political career until 1985 when he returned from his self-imposed exile in Britain, read his 270-page autobiography, *The Story of My Life* (1984). The book is rich in that it sheds light on some of Nkomo's political involvement, which has hitherto been either omitted or distorted for political gains by his opponents and their supporter. Nkomo also allows us to see his vision for an independent Zimbabwe which he thinks is scheduling the ordinary folk as he aptly summarized the purpose of his autobiography when he stated that his book was "a personal record of life that has

The Founding of Zapu, Leadership, Split And Struggle, 1961-69

played a part in history, and it is also the work of an active politician who wishes to see things change for the better in the lives of the ordinary people of this country," *The Daily News*, 6 July, (1999), p. 12.

22. In his book entitled *Political Myth* (London, 1972), Henry Tudor makes a distinction between the popular use of 'myth' as referring to mere illusion and a more deeper meaning which he adopts and elaborately discusses. Tudor states that myths are narrative visions of the past or of the future that have political meaning to a group of people who believe in them. As such, a political myth makes sense of a people's present experience, in situations of a struggle, identifying the enemy and promising victory in the end. Such myths, Tudor asserts, are not mere intellectual inventions, but a product of particular historical circumstances to meet social needs. Thus myths interpreted this way have their roots in real life.

    It can be accurately pointed out that among people where recollections of past events is largely dependent on oral rather than documentary tradition, mythology plays a crucial role in the development of national consciousness. It is in this deeper meaning of myth as provided by Tudor that we are to understand the meaning of myth in this work.

23. The phrase "I am the son of the soil" became part of Nkomo's introductory remarks in most of the rallies he addressed. The use of this phrase was generally meant identify him as one with his audience.

24. Joshua Nkomo, interview by author, 15 July 1994.

25. Nkomo's integration of Christian and traditional beliefs was characteristic of his life. Nkomo was accorded both Christian and traditional rites at his burial on July 5, 1999. To fulfill the traditional rites his body was taken to his village in Kezi, a day before burial, where Nkomo's family elders sought the blessings of their ancestors to have him buried at the Heroes' Acre, Harare, away from his family cemetery at Tshimali Mabunga in Kezi, Matobo, where his father, mother, elder brother Paul and his son Tutani are buried. In order for his body to be buried away from his village, his brothers Steven [Governor of Matebeleland South] and Edward [Education Officer] dug up the soil from the Nkomo family cemetery in Kezi where he was supposed to be buried and took it with them to the Heroes' Acre which traditionally symbolized that although his body was buried away from his village, spiritually he was buried alongside his family in Matobo. At his burial, again in observance of traditional rites, his only surviving son, Sibangilizwe Michael, was given his father's traditional knobkerrie and a spear, which he held, pointed to the ground as he stood by his father's body before it was buried.

    In observance of Nkomo's Christian faith, Catholic Archbishop Patrick Chakaipa and Bishop Ncube of Bulawayo performed Christian burial rites, which included the sprinkling of holy water on the casket and the burning of incense. Even Pope John Paul II, the head of the Catholic Church, showed his high regard for Nkomo's faith by dispatching his special representative, Apostolic Nuncio Peter Prabh, to support the officiating highest-ranking church officer, Bishop Chakaipa at his burial. For detailed information on the infusion of Christian and cultural rites at Nkomo's burial. See *The Daily News*, July 10, 1999, p. 13.

26. Nkomo, *The Story of My Life* (1984), pp. 30-33.

27. Mrs. Julia Hoskin was a clerk at Adams College where Nkomo spent three years working on his High School Diploma. While he was a junior at Adams College, Mrs. Hoskins bought a car, but did not know how to drive, so she hired Nkomo as her driver. In the course of time Nkomo, and Mrs. Hoskin became so close that some as Mr. De Kock, the Dean of Man reported to the school superiors that he suspected the two had an illicit relationship. This, if true, would have been punishable by law since interracial romances were banned in South Africa. When confronted about it, Nkomo told the school's superiors that his relationship with Mrs. Hoskin was that of a mother and a son. There is no reason not to believe Nkomo on this. Mrs. Hoskin, a widow of an army major, was undoubted lonely after the death of her husband, and her bonding with Nkomo as a 'son' comes as no surprise. During the almost three years that Nkomo worked for Mrs. Hoskin they developed a very intimate, non-genital relationship which continued when Nkomo went to Jan Hofmeyer School of Social Work.

28. *Ibid.*, p. 35. Apparently, Nkomo's encounter with Nelson Mandela who was then a student at the Witwatersrand, at the Blue Lagoon restaurant was very significant in his life, for later his daughter would name her own restaurant Blue Lagoon in honor of the meeting between Mandela and her father.

29. Anton Muziwakhe Lembede was a lawyer by profession known extensively for his mass political organizational skills. Although highly educated, he had now problem identifying and communicating with the uneducated blacks, and would invariably refer to himself as the "son of the soil," a self-reference Nkomo would use successfully later when he joined politics. The phrase, "son of the soil," in the Southern African context is generally understood by blacks to be indicative of the connectedness of the one who uses it with land and its people irrespective of their rank in life. Thus, the phrase was part of a consonance with popular black consciousness, which to create a shared structure of feeling with the masses.

30. Later, in his autobiography, Nkomo recounted his reason for involvement in London Conference differently. He convincingly argues that he attended the conference only subsequent to consulting with executive members of the SRANC and having secured their approval, see Nkomo, pp. 40-61.

31. Nkomo, *The Story of My Life* (1984), pp. 64-65. Nkomo confesses that Mike Hove got 30,000 votes when he himself got 15,000. A majority of the black electorate and Asians (Indians) voted for Nkomo and possibly some whites. In that first Federal Election, Mike Hove and Jasper Savahnu, both of whom ran as chosen black candidates sponsored by the UFP, won their seats.

32. The *Ilitshe* was what Mt. Sinai was to the Israelites. The blacks in Zimbabwe believed there were specific, designated mountains where God could be worshiped, and those mountains where this happened were known as *Amatshe*, in the singular, *Ilitshe*.

33. Thenjiwe Lisabe, interview by author, 11 February, 1987, repeated in an interview with author, 26 January, 1998.

34. Thenjiwe Lesabe, interview by author, 24 January, 1998.

35. For posthumous accolades and tribute to Nkomo by both his followers, admirers, and hitherto avowed enemies see *The Daily News* (July 2-6), 1999; *The Guardian* (July

The Founding of Zapu, Leadership, Split And Struggle, 1961-69

9-15), 1999; *Financial Gazette* (July 8, 1999); and *Zimbabwe Independent* (July 2-9), 1999.

36. Nkomo, *Nkomo: The Story of My Life* (1984), p. 14.
37. Terence Ranger, "Whose Heritage? The Case of the Matopo National Park," *Journal of Southern African Studies*, Vol. 15, 2 (January 1989):217-249.
38. As part of the negotiations to end the *Impi YomVukela*, Cecil Rhodes promised the AmaNdebele that they would live in peace and quiet in the Matopos. Also, missionaries assured African entrepreneurial farmers a permanent stay on the church owned farms.
39. *Mirror* (December 27, 1958).
40. *Bantu Mirror* (February 10, 1951); *ibid*.
41. *Home News* (January 12, 1957).
42. Richard Sibanda, interview by author, 26 August 1996.
43. Patricia Cheney, *The Land and the People of Zimbabwe* (New York: J.B. Lippincott, 1990), p. 134.
44. Ntini, interview by author, 7 August 1994.
45. Mlambo, *Rhodesia: The Struggle for a Birthright* (1972), p. 204.
46. John Mpofu, An Interview with Author, August 26, 1987.
47. *Report on the Zimbabwe African People's Union* (Salisbury: Government Printer, 1962).
48. Shamuyarira, *Crisis in Rhodesia* (1965), pp. 202-203.
49. Banana, ed., *Turmoil and Tenacity* (1989), pp. 108, 366.
50. For a list of the places where violence by ZAPU supporters broke-out after the white regime banned their party see *Rhodesia: Struggle for a Birthright* (1972), p. 193.
51. *Ibid*.
52. The two pieces of law, the Unlawful Organization Amendment Act and the Law and Order (Maintenance) Amendment Act, were used to ban ZAPU on September 20, 1962, and to restrict its leaders to specified rural and urban areas.
53. Clearly, Julius Nyerere misread the situation in Southern Rhodesia by thinking that, like his country, and most of the administrative colonies, Rhodesia could only be liberated when the leadership remained in the country. What he did not seriously ponder was the efficient and repressive white machinery put in place to eliminate any nationalists' activities, as well as the presence of white settlers.
54. For a well balanced ZAPU view of the split, especially within the context of the constitutional convention dispute in London and Salisbury, at which Nkomo was singularly held as responsible for accepting a sell-out electoral deal, see Ishmael Mlambo, *Rhodesia: Struggle for a Birthright* (1972), and for a chronological account of the splits leading to this one see Leonard Kapungu, *Rhodesia: The Struggle for Freedom* (1974).
55. Leopold was based in London as the party's Director of External Affairs, a post that was once held by Nkomo before taking up the leadership of the party in October 1965. Other leading opponents who raised opposition at a time when Nkomo and his leadership had already indicated they did not accept parliamentary seat allocations, were Morton Malianga, Vice-President, Robert Mugabe, Publicity

Secretary, Enos Nkala, Vice-Secretary General and Ndabaningi Sithole, and these dissidents composed the cast of dissident two years later, 1963, leading to the formation of ZANU.

56. Melwa Ntini, An interview by author, 27 August, 1987.
57. Ngwabi Bhebe, "The Nationalist Struggle, 1957-62," Canaan S. Banana, ed., *Turmoil and Tenacity. Zimbabwe 1890-1990* (Harare: College Press, 1989), pp. 89-90.
58. Wilfred Mhanda [war name Dzinashe Machingura], interview in Focus (HSF-SA), December 2000. Machingura was a high ranking ZANLA who when ZIPA was formed became deputy to the Army Commander Rex Nhongo [real name: Solomon Mujuru].
59. Nkomo, *The Story of My Life* (1984), p. 116.
60. Some of these dissidents were high-ranking officials in ZAPU. For example, Ndabaningi Sithole who became the first President of ZANU was formerly Treasurer and National Chairman of ZAPU.
61. Nkomo, interview by author, 15 July 1994.
62. Shamuyarira, Crisis in Rhodesia (1965), p. 182.
63. ZAPU Report entitled, "Zimbabwe African People's Union Resolutions of Cold Comfort Farm Conference," n.d. The document is in the possession of the author.
64. *Ibid.*
65. Tshombe in Zimbabwe then was used in reference to a sellout. In the early 1960's a beloved nationalist, Patrice Lumumba was assassinated by Joseph Mobutu, it is believed with the help of Moise Tshombe who later became the Premier of the Congo-Leopoldville. The general belief among African nationalists then was that Mobutu and Tshombe were used by white interests in order to forestall the revolutionary leadership of Lumumba. Tshombe would latter be overthrown by General Joseph Mobutu in October, 1965. Because of his participation in the assassination of Lumumba, Tshombe became known as a sell-out to many blacks in favor of majority rule in Africa and their sympathizers, and so it was that his name became synonymous with the word sellout.
66. A.J.A. Peck, *Rhodesia Accuses* (Salisbury: The Three Sisters Books, 1966), p. 86.
67. The Rhodesian Front in particular was determined to silence black political opposition, and as soon as it ascended the throne in 1962, it promulgated stringent laws with very dire consequences. For instance, it imposed mandatory death sentences for using petrol bombs on either property or people, and these dire consequences were built into the Law and Order Maintenance Act. The Rhodesian Front also stiffened the Prevention Detention Act so that it detained more ZAPU/PCC members than the previous governments.
68. Mzila Moyo, interview by author, 16 June, 1994. August 28, 1994. Although it was difficult to verify how much ZAPU was worth, in terms of finances and property, as compared to other black nationalists movements before it, a majority of my interviewees agreed with Mzila that ZAPU was the richest of all the black organizations to date.

The Founding of Zapu, Leadership, Split And Struggle, 1961-69

69. H. Ellert, *The Rhodesian Front War: Counter-Insurgency and Guerrilla War in Rhodesia 1962-1980* (Gweru: Mambo Press, 1993), pp. 19-20; Kees Maxey, *The Fight for Zimbabwe* (1975), p. 8.

70. *Rhodesia Herald* (13 August 1968).

71. The employment of tradition/culture as a pretext for retaining arms of war (knobkerries, axes, and *imikhonto* was not peculiar to ZAPU alone, Inkatha, Gatsha Buthelezi's movement used the same argument in throughout the 1980's to protect its privilege of carrying what turned out to be weapons of destruction against their opponents.

72. Ishmael Mlambo, *Rhodesia: The Struggle for a Birthright* (London: C. Hurst & Company, 1972), p. 214; Nkomo, The Story of My Life (1984), pp. 104-105. Manyonga was a regional secretary of ZAPU.

73. Peter Stiff, *Selous Scout: Top Secret War* (Alberton: Galago Publishing (Pvt) Ltd., 1982).

74. The ban on hunting of animals was strictly enforced on white farms. In defiance blacks used spears, *indobhi*, and snares to kill animals on these farms. With the promotion of the use of skins to make headgears and sitting mats and bedspreads as a 'badge' of going back to the roots, which at this time was synonymous with being ZAPU, hunting on white farmers' land became widespread. Chenju Nkala, who was a youth member then, and beyond 20 years old, informed me that wearing a skin attire gotten from animals butchered on a white farm was psychologically very rewarding as it was "a small victory for us." Thus, the activity became a demonstration of their manliness and mettle, as it were.

75. Dumiso Dabengwa, Hon. Deputy Minister of Home Affairs, in a paper entitled "ZIPRA and ZIPA in the Zimbabwe War of National Liberation," presented at the University of Zimbabwe, (July 8, 1991), p. 7.

76. Barber, *Rhodesia* (1967), p. 108.

77. Robert C. Good, *U.D.I. The International Politics of the Rhodesian Rebellion* (Boston: Princeton University Press, 1973), p. 40.

78. Mutasa and Shamuyarira, for example, were members of the Capricorn Society, a liberal white-led society.

79. Mlambo, *Rhodesia: The Struggle for a Birthright* (1972), p. 202.

80. ZANU at this time had a membership campaign of its own. The argument between ZAPU and ZANU soon became over who had more members. ZANU engaged in extensive campaigns and set 100,000 as its target number for registered members. To its chagrin, its rallies were attended by less than 300, while its popular opponent, ZAPU drew thousands to its meetings for whom it could not produce documentary evidence. To solve this what developed into a problem in this competition for numbers, ZAPU registered its members, and moved toward declaring its internal wing, PCC, a party.

81. Revelation 20:12 talks about the Book of Life which will be opened on the Judgment Day and those not found in it, it says will be throne out of Heaven. This obviously angered many settlers who considered themselves Christian and apparently considered its use by Nkomo and his party as sacrilegious since they

were considered 'pagans'. To ZAPU, those who were not found in their book of life were considered non-Zimbabweans.

82. Immediately after his arrest, Nkomo was detained at Gonakudzingwa Camp in the Southeast border area for one year. Thereafter he was transferred to Gwelo for one year to serve a sentence for a subversive statement. In 1966, together with Joseph Msika and the late Lazarus Nkala, Nkomo was imprisoned in Gonakudzingwa again where he was refused contact with other people other than government officials. In 1974 as power was slipping through the fingers of the Mozambican minority government, he was moved to Buffalo Range Prison near Triangle for tighter security. Indeed, Nkomo served ten years six months in prison under different conditions, all of which were inhuman. For instance, from 1969-1974, he was allowed only one visit every three months from his wife and children. Also, he was permitted to appear in the public eye on only three occasions: 1965, 1968 and 1972.

83. In fact, Josiah Chinamano and his wife Ruth as well as Joseph Msika, the two men being officials of ZAPU, were arrested and restricted on the same day as Nkomo, and were also restricted at the same location.

84. *Zimbabwe Review* (April 20, 1964), p. 1.

85. *Ibid.*, p. 2.

86. Ellert, *The Rhodesian Front War* (1989).

87. Julie Frederikse, *None But Ourselves Masses vs. Media in the Making of Zimbabwe* (Harare: Penguin Books, 1982), p. 48.

88. Cited from Good, *U.D.I.* (1973), p. 50.

89. Martin Meredith, *The Past is Another Country* (London: Andre Deutsche, 1979), p. 44.

90. Joshua Nkomo, interview by Author, 15 July, 1994.

91. Zimbabwe African People's Union, *The Armed Revolutionary Struggle in Zimbabwe*, Asian-Afro Publications, 55, (1973), pp. 13-14. Ironically, the Smith government depended on troops transferred to the white minority government at the break-up of the Federation on 13 December 1963.

92. Paul Moorcroft, *African Nemesis: War and Revolution in Southern Africa (1945-2010)* (London: Brassey's [UK], 1990), p. 123.

93. In fact, at the declaration of Independence, Britain's position was closer to that of Ian Smith than to that of ZAPU. Britain was willing to give the white regime independence as long as they were willing to promise reform on the part of Africans, and that they would in some distant future introduce a Majority Rule in the country. Smith would have none of this; he wanted unconditional independence based on white supremacy, See Martin Meredith, *The Past is Another Country* (1979), pp. 55-56.

94. Martin and Johnson, *The Struggle for Zimbabwe* (1981); Michael Raeburn, *Black Fire* (1978); Moorcroft, African Nemesis (1990), p. 123.

95. Prior to this attack by ZANU, the O.A.U. had adopted a resolution whereby it gave support to only those liberation movements, which waged effective military and political struggles in their own countries. The support was channeled through the African Liberation Committee which served under the O.A.U. See

The Founding of Zapu, Leadership, Split And Struggle, 1961-69

for information on the support of liberation movements by O.A.U., T. Kapungu, "The OAU's Support for the Liberation of Southern Africa" in Yassin El-Ayouty (ed.), *The Organization of African Unity After Ten Years: Comparative Perspective* (New York: Praeger, 1975), pp. 138-139. On the OAU's and the ALC's position toward Zimbabwe, see Zdenek Cervenka, *The Unfinished Quest for Unity* (London: Julian Friedmann Publishers, 1977), pp. 45-63, 122-127.

96. Martin and Johnson, *The Struggle for Zimbabwe: The Chimurenga War* (1981), pp. 9-12.

97. Simbi Mumbako, "Aspects of the Zimbabwe Liberation Movement, 1966-76," a paper presented at the International Conference on Southern African History, Lesotho, August 1977. When Dr. Mumbako presented this paper, he was based in Zambia where besides serving as one of the ZANU leaders, he worked as a law lecturer at the University of Zambia. He is a Harvard trained lawyer and participated in many ZANU high profile conferences. For instance, he was part of ZANU legal team at Geneva (1976) and Lancaster House (1979).

98. Dumiso Dabengwa, who served as the head of intelligence for ZAPU forces disputed the assertion by ZANU that it was the first to fire shots of liberation in his paper, "ZIPRA and ZIPA in the Zimbabwe War of National Liberation" presented at the University of Zimbabwe, (8 July, 1991). Dabengwa points out that contrary to popular claims, that ZANU started the armed struggle in 1966 in Chinoia, ZAPU in 1965.

99. Keesing's Contemporary Archives 21421, *Times* (4 March, 1966). ZAPU alleged from its offices in Dar es Salaam that fierce fighting had occurred in the Nkayi Reserve in early March.

100. Silwane Bhunkuzo, Interview by Author. Silwane informed this author that he was teaching in the area when ZAPU guerrillas arrived in the area towards the end of February. He reported that these guerrillas, before ZAPU forces battled with settler forces, recruited him and two other teachers from two different schools. Subsequent to the March battle, he left with a group of six guerrillas who were part of that battle.

101. Chimurenga is a Shona word, which refers to the uprisings against the white settlers in the late 1890's. Some historians like Terence Ranger have posited a continuity thesis between these uprisings and the liberation war that lead to the independence of Zimbabwe. See, for instance, Terence Ranger, *Revolt in Southern Rhodesia* (London: Heinemann, 1967).

102. Ken Flower, *Serving Secretly* (London: Murray, 1987), p. 106.

103. Cited in Good, *U.D.I.* (1973), p. 235.

104. Philemon T. Makonese, *Africa Quarterly* (Vol. 10, 1970), p. 50.

105. Zimbabwe African People's Union, *The Armed Revolutionary Struggle in Zimbabwe*, p. 15.

106. Makonese, p. 50.

107. Kees Maxey is one of the authors who believed that Rhodesia first involved foreign troops on its soil after ZAPU and South African National Congress cadres *uMkhonto We Sizwe*, (the spear of the nation) first joined forces against the Smith regime in July 1966, Maxey, *The Fight for Zimbabwe* (1975), p. 66.

108. Maxey writes that ZAPU forces engaged the regime forces in seven battles in 1966, (Maxey, pp. 54-62). This source also records these engagements in detail and is well documented. However, his sources are one sided as he depended primarily on

Rhodesian sources, mostly government owned newspapers. It is useful, however, in that it documents some of the battles, which the Rhodesian government chose to disclose between its forces and those of the nationalist parties.

109. Black Moses, interview by author, 10 August 1997.
110. Dingilizwe Dewa, interview by author, 24 December 1996.
111. Ellert, *The Rhodesian Front War* (1989), p. 18.
112. The type of weapons ZAPU insurgents used during this time were learnt from the military equipment that was carried by one of the two group of cadres that crossed the Zambezi River at Feiri, opposite Kanyemba in northeastern Rhodesia. These groups, instead of landing in Rhodesia, drifted into Mozambique, where the kind of military equipment with which they were armed was learnt.
113. Dabengwa, "ZIPRA and ZIPA in the ZIMBABWE WAR of National Liberation" (8 July 1991), p. 9.
114. Ellert, The Rhodesian Front War (1989); Peter Stiff, *Selous Scouts: Top Secret War* (Alberton: Galago Publishing [Pvt] Ltd., 1982). The versions given by these two sources are different, and of course both represent the official voice since both men served as members of the Rhodesian security forces. However, Ellert tends to be a bit more liberal in his narration of the war occurrences of the two.
115. *Ibid.*
116. Silwane Bhunkuzo, interview by author, 27 August 1987.
117. Sigawugawu, interview by author, 13 May 1995. Sigawugawu is one of the guerrillas who participated in this contact.
118. These liberals included John A. Conradie, and Ivan G. Dixon, both of whom were sentenced for the possession of hand grenades, and George Brind who was sentenced for publishing, outside the country, an article likely to spread alarm and despondency among the white population. All the three whites were charged under the notorious Law and Maintenance Act of 1960. Giovanni Arrighi, an Asian lecturer at the University of Rhodesia, led the ring of liberals. The only people among this ring, which also included John Reed to escape arrest, were Arrighi and Reed.
119. In 1968, a lone guerrilla shot at a white family through a window of their house in Harare, and the family barely escaped death, *Rhodesia Herald* (7 December 1968).
120. Richard Sibanda, interview by author, 26 August 1996. Sibanda was a local leader of the Zimbabwe Church of Orphans from 1965-1968. In an interview with the author he reported how he, and some church leaders of his local church used to ferry weapons and cache them, among other things.
121. Stephen Ndlovu, interview by author, 24 July, 1996. Rev. Stephen Ndlovu, was a former teacher and former Bishop of the Brethren in Christ Church.
122. Some of the German and Italian prisoners of war in the 1940s were imprisoned in Salisbury, Rhodesia, where they were housed at the Beatrice Cottages near Mbare. Upon release, they were integrated into the white community and enfranchised. These were the people who were against every tenet of freedom and democracy. Nkomo, on more than one occasion, reminded Zimbabweans about this paradoxical situation, Mlambo, *Rhodesia: The Struggle for a Birthright* (1972), p. 198.

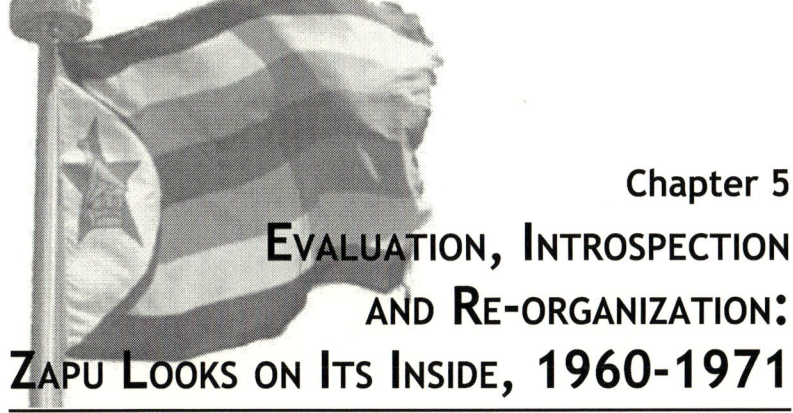

Chapter 5
EVALUATION, INTROSPECTION AND RE-ORGANIZATION: ZAPU LOOKS ON ITS INSIDE, 1960-1971

In this chapter, I begin with evaluating ZAPU's activities in the late 1960s with a view of understanding the effectiveness of its strategies and the fulfillment of its goals, focusing mostly on the years between 1964 and 1970, when all hope of a negotiated solution regarding majority rule were abandoned by the black nationalists. In the previous chapter I stated that ZAPU, to a certain extent, fulfilled some of its major goals, which were to undermine security morale, organize support among the rural population and to begin to build an intelligence network.

However, I observed that militarily ZAPU did not win, although this was not their goal. Theirs was to fight only in self-defense. In evaluating ZAPU's strategies and goals during the 1960s, I raise the question: how effective was ZAPU's prosecution of the struggle during this time? A question may be raised at this point as to what objective yardsticks I use for measuring the revolutionary success of ZAPU or judging its goals as revolutionary.

Several writers have made the distinction between the nationalists who struggled and were granted independence by administrative colonies, and those that had to wrest power from settler colonies through armed struggle. According to these writers, in settler colonies nationalists' combatants did not only engage in an armed revolution but a social and national one as well.[1]

Basil Davidson[2] and John Saul[3] are two good examples of such writers. The two writers agree on the two features which they say are essential in any struggle that results in the social and national revolution. Saul says it is important that the gap between the leaders of the revolution and the majority of the peasants be closed. Davidson says the same thing but in a different, and perhaps clearer way. Davidson says leaders of a revolution should live among their people, and mobilize them for the struggle, in other words work towards winning the peasants' hearts and minds.

By living with the people, Davidson correctly points out, leaders acquire an understanding of the economic, political and social hardships and aspirations of their people. Davidson then points out the second element as the 'deepening of national consciousness.' He saw this process as helping in the strengthening of national unity that could overcome factionalism, be it ethnic or otherwise. The overcoming of factionalism is important because it allows, among other things, armed insurgents to operate in operational theaters far from their homes or people of their own ethnic group.

Davidson says such a revolution first occurred in the Continent of Africa in Guinea Bissau, and was prosecuted by the "Partido Africano da Independencia de Guinea e Cabo Verde" (Portuguese rendered in English, African Party for the Independence of Guinea and Cape Verde, PAIGC) under the leadership of Amilcar Cabral.[4] Like other writers such as Saul,[5] he also points to the parallel situation that obtained in Mozambique. However, the idea of mobilizing people in the countryside, and win them over to one's side as a guerrilla movement was not original with Davidson and Saul.

Guerrillas were, in fact, exposed to such teachings long before these two writers had their works published when they received training in Cuba and also in China where they got exposed to the principles of successful guerrilla warfare as espoused by Mao.[6] Although ZAPU cadres did not continue to be directly exposed to Chinese instruction after 1965, like their counterparts ZANLA,[7] they continued to use the tactics.

Thus, this relationship brings together what Fanon described as the "separate dialectic" of mass (largely rural) protest and urban-based elite political organization. Otherwise, as Saul pointed out, politics in the African national movements would be dominated by

[A]n educated elite, a petty bourgeoisie ... [concerned with] gaining privileged access for themselves [with the masses separate and manipulated by ethnic symbols and competitions, and by the faintest] of nationalism, the most meaningless of African socialism.

Parenthetically, it is important at this point to mention that the leaders of ZAPU were drawn from the ranks of urban and professional Africans some of whom had attended University, and so were some of their cadres.[8] Saul's observation clearly indicates that even after nationalists have decided to pick up arms against an oppressive regime, the tendency for the struggle to use a putschist approach still exists. Also existing are the chances of the struggle to be removed from the general masses and also for it to be unduly inclined to factional fighting, and infighting. According to this model then, success is how integrated the leadership is with its masses,' and the depth of political consciousness.

In a situation of an armed struggle, the guerrilla, as has been noted, becomes the social revolutionary who helps in the bridging of the gap between nationalist leaders and the masses, as well as helps conscientize the general population about their grievances against the government, after living among them, and learning of these grievances from them. As such, for ZAPU insurgents to be judged as successful during this era under study, they should be seen to have successfully lived among the African masses, learned about their grievances against the white regime, and tried to problematize their issues.

Evaluation, Introspection and Re-organization

The second section looks into ZAPU's self-prognosis in light of its military operations of the last five years of the 1960s. Specifically discussed in this area are Jason Moyo's evaluative contributions and his recommendations as well as James Chikerema's response to Jason Moyo's prognosis. Moyo's recommendations form the second section of my discussion in this chapter. The major results of this self-prognosis were splits within the party, and these crises form the third section of my discussion. I also try to understand the causes of the two splits which occurred around this time.

5.1 STRATEGIES AND GOALS OF ZAPU: AN EVALUATION

Since I have already alluded to some of ZAPU's goals and strategies in the previous chapter, and at the outset of this one, for the sake of evaluation I will choose only some and not all of them for evaluative purposes. These are:

1) Mobilizing and politicizing the masses to participate in the struggle;

2) Provide intelligence system upon which the guerrillas would rely for information and coordinating contacts; and

3 To establish groups inside the country that would provide food, medicine and clothes to the guerrillas, and later, to provide logistics to the South African ANC forces.

5.2 MOBILIZING AND POLITICIZING THE MASSES

The masses were organized to essentially do the following: join the armed struggle and provide succor, clothing and food to ZIPRA forces, and starting from 1967, to ANC forces as well. Also, they were to help in the ferrying of weapons to various places around the country where they were to be cached for later use.

As we have pointed out in the preceding chapter, ZAPU forces achieved some qualified success in organizing people to participate in the struggle by recruiting some able bodied youths to go abroad for military training. The newly recruited went to Zambia where they were distributed among different sympathetic countries for training. Also, we observed that not everyone left for training abroad, some trained on the operational theater, on the job, and never left the country till independence. These were trained first on sabotage, and as time progressed, on the use of firearms.

Some locally trained saboteurs like John Mpofu were so good at it that they ended up coordinating both local and external trained saboteurs. John Mpofu, a self-employed carpenter, in 1962-3, coordinated the sabotage activities of both local and external, trained groups. He provided both groups with the materials they needed for their sabotage actions, and at the same time kept in touch with the Headquarters in Lusaka. At the same time, Mpofu continued with his normal life of a carpenter.[9]

As Allert points out, internal saboteurs were very difficult to detect as most of them did not have any criminal records, and were therefore trustworthy workers. As such, it was difficult for the security to think of them as part of the struggle. The saboteurs created a lot of damage while maintaining their businesses in normal ways. These men did not go abroad for training; they were trained inside the country, contrary to the belief by such people as Ellert that these people acted independently.[10]

Also, the locals helped in the transportation of weapons to forward bases where they were cached for future use. ZAPU actually utilized people in all walks of life in the transportation of weapons to forward bases as well as in distributing them to saboteurs already situated in various parts of the country. A good example is that of Phineas Shava, a clergyman with the Salvation Army where he served as a major. Shava smuggled weapons to his home in Fort Victoria in a lorry carrying fish.

Using his home as a base, he distributed some of these weapons by motorcycle to a distributing place in Salisbury.[11] ZAPU also utilized the services of radical white and Indian (Asian) supporters whom it organized into cells. One such cell existed at the University College in Salisbury and was led by an Indian (Asian) lecturer, Prof. Giovanni Arrighi and included Europeans among whom were John Conradie and John Reed.

The cell included Africans as well, and was not limited to University lecturers only. Europeans and Indians supporters of ZAPU who were led by Giovanni at the University College distributed grenades, reported on the deployment of the Rhodesian security forces and selected European white farms to be attacked by ZAPU insurgents.[12] The involvement of whites in the struggle proved to the world that ZAPU clearly defined its struggle as one against an oppressive regime as opposed to one against whites as a racial group.

Also, ZAPU'S infiltration of cities and towns to organize cells and to sustain an inflow and outflow of information should be ample proof of this party's operational skills and also its ability to politically mobilize the general population. Simultaneously, guerrillas explained to the people why they were fighting and also provided reasons for them to join the struggle. Sigawugawu, one of the locally trained cadre, in the 1960's, told of times when ZIPRA forces, in threes and fours, visited people in the village teaching them about the evils of colonization, and telling them why they should fight. Thus, ZAPU fighters interpreted to the masses their desire to repossess their lost land as a means of production as well as a basis of wealth.

Thus, land again, just as it was in during the war of "uMvukela," became the core of ZAPU's revolution. Moving from home to home, as if it were missionaries doing village visitation in an African rural area, ZAPU forces visited villagers with their revolutionary gospel.

Sigawugawu noted:

Evaluation, Introspection and Re-organization

Comrades used to visit my place at night, and sometimes during the day on weekends. I would invite cell leaders in the area to come and listen to them talk about how we lost our land and why we should fight to get it back. We would keep the groups small, and those of us who received this training, spread the revolutionary word to our members. These teachings contributed to my leaving teaching and joining the war on the side of the people.[13]

The insurgents were not only teachers, they were students as well. They moved among the masses and learned from them their problems, as well as ways of fighting the enemy. Indeed, testimonies of ZAPU forces learning and educating the masses in the rural areas during this time abound. Such personal accounts of witnessing ZAPU cadres involved in mobilizing and politicizing the masses negate the popularly held view that ZAPU forces, at least between 1965 and 1970, did not politically educate and organize the masses for the purposes of participating in the prosecution of the armed struggle.[14]

This was the position that Davidson maintained about the nationalist movements in Rhodesia from 1966 onwards. He asserts that ZAPU, like its counterpart ZANU, sent its armed units into the operational theater without prior contact with the masses, consequently, they all ended up in failure.[15]

However, Davidson acknowledges that there was eventually a change in the strategy of war by ZAPU, so that it started working with the masses. He, however, erroneously dates this from the period after 1974.

As has already been observed testimonies by both guerrillas and people who formed cells at that time strongly contradict Davidson's observation.[16] Saul sets the date of radicalization of the Zimbabwean nationalists, by which he meant essentially their involvement with the masses in the struggle against the regime, even later than Davidson, by 1976. In other words, before 1976, Saul saw the Zimbabwean liberation movements' approach to war as having been militaristic. Clearly, ZAPU forces right from the outset were aware that success in armed resistance was unlikely to be achieved until it took on the form in which the masses were organized, and that for organization to occur, politicization was necessary.

However, this is not to say ZAPU was free from elitist thinking. Although, by and large, the notion of being a people's party was practiced, even by the cadres on the operational theater, there was always a section of its supporters who were self-anointed victims of an elitist, ego-centric thinking inclined to losing touch with the masses and fighting on ethnic grounds. Such occasions were exemplified by the intra-ZAPU crisis, which resulted in the Acting President, Chikerema, forming a party of his own.

Thus, on the organizational and agit-prop (agitation and propaganda) level, ZIPRA openly aroused the rural masses to discontent. The more responsive ones were discreetly organized, at first as sympathizers, later as helpers, and finally as members of the revolutionary cells involved in clandestine sabotage or armed forces. Essentially, this was an agit-prop phase. Success in this area, though in fits and starts, was achieved.

The success in terms of numbers of people who responded to the teaching of guerrillas at this time is difficult to establish. However, from the confession of some who worked as cell leaders we can safely conclude that, indeed, the forces were able to recruit, train and organize cells as part of their support system during these years. However, the recruiting was not easy for two basic reasons: one, the regime had its own informers in the rural areas in the form of chiefs and headmen.

During the first years, the regime had people in the rural areas that served its interests.

To these chiefs and headmen, as much as to the white settlers, ZAPU to the extent that it represented Black Nationalism, posed a serious threat. At this level, the war was over the hearts and minds of the rural population who till the early 1960s were firmly under the influence of the chiefs. But after the "Indaba" when some chiefs endorsed Smith's UDI,[17] a battle over the allegiance of people in the rural areas between the black nationalists and the Africa traditional leaders intensified. Consequently, both the regime and these traditional leaders jointly worked at presenting the latter as the bona fide representatives of blacks and not the educated ZAPU nationalists and their armed forces. Characteristically, this first group, the traditional leaders, in turn reported to the authorities the presence of insurgents in their areas as soon as they got some information on them.[18]

Two, government had policemen and some government informers planted within the community. Most of the security forces were deployed in some of these areas before UDI, for the purpose of thwarting any efforts of rebuilding nationalists' parties. The environment was not very hostile for their operation since there was little resistance from the people at that time. Immediately after the UDI, more security people poured into the rural areas to keep order when rural areas erupted in violence, with disgruntled rural people cutting farm fences and filling up dip tanks in protest. These were supplemented by chiefs' messengers and policemen who spent most of their time drinking beer with people in the village, which made it easier for them to gather information on the existence of suspicious people in the area.[19] It is against this background that we can appreciate the importance of internal saboteurs and locally trained guerrillas.

In short, the problem with which the guerrillas were faced at this point of the struggle could at minimum be solved by the elimination of individuals likely to give information on their presence and movement to the securing forces. Alternatively, they could frighten these informers to silence. The general wisdom of guerrilla warfare that says in a situation where there are many informers, "you kill one you frighten hundreds" has more relevance to this initial stage. This particularly applied to regime supporting chiefs, kraal heads, chief policemen and government informers. Only then, could the insurgents have security living among the masses.

Supplying food and clothes went on in fits and starts as well, because of the same reasons as mentioned above. The locals however succeed in doing it, and even provided shelter to ANC guerrillas. Chris Hani, for instance, and his

Evaluation, Introspection and Re-organization

colleagues, received help from the locals to escape to Botswana after the Luthuli Detachment battle in the Wankie rural area.[20] Unfortunately, Hani and his colleagues were arrested, disarmed, charged with illegal possession of weapons, and detained before he and some members of his group made their way back to Zambia.[21]

In such areas as Tsholotsho and Wenlock, the existence of the Zimbabwe Church of Orphans, gave guerrillas an added advantage of instilling mass information and recruiting people to provide shelter, food and clothing. However, in some cases, the guerrillas brought their own food, since they were aware of how difficult it was to penetrate the community because of the existence of informers and security people in those communities. In some instances, guerrillas had their hideouts in isolated areas, and lived in large numbers so that any supply of food by the locals was difficult.

A good example of this situation was when insurgents camped in Vietcong style camps in Sipolilo in 1968. In the first place, the joint ZIPRA/MK Commando numbered too many people, more than 150 insurgents at any given time, and they used a base that was far removed from the community. This was land reserved as Parkland, and consequently, there were no villages on it. Villages were very far from this park. In this case, they had to bring their own food and clothes initially, and as time went on, they began to send some of their men in small numbers to secure food from the locals.

The third reason for incursions during this era was to provide logistics to the ANC forces.[22] It has been pointed out how this 1967 alliance provided the excuse for South African troops to support Rhodesian counter-insurgency. However, joint commandos involving ZIPRA and the ANC forces became a controversial issue not only to the natural enemies of ZAPU but to its allies in the struggle as well. When the first contact between a joint-commando of ZIPRA and ANC forces occurred, ZANU condemned it saying it was a poor strategy that would give Rhodesia a pretext to invite South African forces. ZANU erroneously believed ZIPRA and MK alliance was a "domino" type-strategy whereby they would attack Rhodesia first, and when it fell, then attack South Africa, and therefore advised the MK to concentrate on South Africa:

> *In guerrilla warfare we must strive to spread the enemy forces so that we can wipe them out one by one. The greatest help we can get from ANC is for ANC to wage intensive guerrilla warfare in South Africa. If ANC can pin down the whole South African force within South Africa, then Zimbabweans shall be left with Smith alone without South African aid ... as it is now, the ANC and PCC-(ZAPU) alliance has made it easy for Smith and Vorster to unite and concentrate their forces to slaughter Zimbabweans.*[23]

ZANU's definition of this alliance was fundamentally incorrect on two accounts: 1. On the account that the alliance would encourage an alliance between the Rhodesian and South African regime because an alliance involving the two was already in place; and 2. that ZAPU and the ANC meant to implement a "domino" type-strategy.

The 'Unholy Alliance' between Rhodesia, South Africa and Portugal was firmly established between 1959 and 1962, the year the Rhodesian Front assumed the leadership of the country. It was Dr. Verwoerd, the then South African Prime Minister, who in 1959 first raised the notion of co-operation. The kind of co-operation that Verwoerd introduced was that of a Southern Africa Common Market, positing that a common market should be developed including South Africa, its Bantustans and the two Portuguese colonies, Angola and Mozambique.

This discussion led to talk about military cooperation that by 1961 was already widely rumored. In April, 1962, Kenneth Kaunda, who then was leader of the United National Independence Party of Northern Rhodesia, repeated the same allegations about a tripartite defense agreement between South Africa, Portugal and Rhodesia. Characteristically, both South Africa and Southern Rhodesia, the latter through its Federal Prime Minister, Sir Roy Welensky, denied these allegations. Welensky supported his denial by pointing out that the Federation could not legally enter any alliance without approval by the British Government.

However, Welensky in a journalistic throw away line gave away the truth when he confessed in the British paper, the *Guardian,* that the Federation was fully responsible for its own defense.[24] Cooperation between South Africa and Rhodesia was undoubtedly an easier one given the strong relationship ties that existed between the whites in these two countries. A commentator in the *Rand Daily Mail* (19 July 1965) succinctly characterized this relationship when he remarked:

> *Historical and demographic links were strong. More than half the white Rhodesians or their fathers or mothers came from South Africa. Many family ties span the two centuries. Every year, thousands of Rhodesians spend their holidays in South Africa, and the major part of Rhodesia's tourist traffic comes from South Africa.*[25]

There is also evidence of conferences involving the South African, Angolan, Mozambican and Rhodesian air force commanders and military beginning from 1962. According to Jose Ervedosa's 1966 report before the United Nations Committee of 24, officers of the Royal Rhodesian Air Force met with officers of Angola's 2nd Air Force Region in Salisbury and in Luanda in February 1962.[26] Clearly, ZANU's fear of South African involvement in the Rhodesian war as a result of the alliance between ZIPRA and the MK was unfounded.

By 1967, ZAPU alleged that there were South Africa soldiers in Rhodesia. Although they could be debate as to the number of South African troops involved, there is no question as to the fact that their presence preceded ZIPRA/MK alliance. South Africa would increase its military presence in Rhodesia so that by 1974 it had four thousand soldiers, supported by armored cars and helicopters. In 1975, South African police and troops were officially

Evaluation, Introspection and Re-organization

withdrawn from Rhodesia, but large numbers secretly remained. From 1967 on, South African support for Rhodesia included the loan of aircraft, that later would be used for carrying out cross-border bombing attacks on Zambia and, later, Mozambique and Angola.

South Africa also supplied almost all of Rhodesia's military equipment, from ammunition to heavy weapons systems.[27] It is important to point out that throughout the war, South Africa denied it had deployed its military in Rhodesia. Because it did not want it known that it had deployed its defense forces, its troops fighting with the Rhodesian forces were either seconded to the Rhodesian forces and dressed in their uniforms or disguised as policemen.[28]

While it is true that the accusation against ZAPU's involvement with the ANC in the implementation of the domino type strategy was unfounded, the "domino" principle was not completely unknown in Africa, especially with reference to the on-going struggle in Rhodesia. In 1963, in Dakar at the founding of the Organization of African Unity (O.A.U.), for instance, and in a private conversation with the black South African nationalists, Ahmed Ben Bella, the Prime Minister of Algeria, introduced the notion of the domino strategy. He said that notion was "based on the straightforward military notion of knocking off the weakest enemy and moving step by step towards the strongest."[29]

One of ZAPU's own, Saul Gwakula Ndlovu, gave a convoluted view about the alliance between ZAPU and ANC. In his explanation, Ndlovu implied that ZAPU meant to provide logistics to MK, but also stated that the alliance meant to fight white Rhodesians first, so that with their fall, South African whites might be demoralized.

Ndlovu wrote:

> *The moving spirit of the ZAPU-ANC alliance was [and still is] the human rights. If the ANC cadres had succeeded in passing through Zimbabwe undetected and had crossed the Limpopo River to South Africa, that would have been best for the oppressed masses of both Zimbabwe and South Africa; if they had failed to pass through and were intercepted by the enemy [Rhodesian, South African or Portuguese] inside Zimbabwe and had to fight, the better for the struggle as a whole; if, however, they had not met a single enemy troop and had established themselves solely in Zimbabwe and later managed to overthrow the Rhodesian regime, that would have been good for the liberation of Southern Africa as a whole.*[30]

This was partially true. ZIPRA, however, had to wait until after independence to clearly explain the reason for its joint-commandos with the ANC cadres, and Dumiso Dabengwa, who then was the Deputy Minister of Home Affairs, did this. So far as ZAPU was concerned, the joint venture was to provide logistics to the MK by ZIPRA escorting ANC forces to the Rhodesian border with South Africa. The reason for providing escort was so that ZIPRA could introduce the ANC cadres to the masses on whom they were to rely for food, and sometimes shelter, and also to avoid misunderstanding among the same in the event there was contact between an exclusively ANC force and a Rhodesian force.

ZIPRA was afraid confusion would have arisen among the general African population as to why the ANC forces were fighting on their soil. The ANC forces were warned to avoid contact with the Rhodesian forces and not to fight unless in self-defense. On some occasions ZIPRA did, indeed, succeed in accompanying ANC fighters to the Limpopo.[31] It can be reasonably argued, therefore, that ZIPRA had a qualified success in accompanying ANC forces through Rhodesia, and also in introducing them to the masses in the rural areas, which in turn helped the cadres as they moved across the country to the border.

Lest a wrong impression be formed based on this rendition of ZIPRA's operation, it is important to point out that the insurgents did not achieve complete success in meeting their goals. Some got arrested or killed before they reached their target destination or reached contact cell groups. Even their provision of logistics to the MK was not always successful. Rhodesians did, indeed, on some occasions intercept communications between guerrillas and also between guerrillas and their command in Lusaka. On such occasions, they found themselves either apprehended or killed by the enemy forces.

The Rhodesians did not depend on intercepted communications only. They planted their own informers in the community to gather intelligence information on the movement of the guerrillas, and sometimes guerrillas themselves compromised their presence.

If anything, the 1967 joint ZIPRA/MK contact with the Rhodesian forces introduced a new phase in the war situation in Rhodesia where South Africa openly stated its military involvement in Rhodesia and its resolve to punish Tanzania and Zambia for harboring ZAPU and ANC insurgents, and so did Rhodesia. In a matter of a few days after the first contact between the Rhodesian army, Mr. Wrathall, Rhodesia's Deputy Prime Minister, issued a stern warning against Zambia for harboring "terrorists."[32] As if not to be outsmarted in October, the South African Prime Minister Vorster threatened Zambia with violence that it would be hit "so hard that [it] will never forget it."[33]

The 19 August outbreak of fighting between these forces also further exposed Britain as a toothless bulldog whose protest were not taken seriously by South Africa, the main backer of Rhodesia. After South Africa announced it had sent a police force -- understand troops -- to Rhodesia, Britain protested. But Vorster simply chided:

> *South Africa would act against overseas trained terrorists in every territory where it is allowed to, [and that] South Africa police [understand soldiers] would remain in Rhodesia as long as they are allowed and as long as it was necessary.*[34]

South Africa's open challenge to Britain, and the passive response by the latter, was in some way a victory over the war for international hearts and minds. Up to this point there were still some African countries that were part of the

Evaluation, Introspection and Re-organization

O.A.U. that still believed Britain would at one point turn around and force Rhodesia to accept majority rule. It was within this context that the O.A.U. secretariat voiced some displeasure with the British government's failure to crush the illegal Smith regime.

Most of the O.A.U members hardened their attitude against Britain denouncing her for playing fiddle while Africans got politically trodden by the Smith regime which, according to the O.A.U. General Secretary, "had continued to thrive politically..."[35] After this incident, Smith felt sufficiently secure to bluff Britain's attempt to find a solution to its political crisis.[36]

ZIPRA was keenly aware of the fact that the ultimate war-winning factor was intelligence. Therefore it put in place a courier system as part of its organizing of the masses. As has been pointed out, the courier system was established by the guerrillas for the reason of gathering information about the enemies' movements in their operational theater. Key to this intelligence system was the role of the *umjibha*.[37] A simplistic definition of the role of *umjibha* would be mediating between the guerrillas and the peasants.[38]

However, the *umjibha* role, seen in its multifacetedness, was more complex than that. He was an intelligence and counter-intelligence person, a security person in the community and sometimes a soldier fighting along side the full time guerrillas. The umjimba organized political meetings and politicized the general population. He also was a link for the full time guerrillas with mainstream economy in that he was used to purchase things for the latter, and in some instances to sell things on their behalf. This was very true in such areas as Sadawana in Belingwe where guerrillas acquired emeralds and used the *umjibha* to sell it on their behalf.

The guerrillas, in turn, used this money to purchase food and some of their basic *umjibha*. They also got some money collection from cell leaders to give to the guerrillas. The *umjibha* did not collect money from people himself, this was done by the cell leaders. The *umjibha* collected money only when the cell leader sent him.[39]

In so far as politicization was concerned, unlike his counterpart the ZANLA *umjibha*, who used mass all-night pungwes (rallies) to instill such information,[40] ZIPRA umjimba addressed people in very small groups of no more than ten people at a time, excepting in church situations, and usually it was during the day.[41] The idea was to avoid detection and situations in which Rhodesian soldiers killed the innocent unnecessarily. This was the approach of the ZIPRA forces, which tried by all means to avoid using civilians as human shields. The same could not be said about ZANLA, which addressed villagers in large groups, sometimes with calamitous results.[42] However, this approach, by ZANU, had its own limited success.

At this point it is natural to ask: what were the qualifications of a ZIPRA *umjibha*? In many ways he possessed the same qualities as an ideal guerrilla as described by Che Guevara. Guevara said that a guerrilla's familiarity with the terrain of his operation must be absolute. Thus, he must know friendly and unfriendly houses, all the access, retreat and closed footpaths, indeed, know the theater of operation as well as he did the back of his palm. People's support must be absolute, Che said. Also rapidity of maneuver was equally critical.[43]

The knowledge of people in the area was so crucial for the *umjibha* because with that knowledge he could tell strangers from non-strangers. An *umjibha* would invariably quiz every stranger in the area to determine if he or she was a government informer. If one was discovered to be an informer, he was either handed over to the regular guerrillas or killed by the *umjibha* with the help of his youth members. In this sense, they were counter-intelligence agents, and as intelligent agents they collected information about the movement of security forces. Also, *umjibha* provided ZIPRA with contact information (information on the movement of security forces, their size, and type of weapons the security forces were carrying).

This kind of information helped the insurgents find the security forces by knowing their location, or likely actions in advance. Background intelligence information was largely left to the fighters and the research team in Lusaka.[44]

It must be made clear that during this period under study this system was still in its elementary stage, but all the same had started working despite its teething problems. *Umjibhas* were used at various local party structure levels by cell leaders to convey messages to guerrillas, or to disseminate messages from cell, district, or provincial underground ZAPU leaders to the general membership. Since in some of these areas chiefs were no longer effective in keeping peace in the community, ZAPU cell leaders stepped into that role. *umjimba* became his messenger and policeman.

Thus, the *umjibha's* role was a very delicate and dangerous one, sometimes more dangerous than that of a regular guerrilla. He was not a complement but an integral part of liberation war of Zimbabwe and an agent of stability in the absence of police in the community.

Obviously, and contrary to the assertion by Cliffe, Mpofu and Munslow that ZIPRA did not establish an administrative network of the *umjibha,* committees and subcommittees, and that its *umjimba* did not possess any political power,[45] the *umjimba* did possess political power, and his activities were politically systematized, just as much as the activities of the local population were.

In fact, the *umjibhas* were recommended to the cadres by their respective cells, and it was very rare for the guerrillas to turn them down. This then raises a question about how well integrated the people were with the insurgents, and the whole ZAPU movement. The degree of closeness between the general population and the guerrillas varied from operational theater to operational theater. Where the environment was more hospitable to them, the guerrillas got to trust people more than in areas infested with government agents and uncooperative community people.

Terence Ranger's and Norma Krieger's works well sum up this basic relationship that existed between ZIPRA and black people on the ground.

Evaluation, Introspection and Re-organization

Although both of these authors were discussing ZANLA in this context, the same could be said of ZIPRA as well. To Ranger, the relationship between the people and guerrillas was that of close symbiosis, one in which the people themselves were able to help in the shaping of official ideology regarding land and a better deal for peasant producers in situations where ideology was not spelt out clearly.[46] Krieger drew attention to tensions and collaboration between peasants and guerrillas, a relationship she asserted was marked by benevolence as well as force on the part of the insurgents and support on the part of the peasants.[47]

Creating an intelligence system and then building up the flow of intelligence through it was, however, very difficult for ZAPU fighters mainly because of the hostile environment in their theater of operation. To succeed in having people participate in the system, ZIPRA needed to develop a climate of public confidence on two levels:

1) Confidence that they would in the end win; and
2) Confidence that the community people who co-operated would have their identities kept secret from the enemy security forces and police, and also that they would be protected.

Right from the word go ZIPRA won the hearts of the local population by the way it defended itself against the enemy. What Cliffe, et alia, said of ZIPRA in the 1970s was actually true of this force in the late 1960s. They assert that:

> *To sustain high morale and enthusiastic support for ZAPU in the local population, the ZIPRA guerrillas relied...on their military operations. Through their effective attacks on enemy installations and camps they generated a high degree of political affinity with the local peasants....*

> *In the ZIPRA operational areas, many people talk about the guerrillas as if they possess mystic power to demolish the enemy forces with ease. Having had the bangs and seen `security force trucks burning and soldiers dying and bleeding,' the peasants regarded the guerrillas as possessors of extraordinary power that had never been known before. Since the performers of this `mystic power' had been sent to `perform it' by Joshua Nkomo, his name also became associated with some inexplicable legend, `possessing extra-ordinary power' to conquer and liberate Zimbabwe.*[48]

Contrary to the opinion of some scholars, who believed that the regime was winning, the Rhodesians were losing in the field despite their operational ingenuity. As ZIPRA forces increased in professionalism, they managed to expose operational weaknesses on the part of the Rhodesian forces. Barry M. Schuzt and Douglas Scott, albeit guardedly, well captured the increase in ZIPRA professionalism and the corresponding exposure of weaknesses in Rhodesia troops when they observed:

> *Not long after this foray [the 1967 battle], ZAPU contingents became active along the Zambezi River in far north/central Rhodesia. Their hit and run*

tactics were not overtly impressive, though they did cause one high ranking white Rhodesian commander to comment in 1969 upon the guerrilla's rapid rate of improvement in military capacity. He further pondered the fate of the Rhodesian troops [white and African] in maintaining this developmental pace. He frankly could not conceive of white Rhodesian military defense without increasing amounts of South African support.[49]

The result was that Rhodesian forces failed to totally annihilate the guerrilla forces with their tactic of mobile engagement of their enemy. Thus, despite the fact that the guerrillas could not score a total victory in military terms against the Rhodesian Forces, and from a military perspective, even suffered some defeat, their losses were not palpable. Instead, the RSF, as the 1960's drew to a close, was increasingly losing the initiative because guerrilla numbers were rapidly increasing. Thus, the RSF came under military strain earlier than the 1972 date some scholars have posited.

ZIPRA's major success was in the area of its psychological warfare against the Smith regime. The sheer bravado on the part of the guerrillas of facing an enemy with almost unlimited military resources of heliborne troops and fighter planes was winning points for them from the peasants. The RSF, as compared to the ZIPRA forces, was formidable in military strength and numbers. In accordance with its militaristic approach to the political conflict in the country, the Rhodesian regime built a huge army, essentially to counter guerrilla insurgents.

The regime force was composed of five major army units, namely the Rhodesian African Rifles consisting of blacks but with white head officers, the Special Air Service (SAS) considered an elite commando/paratroop unit, Rhodesia Light Infantry, an exclusively white unit, Grey Scouts composed of racially mixed horse riding infantry, and the predominately black Selous Scouts, a notoriously infamous tracker unit which often posed as guerrilla forces. Assisting these units was the British South African Police (BSAP), territorial forces on short stints of duty, national servicemen and reservists.[50] The Rhodesian army, as has already been pointed out, was assisted by foreign troops, most of which came from South Africa.

Thus, instead of embarking on reforms as a strategy to win the allegiance of blacks, Smith flexed his military muscle. He poured the army into the community, aided by such oppressive legislation as: the Unlawful Organization Act, the Preventative Detention Act and the Law and Order Maintenance Act, all of which had survived the so-called liberal constitutional era of Whitehead.[51] Clearly Smith seemed to disregard the tested wisdom that counter-guerrilla warfare is eighty percent social and political and only twenty percent military.

This approach comes as little surprise given that all of the Rhodesian forces, including their South African helpers, were trained in 'classical' warfare, and only a handful were trained in counter-insurgency warfare.[52] Even some of those with the counter-insurgency experience, like the bulk of the white soldiers

Evaluation, Introspection and Re-organization

and the general white society, had bought into this military solution to the problem of insurgency. MacIntyre, for instance, believed in the "grabbing of the balls" approach ahead of the hearts and minds campaign. Others, like Ken Flowers, according to his own confession, insisted on a campaign of winning the hearts and minds of the local black population.[53]

Because the Smith regime bought into this "grab them by their balls" tactic, it quickly lost the war of hearts and souls. It was within this context that Ellert asserted that the white regime lost the war during this period. For Smith to have won this psychological warfare, it was necessary that he won the support of the peasants first. Perhaps social reform and political development would have helped him in some way to postpone the arrival of the apocalypse. This Smith could have done by merely conceding the principle of majority rule and introducing some social reforms in the black communities. Instead, and increasingly, the RSF reverted to brute force in their endeavor to discourage the general black population from supporting ZIPRA forces. By losing the psychological warfare, Smith handed victory to the nationalists, despite whether or not his forces did well in the use of arms.

For counter-revolution to succeed, as noted by Robert Taber in his book, *The War of Flea*,[54] it has to eliminate the promise of the revolution by proving that it is unrealistic. If anything, to peasants and black urbanites, ZIPRA and its wars were real and realistic, and so was the movement's victory as the goal of the revolution.

Clearly, ZAPU guerrillas waged a far more psychological warfare than their opponents. ZIPRA saw the struggle in terms of its wider social and political context. This, however, does not mean that the Rhodesians were unaware of the importance of balancing the two vital components in a battle situation: use of force of arms and psychological warfare. The Rhodesian Ministry of Information tried every trick in the book, from the use of film and print media to try and persuade the African population to see things from their own way.[55]

However, because of their selfish life-style, which deprived Africans of almost every right, they lacked legitimacy[56] in the eyes of the latter. Consequently, the settlers' psychological warfare messages fell on deaf ears.

In contrast, ZIPRA forces had the advantage of understanding the psyche of the people on the ground. Prevailing social conditions prepared the peasants' hearts for politicization by the guerrillas. Issues such as education, health, land alienation, low wages, political oppression, welfare discrimination and social inequalities formed the fundamentals of the recruits' political curriculum. The peasants' aroused consciousness of their dire social conditions was further sharpened by the stark contrast between their ugly situation and that of the whites. The settlers saw themselves as God's elects and encapsulated all their divine privileges in the notion of "lekker lewe" (the sweet life).[57] Using the ZOC, guerrillas, *umjimbas* and other ZAPU operatives increasingly became vociferous in defense of the oppressed's rights, and outspokenly critical of white attitudes which considered blacks as ungainly and always ignorant. According to ZAPU, white leadership and its general population neither understand nor showed any desire to comprehend, the thinking of Africans, let alone their politics largely born out of a rural and not a proletariat population.

ZIPRA also achieved success in establishing a connection between the people's struggle and traditional religion, thereby tapping into the spiritual world of a people totally sold out to religion. By this time, the peasants already believed in Nkomo, their leader, as having some mythical powers that had been bestowed on him by the *Ilitshe*. The guerrillas' performance in the 1967 and subsequent contacts, given their disadvantaged position, earned them mythical status, which the peasants quickly attributed to ZAPU's being assisted by *Ilitshe*.

A comparison of the military potentials of the two military groups involved in the conflict reveal the following: the regime had fighter planes and cars, training facilities close to the fighting theater, numerical advantage and assured sources of food. ZAPU guerrillas had none of these advantages. Thus, the Rhodesians were in a much better position to prosecute the war. In spite of their disadvantage in combat potential, ZIPRA had in their arsenal a powerful weapon, which they had nurtured and forged with the help of their leaders.

This weapon was their traditional religion. They acquitted themselves as sons of the soil who respected their traditions, religion and their leader, whom many blacks already believed had been appointed by *Ilitshe le Dula* (God resident in *Dula*) because of their success in the prosecution of the struggle. However little the success, peasants immediately attributed the guerrillas' success to *Ilitshe's* help. Guerrillas themselves asked elders to intercede for them before the *Ilitshe*. Thus, religion became a dynamic force not only in inspiring guerrillas to fight despite great odds against them, but also in molding a relationship between them and the community.[58]

Still a question can be raised as to why ZAPU did not fully accomplish all of its goals during this time. The position of this writer here is that ZAPU did not suffer a total failure between 1965 and 1970, but rather that it was confronted with some teething problems that were characteristic of every evolving movement at its elementary stages.[59] Several theories have been advanced in an attempt to account for the setbacks guerrillas suffered during this period. All of them could be roughly summed up into two: disunity among nationalists and guerrillas' lack of ideology, poor tactics and training.

From 1963, when a split occurred in the ZAPU party, the history of the black, nationalist movement became strewn with a whole series of conflicts. This split was indeed the mother of all divisions in that it marked the beginning of factional fighting between nationalists, and planted a seed for post-independence ethnic cleansing by the ruling dominantly Shona party, ZANU. Undoubtedly, during the time when ZAPU/PCC and ZANU were still operational within Rhodesia immediately following the split, the struggle for majority rule was

Evaluation, Introspection and Re-organization

severely weakened as these groups concentrated on their factional fighting, and focused little on the struggle against the regime.

Smith, as has been previously observed, took advantage of this infighting by routinely trying to crush organized nationalist movements, and further divide black people in order to diminish their resolve for majority rule. The white regime exploited the differences between the nationalists as one of the ZANU nationalist observed:

> *The government and its police played their cards cleverly ... the government refrained from commenting in any way which might have unified the parties, and enjoyed watching the rivals fight the issue out. The police patrols in the township were for months cut to a minimum, to allow this party warfare to gain hold.*[60]

Historians continued to point to this factor of disunity as one of the causative factors that debilitated nationalists' struggles for majority rule, and also contributed to what some scholars described as the defeat of the pre-1970 insurgency.[61] The line of argument by these scholars is that the division between ZAPU and ZANU meant that they did not share a common ideology, and therefore pursued different goals, the result of which was a weakened focus on the majority rule goal. However, the alleged absence of ideology should not have been a problem since sharing a common goal of majority rule should have been enough to allow the nationalists to engage in effective political action.

The question of disunity is therefore important here for other reasons than as a determinant factor in the effectiveness of guerrilla warfare in the pre-1970 period. Rather, the question of disunity was important because of the light it shed on the ZAPU split in the early 1970s, the post-independence political and military persecution of ZAPU, and black nationalism in Rhodesia then, and Zimbabwe today.

Hopefully, a critical review of these hypotheses that have been propounded in an attempt to explain the causes of the split in ZAPU will contribute to our analysis of the preceding immediate three issues raised here. As such, what is important here is trying to understand the cause(s) of the 1963 split which seems to have had very destructive implications for black Nationalism in Zimbabwe.

5.3 Analysis of the Mother of all Splits

The question therefore is what were the causes of the 1963 mother of all splits? As has been pointed out in Chapter IV, several hypotheses have been advanced to try and explain what caused ZAPU split in 1963 that resulted in the founding of ZANU. This conflict has been explained in terms of differences such as in ideology, personality, and ethnicity, by which each group may be distinguished.[62] On their part, ZANU members reported as the initial causes of the split, lack of confidence in Nkomo's leadership, and their support of a policy of prosecuting the struggle within Rhodesia rather than depending on international support. As will be shown later in this chapter, after the split, ZANU engaged in both tactics, a testimony to the fact that there was no ideological difference between the two.

Also implied, as the possible reason for the breakaway party was the alleged inactivity of the liberation movement since the banning of ZAPU. This reason was given on August 8, 1963, when Ndabaningi Sithole, the leader of the new party, announced his ten-man national executive. In the same announcement, Sithole tried to draw some ideological distinction between ZAPU and his new party.

Sithole asserted:

> *For the last 11 months we have not had a political party in the country and the result has been a political stalemate that in turn has caused confusion through the rank and file and the present political crisis within the nationalist movement.... From now on our nationalist struggle will be carried on in the name of this party. ZANU closes a chapter of evasive, shortsighted exclusive and short politics. It opens a new chapter of politics in confrontation, foresight, inclusiveness and willingness to suffer in order that freedom may be established.*[63]

There can be no question that most of these allegations against Nkomo were untrue as could be seen in that, other than high flown radical rhetoric from the new party leaders, ZANU's strategies were similar to those of ZAPU. ZANU failed to come-up with new strategies supporting its militant rhetoric, and resorted to, as Nkomo noted, "plagiarizing its mother party's (ZAPU) strategies and goals." For instance, both parties had great faith in the fairness of the courts to decide in their interests, they engaged in foreign-diplomatic activity to secure international support as well as struggled inside the country to try and secure majority rule.

Both parties tried to enlist the help of Britain in preventing the CAP from transferring its armed forces to the Smith government.[64] And ZANU, like ZAPU, voted with their feet and went to Zambia after they were banned. With an obvious similarity in strategies, goals and tactics, the ideological differences as an argument explaining the split in ZAPU falls by the wayside.

ZAPU, however, advanced its own reasons as to why it favored mostly foreign diplomatic strategy in fighting against the Southern Rhodesia regime, especially after it was banned. In light of government repression, it argued, the best strategy was to organize externally, keep the unity by forming a government in exile and create an underground organization as preparation for guerrilla struggle. For this approach, ZAPU received extensive criticism from some scholars who simply enjoyed arm-chair speculations disregarding the extremely repressive nature of the Southern Rhodesian government and the status of this country vis-à-vis Britain.

We have already pointed out that the constitutional status of Southern Rhodesia before the implementation of the 1961 constitution was genuinely confusing. Britain claimed to exercise reserve powers over a colony described as self-governing. Add to this Smith's claim, after the Unilateral Declaration of

Evaluation, Introspection and Re-organization

Independence on November 11, 1965, that the 1961 Constitution secured this country independence. This dilemma, obviously presented ZAPU with a strategic predicament. If Southern Rhodesia was independent as Smith claimed, then ZAPU was to create an armed group to wrest power from Ian Smith from within.

However, if it were a non-independent colony of Britain, as ZAPU believed it was, then its foreign diplomatic offensive was relevant and appropriate. This approach is in recognition of the fact that the opponents can achieve the end of a colonial rule without necessarily establishing military superiority, while the demise of an independent regime is unlikely without the use of military force.[65]

With ZAPU leadership experiencing difficulties in organizing within Southern Rhodesia as a result of a repressive environment emanating from draconian laws, it is not surprising that they decided to concentrate mainly on foreign diplomatic approach to the problem of black disenfranchisement. So, for many ZAPU people and its leadership, all the reasons advanced by the dissenters as a basis for the split were a mere pretext.

Another of the psychological factors to explain divisions within ZAPU were personality differences, which expressed themselves in intense personal ambition. Supporting the position of officiousness as a basis for the split, as was asserted by Ntini in the previous chapter, Dumiso Dabengwa, once stalwart ZAPU member, the Minister of Home Affairs, in a paper presented at the University of Zimbabwe on July 8, 1991, said,

Largely those who harbored secret agendas and who had been waiting for an opportunity to promote their personal ambitions by dividing the organization engineered the 1963 split in ZAPU.[66]

In hindsight, Nkomo, in his autobiography asserted that his opponents opposed his leadership largely on ethnic grounds. Commenting on the contents of a paper that was snatched from one of the dissidents in Cairo by Joseph Msika who remained loyal to ZAPU, Nkomo pointed out that Washington Malianga did not intend for Msika to see the letter. An extensive citation will help provide background against which to understand Nkomo's allegation of tribalism.

He wrote:

Joseph Msika, then deputy treasurer of ZAPU, had ... a disturbing experience. He saw one of our colleagues, Washington Malianga, nervously hiding away a printed document.... Msika snatched it away and read it. He found it was a circular openly urging ZAPU to bring the 'majority tribes' to the leadership of the party, and to get rid of 'Zimundebere,' which is a derogatory term in the Shona language for 'the old Ndebele man.' That meant me.[67]

Also, some academicians have asserted that Nkomo lacked charisma among the educated, although Nkomo himself was an intellectual. A. H. Tony Rich has compiled a useful brief survey of letters in the *African Daily News* lending evidence enough to this false dichotomy which presented Nkomo as favored by non-intellectuals and ZANU by intellectuals.[68] Although there can be some explanatory value in these personality-based hypotheses, they do not, however, explain adequately the cause of the split. Emphasis on personality obviously favored liberation struggle opponents by focusing people's attention on adjusting personalities (as in behavior modification) as a way of solving social ills.

Ethnic differences within the nationalist membership as a cause of division in ZAPU provide probably the most serious explanation of the split between the two groups. Despite denials by some scholars who either are less informed on issues of ethnicity or are mere sympathizers of ZANU, ethnicity did, indeed, play a very critical role either as a basis or an instrument for the first split of ZAPU. If tribal differences are to be proven as an acceptable explanation for the split in the nationalists' movement, one factor must be established.

It has to be shown that the differences between ZAPU and ZANU corresponded with tribal divisions. When discussing the rivalries between ZAPU and ZANU, some scholars who downplay the negative role of ethnicity have tried to point out that there were AmaNdebele and Shona in both party executives. However, they fail to point out that the ZANU executive had only one Ndebele, Enos Nkala.[69] Otherwise, it was exclusively Shona and would remain like that for many years.

The element of ethnicity, as a matter of fact, dogged ZANU till the day of independence, even as a government. John Makumbe, a University of Zimbabwe political scientist, himself a Shona, once noted, "the current government under Robert Mugabe [Zanu] is known to be quite viciously tribalistic."[70]

Thus, Nkomo's allegations may very well be true. Nkomo himself steered clear of ethnicity and argued on the basis of national liberation. His executive was for that matter mostly Shona and he is known to have fought hard against tribalism for many years.[71] ZAPU continued to draw support from urban and rural areas with large concentration of AmaNdebele and Shona alike. Thus, it can be said ZAPU remained a national party while ZANU remained an ethnic-centered one. Even Enock Dumbutshena, a ZANU insider and Shona, was keenly aware of the tribalism existing in ZANU, in contrast to the non-tribal stance of ZAPU. He wrote:

> *The Rev. Sithole's...ZANU tried to divide the Africans of Zimbabwe into political groupings according to tribal affiliations. The Shona, who constituted 96 per cent [sic] of the five million Zimbabweans rejected Sithole's tribal politics and stuck with Joshua Nkomo whom Sithole's followers had branded Ndebeles.*[72]

Smith, again, used this tribal division to his advantage. On 26 August, 1964, when he banned both PCC and ZANU, Smith dwelt at length on the subject of tribalism as the source of interparty fighting.[73] In one way he was right; tribalism, especially by ZANU had become a source of conflict.

The picture that emerges from this observation is that those who saw the major cause of the 1963 split of ZAPU as a result of the activities of those who were concerned with narrow tribal nationalistic liberation were on the correct path, compared with to those who either down-played or totally ignored tribal sentiments. Evidence abounds of the enormous strength of tribalism or narrow

Evaluation, Introspection and Re-organization

ethnic nationalism as a divisive factor. One such example is the Soviet Union that collapsed not because of the shortcomings of communism but because of narrow nationalistic aspirations of its nationalities.

What then were the real reasons for the split? Was it because the founders of the new Party, ZANU, wanted to prosecute the armed struggle from inside Zimbabwe or their dissatisfaction with the leadership of Nkomo as they claimed.[74] Or was it because of the officiousness and tribalism of the founders of the new party as claimed by ZAPU leadership and some of its members? Both of ZANU's reasons seem to diminish under what actual happened.

We now know that ZANU literally plagiarized ZAPU's goals and strategies despite its claim to espousing a different radical path, and that they voted with their feet once their party was banned, less than a year after they pledged themselves to prosecuting the struggle within the country. This leaves us with the claims which ZAPU made: officiousness, tribalism and the other charge ZAPU leveled against ZANU, which was their claim that ZANU was being used by America to divide the African people.[75] While there is reason to believe in the first two as motives for the founding of ZANU, it is hard to believe that ZANU was sponsored by America given the fact that it followed a similar revolutionary strategy as ZAPU.

Evidence exists to substantiate the argument of correspondence between ethnic and factional divisions between ZAPU and ZANU in 1963. It would appear that ethnic differences played a causal role in this division, especially in the absence of ideological differences. Again, be that as it may, that the two parties suffered from disunity during 1963-1970, no evidence exists to show that the nationalist movements suffered some of their setbacks and defeats because of it.[76]

5.4 Poor Tactics and Training

Some scholars attributed what they saw as absolute defeat of the nationalist forces to tactical errors, cohesiveness of the white community[77] and army, poor tactics as well as training on the part of the guerrillas.[78] As has already been pointed out elsewhere in this chapter, the incompetence of the ZIPRA forces was often exaggerated by government reports and some scholars who uncritically used government sources to write on the liberation war.

5.5 Gathering in the Sheaves: A Time for Prognosis for ZAPU

The years 1969 and 1970 are generally considered as years of a lull in terms of ZIPRA incursions into Rhodesia. Some scholars allege that there was a slackening in the tempo of the war over a period of these two years, and they attribute this change in the tempo of the war to intra-party conflicts. In no way should this be understood as meaning that there were no incursions undertaken during these years however.

According to some scholars, from 1969 to 1970, ZAPU was relatively inactive in terms of its military engagements. These scholars go further in support of their assertion to state that because of the movement's inactivity, the O.A.U. threatened to cut off funding if ZAPU did not become more active in the war.[79] Some ZAPU officials who were part of this crisis question the accuracy of this accusation. They say the closest O.A.U. came to cutting off funding was to promise them a better funding if they joined with their co-patriots ZANU instead of continuing with their joint-military venture with the South African ANC. After all, ZAPU funding by O.A.U. at this point was very minimal, even the provision of training so that such a threat would not have meant anything.

ZAPU still depended largely on Russia and its allies. This is evidenced by the fact that when in the 1970's ZAPU increased its military incursions, Russia had increased its military assistance.[80] Thus, contrary to the assertion of a cessation of incursions into Rhodesia, ZIPRA continued to launch tenacious attacks on the Rhodesian and South African troops with some measure of success in inflicting some casualties on the later.

Although it was the goal of the guerrillas to avoid positional war, they sometimes found themselves forced into such situations.[81] When such situations occurred, the Smith regime invariably had problems flushing the guerrillas out, and it was only when it brought in the Air Force that the RSF eventually had the upper hand. Thus, the Air Force gave the RSF the advantages of strike-power and mobility. Also, the RSF could easily bring in fresh reinforcements and evacuate their injured with speed since they were well-equipped.[82] Thus, the lack of heavy weapons to bring down Rhodesian military planes greatly disadvantaged ZIPRA in the 1960s into the early part of 1970s.

However, ZAPU's military efforts were reduced as a result of the crisis obtaining within the movement's ranks. The crisis precipitated the party's major self-prognosis instead of a routine and on-going one. According to Edward Ndlovu, a deputy national secretary of information, self-evaluation was a routine so that they would have done it even without the prevailing crisis at that time. He, however, said that the 1970 and 1971 leadership crisis contributed towards the timing and magnitude of the ZAPU's self-prognosis. Thus, in response to the crisis, three documents were generated which to a large extent ended up addressing the question of leadership in the party. The three documents will be discussed later, after examining what might have contributed to this crisis that in turn led to a major self-diagnosis.

The 1970/71 ZAPU crisis was possibly caused by two factors: Chikerema's, ZAPU's Acting President, unauthorized filming of ZIPRA forces as they crossed into Rhodesia,[83] and also his subsequent efforts at unilaterally uniting ZAPU with ZANU. Differences within the external wing of ZAPU that was based in Zambia began to emerge as early as 1967 when Chikerema started to negotiate with ZANU for unity without consulting with other national executive members. After all, the other national ZAPU leaders felt that negotiations aimed at bringing together the two parties could only be done with the blessings of

Evaluation, Introspection and Re-organization

their larger membership and also their leader, Nkomo, who was at that time languishing in Smith's prison.

As the Acting President Chikerema felt slighted and with the support of his loyal lieutenant, George Nyandoro, started taking unilateral decisions on behalf of the party without consulting with other executive members. The intrigues around the question of loyalties and decision-making went pretty much unnoticed by a larger percentage of outsiders until the incident of filming, which brought the crisis to a head.

Early in 1969, Chikerema took a group of foreign journalists on a tour of ZAPU military camps, and on January 1, 1970 he screened a documentary on ZIPRA that was shown to overseas audiences, in Britain and West Germany. From a tactical and military standpoint, this action by Chikerema was unconscionable as it compromised ZIPRA's military strategy as a guerrilla movement and also exposed its incursion routes into Rhodesia. Worse still, it exposed the identity of guerrillas to Rhodesian and South African intelligence, which probably purchased the film.

Zimbabwean nationalists and supporters, irrespective of their party affiliations who saw the film were shocked and angered by its authorization. Not only did this act of Chikerema anger Zimbabwean nationalists, but it embarrassed and infuriated the Zambian government as well, on whose soil the film was shot without its authorization.

Angered by such blatant publicity of guerrilla activities, Jason Moyo, the national treasurer and second in command in the military department, released a document entitled the "Observation on Our Struggle" in which he accused Chikerema of dictatorial and irresponsible practices. Moyo also criticized what he saw as the infiltration of ZAPU by the Zambian intelligence units and self-indulgence and indiscipline of the ZIPRA forces.[84]

Moyo complained in this document of specifically "a steady decline of a serious nature in [ZIPRA's] military administration and army," and open repudiation of authority in the camps and attempts "to justify demobilization of the army."[85] This statement Moyo made in response to challenges to his assertion where he likened guerrilla trainees to those of any army, and, who as such, should not expect to arrive on decisions through a democratic process.

To rectify the situation, Moyo proposed a general review of ZAPU's military strategy and that three members of the Military Command be added to the War Council, a council mostly composed of political rather than military personnel. Evidently, by this proposal Moyo was correctly asking for a greater role in the planning of the prosecution of the armed struggle for the military trained, while not excluding those without such training completely. The restructuring Moyo rightly claimed would strengthen the War Council.

Chikerema came out as defiant as ever. He responded with such an assertion of personal authority that, according to Owen Tshabangu, one of the ZIPRA cadres at that time, revealed the degree of the "naked power struggle and mutual vilification in ZAPU".[86] Chikerema charged that Moyo and his supporters had been plotting "to remove [his] authority over [his] departments" as Nkomo's deputy. Denying any legitimate authority besides himself, however agreeing with Moyo that there was a decline in the ZAPU forces, Chikerema continued:

> *The whole of this document, from beginning to end, states a position of calculated hypocrisy, calculated maneuvers for positions and influence in the party and army. It is intended to protect clans and tribal corruption in the Party and Army. It is not a truthful analysis; it is not a revolutionary heart searching of the ills that have befallen the Party and the Army. Yes, Comrades, the Party and the Army are in dismay. It has no commander. It has no administration. It has no team spirit. It is corrupt, and therefore not sincere to its objectives.*[87]

While Chikerema agreed with Moyo on the decay suffered by the movement's army, he, however, did not blame the political leadership for it but the military one. In other words, it was Moyo and not Chikerema who was to blame for corruption within the forces. Also, Chikerema claimed that as ZAPU's acting President, it was he and not the collective council who had the overall responsibility of running the movement. To Chikerema the basis for the challenge of his leadership was obvious, tribalism.

At face value, Chikerema's charge would make logical sense given that the division pitted Chikerema, who was supported by George Nyandoro, both of whom were Shona, against Jason Moyo, George Silundika and Edward Ndlovu, all of whom were AmaNdebele. In fact, even some scholars have concluded this particular incident could be said to have had a solid tribal basis.

There is, however, no evidence to prove that Moyo and his colleagues acted in any way out of tribal motives. After all, ZAPU national executive remained overwhelmingly Shona. What appears clear though is that Chikerema used the already politicized ethnic identities to cover up for his dictatorial and irresponsible tendencies. Although tribalism became a major factor later, particularly on the part of the Chikerema group, it was never the main cause of the crisis.

Predictably, Chikerema rejected Moyo's criticism and suggested solutions. He then dissolved the military command, and relieved Moyo and his supporters on the executive committee of their offices. All the offices were now concentrated in Chikerema's person although Ndlovu believed Chikerema in practice tried to run the party with the help of his loyal supporter Nyandoro.

Stung by Chikerema's unrepentant reply, and what they considered a high-handed manner of dealing with the crisis at hand, Moyo, Ndlovu, and Silundika, challenged the former's right to remove them, and in a non-conciliatory tone, attacked, again what they saw as an unhealthy concentration of power in one person.

They equally defiantly wrote:

> *We will not have ZAPU run the way Banda runs the Malawi Congress Party as a personal estate. In fulfillment of our national obligation we declare, without*

Evaluation, Introspection and Re-organization

fear or favor, that comrade Chikerema's reckless bid for personal power in the Party ascertained in no document ... is null and void.[88]

After dissociating themselves from Chikerema and Nyandoro, Moyo, Ndlovu and Silundika appealed for a collective leadership by the National Executive, which included the former. By not excluding Chikerema and Nyandoro, the three showed that they were not opposed to the former's participation in leadership as long as they supported the democratic process.

The sad result of this crisis was friction between the two hostile groups, ending in violent encounters and murders. By end of March, 1970, ZIPRA was divided between the two leaders, Chikerema and Moyo. While Chikerema's supporters could be identified as exclusively Shona the same could not be said of those who supported the Moyo group. Contrary to what some scholars saw as a neat division of the ZAPU army from top to bottom along tribal lines,[89] the Moyo group, like the ZAPU of 1963, retained a national character in that its composition was a microcosm of the black population of Zimbabwe.

Throughout the crisis, the ANC and the Soviet Union supported the Moyo group, mostly for its national composition. When the Moyo group refused their removal from their posts, the Murewa cabal of Chikerema supporters attacked them, and soon a battle ensued with guerrillas using knives, axes, stones, guns, clubs and hoes.[90]

Kenneth Kaunda, then President of Zambia, intervened and forced the two groups to settle by threatening to expel ZAPU from his country. The patching up of differences between the two feuding factions was, however, nothing more than a marriage of convenience, as the Chikerema group would leave ZAPU to join a new party the Front for the Liberation of Zimbabwe (FROLIZI) the following year in October, 1971. The formation of FROLIZI will be discussed later.

Twice within a decade ZAPU suffered an internal conflict resulting in the shedding of blood among its supporters. Chikerema was trying to fit into Nkomo's shoes, unfortunately for him, he was not as personable as Nkomo. Nkomo was the glue that held the party together. His leadership style derived from his personal authority and he had charisma Chikerema did not have, and when he tried to imitate him Chikerema failed dismally.

There was also some ideological basis to the conflict. While the ZAPU executive members believed that unity with ZANU would be helpful, they differed on its timing and modalities of introducing it. Elsewhere in this chapter it was pointed out that most of the ZAPU leadership believed such a unity should occur with the participation of its leader Nkomo and also the larger ZAPU constituency consisting of the party's general membership. Chikerema did not see the point in involving supporters in Rhodesia in deciding on the merger. Aware of such resistance, Chikerema went it alone and started negotiating for the unity of the two parties secretly.

After the crisis came to the open Chikerema aggressively pursued unity with ZANU. Because of tribal sympathies, ZANU agreed to negotiate with him on a technicality that he was the Deputy President of ZAPU. But the fact of the matter is that he was then representing a very small group among ZAPU people and had no mandate from ZAPU to negotiate for unity with ZANU.

As the African adage goes, the leopard cannot change its spots, soon Chikerema began to show his insidious, tribally inspired motives. While officially negotiating with Chitepo and Mudzi, he met secretly with his own Zezuru compatriots Shamuyarira and Mutizwa, both of whom were members of the ZANU Supreme Council (DARE). The situation became ludicrous when Chikerema leaked to British journalists, according to one jurist supporter of ZANU, the news that:

> *Sithole and Nkomo had stepped down in favor of Mugabe; the prestigious Secretary-General of ZANU in Salisbury prison-who like Shamuyarira and Mutizwa was from Chikerema's tribe and region. The tribal and regional overtones in Chikerema's strategy were bound to raise questions about his real motives. Annoyance turned into fury when Sithole managed to smuggle out a letter denying any communication with Nkomo, let alone an agreement.*[91]

Once ZANU saw Chikerema for what he was, a tribalist, they immediately discontinued negotiations with him by action of a review conference held on August 18, 1971. Chikerema's misrepresentations about Nkomo stepping down in the name of unity and choosing Mugabe as leader of the merged party raise many questions about his allegiance to Nkomo. Undoubtedly, a picture that emerges here is that of a Zezuru group fighting for the hegemony of black Nationalism, and fanning tribal animosity as a way of attaining it.[92] Would ZANU have turned down the offer of unity with the Chikerema ZAPU faction if it was the largest as Moyo's was? Probably not.

Chikerema, to the extent that his faction was small and exclusively Shona, was no political asset to ZANU. ZANU needed someone with clout within ZAPU who could help in making it a national rather than an ethnically based movement by bringing with him different ethnic groups. Worse still, Russia, which was the major supplier of weapons to ZAPU, supported the Moyo faction that considered itself a true representative of the original movement.

While it can be said that the departure of Chikerema dealt ZAPU a blow that temporarily disrupted its organization, its effects paled in comparison to the split that was later led by some of the ZAPU military cadre. After futile, repeated appeals to the ZAPU Headquarters for the resolution of the leadership problem, in February of 1971, forty ZIPRA combatants signed and sent a letter to the OAU criticizing ZAPU leaders in exile and calling for a conference.

Among other things, these cadres charged they had been abandoned by party leaders in transit camps where some of their commanders enforced overly strict rules for trainees, while [they themselves] were "sitting under the shade and listening to the latest top tunes in the pop charts."[93] They charged that because the Party leadership had abandoned these camps, recruits had spent up to a year doing nothing because the leaders were preoccupied with their petty

Evaluation, Introspection and Re-organization

and selfish leadership in fighting, which they characterized as "tribal squabbles of the leaders."[94]

The OAU disregarded these cadre's appeals. Frustrated by their being ignored by what they considered to be their ultimate court of appeal, the dissidents took matters into their hands and on March 11, 1971 kidnapped several of "Dengezi" leaders, including Jason Moyo and Edward Ndlovu. They also tried to kidnap members of the Chikerema group, a rival group to the "uDengezi." The reason for the attempted and real kidnappings was to try and force the issue of a Conference with the leadership. With such pandemonium on its soil, the Zambian government had to take action. It appealed to the dissidents for the release of its detainees and further promised to call for a Conference involving all the ZAPU guerrillas to be held on "a neutral ground"[95] where they could freely express themselves on the leadership crisis.

The captives were released and the Conference held, with the Zambian Minister of Home Affairs Aaron Milner, a colored Rhodesian, serving as chairperson. In preparation for this meeting, the guerrillas presented their agenda that called for a kind of suspension of the present leadership until the issue was finally settled, once and for all, by the people of Zimbabwe in a Congress chaired by the National leader, Comrade Joshua Nkomo, as soon as that would be possible.[96]

Further, the agenda called for the discussion of such issues as codes of behavior of ZAPU leaders and the cadre, party ideology and general protocol within the organization. Milner quickly rejected the agenda claiming, and correctly so, that they as exiles could not discuss the question of leadership, and that anyone who opposed his agenda would be dealt with "ruthlessly."[97] Clearly the Zambian government did not want any further problems on its soil, and hence, it unilaterally decided to side with the leadership of the party and disregard the grievances of the cadres included in their agenda. The crisis had gone too long, for almost three years now starting with Chikerema's unilateral decision to film ZAPU insurgents.

It soon became obvious to the cadre leaders that Milner took sides with the ZAPU leadership. Both sides dug in their heels and refused to budge with the guerrillas insisting that all relevant issues including their agenda were legitimate topics of discussion. Milner, in time, lost it and accused the guerrillas of organizing a coup against Nkomo, and thereby breaching ZAPU constitution and the Cold Comfort Farm Resolutions of 1963.

The conference soon reached an impasse after which the Zambian government detained at least forty dissidents and deported 129 to Rhodesia, accusing them of being foreign agents. Some of those who were detained in Zambia were offered scholarships by Britain and left to study there.[98] Like the Zambian government, the external ZAPU leadership believed that the Mthimkhulu (the March 11 movement leader) was a creation of Britain, the country that agitated for their release and ultimately offered them scholarships on its soil. Dumiso Dabengwa commenting on the movement wrote:

> Many members of the group [March 11 Movement] were flown to Britain. There was Intelligence information before the 1971 crisis that the group already had links and contacts with Britain that influenced the group through some journalists and other personalities.[99]

Whether or not the group was sponsored by external forces whose interests were inimical to those of ZAPU is difficult to determine. However, it can be said that the Movement's desire to discuss the leadership crisis, party's ideology and organization was legitimate given the confusion and squabbles going on within the party at that time. However, the Movement then did not attain its goals because it did not have a wide support base from among the cadre, absolutely no support from ZAPU members in Zimbabwe and equally critical, no support from the Zambian government. Undoubtedly, their tactic of kidnapping the popular leadership of *uDengezi* further isolated them from the critical support they needed.

This crisis was permanently concluded when Chikerema split from ZAPU and recruited disgruntled ZANU leaders to join a newly found, short-lived party, Front for the Liberation of Zimbabwe (FROLIZI). Kaunda and Nyerere, the two main supporters of ZAPU and ZANU, were determined to see these two nationalist parties unite so that they could eliminate what they saw as a weakness of division and failure to present a formidable challenge to the Smith regime. After repeatedly and futilely appealing to ZAPU and ZANU to unite, the two Presidents warned they would expel the recalcitrant parties from their haven. This threat of expulsion finally paid off.

On October 1, 1971, a group of members from ZAPU and ZANU announced at a Lusaka Press Conference that ZAPU and ZANU had merged to form FROLIZI. A former ZAPU military commander, Shelton Siwela, was chosen the chairperson and leader of the new party with Godfrey Savanhu, formerly ZANU, as its Secretary-General. However, the main factions of ZAPU and ZANU, under the leadership of J. Z. Moyo and Herbert Chitepo refused to join the still-born Front, and the party tacitly supported by the two Presidents crumbled like a paper house. Also key to the party's collapsing was the squabbling within the party soon after Chikerema joined it.

In the spring of 1971, under growing criticism, which some members allege was inspired by Chikerema, Siwela resigned and was replaced by the former.[100]

In fact, the 1970-1971 crisis had four major results: one, Chikerema split from ZAPU and founded a new party FROLIZI; two, the March 11 Movement was formed under the leadership of Mthimkhulu and was forced to leave the party,[101] robbing the party of one of its best trained cadre; three, Jason Z. Moyo remained the leader of the main ZAPU party.[102]

Astute strategist that he was, Moyo, following the 1970/71 crises decided to reorganize the organization. The first thing Moyo did was to reorganize the

Evaluation, Introspection and Re-organization

army that had been destabilized by the crisis. Although ZAPU had forces in the field against Smith as early as mid-1960s, ZAPU did not refer to its army as ZIPRA until after its reorganization in 1971. Moyo convened a one week consultative meeting at which the entire structure of ZAPU was reviewed and also the military activities of the party from 1965-1969.

One of the major results of this meeting was the creation of a Revolutionary Council, which became the highest ZAPU committee outside Zimbabwe. This committee was also responsible for the formation of the Zimbabwe Liberation Army. The council consisted of all members of the national executive committee and all members of the command structure of ZAPU's military wing.[103]

ZAPU immediately showed its steel resolve to prosecute the war of liberation, and this could be easily deduced from the tasks it assigned to the Revolutionary Council. The council was charged with:

1) Organiz[ing] the entire liberation campaign and the ZAPU's political strategy inside and outside the country aimed at gathering resources required for a successful armed struggle.

2) Review[ing] from time to time the military strategy of the party and align[ing] it with political objectives of the national struggle for independence.[104]

The fourth result of this crisis was ZAPU's loss of its strategic contact with FRELIMO. This subject will be discussed elaborately later. At this point, suffice it to say that, if ZAPU had succeeded in using FRELIMO liberated zones as pads to launch incursions into Rhodesia, it would have had a vast advantage of a long border that could be easily crossed as compared with the Rhodesia/Zambia border where guerrillas had to cross the formidable Zambezi River on inflated rubber boats.

With this major review and reorganization, ZAPU was now ready to move into the next state of its liberation war, that basically involved the force of arms and diplomacy.

5.6 SUMMARY AND ASSESSMENT

Just as much as ZAPU had entrenched itself within the Zimbabwean black masses before it was banned in the country, by the end of the 1960s, ZAPU forces had won the hearts and minds of the same by 1970. Also, as the 1960s decade came to a close, ZAPU had moved from the throwing of stones, use of petrol bombs to the use of trained men who received their training in African states as well as the Soviet Union and its Socialist allies. Although the OAU did support ZAPU, its material support was very minimal and also stopped short of military support.

Also it has been shown that, contrary to the general belief by some scholars who claimed that ZIRPA's operations during this era were amateurish and not well coordinated, the group carried out a smart war and refused to be moved from its goal to fight only in self-defense. By and large ZIPRA succeeded in organizing in the country a courier-system on which the guerrillas would rely for coordinating contacts and information, recruitment of military personnel for military training abroad, cache weapons, escort their South African comrades through Rhodesia, mobilize the masses for war, and secure clothes, medicines and food for the guerrillas. ZIPRA, despite the huge size of the Rhodesian Army, continued to enjoy a strategic and tactical initiative most of the war. They were small and mobile.

Above all, ZIPRA won the war of hearts and minds of the black majority, and the Rhodesian regime that had turned to a strategy of implementing martial law and punitive destruction upon the black masses totally lost the war because of its almost exclusive dependence on force rather than on psychology. Clearly, the idea of peace through a full military victory over ZIPRA was proving to be illusory.[105]

Britain, although it bore a large share of historical responsibility over the country, applied half-hearted measures towards bringing peace in Rhodesia by introducing, first, the 1961 constitution, and later, the Tiger and Fearless talks. It, however, seemed not interested in enforcing comprehensive sanctions against the Smith regime,[106] so that Smith would not have the capacity to block the implementation of genuine negotiations with black nationalists.

Smith needed to be isolated for any efforts of negotiating for majority rule to have succeeded. Absent of this condition, all these talks that were sponsored by Britain, which took it upon itself to speak for blacks, even launching a new round of talks with the Smith regime, were an illusion.

By the close of this period, ZAPU had suffered yet another split. ZAPU's unity was put to test once again, this time affecting its external wing, however, with potential to affecting the party's followers inside the country. The split led to the formation of FROLIZI. It has been shown in this chapter that the split was fuelled by tribalism and also by a dictatorial leadership that had gotten out of hand.

The March 11 members, who for the most part were well-intentioned ZAPU members, got dismissed, arrested and sent back to Rhodesia to meet with sure death, an action that gave ZAPU a black eye.[107] The organization's leadership, most of whom had fought inside Rhodesia, was taken and offered refuge with full scholarship by Britain which believed the group would be certainly hanged if it were to be sent back to Rhodesia.

The sending of part of the otherwise faithful members of the party to their certain death in Rhodesia, besides showing how totalitarian the leadership of the party under Chikerema had become, shone light on the failure of the party to undertake a serious public relations scrutiny. It also showed the movement's failure to negotiate and compromise in order to reconcile with some of its genuine and well-intentioned members. With patience and scrutiny ZAPU would have been able to weed out the Smith infiltrators who already were in the group, and redeemed those who were bona fide ZAPU members with legitimate concerns.

Evaluation, Introspection and Re-organization

The 1970-1971 crisis in ZAPU, however, had some positive results as well: the evaluation of ZAPU's insurgency tactics, leading to the production of the operational program entitled "[The] 1970 Program of Recruitment, Training and Deployment." The program was foundational for the 1970s operational strategy of ZAPU. However, this program was not implemented in full until after 1972. But some of it, such as the strengthening of reconnaissance units, who in turn managed to carry out covert contacts upon whom the insurgents depended, the deployment of guerrillas based on planned operations and the deployment of small units with instructions to avoid taking on the RSF, were immediately implemented.

Having fulfilled some of its operational goals, albeit in an imperfect way, and having survived two splits, ZAPU was ready to step-up its twofold strategy, armed struggle and negotiations, as the 1970s dawned. Even at this point, the warpath was used by ZAPU as a means of forcing the British government to impose a political solution on the Smith regime that favored majority rule.

Endnotes

1. ZAPU insurgents saw themselves as social reformers and not simple combatants in a militaristic sense. The meaning of a guerrilla as it was understood by ZAPU insurgents was reminiscent of the way the term was used by Ernesto Che Guevara in an article, which appeared in the daily *Revolution* (February 19, 1959) only fifty days after the victory of the Cuban Revolution. In that article, Che defined a guerrilla as a social reformer, one who takes up arms as an angry citizen, and fights to change the social system.

2. Basil Davidson, *Africa in Modern History, A Search for a New Society* (London: Allen Lane, 1978).

3. John S. Saul, "FRELIMO and Mozambique Revolution," in G. Arrighi & J. S. Saul, *Essays in the Political Economy of Africa* (New York: Monthly Review Press, 1973).

4. *Ibid.*

5. John S. Saul, op. cit.

6. ZAPU sent some of its cadres for training to Nanking Academy, Peking for training in between 1964 and 1965. However, after 1965, no record exists which point to ZAPU training their cadres in China. It is known, however, that its counterpart, ZANLA continued to train in China and also to receive training from the Chinese on African soil. Josiah Tongogara, the late brilliant ZANLA commander who led a group of eleven ZANLA recruits for training at Nanking Academy in 1966, after 1972 introduced a drastic change in the strategy of war on the part of ZANLA by introducing the process of mobilization and politicization along the lines of Maoism, as part of training. See Michael Raeburn, *Black Fire*, (Gweru: Mambo Press, 1981), p. 41; Martin and Johnson, p. 11 and Pandya, p. 89.

7. Chinese instructors came to ZANLA guerrilla camps in Tanzania to train recruits in sabotage and other tactics.

8. Nkomo and Chinamano were University graduates, Silundika and Chikerema were expelled from University, Dumiso taught before he left for military training, and even got admission to University in South Africa, after all, most of the fighters between 1964-1970 were working in industry when they left the country.
9. Ellert, *The Rhodesian Front War* (1989), p. 8.
10. *Ibid.*, p. 9.
11. Maxey, *The Fight for Zimbabwe* (1975), p. 60.
12. *Ibid.*, p. 38.
13. Sigawugawu, An Interview with the Author, 14 August 1996.
14. See Lionel Cliffe, Joshua Mpofu and Barry Munslow, "Nationalist Politics in Zimbabwe: The 1980 Elections and Beyond," in *Review of African Political Economy* (May-August, 1980), p. 55.
15. See Basil Davidson, *Africa in Modern History, A Search for a New Society* (London: Allen Lane, 1978), Chapter 31.
16. It is understandable why so many western scholars and those who later adopted their approach to gathering evidence thought that ZAPU had no contact with people. To most western scholars, what is not supported by documentary evidence either is not true or does not exist. I have already mentioned that ZAPU rarely published most of its activities, more so for security reasons. In this situation, it makes sense that they did not want to reveal their involvement with the locals. Such publicity would have further encouraged the regime to victimize the locals.
17. According to a detailed report on the Indaba by ZAPU which appeared in its publication *The Review* (5 November, 1964), the chiefs were told that the regime expected absolute obedience from them, that any diverging from its directives would have them replaced by chiefs who would be willing to abide by government orders. Paradoxically, the interpreters at the indaba were whites. The chief who gave information to ZAPU said that most of the chiefs had no part in the final statement that was produced by the conference, claiming it was produced with Chiefs Kayisa Ndiweni of Ntabazinduna and Zvimba of Zvimba.

    The insider's report aside, one can get the sense of the pressure the regime brought on the chiefs to attend this "indaba" from reading a government news paper accounts in the *Rhodesia Herald* (4 November 1964). Sigombe Mathema of Wenlock became one of the victims of these threats because he did not attend the "indaba." He was replaced and finally detained.
18. *Ibid.*, pp. 61-62.
19. Joshua Moyo, An Interview with the Author, August 28, 1994.
20. Not all of the MK cadres escaped from Rhodesia. Some were killed and others were arrested. Some of those who were arrested in this 1967 battle were sentenced to death, spent two years on death row before their death sentences were commuted to life imprisonment. Most of these former MK soldiers were released under the general amnesty declared by Robert Mugabe in 1980, when Zimbabwe became independent.
21. The 1968 Wankie Campaign had a symbolic value for the ANC despite the fact that in military terms this battle was a fiasco. The Campaign became "Umkhonto we Sizwe's" mythology, which marked the beginning of a new and critical phase of

Evaluation, Introspection and Re-organization

the armed struggle. The news of the battle created heroes whose stories inspired the South African black recruits. Among these were Paul Petersen, a colored former medical student from the University of Cape Town who also blossomed as an intellectual when he started publishing articles on political theory. Petersen was also known as Basil February. Legend has it that after he had been seriously injured in the heat of the Wankie Campaign, he told his comrades to leave him with a "She" machine gun so he could fight to his death. That particular machine gun was manufactured in Czechoslovakia, and since then it was named after Petersen in ANC circles, and was known as the "She Petersen." Another prominent victim of this battle was Patrick Molaoa, who despite the fact that at that time he was a member of the ANC National Executive Committee, and therefore could have avoided combat, decided to fight.

Others escaped to South Africa as planned, and to Botswana and Mozambique. These received help from the locals as they went across Rhodesia. Among those who succeeded in making their way to South Africa were Daluxolo Luthuli, known as `Kenken.' He was later arrested, sent to Rhoben Island and afterwards joined Gatsha Buthelezi of *iNkatha*. Leonard Nkosi, who was later betrayed by one of his family members, subsequently joined the enemy forces. Nkosi was, however, shot and killed by ANC guerrillas in the 1970's while in bed with his wife. Chris Hani escaped to Botswana. Another ANC guerrilla, Lennox Zuma, escaped to Mozambique, where he joined FRELIMO and served under a variety of assumed names.

(Stephen Ellis and Tsepo Sechaba, *Comrades Against Apartheid: The ANC & South African Communist Party in Exile*, London: James Curry, 1992), p. 50.22.

Dumiso Dabengwa, "ZIPRA and ZIPA in the Zimbabwe War of NATIONAL LIBERATION," a paper presented at the University of Zimbabwe (July 8, 1991).

23. *Zimbabwe News* (30 September, 1967), published by ZANU in Lusaka.
24. *Guardian* (23 January 1962).
25. *Rand Daily Mail* (19 July 1965).
26. Testimony of Jose Ervedosa, report of the United Nations Committee on Colonialism, 1966.
27. P. L. Moorcraft & P. McLaughlin, *Chimurenga! The War in Rhodesia 1965-1980* (Johannesburg: Sygma Books, 1982), p. 167-168; IDAF, *The Apartheid War Machine: The Strength and Deployment of the South African Armed Forces Fact Paper on Southern Africa*, No. 8 (London: IDAF, 1980b), p. 65.
28. R. S. Jaster, *A Regional Security Role for Africa's Front Line States: Experience and Prospects Aldelphi Papers No. 180* (London: International Institute for Strategic Studies, 1983), p. 19.
29. Colin and Margaret Legum, *South Africa: Crisis for the West* (New York: Praeger, 1963), p. 4.
30. Saul Gwakuba Ndlovu, *Zimbabwe: Some Facts About Its Liberation Struggle* (Lusaka: Zimbabwe African People's Union, 1973), p. 42.
31. *Ibid.*
32. *Times* (London, 26 August, 1967).
33. *Evening Post* (17 October 1967).
34. *Transvaler* (25 September 1967).

35. Cited from S. O [lu] Agbi, *The Organization of African Unity and Diplomacy, 1963-1979* (Ibadan: Impact Publishers Nigeria Limited, 1986), p. 78.
36. Smith was not threatened at the 1968 talks with Britain where the latter tried to play tough. Talks collapsed because Smith felt nothing would happen to his government even if he did not accept the British proposals.
37. Joshua Nkomo, Interview by author, 26 July 1995.
38. Lionel Cliffe, Joshua Mpofu and Barry Munslow, "Nationalist Politics in Zimbabwe: The 1980 Elections and Beyond," in the *Review of African Political Economy*, No. 18, (1981):52-53. For more discussion of the different roles played by the *umjimba* in the liberation war, see Norma J. Kriger, *Zimbabwe's Guerrilla War: Peasant Voices* (Cambridge: University Press, 1992), pp. 179-191. In this book though, the discussion is largely that of the role of the *umjimba* within the ZANU structures. However, some of these roles corresponded with the roles played by their equivalent in ZAPU, such as carrying information between the guerrillas and peasants.
39. Sigawugawu, interview by author, 14 May 1996.
40. Cliffe, *et al*, "Nationalist Politics in Zimbabwe: The 1980 Elections and Beyond," *Review of African Political Economy* (1981):53; Alec J.C. Pongweni, *Songs that Won the Liberation War* (Harare: College Press, 1982).
41. Jeremy Brickhill, "Daring to Storm the Heavens: The Military Strategy of ZAPU 1976 to 1979 in Ngwebi Bhebe and Terence Ranger, *Soldiers in Zimbabwe's Liberation War* (London: James Currey, 1995, pp. 68-70); Dingilizwe Dewa, An Interview, August 24, 1996; Stephen Ndlovu, Interview with the Author, July 24, 1996. Ndlovu, as a minister of religion, and bishop of the church told of how ZIPRA would organize people in churches. This, he said, was made easier by the fact that to a certain extent churches as places of worship still enjoyed some freedom from harassment by the state, especially the mainline churches.
42. The ZANLA forces as one of their major methods of political conscientizing and recruiting people in the rural areas used "pungwes," nighttime political rallies (Josiah Tungamirai, "Recruitment to ZANLA: Building up a War Machine," in Ngwabi Bhebe and Terence Ranger, *Soldiers in Zimbabwe's Liberation War*, London: James Currey, p. 42). The major drawback of this method of recruitment was that such gatherings could be easily detected by security forces, resulting in civilians being killed.
43. Ernesto Che Guevara, "What is a "Guerrilla?" in *Revolution* (February 19, 1959).
44. Military intelligence can be divided into two parts: background and contact information. Background information involve monitoring broadcasts and publications, studying statistics and facts. Contact information is on the movement of the enemy forces, the kind of weapons they are carrying, where there are located, and their likely actions and intentions. Both kinds of intelligence information can be gathered from technical sources, e.g. intercepts, or from informers who are part of that community.
45. Lionel Cliffe, Joshua Mpofu and Barry Munslow, "Nationalist Politics in Zimbabwe: The 1980 Elections and Beyond," in *African Review of Political Economy* (May-August, 1980), pp. 56-57.

Evaluation, Introspection and Re-organization

46. Terence Ranger, *Peasant Consciousness and Guerrilla War in Zimbabwe* (London: James Currey, 1985).

47. Norma Kriger, "The Zimbabwe War of Liberation: Struggles Within the Struggle," in *Journal of Southern African Studies*, Vol. 14 (1988): 304-322.

48. J. M. M. Mpofu, "The February 1980 Zimbabwe Elections: The Matebeleland North and South Provinces," Conference on Zimbabwe, Leeds University, June 21-22, 1980. In the previous chapter evidence was provided on the courage with which a joint ZIPRA/MK commando fought against the regime forces, and at one point putting the Smith soldiers in flight and capturing their weapons. In most instances, contacts were protracted, and the fights fierce.

49. Barry M. Schutz and Douglas Scott, "Natives and Settlers: A Comparative Analysis of the Politics of Opposition and Mobilization in Northern Ireland and Rhodesia," *Monograph*, Vol. 12, no. 2 (Denver: University of Denver, 1974), p. 39.

50. James K. Bruton, "Counterinsurgency in Rhodesia," *Military Review 59* (March 1979): 32-38. The Rhodesian army had 3,500 men, and it was organized into two battalions, the Rhodesian African Rifles, about 1,000 men, and the all white Royal Rhodesia Regiment. By 1969, the Air force was composed of about 1,000 soldiers, and these were organized into seven squadrons, with approximately 80 aircraft. The territorial force was composed of about 10,000 white males. The territorials were called up to do nine months of national service at any given time. The BSAP was 6,400 men-strong. The BSAP was complimented by the reserve police force, which served on a temporal basis. This force, that was largely white, experienced a dramatic increase in the 1960s. By 1970, its white composition had risen to approximately 28,500 (Richard Booth, *The Armed Forces of African States*, Adelphi Papers No. 67 (May 1970) and International Institute for Strategic Studies, *The Military Balance, 1969-1970* (London, 1970), p. 53. For an informative source on the evolution of the Rhodesian forces, see Lewis Gann, "From Ox Wagon to Armored Car," *Military Review 48* (April 1968): 63-72.

51. Robert Good, *UDI: The International Politics of the Rhodesian Rebellion* (London: Faber and Faber, 1973), p. 37.

52. The Rhodesian troopers who had some experience in counter-insurgency operations at Malaya in the 1950s, and those who rose to be officers of high rank in the Rhodesian Army were Lieutenant-General Peter Walls, Colonel John Hickman and Lieutenant-Colonel `Derry' MacIntyre.

53. Ken Flower, *Serving Secretly: An Intelligence Chief on Record. Rhodesia into Zimbabwe 1964-1981* (London, 1987), pp. 114, 111-112, 120-125.

54. Robert Taber, *The War of the Flea: A Study of Guerrilla Warfare Theory and Practice* (New York: L. Staurt, 1965).

55. For a very insightful and informative book on the use of psychological tactics by all groups involved in war in Rhodesia see Julie Frederikse, *None But Ourselves: Masses vs. Media in the Making of Zimbabwe* (New York: Penguin Books Ltd., (c) 1982, 1984).

56. Roughly speaking, there are four factors that are critical to the success of any political movement involved in a struggle: legitimacy, non-violent pressure resistance, violent resistance and global political and economic changes. All these facts do not have to obtain in every given situation of struggle in the exception of

57. Richard Sibanda, Interview by author, 26 August, 1994. Richard Sibanda, an historian by training was one of the Zimbabwe Church of Orphans officials. The church met at Emhlahlandlela by Mt. Buze. In this interview Sibanda informed this writer that the preaching was met to show the injustice in the distribution of wealth in the country, a situation in which whites appeared to be having everything, most of which was ill gotten. Sibanda said his church contributed "greatly in raising black's consciousness regarding their oppression".

58. For functions of the *ilitshe* and pilgrimages to the same by guerrillas see chapter IV.

59. Michael Raeburn, *We Are Everywhere: Narratives From Rhodesian Guerrillas* (New York: Random House, 1978). Although Raeburn suggests to his readers that guerrilla incursions up to 1970 should not be seen as absolute failure, the tenor of his whole discussion, however, suggests the opposite, that the guerrillas' attacks were a dismal fiasco. This does not surprise this writer at all in light of the fact that Raeburn was one of those people who would not see anything good coming from ZAPU. It makes sense to see him draw such conclusions regarding pre-1970 guerrilla armed struggle since most of it was carried out by ZAPU

60. Shamuyarira, *Crisis in Rhodesia* (1965), p. 189.

61. Ibid., Jeremy Ginifer, *Managing Arms in Peace Processes: Rhodesia/Zimbabwe* (New York: United Nations, 1995), p. 7.

62. Masipula Sithole, "State Power Consolidation in Zimbabwe," in *Afro-Marxist Regimes: Ideology and Public Policy*, eds., Edmond J. Keller and Donald Rothchild (Boulder: Lynne Rienner Publishers, 1987), pp. 86-87; Richard Gibson, p. 174; Martin and Johnson, *The Struggle for Zimbabwe* (1981). For a detailed analysis of the ZAPU-ZANU split, see an account of a ZANU nationalist Shamuyarira in his *Crisis in Rhodesia* (1966). See also Masipula Sithole, *Zimbabwe Struggles*, the chapter entitled "Contradictions in ZAPU," pp. 27-46, especially the document by Ndabaningi Sithole, leader of ZANU at the time of the split, appearing on pp. 31-34.

63. *The Rhodesia Herald* (August 9, 1963).

64. See Day, *International Nationalism* (1967), pp. 22-103; and for a apparent differences between ZAPU and ZANU see Christopher Nyangoni and Gideon Nyandoro, eds., *Zimbabwe Independence Movements: Select Documents* (New York: Barnes and Noble, 1979), pp. 64-113.

65. On the tactical differences in fighting a colonial administered state and an independent, domestic one see Robert Taber, *The War of the Flea* (Suffolk: the Chaucer Press, 1970), pp. 90-91; Kenneth W. Gundy, "Black Soldiers in a White Military: Political Change in South Africa," *The Journal of Strategic Studies*, 4, (September 1981): 296. ZAPU's optimism in a peaceful transition to majority rule by Britain in its colony was not without examples. Several West and East African countries had received their independence without any use of military force by the African population.

66. Dumiso Dabengwa, "ZIPRA and ZIPA in the Zimbabwe War of National Liberation," paper presented at University of Zimbabwe, July 8, 1991, p.6.

Evaluation, Introspection and Re-organization

67. Nkomo, *The Story of My Life* (1984), p. 113.
68. A. H. Tony Rich, "Social, Ethnic and Regional Factors in the Development of Zimbabwean Nationalist Movements, 1963-80," Ph.D. Dissertation, University of Manchester (May 1983d), pp. 82-86.
69. Before the split in 1962, the ZAPU Executive had ten Shona people and four AmaNdebele. In 1963 after the split, ZAPU had ten Shona people and six AmaNdebele, and ZANU, fourteen Shona people and one iNdebele. The ZANU executive stayed almost exclusively Shona to the time of my writing and ZAPU continued to have a multi-ethnic executive committee to the time it merged with ZANU. Two things are very clear from the reading of ethnic representation in both ZAPU and ZANU respective. One, because ZAPU's membership remained even after the split, and throughout the 1960's, we can safely conclude that tribalism played a role in the split not on the part of the membership but that of the dissenters. Two, the split could not be correctly attributed to dominance of the AmaNdebele on the ZAPU executive committee so that we could interpret it as a reaction of the Shona people to such dominance. Third, that the ZANU executive was overwhelmingly Shona. The can be no question that the founding members of the ZANU party were mostly led by personal ambitions and sheer opportunism which in turn, brought to the fore the expedience of tribal politics.
70. *Voice of America*, June 19, 1996, 10:45 AM EDT (1445 UTC).
71. *Voice of America*, June 19, 1996, 10:45 AM EDT (1445 UTC).
72. Enock Dumbutshena, *Zimbabwe Tragedy* (Nairobi, 1976).
73. See also L. H. Gann, *History of Southern Rhodesia: Early Days to 1934* (London: Chatto & Windus, 1963).
74. Mai Palmberg, ed., *The Struggle for Africa* (London: Zed Press, 1983), p. 187.
75. According to a US State document, Declassified E.O. 11652, Sec. 3(E), 5(D), 5(E) and 11, March 1, 1978, written in July 12, 1963, the US Consulate General at Salisbury, quoting what he called a "reliable source" reported that Nkomo charged that the U.S. Embassy at Dar es Salaam was responsible for the ZAPU split. Although Nkomo on behalf of ZAPU produced no documentary evidence to support their allegation, one can understand why ZAPU would think United States supported the dissidents. US consulates in Salisbury during the early 1960's did not speak kindly of Nkomo. In fact they favored Ndabaningi Sithole and Robert Mugabe. For instance, in this document Sithole is described as more intelligent and resourceful than Nkomo who is characterized as "impatient ... phlegmatic, [and] luxury-loving...."
76. Disunity is not always a source of weakness. It is also important to note that ethnic consciousness is not necessarily a bad thing as it can be foundational to the formation of the notion of nationalism.
77. J. Bowyer Bell, "The Frustration of Insurgency: the Rhodesian Example in the Sixties," *Military Affairs*, Vol. 35 (February 1971): 1-5.
78. Ginifer, p. 7.
79. Martin and Johnson, *The Struggle for Zimbabwe* (1985), p. 223.
80. *Africa Contemporary Record* (1975/76): A103-A 111; Keith Somerville, "The Soviet Union and Zimbabwe: The Struggle and After," in R. Craig Nation and Mark

Kauppi, eds, *The Soviet Impact on Africa* (Lexington, MA: D.C. Heath & CO., 1984), p. 202. For a detailed account on Russia's moral, training and military support to ZAPU through out the armed struggle period see Daniel Robert Kempton, "Soviet Strategy Toward African National Liberation Movements," a Ph.D. Dissertation, University of Illinois at Urban-Champaign.

81. Two examples of situations where ZIPRA found itself fighting a positional war are in the Sipolilo area where they fought in the Vietcog style underground hideouts and in the Wankie area in 1967, in their first joint-military campaign with MK. In both instances, only after the engagement of the Air Force, did the RSF have an upper hand.

82. Raeburn, *We are Everywhere* (1978), p. 198.

83. Gibson, *African Liberation Movements* (1972), pp. 169-174.

84. *Ibid.*, pp. 169-170.

85. J.Z. Moyo, "Observation on Our Struggle," in C. Nyangoni and G. Nyandoro, eds, *Zimbabwe Independence Movements* (1979), p. 143.

86. O[wen] Tshabangu, *The March 11 Movement in ZAPU: Revolution Within the Revolution* (Heslington, 1979), p. 29.

87. James Chikerema, "Reply to the Observation of our Struggle," (17 March 1970), p. 4. A copy of this document is in possession by the author.

88. J.Z. Moyo, E. Ndlovu and T. G. Silundika, "On the Coup Crisis Precipitated by J. Chikerema," 21 March 1970, p. 4. A copy of this document is in the author's possession. The document was reprinted in Nyangoni and Nyadoro, 1979.

89. Martin and Johnson, *The Struggle for Zimbabwe* (1981), pp. 29-30.

90. *Ibid.*, p. 30.

91. Simbi Mubako, "The Quest for Unity in the Zimbabwe Liberation Movement," in *Issue*, Vol. 5, Number 1 (Spring, 1975): 10-11.

92. For a detailed account on Chikerema's tribal inclinations and negotiations with ZANU and his tribal men, see *ibid.*

93. Owen Tshabangu, *The March 11 Movement in ZAPU: Revolution Within the Revolution* (Heslington, 1979), pp. 8-9.

94. *Ibid.*, p. 38.

95. *Ibid.*, p. 46.

96. *Ibid.*, p.47.

97. *Ibid.*, pp. 47, 49.

98. *Ibid.*, pp. 49-62.

99. Dumiso Dabengwa, "ZIPRA and ZIPA in the Zimbabwe War of National Liberation," a paper presented at the University of Zimbabwe, (July 8, 1991) pp. 20-21.

100. Peter Mugurwa, An Interview by the author, August 10, 1992. Mugurwa was a member of FROLISI from the time it was formed to the time it folded-up. He was one of its fighters who made several incursions in to Rhodesia on its behalf. He was among those who went back to ZAPU after the Front died.

101. Dabengwa, "ZIPRA and ZIPA in the Zimbabwe War of Liberation" (1991), pp. 19.

Evaluation, Introspection and Re-organization

102. *Ibid.*
103. *Ibid.*, p. 21.
104. *Ibid.*, pp. 21-22.
105. Britain was, at this point, in 1970, thinking of trying negotiations on the basis of the Rhodesian 1969 constitution, which it wanted to test by holding a referendum on it among the black population. Clearly, Britain had finally convinced itself that any credible and successful peace depended on peaceful negotiations and engaging out-spoken black Zimbabwean civil society, and hence their beginning to organize for talks leading to the 1971 referendum.
106. More than 25 UN Resolutions, including selective UN sanctions in 1966 and comprehensive ones in 1968 [The Parliament of the Commonwealth of Australia, *Zimbabwe: Report of the Joint Committee on Foreign Affairs and Defense* (Australia Government Publicity Services, Canberra, 1980), p. 41.] These sanctions did not seem to have any effective impact for the most part of this period because Britain stood against their enforcement and even connived at sanction busting. The British government watched as South Africa materially assisted Rhodesia, and the United States purchased chrome without raising so much as a finger for the violations.
107. According to one March 11 informant, the Mthimkhulu (March 11) group consisting mostly of degreed cadres angry with Chikerema's use of tribalism as a tool to divide the cadres, mutinied and tried to arrest the top leadership to resolve the internal crises that had, to a large degree, crippled ZAPU. According to his version, this group consisted of loyalists who wanted progress and could not let tribalism divert the course of liberation. This, indeed, was a black eye for ZAPU.

Chapter 6
THE STORM AND THEN SPEARS TURNED INTO PLOWSHARES: ZAPU GOES ON MILITARY AND THEN PEACE OFFENSIVE, 1972-79

This chapter looks into the military activities of ZAPU, and its military strategies and goals after 1970 as well as its participation in negotiations leading to the first majority rule elections in 1980. Because the process of negotiations involving ZAPU has been extensively covered in scholarly literature,[1] In this work an inordinate space will be accorded ZIPRA's military activities rather than its party's negotiation process. Much time will be spent discussing ZAPU's military approach to solving the political question of Rhodesia, basically, because there is very little scholarly work out there on the subject.

6.1 ZAPU Storms the White Haven: 1971-79 Guerrilla Warfare

Even during the midst of its critical moments of leadership crisis in 1970, ZIPRA operated in Rhodesia, springing deadly ambushes and laying land mines, essentially employing the open up and then melting into the bush, community or night. ZIPRA could afford melting into the community because by 1970 it was well ensconced in the local population.[2]

From 1966, and on, ZIPRA worked at establishing a supportive civilian structure, involving a network of contact personnel and the courier system of *imijibha*. Thus, ZIPRA made careful preparations for the subsequent military campaign: politicizing, and in a limited way, militarizing the rural population, establishing security procedures and infiltration and escape routes. They cached arms and recruited porters. ZIPRA also established some alliances with movements with similar goals for inspirational, logistical and tactical reasons. The 1970's would witness all those years of preparation coming to fruition.

Thus, for the most part in the late 1960's ZIPRA concentrated on preparing the masses for the guerrilla offensive of the 1970's. In that direction, ZIPRA invested in systematizing its party's political activities of organizing its black supporters, and avoided positional confrontations as it sought to prepare hospitable military and political bases among the local black population. Its infiltrations were concentrated mostly in the northeast and western part of the country. During the early 1970's ZIPRA would dominate much of the northwest,

west, southwest and Midlands while their comrades in arms, ZANLA, operated mainly in the east, northeast and south east of the country.

In the late 1960's ZAPU voluntarily entered an agreement of joint operations with first ANC's MK then on paper, with ZANLA, at the same time as it [ZAPU] was starting its joint military campaign with FRELIMO. OAU intensified its efforts to unite ZIPRA and ZANLA after the former entered an alliance with the MK. In 1967, the African National Congress of South Africa approached ZAPU with a proposal for joint operations.

ZAPU agreed, although the purpose of this joint operation was not for carrying out joint military attacks on the Rhodesian forces but for logistics. The joint campaign, however, did not receive wide support among the African states that thought that ZIPRA should have united with its own fellow nationalist guerrillas, ZANLA. Accordingly, the OAU Liberation Committee organized a meeting at Mbeya, Tanzania to discuss the merging of the military wings of ZAPU and ZANU.

Frontline Presidents supported the move of the OAU. ZAPU did not favor the unity because it did not see any military advantage in it given that ZANU had a very small number of trained men, and did not have significant support inside Zimbabwe. Further, ZANU had a hard time recruiting Zimbabweans for training both inside and outside Rhodesia. ZAPU therefore concluded:

> *[T]hat it would be imprudent to unite with an organization whose armed wing consisted only of the command element and a few other people who continued to be sent on for training and re-training without doing the actual fighting.*[3]

However, confronted by a situation in which their host African countries favored the unity, ZAPU had to sign the pact. According to the pact, ZAPU and ZANLA were to deploy their guerrillas under the Joint Military Command whose leadership consisted of a joint military leadership charged with implementing the Mbeya agreement.

Since ZAPU got cowed into accepting the pact because it was afraid of risking the loss of its bases if it were to openly boycott the Mbeya conference, it decided to undermine its implementation by assigning commanders of lower rank to the Joint Military Leadership. Senior commanders like Akim Ndlovu, Dumiso Dabengwa,[4] Alfred Mangena, Lookout Masuku and Elliot Sibanda[5] were left out. Chikerema who was the Acting President of the party even went to the extent of not attending and advising Jason Moyo whom he delegated to make sure the agreement did not go beyond just being a paper agreement.

Clearly, the OAU's approach of trying to unite ZAPU and ZANU when there was no mutual political will on the part of the parties concerned was ill advised. More so because there was no material basis for it, so far as ZAPU was concerned.

Instead, ZAPU was interested in pursuing its joint-military campaign with FRELIMO because of the military advantages created by such a joint-campaign. It was even easier for ZIPRA to join hands with FRELIMO because they were

The Storm and Then Spears Turned into Plowshares

both supported and got arms from the Soviet Union whereas ZANLA was supported by China. Consequently ZIPRA's war tactics were similar to those of FRELIMO. At the same time as the OAU was trying to impose unity on the Zimbabwean Liberation forces, ZAPU was talking with FRELIMO on a possibility of joint operations for the opening of the Tete Corridor.[6]

The opening of the Tete Corridor would have helped ZAPU considerably with the difficulties of infiltration into Rhodesia. Incursions from Zambia were very difficult because the guerrillas had to cross the forbidding Zambezi River, infested with crocodiles, hippopotami and poisonous snakes. That meant that guerrillas had to sometimes compromise their presence when they shot at attacking animals as they crossed the Zambezi River.

Also, it was easier to monitor the crossings from the River and to mine possible crossings, which were not too many. Joint operations with FRELIMO would have given ZIPRA the advantage of crossing into Zimbabwe on land and under the cover of a range of mountains covered with trees and rugged landscape suited for guerrilla operations. Besides, the 150-mile border was very porous at this point in time.

In addition to the long border that could hardly be effectively monitored by RSFs, were patches of black reserves that were 40 miles wide, immediately after the border into Rhodesia. These reserves could have more than likely provided support, shelter and succor to the ZIPRA cadres operating in their area. Instead, by mid-1973, people in this area were giving support to ZANLA forces which were already operating in their area.[7]

Thus ZIPRA preferred to unite with FRELIMO primarily for this reason. At this point, ZIPRA's involvement with FRELIMO was far advanced as noted by Dumiso Dabengwa:

> *Through field commanders like Robson Manyika, ZAPU was very actively assisting FRELIMO with logistics and transportation of its personnel for the opening of the Tete Corridor. We were looking forward to its completion because at that stage we were getting reports from our men who had survived the Sipolilo Campaign and had gone underground and were working on farms in the entire Northeastern part of Zimbabwe. The men were sending regular reports of completed reconnaissance and had large numbers of recruits that they didn't know how to send....[8]*

However, as was pointed out in Chapter V, ZAPU lost its contact with FRELIMO during its leadership crisis of 1970/71. Unbeknown to the ZAPU hierarchy, Robson Manyika, one of ZIPRA's highly trained guerrillas, who had been tasked with leading ZIPRA men who were helping in the opening of the Tete Corridor showed the plans to ZANU after which he and Rex Nhongo (who has changed his name to Solomon Mujuru since independence) defected to ZANU.

According to Sibiya Mpofu, one of the ex-ZIPRA combatants involved in the FRELIMO joint-campaign, Manyika made FRELIMO believe he was still with ZAPU. In actuality, Manyika had changed parties for a considerable length of time before he disclosed his new affiliation when he already had built a big army for ZANLA.[9] This was a significant tactical loss for ZIPRA.

This meant that with the beginning of the 1970's, and throughout the war period, the thorn in ZIPRA's side was the crossing of the Zambezi River. Again, as it opened the new decade of the 1970s, unity with its ZANLA brothers and sisters was still a far-fetched dream. Despite these shortcomings, ZIPRA, through the rattling of its gunfire, the bangs of its heavy artillery, its budding but robust propaganda and its political commissariat system had managed to lay a solid foundation for its major incursions and mass recruitment of the 1970's.

The opening of the Tete Corridor in Mozambique for ZANLA became a blessing in disguise for ZIPRA. When ZANU left to open its training bases in Mozambique, Zambia bequeathed all ZANLA bases to ZIPRA although the expulsion of ZANU from Zambia would come later after the assassination of its leader Herbert Chitepo in Lusaka in March 1975. At this point only some bases were left vacant.

This provided ZAPU with more training bases to accommodate the many recruits ready to be trained, but who could not be moved to Zambia immediately because of little space. It also spread the RSFs. Up to 1970 RSFs were concentrated on the North West, West, and along the Zambezi River. With the opening of the new Frontier in the East, Smith had to move his troops to the border of Mozambique. Thus, at this point war had been brought into the rural population in the affected areas and the masses had been politicized, and thereby making it not difficult for the regime soldiers to receive any co-operation from them.

The work that Manyika and other ZIPRA forces did with FRELIMO on the northeastern part of Rhodesia before he defected to ZANLA was, however, critical in preparing the ground for military operations that ensued in the early 1970's. Terence Ranger, at a conference on Liberation Movements in Zimbabwe, described the nature of ZIPRA's involvement during this time:

> *According to Dabengwa's oral presentation, preparations for this northeastern offensive had been on hand between ZAPU and FRELIMO since 1969 and ZAPU emissaries had made contact with underground agents in the area in readiness for infiltration. Robson Manyika, now acting for ZANU, later mobilized these agents.*[10]

There is no reason to doubt Dabengwa's assertion given that some of ZAPU's initial infiltration were in that part of the country and also since it is the case that ZIPRA was indeed at one time involved with FRELIMO, helping it with logistics in the opening of the Tete corridor. Thus, to some very significant extent, ZIPRA prepared the way for ZANLA's operations of the early 1970's so that what the latter did was to ride on the crest of the wave. Since ZIPRA was truly national in its character, more so during the 1960's, language posed no barrier for some of the cadres, such as Robson Manyika, came from that region.

6.2 The Reign of Land Mines (Ibhabayila),[11] 1970-1975

Subsequent to the meeting which Moyo led immediately after the 1970/71 crisis, and under the guidance of the Revolutionary Council ZAPU did major reorganizing and building up of the ZIPRA forces, especially between 1972 and 1974. The year 1971 saw an increase in the use of land mines by the ZIPRA forces, a strategy it widely adopted in 1970.

ZIPRA planted land mines on the access roads to the South African camps in the Mana Pools Game Reserve. In fact, operations during this year, through 1973, were mainly focused on sabotage and on frustrating the RSFs by making roads inaccessible by mining them. Indeed, this was not what Godwin and Hancock erroneously characterized as "only a pinprick in our sides"[12] when they described ZIPRA attacks of the 1970's.

Land mines took their death toll on the part of the Rhodesian and particularly the South African troops, and even those that were detonated outside the South African camps claimed their own fatalities.

Expanding on the failure of the South African troops to ward-off the fatal attacks waged against them by the ZIPRA forces, Ellert, attributed this failure to the troops' lack of discipline, indeed, the dereliction of duty. He asserted:

The South Africans made it very easy for the guerrillas to score successes against them. A classic example of dereliction of duty with fatal results occurred during 1971 when a number of young inexperienced constables [understand soldiers], overcome with fatigue during a mid-morning patrol along the banks of the Zambezi River upstream from the Victoria Falls, decided to have a swim. Stacking their rifles in a pile, the Constables [understand soldiers] stripped off and dived into the cooling waters. Observing [them] was a ZIPRA patrol and the constables [understand soldiers] paid for their carelessness with their lives.[13]

Despite this playing down of the seriousness of the situation by Ellert, the regime itself was undoubtedly aware of the gravity of the situation. The new offensive by ZIPRA, combined with that of ZANLA, led Prime Minister Smith to warn the public in December 1972 that the situation was "far more serious than it appear[ed] on the surface."[14]

In response to what Smith perceived to be a serious situation, he, on July 1, 1972, formed the Rhodesian Armored Car Regiment, and increased his armed forces so that by December 1972 its regular army and Air Force stood at 4,700 men, and these were supported by thousands of territorials, the BSAP and at least 3,000 paramilitary South African Police who had been operating in the country since the 1960s.[15] In fact Smith felt the heat as early as the late 1960s.

On January 30, 1969, his Minister of Defense announced that the number of the Rhodesian Light Infantry (RLI) was to be increased, and the number of paratroopers doubled.[16] Arguably these are not preparations made in times of peace and when a sense of security prevails. ZAPU forces obviously were giving the regime's military a run for its money, although the government down played their effectiveness.

The Zimbabwe African People's Union 1961-1987

As ZIPRA unleashed a reign of land mines on its enemies, it also busied itself with building up a network of subversive cells and arms caches throughout Rhodesia. The cadres at this point, in 1974, operated clandestinely, mainly from Botswana, and cached weapons throughout the rural areas of Matebeleland. This network was also responsible for recruiting for guerrilla training.

The operation became known as the 3-2-3 networks because it involved the infiltration of very small units who worked closely with "imijibha" and already established cells within the country.[17] The professionalism and dedication of those involved in these internal networks is well captured by Barbara Cole when she observed:

> ZIPRA had planned it all very carefully. They had devised a series of secret signals to enable one person to recognize the next in the chain. It was a cutout network so that if the security forces picked one man he could not pinpoint the others.[18]

The purpose for planting weapons and ammunition throughout the areas where ZIPRA operated was two-fold. One, and the immediate one, it was to make weapons available to the locals, like land mines which were extensively used by the locally trained *umjibha*. Francis Sibanda gave information about this:

> The immediate purpose of caching weapons throughout the rural areas in our operational theater was to make them readily available to our local supporters who had been trained in their use. These internal recruits laid mines and increasingly some of them became efficient with the use of weapons, and carried out ambushes.
>
> The second reason was so that guerrillas could replenish their supplies. In some cases where it was difficult for guerrillas to get to a given target location without being detected when carrying weapons, they went without weapons to avoid being spotted and these cached weapons became available to them. Most times these were people who were operating in places where they were either born or grew-up.[19]

Sibanda's observation yields a very important point that is generally missing in the mainstream literature on ZAPU as a liberation group, and that is the increasingly extensive involvement of black local Zimbabweans in the liberation's armed struggle. Clearly ZIPRA was cognizant of their being an integral part of the armed struggle from the beginning of their operation, and as time went on, they encouraged the locals mass involvement in the armed struggle as fighters, and not only in supportive roles.

The second and long-range reason for the planting of weapons post-1970 was in preparation for what came to be known as the Zero Hour. The thinking was when the time was ripe for the implementation of the Zero Hour the locals would use these weapons to create a chaotic situation as the conventionally trained army rolled in tanks on beachheads across the Zambezi River. Thus, in addition to the use of mines, ZIPRA this time also engaged in a campaign of ambush, especially along the Zambezi River.

The Storm and Then Spears Turned into Plowshares

This time the attacks by ZIPRA were handsomely complimented by that of its compatriot, ZANLA which was successfully prosecuting a guerrilla warfare in the newly opened Mozambican front, and by 1974 the combined and yet uncoordinated military pressure by both ZIPRA and ZANLA, coupled with pressure from South Africa, forced Smith to open negotiations with the black nationalists.

The South African inspired detente led to two important developments, one of which was positive and the other negative so far as the struggle was concerned. On the positive note, it resulted in the release of leading nationalists like Joshua Nkomo on the part of ZAPU and Sithole and Mugabe on the side of ZANU in order to prepare for negotiations. More negatively the opening up of negotiations resulted in the de-escalation of the military campaign on the part of the nationalist groups. As part of the agreement to enter negotiations, a cease-fire was announced, and nationalists' leaders released in December 1974. The cease-fire did not work as guerrillas continued to make military incursions into Rhodesia. The Smith regime in fact initiated the bad faith by not releasing some nationalists who were expected to be taken out of detention.

Using his popularity, Nkomo made a call for more recruits to join the fighting ranks in Zambia. The call was handsomely rewarded as recruits began leaving the country for training at a rate of 3,000 a month.[20] On August 1, 1975 South Africa officially withdrew its military and police units from Rhodesia as a gesture of good faith and a show of seriousness for a negotiated settlement.

Another reason Vorster withdrew its forces was as a *quid pro quo* for Kaunda's cooperation in the implementation of the cease-fire and his support for South African inspired negotiations. However, a large number secretly remained in the country.[21] Under the codename Operation Polo, pilots, helicopters and ground support crews were not withdrawn and only these were publicly known to have been operating in Rhodesia.[22]

The official withdrawal of South African troops at a time when thousands of young black Zimbabweans were leaving the country to join liberation forces shook the Rhodesian government. For ZAPU, this injection could not have come at a more propitious time. Cubans and the Soviets started arriving in Angola to fight on the side of the MPLA in order to help defend the later from the invading South Africans who were fighting on behalf of UNITA.

Since ZIPRA was friendly with the MPLA and since it received some training and material support from both the Soviet Union and Cuba, the coming of the latter to Angola therefore meant that ZIPRA was now going to receive training not too far away from its bases, and as such ZAPU could send more people for training.

Other than the benefit of a dramatic increase in the number of recruits during the cease-fire period of 1974/75 there were not immediate benefits on the war front. Thus, 1974/75 were years when ZIPRA lost the gains and initiatives it had secured through the use of land mines and ambushes during the early part of 1970s.

In 1975 military casualties were even fewer than the previous year, and the low number in the deaths of the enemy was attributable, according to Michael Raeburn, to preoccupation by the nationalists with trying to make up their divisions since the collapse of the Lusaka Negotiations of December 1974, and the de-escalation of the guerrilla attacks as a result of the restraining act by the Frontline Presidents who were still hoping to persuade Vorster, the South African President, to put pressure on Smith to get back to the negotiation table.[23] At this time ZANU was involved in its own internal convolutions, which will be treated in detail later in the chapter.

Before the military slow-down on the part of ZIPRA in 1975/76 years, ZIPRA had transformed itself into a national movement of liberation, and had moved beyond only engaging in a preparatory process of war, and demands for equal representation towards a nascent concern for mass involvement in fighting the war so that it would become impossible for the RSFs to move around the country with impunity, and even for the government to organize people in administratable units.

The war for political allegiance intensified, especially in rural areas that after 1970 became the locus of the armed struggle. At this point the many rural people, who prior to this time questioned the use of armed struggle as a means of attaining majority rule, accepted it as an effective and legitimate means both for the attainment of broader transformational goals and gaining majority rule.[24] The *Ibandla leZintandane* (Church of Orphans) in most of the Matebeleland south and north provinces continued to present political free space where political sermons geared at making people aware of their socio-economic and political deprivations were presented. Also, the church was used for transmitting messages from ZAPU leadership.

To destabilize the movement of the Rhodesian troops in the rural areas, ZIPRA and its locally trained sympathizers laid mines and ambushed troops. To destroy governmental administrative structures in the rural areas ZAPU politically organized the rural population to refuse to co-operate with the former. The drama was most visible in the rural people's resistance against the formation of Councils, the smallest governmental administrative unit of the rural blacks.

The year 1971 witnessed the peak era for the formation of African Councils. In that year, forty Councils were formed. Excited by this mushrooming of councils, the Secretary for Internal Affairs confidently predicted similar growth for 1972. This was not to be, and to the chagrin of the Secretary, the rural population started to lose interest in councils, even those who had requested them the previous year. As a result of this lack of interest, only twelve councils were established the whole of 1972. The decrease was largely due to the increase in ZIPRA and ZANLA insurgency, but for the early part of that year, due to the activities of the ZIPRA forces and a corp of its party's political evangelists who

The Storm and Then Spears Turned into Plowshares

strongly preached against the formation of these councils. Some schools, clinics and mission stations in the rural areas were closed down as well. The process of closing down all these institutions would intensify as the years wore on.

ZAPU wanted to make the country ungovernable, and shutting down councils was one of the effective ways to do so. The *Ibandla leZintandane*, echoed the words of the ZAPU leadership for the reversal of the extension of regime administrative apparatus into the rural areas. The Smith regime responded by harassing church members, most of whom were ZAPU officers.

Simon Nkala, a church committee member who would become a councilor after the 1980 elections, related to the author how he and the other church members were harassed by the Smith's Special Branch subsequent to a church service at which the preacher Richard Sibanda, a ZAPU chairperson, who too became a councilor after independence, presented a revolution-inspiring message concluding with the words, "a people has a divine right and a duty to fight back if the system is unjust."[25] He informed:

It was on the first Sunday of the month of August, 1972 when immediately after church service we were harassed by the Special Branch, all of our church leaders were taken separately for questioning by two Special Branch guys, while the remaining three remained searching all the church members, even children, taking down their particulars and some had their Bibles confiscated especially if they had some written notes on them. Teenagers got harassed more, as they were thought to be potential guerrillas.[26]

Nkala made it clear that in addition to providing inspiration to the black population to support the armed struggle in whatever way possible, the church also provided a rationale for doing so. He recalled a sermon that was preached on a Sunday, April 1972, by a visiting preacher Mtshumayeli Sibanda, a firebrand ZAPU organizer who served ZAPU at branch, district and Provincial levels at different times. The title of the sermon was "You Reap What you Sow." Applying his message for the day to the political situation, according to Nkala, Sibanda said:

The Smith regime has sown violence, a violence of a greater proportion. Consequently, we can no longer satisfy ourselves with blowing up pylons if we are to bring sense to this government. Our forces of justice will have to match this violence with the might of force proportionate to the one it uses against our people at the least.[27]

Such a statement might be disquieting to some members of the Brethren in Christ Church, a pacifist denomination, and the church to which Mtshumayeli Sibanda and most of the *Emhlanhlandlela Ibandla Le Zintandane* belonged. They would see Sibanda's advocacy for violence as inconsistent with church doctrine. However, one would contend, as members of the church of orphans did, that Sibanda, and the rest of the church membership that supported ZAPU and its path of revolutionary violence, was acting in a morally acceptable manner, especially in light of the absence of any peaceful means of ushering in a dispensation of justice and peace. As the conservative philosopher Van den Haag well put it:

> [D]isobedience to law, ranging from civil disobedience to revolution is justified only if citizens have no legitimate ways to freely elect or oust the government by majority vote, i.e., to participate in the law-making process.... Those who are hopelessly and permanently bereft of the right to persuade and vote are under no moral obligation to obey laws imposed on them.[28]

What emerges from Nkala's account of the war is an obvious conclusion that state violence was the main source of blacks' hostile attitudes against the government of the day, and also the depth of anger against the Smith regime and those who supported it, the army, police and ruling class. To these Christian men and women, the war was just because it was against an unjust system and there was a divine duty to fight it. The clarion to bear arms against the regime was also a matter of complying with the orders of the top leadership, which called for an armed struggle as a matter of necessity.

ZAPU, mostly using its guerrillas and the *Ibandla leZintandane*, effectively urged the rural population not to pay fees for cattle dipping, education, staff salaries or any rates related to the promotion of councils. Guerrillas and *imijibha* also helped in closing down already existing councils by burning such symbols of these councils as beer halls, taking money from them to support the struggle, or sometimes killing the council staff.

In addition to attacking councils, ZAPU forces attacked white farmers to whom the regime gave financial inducement in order to use their farms to establish area defense systems. Consequently, ZAPU's policy was that white farmers were legitimate targets for its forces. For their part, rural blacks living close to the farms engaged in such tactics as fence-cutting and poaching-grazing tactics. The kind of tactics which James Scott called the weapons of the weak.[29]

As has been observed elsewhere in this chapter up until 1974/75, ZIPRA dominated the prosecution of the nationalist war against the Smith Regime. ZANLA forces were still very small in number and poorly armed.[30] By 1971 the number of ZANLA forces jumped from about a hundred cadres to about two hundred.[31] The windfall for ZANU came as a result of the leadership crisis in the external wing of ZAPU. Most of the defectors from ZAPU to ZANU involved cadres at the Morogoro Camp in Tanzania, and it robbed ZAPU of such seasoned and well trained soldiers as David Todlana, who had received advanced training in both Russia and Bulgaria, and was later Head of Wampoa College, a Marxist Leninist school which trained trainers and was started by ZIPA, Rex Nhongo, who would become commander of the ZANLA forces after the death of Togongara, Robson Manyika, the deputy commander of the ZIPRA forces, and Thomas Nhari, who too had received some training in Russia.[32]

Despite the windfall, however, ZANLA continued to be essentially inactive up to late December of 1972. Much of ZANLA's inactivity was due to its lack of recruits, a problem that dogged it until the late 1970s.[33]

Despite this significant loss in terms of talent, ZAPU forces still remained superior in number, better armed, more disciplined and carried out most of the ferocious attacks on the regime forces. By 1977 ZAPU had infiltrated about 2,000 of its veteran soldiers[34] and ZANU still had recruiting problems, and moreover it had lost some of its cadres as a result of its own internal convolutions. Up to the formation of ZIPA, ZANLA still had under a hundred men in arms operating in the Northeast part of the country[35] where it was largely based. ZANLA's only major accomplishment at this stage was its December 23, 1972 Altina farm attack on a farmer and his family. This attack was of great importance, not because of its military accomplishment, but because it signified a sharp shift in the war strategy of the early 1970s from the attack on soldiers to the attack on white civilians (soft targets). Since 1966, ZIPRA had targeted soldiers and policemen, the armed Smith personnel.

Although it was the party's policy to target farmers as well, they rarely attacked soft targets at this point in time, and even if they were to do so, it is likely the Regime would have kept mum over it for it did not want to credit ZIPRA with any success at all. ZANLA however in contrast, repeatedly attacked farmers from that time on, and made no secret of it.

Fearful of the opening of a second front, the Rhodesian regime concentrated its soldiers in the northeastern part of the country the area that ZAPU had explored for the short time it was working with FRELIMO. Stealing a page from the neighboring Portuguese regime, Smith gathered the local population into *aldeamentos*, what came to be known in Rhodesia as protected villages. The idea was to isolate guerrillas from the local population. Using the powers introduced on May 18, 1973, the government moved Africans in the Northeast part of Rhodesia into protected villages.

By late December 1973, 8000 Africans had been forcibly removed from their homes near the border with Mozambique into holding camps near Gutsa before they were settled in three PVs. On April 5, 1974 the government accused 200 blacks in Madziwa Tribal Trust Lands south of Mt. Darwin of collaborating with 'terrorists' and as a punishment, moved them to Bietbridge[36] in Matebeleland, an area dominated by Venda/Sotho people. The movement of this population that mostly supported ZANU would be to the advantage of the ZANLA forces towards the end of the war when they infiltrated Matebeleland by providing them with the necessary shelter and succor.

Because of a lot of similarities between the Mozambican and Rhodesian experiences, and the fact that the latter's programs were directly inspired by the former's, its discussion should help in the understanding of how PVs worked for the Rhodesians. As has already been pointed out the PVs' strategy was once vigorously implemented by the colonial Mozambican regime, first, in the Tete region towards the end of the 1960s and by 1973 throughout the country. The colonial Mozambican regime moved the locals in the Tete region into "aldeamentos" as part of its strategy of fighting FRELIMO, which was increasingly gaining military ascendancy in the region. Their villages were burnt and they were taken into fortified camps which the regime called "goat pens." Here, blacks were monitored by militia forces, and entry and exit were strictly supervised.

Again the intention was clear: to take away as it were the "water" (local black population) in which the "fish" (guerrillas) swam so as to drive the latter off their sources of support and succor. The scheme was so massive so that by end of 1970 there were 45 *aldeamentos* in Tete with 26,059 people, and space was ready for every African in the Tete region by end of 1973. By September of 1973, according to an interview given by the Governor General, one million people throughout Mozambique were already in *aldeamentos*.[37]

Unfortunately for the government when it moved the locals, FRELIMO guerrillas were already part of the community so that they too were included among those rounded up into PVs. Thus the guerrillas used these PVs as safe havens. During the late 1971-1973, those moved into these PVs included ZANLA members since they too already had integrated into the civilian population.

The removals of the black population in Mozambique by the white regime affected Rhodesia in two major ways: one, there was an influx of refuges who crossed into the country to avoid the loss of their stock and some of their property.[38] Second, ZANLA guerrillas easily slipped across the border among bona fide refugees from Mozambique and settled among their own communities, especially in the northeast of the country. This meant that by the time Rhodesia created its own protected villages, among the people who were moved into these camps were ZANLA, and sometimes ZANLA/FRELIMO guerrillas themselves, and therein laid the ineffectiveness of such *aldeamentos* in Rhodesia.

Like his counterpart the Mozambican leader, Smith's plan was to flush out the ZANLA/FRELIMO insurgents before they found roots among their people. FRELIMO gave the necessary logistical support to ZANLA, the same kind of support that it had previously offered to ZIPRA. FRELIMO by this time was already scoring success against the Portuguese south of the Zambezi, so that the area was, by and large, a liberated zone. This made it possible for ZANLA to strike and slip across the border undetected.

In March 1978, after the signing of the internal agreement, PVs were closed down.[39] The reasons of their closure were the same as those that caused the failure of "aldeamentos" in Mozambique which were, in addition to opening PVs in the most guerrilla subverted areas, lack of financial, material and human resources to implement the program. Also the place was poorly policed.[40] Above all, the people who were put in these PVs detested them and fought against their existence. Because of such revulsion against the PVs some people left them. The Mrewa, Mtoko and Mudzi district PVs suffered such a fate in December 1978 when all villagers left and settled elsewhere.

The Storm and Then Spears Turned into Plowshares

Clearly, Rhodesians, though some of them had fought in Malaya where the British successfully used PVs as part of their strategy to fight the Chinese, were not ready to emulate the Malayan experience. Instead they chose the Mozambican one that naturally led to a debacle. Although the Rhodesians thought of themselves as using the Malayan experience of PVs, what they totally ignored was that in Malaya the majority Malayan liked and supported PVs in which they were put because they protected them against a Chinese minority. This could not be said of both Rhodesia and Mozambique.

Another reason Rhodesians fought the ZANLA/FRELIMO insurgents was because they did not want FRELIMO opening forward bases on its own soil. As guerrilla war activities increased in vicinity of the Bindura area, Rhodesia put in more and more of its soldiers. In 1973, a military campaign, code-named Operation Hurricane futilely tried to operate into Mozambique. FRELIMO frustrated the Rhodesians by laying land mines and effectively ambushing them. As a matter of fact, FRELIMO had been operating in the north-east part of Rhodesia before 1970, and it was only in August of 1971 that the RSF officials reported their first contact with them, and in November 1979 the RSFs officials reported intercepting a column of local porters helping with the transporting of weapons,[41] an indication of how well integrated into the society FRELIMO already was by this time. Clearly, ZANLA benefited a lot from their co-operations with FRELIMO since the latter was very familiar with the terrain.

Three crucial events that had a direct impact on the prosecution of the war in Zimbabwe occurred during the following year, 1974: First, the Selous Scouts were formed; Second, Mozambique fell to FRELIMO and a second front, manned by ZANLA/FRELIMO was formed;Third, a cease-fire was declared and followed by an ominous lull. The Selous Scouts, a unit that was named after the nineteenth century settlers' hero-scout and hunter, had as its main purpose penetrating and operating as insurgents behind the lines. The security forces would masquerade as insurgents to the rural population for the purpose of gathering intelligence on the nationalist guerrillas, and once they located them, they talked-in a fireforce on them by radio while maintaining their cover with the locals. The group consisted of no more than six people and was a mixed group of blacks and whites. To hide their identity, white soldiers blackened themselves with "Black-Is-Beautiful" camouflage cream. As the year wore on, the unit incorporated `turned' guerrillas.

Initially, the plan worked well, and the Rhodesian forces killed many insurgents with the help of the Selous scouts. However, more times than not, white soldiers could not successfully hide their identity. Besides color blacks could tell whites from their own kind by subtle differences in the size of lips, nose-shape, by movement, shoulder-shape and other mannerisms. Blacks in the Rhodesian army, however, did so well in the deception, and hence the unit became increasingly black in its constitution. The scouts became the most feared unit of the Rhodesian military by rural people. They were especially successful operating against ZANLA in Bindura and the Ngarwe and Pungwe areas in 1974 as assassins, murdering leading black leaders in and outside of Rhodesia throughout the war period.

As ZANLA/FRELIMO and some ZIPRA forces ambushed RSFs in the part of the country, ZIPRA continued to harass the enemy forces in the northwestern part of the country. On January 8, 1973, in the north west part of Rhodesia, a South African military truck detonated a ZIPRA land mine near Victoria Falls and resulted in the death of two South African soldiers. Of those injured, three were Rhodesians and the rest were South Africans. Four days earlier, an army truck had detonated a land mine near Centenary in the northeastern part of the country, and its occupants were injured.[42] Thus, it was because of ZIPRA infiltrations from Zambia resulting in the loss of lives on the part of Rhodesian soldiers, that Smith closed the border with Zambia, and demanded that Kaunda stop supporting guerrillas. The closing of the border, however, did not stop ZIPRA incursions on the regime forces.

Despite the concerted efforts of Rhodesians and Portuguese to prevent Mozambique from falling into the hands of FRELIMO, it finally did in 1974. Naturally, after the fall of Portuguese rule in Mozambique, a second front was opened, necessitating the expansion of a number of Rhodesian military units. This also meant that the regime troops were now thinly spread. Efforts to cut-off the rural population by putting them in Protected Villages were not working.

Immediately upon taking power, the FRELIMO government threatened to reduce half of Rhodesia's supply lines to the sea. Despite its claim that its forces and that of Rhodesia were winning the war against guerrillas, South Africa realized the implications and forced Smith into a detente with the black forces. The odds were clearly against Rhodesia now, with ZANLA having the whole of Mozambique as a safe haven in the east and ZIPRA attacking from the North.

By early 1974 ZAPU had established a headquarters in Francistown, Botswana; by March 1974, the Rhodesians knew of it. The purposes of the Francistown office were, among other things, to direct the infiltration into Rhodesia of ZIPRA's intelligence agents, to serve as a recruiting agency and organizational center for ZIPRA, and to serve as a routing center for guerrilla arms and supplies. Rhodesia, which was already engaged in desperate efforts to stop the ZANLA forces from opening a second front were suddenly confronted with another possibility of a third front, this time in South-western Rhodesia. Rhodesia also feared the threat posed by such a presence to its critical lines of communication with South Africa, and it immediately deployed the Selous Scouts to try and neutralize the situation. This threat and the threat posed by the independence of Mozambique pushed South Africa to seek for a political solution to the problem of Rhodesia by forcing Smith to a settlement. The agreement to negotiate led to a cease-fire. Although all parties did not adhere to the cease-fire conditions, fighting scaled down while the politicians sat around the negotiation tables.

The Storm and Then Spears Turned into Plowshares

6.3 Ominous Lull, 1974-76

The ominous lull provided by the cease-fire gave ZIPRA an opportunity to regroup, resupply, recruit and reorganize. It was during this period that ZIPRA reopened[43] a forward office in Francistown, and from it recruited many people for the struggle in South-western Rhodesia. Schools closed down, and hundreds of students left via Botswana to join the struggle. This was ZAPU's biggest trainee campaign that reached its apex in January 1977 when students from Manama Mission left en mass to join the struggle via Botswana. In fact, 1976 and early 1977 saw an exodus of mature students from Mtshabezi Mission Teachers Training College had moved earlier to United College in Bulawayo, Matopo, Wanezi, all Brethren in Christ schools, and Mpadeni, Cyrene, and Tengwane. This meant more literate guerrillas who could easily read directions and maps, all essentials of good soldiering.

ZAPU also used this lull to train its fighters in conventional warfare. These cadres were trained in Angola, Mulungushi (Zambia) and Ethopia. Their basic training included field craft, fitness, self-defense, communications, security, close quarter combat, weapon handling, raids, ambushes, mine warfare, reconnaissance, and obstacle crossing. Political education was given to all including non-officers. The training for officers, and other specialized units, involved more training in other areas, some of which were as Frontier Commanders (Border Guards) at battalion level, and included individual, section, platoon, company, battalion up to Brigade operations. Also provided were air defence, signals, chemical warfare, artillery, security, joint-operations, interrogation, border patrol, political economy, local administration and airport security training.[44]

For the first time it put about a thousand women in training. These women were based at the Mkushi Camp and most of them received their training from their own comrades who themselves had received training at Angola under Cubans. By September 1978 there was a standing regular army of 1,000 women at the Mkushi Camp, with a 1,000 more in training.

The training for women was very rigorous, and extensive. ZIPRA women:

Spent six months learning bayonet charging, combat tactics, logistics, foot and rifle drill, camouflage and concealment in the bush, weapon handling and firing a variety of rifles and rocket launchers, ambushing and skirmishing, guerrilla warfare administration and urban warfare.[45]

Commenting on the resistance the elite Rhodesian forces received from the women camp at Mkushi Barbara wrote:

Those [women] who fought back were very aggressive, far more so than the women at Chimoio. There was no question in anyone's mind that they knew how to use their rifles.[46]

In all, women constituted ten percent of the ZIPRA forces. They formed a unit of their own, the ZIPRA Women's Brigade. This was a self-contained, conventionally trained infantry brigade with its own female commanders, communications, engineers and all other support services basic to an infantry brigade.

The time was also used to bring in weapons and to set-up a security system around camps where the Party had sensitive information. Most of the weapons at this time came via Angola. Because Zambia preferred to keep ZIPRA's heavy weapons in the national stores, a serious handicap in ZIPRA's self-defense from Rhodesian Air strikes, ZAPU smuggled some of its heavy weapons from Angola to its various camps in Zambia, especially those with troops, unbeknown to the latter. The stored weapons could only be issued on requisition. Because there was a general lull from war Zambia' vigilance was lax so that camps were basically not under constant monitoring, especially at night.

Also ZAPU utilized this lull to try and forge unity with ZANLA so that together they could carry out joint-military campaigns against the Smith regime. This was the time when ZIPA was formed.

6.4 Come Let Us Dance Together: Another Military Alliance Between ZAPU and ZANU, at the Invitation of ZANU,[47] 1975-1976

There is a sense in which it can be said that the birth of ZIPA was a product of a confluence of interests of all the parties involved in its creation, but less so, of the parties that constituted it. Despite the fact that the Frontline presidents, particularly Nyerere and Machel, knew very well of the intransigence of the Rhodesian regime, they were confident the end of the war was at hand. Other events in and around the country warranted such optimism. Rhodesian troops were scrabbling for personnel as they were thinly spread across the country. The opening of another front in Botswana early in 1974 by the ZIPRA forces further added to the desperation of the Rhodesians.

The northeastern part of Rhodesia had once again become a hot spot, with Rhodesians receiving a beating from both ZANLA/FRELIMO and ZIPRA. This then meant guerrillas now had three fronts from which to prosecute the war, and the south-eastern and south-western ones posed greater concern and danger as they were close to strategic commercial and communication lines between Rhodesia and South Africa.

Smith's reaction to the events showed how seriously he regarded them. Police and army leaves were canceled over Christmas and territorial troops and police reserves were called up. National service was extended from nine to twelve months. In early January 1973, he closed the Zambian border, and in the following weeks announced a series of draconian measures against any African aiding the guerrillas. Yet the guerrilla campaign continued and intensified, with a clear deterioration in white security position in areas as close as thirty miles from Salisbury. The costs thus imposed on the regime must greatly encourage African guerrilla leaders about the future.

The Storm and Then Spears Turned into Plowshares

> *To support the Rhodesian Army of 4,000 men (plus a new battalion to be formed), an estimated 10,000 militia, 8,000 police and 35,000 police reservists, the fiscal year 1975-76 budget called for a $95 million expenditure, an increase of almost 25 percent, with an additional $21 million for barracks and road building programs along the border. And, in addition to these fiscal costs, military service requirements have been strengthened.*[48]

To the Front Line Presidents this clearly meant that a hand-over of political power to the black nationalists was imminent, just a question of time. Their hope was further raised by South Africa's concerted effort in helping pressure Rhodesia to work for a negotiated political settlement. As the strongest and leading supporter of the Smith regime, the FLP figured, with South Africa now pushing for an end to war, peace was surely about to arrive. South Africa had already proven its good intentions to them by securing the release of the black nationalists whom they supported.

It was this hope of a dispensation of freedom and majority rule which got the FLPs, particularly Nyerere and Machel, thinking about heading-off potential military problems once independence was secured. Their main concern became to avert possible military conflicts between the ZIPRA and ZANLA forces, and the way they were going to do it was by uniting these two forces before independence. The question of political leadership was going to be resolved after independence. The FLPs were quite cognizant of the fact that the problem of political unity was a particularly vexing one, as Kaunda, Nyerere, and Khama, in conjunction with the OAU had failed to solve it immediately after the split between ZAPU and ZANU in the early 1960s.

At this point they did not entertain any hope of seeing these two parties coming together before independence. Nkomo would express a similar sentiment on December 6, 1976 when asked by the *Rhodesia Herald* why he was in the Patriotic Front with Mugabe. For Nkomo the *raison d'etre* for joining the PF was to avoid "fighting between ZAPU and ZANU."[49]

Nkomo stated:

> *We don't need fighting between ZAPU and ZANU. We don't want our people to wage war after finally getting the freedom they have strived to achieve for years.*[50]

Sensing the exigent need to unite, at least the fighting forces in order to avert potential post-independent civil war, the FLPs brought pressure to bear on the two parties to form a joint fighting force. Thus the initiative to have a nationalist united force came from the Front Line Presidents (FLPs) who in turn worked through Col. Hashim Mbita, the head of the OAU Liberation Committee.

It must also be pointed out that, paradoxically, the FLP sponsored the notion of a unified force because it had given up on the prospect of peaceful negotiations, especially after the collapse of détente, and South Africa's attempts to dethrone the Angolan government of Agastino Neto. They concluded that the only way majority rule could be achieved was through the use of force. Nyerere represented their collective sentiments when he said:

> *We are forced back to the alternative strategy outlined in the Lusaka Declaration of 1969-support for non-peaceful methods of struggle. Unfortunately, but inevitably, the armed struggle in Rhodesia will have to be resumed and intensified until conditions are ripe for realistic negotiations.*[51]

Nyerere and Machel approached ZANU first with the idea of unity. Although ZANU was always suspicious of ZAPU's intentions whenever the subject of unity was brought up, this time there was reason to believe it was more inclined to accept a unity arrangement. ZANU was going through its own internal convolutions, a situation similar to one with which ZAPU was confronted between 1969-71.

The first major incident to spark internecine conflicts and killings within ZANU was the murder of its Chairman, Herbert Chitepo, on March 18, 1975 in Lusaka. Soon thereafter the major question became, who might have killed Chitepo. Several speculations were advanced, from Smith agents to agents within the party itself inspired by tribal interests. The speculation ultimately accepted interpreted this murder as a result of a power struggle among the Shona subtribes within ZANU. The International Commission set up by Zambia arrived at a similar conclusion.

Consequently, the murder resulted in numerous arrests of ZANU supporters. For instance, on the day of his burial fifty people were arrested and all the ZANU bases in Zambia were cordoned off by the Zambian security.

> *[In all] 1,550 [ZANU people] were detained for a time after Herbert Chitepo's death....Virtually the entire ZANU High Command was in prison, facing charges of murdering Chitepo and 59 guerrilla cadres.*[52]

The second incident involved Thomas Nhari's,[53] mutiny within ZANU in November-December 1974. The rebellion pitted some ZANU field commanders against some top ranking ZANU military brass. The mutineers complained about their shortages of supplies in their fight against the regime in the Northeastern part of Rhodesia. In fact, the mutiny started in a camp inside Rhodesia and spread back to involve the ZANU leadership in Lusaka, Zambia.

Most of the field commanders had been fighting in that area since December 23, 1972. When they concluded they were not being heard and that no one in the ZANU hierarchy was willing to respond to the problems they were facing at the Mozambican Front, the Nhari group kidnapped nineteen ZANU members in Lusaka, and demanded to talk to the *DARE,* the civilian command. Instead, ZANU sent in a hot-extraction team, rescued the hostages, tried and executed the kidnappers.

The net result of these two dramatic convolutions within ZANU in the late 1974 and early 1975 was that it undermined the military progress it had made since December 23, 1972. Because of their weakened position any talk of unity with other comrades-in-arms should have been appealing, at least in hopes that

The Storm and Then Spears Turned into Plowshares

it would have helped them mend their internecine quarrels. After all ZAPU had no problems with modern weaponry, and their execution of the war was more professional and disciplined. At least Thomas Nhari, the leader of the rebellious hard core and battle tested cadres felt that way, although some people felt he was in the employ of the Smith regime.

For ZAPU, the idea of having a base in the northeast part of the country where they would not have to contend with the formidable Zambezi River should have been appealing. In addition, they too hoped a united military unit would go a long way in resolving old divisions between the two fighting forces.

Thus, the lunching of ZIPA was done when most of the ZANU leadership was in prison. ZIPA therefore should be understood against this backdrop. ZIPA was formally constituted in November 1975. This was after Nkomo had authorized J.Z. Moyo to engage ZANU people in unity talks, and after ZANU intermediaries, one of which was Simon Muzenda, had consulted and secured agreement from their own men including Josiah Tongogara, the Commander-In-Chief of the ZANLA forces, who then was in prison waiting for his trial for Chitepo's assassination. The creation of ZIPA should also be seen as an attempt to forming a unified command for the purpose of the prosecution of the armed struggle.

Accordingly, a Joint High Command was formed to direct the activities of this united force. According to Dumiso Dabengwa, a participant in the shaping of this agreement from ZAPU's side, these were the elements of the agreement:

We finally agreed that ZIPRA and ZANLA would be brought together to form ZIPA...which was to be led by ZANLA's Rex Nhongo as Commander with Nikita Mangena as Deputy Commander and Jevan Maseko as Chief of Staff. ZIPA was to operate from Mozambique. It was agreed that ZIPRA elements in Zambia would operate under the auspices of ZIPA....[54]

The final composition of the Joint High Command had nine representatives from each side and it appeared as follows:

Army Commander	Rex Nhongo (ZANLA)
Deputy	John Dube (ZIPRA)
Political Commissar	Alfred Mangena (ZIPRA)
Deputy	Dzinashe Machingura (ZANLA)
Director of Operations	Elias Hondo (ZANLA)
Deputy	Enoch Tsangano (ZIPRA)
Security & Intelligence	Gordon Munyanyi (ZIPRA)
Deputy	James Nyikadzinashe (ZANLA)
Director of Political Affairs	Webster Gwauya (ZANlA)
Deputy	David Moyana (ZIPRA)
Director of Logistics & Supplies	Report Mpoko (ZIPRA)
Deputy	Edmund Kagure (ZANLA)

Director of Training & Personnel	Ambrose Mutinhiri (ZIPRA)
Deputy	Parker Chipoera (ZANLA)
Director of Medical Services	Augustus Mudzingwa (ZIPRA)
Deputy	Tendai Pfepferere (ZANLA)
Director of Finance	Saul Sadza (ZANLA)
Deputy	Dingani Mlilo (ZIPRA)[55]

By the end of December of that year, ZIPA had infiltrated Rhodesia through Gaza and Tete and had disrupted communication links with South Africa. Each area was under a ZIPRA and ZANLA Commander, and they were instructed to report to Machel every two weeks.[56] Clearly, FLPs wanted to be seen as the political leaders of ZIPA. This was their creation, and they were going to protect and guide it. With these attacks, war had restarted after the slackening in tempo in 1974 and most of 1975 caused by the ongoing talks and convolutions within the ZANU party.

However, the most glaring problem with the unity was that it favored ZANU. For one, its leader was ZANU and the FLP leader who directed and hosted it was a strong supporter of ZANU. ZAPU was reluctant to be part of the unity agreement, and was apparently pressured to accept it for the reason of "persuad[ing] OAU Liberation Committee to release weaponry that it was withholding pending the unification of the liberation movement."[57] To Nkomo, ZIPA was a ZANU creation, and this can be hardly disputed given its structure and control.

There are, however, some authors such as David Moore[58] who saw ZIPA as truly independent of both parties. Such a view is as generous as it is ambitious. Undoubtedly, some ZIPA cadres tried to act independent of either parties,[59] but when they openly defied Mugabe,[60] (after the release of ZANLA's traditional military leaders) he, aided by Machel, ended ZIPA's life, a clear proof that Mugabe and Machel directed it. Thus, ZIPA was stillborn.

Contrasting this pessimistic view was that of the OAU that viewed ZIPA as a third force and lauded it as the military liberator of Zimbabwe. Nyerere who called it "a new force that has emerged in Zimbabwe" shared this perception.[61]

The jubilation over the unity was short-lived, as ZAPU refused to dance anymore and began threatening to walk out of the ball room as early as December. The major bone of contention was an ideological one regarding training and strategy. Dabengwa succinctly captured ZAPU's complaint about the unity when he wrote:

> *ZIPA developed problems soon after its formation largely because of disagreements over strategy. ZIPRA command elements found that ZIPA strategy to be completely disjointed. For example, disciplined ZIPRA commanders were shocked to find ZANLA deployed people inside Rhodesia who were not well trained or even completely untrained. Some recruits were trained using sticks and were only given a gun on the day of crossing into Rhodesia.*

The Storm and Then Spears Turned into Plowshares

> *Most of these people were literally butchered by the enemy ...As a result ZIPA began to collapse in 1975 and ZIPRA elements were victimized, some of whom were... shot in cold blood by ZANLA forces in Mozambique and Tanzania. Others who managed to escape returned to their original bases in Zambia.*[62]

The total collapse of ZIPA as a unity between ZIPRA and ZANLA would not occur until towards the end of June when violence broke out between the two forces in Morogoro and Mgagao camps in Tanzania. Tensions between the two forces making up ZIPA arose because of a number of reasons ranging from arguments over cooking duties to the use of Chinese in camps as trainers. The increasing role of Chinese as trainers was not so much of a problem to the ZIPRA cadre though. The problem was the kind of training ZANLA underwent. In fact this seems to be one of the main sources of dissatisfaction among the ZIPRA cadres who had joined ZIPA. They complained that most of their ZANLA counterparts were poorly trained and others had no training at all. This then meant that the ZIPRA group did a lot of the fighting, and had to contend with numerous deaths, mainly from the ZANLA side.

Led by one of its commanders, Alfred Nikita Mangena, ZIPRA finally pulled out alleging that ZANU was intent on eliminating it.[63] This marked the end of any attempts to unify the two nationalist military groups until after independence. ZIPRA would move on to plot its own strategy of prosecuting the war of liberation.

Some scholars have tried to blame the collapse of ZIPA on Nkomo. One of these scholars is Andre Astrow who asserts that divisions between ZIPRA and ZANLA forces within ZIPA were, in his words, "exacerbated by Nkomo's attempts to arrive at a settlement with Smith."[64] For some reason Astrow totally disregards the obvious role played by Machel, Mugabe and his ZANU colleagues, in breaking-up ZIPA. After all, it was ZANLA'a forces that refused to allow Nkomo to visit ZIPA camps in Mozambique. Undoubtedly, the blame on Nkomo for the demise of the unity of the ZIPRA and ZANLA forces is totally misplaced.

However, there is evidence pointing to the fact that Nkomo was suspicious of the goals of ZIPA that he saw as a creation of ZANU[65] aided by the two FLPs, Machel and Nyerere, ZANU's patrons. In that direction, there was no political will or desire on the part of ZAPU to participate in the experiment.

Thus, ZIPA failed largely because the two parties were not united politically. Sensing this weakness the Frontline states then pushed the two parties into a political marriage of convenience under the umbrella name the Patriotic Front (PF). Despite its being primarily a marriage of convenience, the PF was effective in peace negotiations. ZAPU at this point had no alternative but to work on a new strategy by which to prosecute the armed struggle.

6.5 THE SHARPENING OF SPEARS: ZAPU'S NEW WAR STRATEGY, 1976-1979

Once ZIPRA withdrew from ZIPA, towards the end of 1976, the external wing of ZAPU under the leadership of its Vice President, Jason Moyo decided to go back to the drawing board and map out a new military strategy. By 1976 ZAPU had been at war for more than ten years, and its strategy had evolved from the use of homemade bombs and missiles (stones and sticks) to sabotage to the use of land mines. ZIPRA forces had become specialists in the practice of boosting or laying one mine on top of another to enhance/double the blast effect.[66] ZIPRA's favorite land mine of choice during the early 1970s was the Soviet TM-47. What was praiseworthy of ZIPRA's use of land mines was that they gathered sufficient intelligence on the ground reconnaissance before they would lay mines. The reason for carrying out this ground reconnaissance was so that they could avoid killing civilians, which they managed to do most of the time. While the number of ambushes and land mine incidents were fewer after the end of December 1972, and their scale of operation smaller than that of its counterpart, ZANLA, ZIPRA guerrillas were better trained and armed and were able to start well-planned and well-led operations.[67] Their biggest asset was discipline and control both of which are indispensable qualities for cohesion in the army.

With all their increased sophistication and professionalism in the use of weapons, ZIPRA had a great liability in the operational theater in that they could not bring in heavy weapons to defend themselves from RSF aircraft. ZAPU's Consultation conference of 1976 sought to deal with these military liabilities among other things. For one to fully understand changes happening within the externally led ZAPU during this era, it is vital that they comprehend its organization (see figure 6.1.)

At the Consultation Conference, Jason Moyo provided a discussion paper that he had helped craft, and that working document would be his last major contribution to the struggle before his assassination by a parcel bomb on January 22, 1977. This was Moyo's strategy document that would shape ZAPU's war strategy to the end of the armed conflict. The title of Moyo's document was "Our Path to Liberation."[68]

Right from the outset the document raised two crucial issues. One, Moyo reflected and continued the debate on ZAPU's military strategy. Second, the document raised a very taxing question about the precise goal of the nationalist movement. It then went on to assert that the negotiations that were going on at the time of its writing were aimed at:

> *[Installing] an interim African government acting as caretakers for the imperialist interests [in an endeavor to] prevent genuine independence and transfer of power to the people.*[69]

The Storm and Then Spears Turned into Plowshares

Figure 6.1: Military Intelligence Structure from 1970 and On.

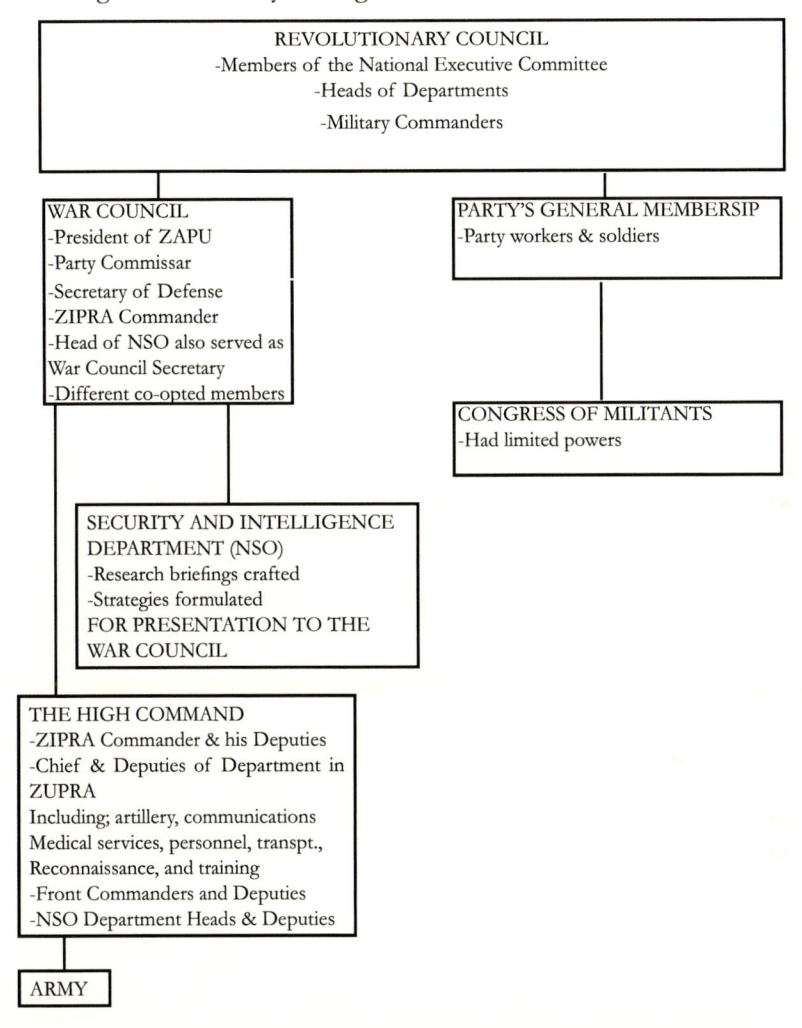

```
REVOLUTIONARY COUNCIL
-Members of the National Executive Committee
-Heads of Departments
-Military Commanders
```

```
WAR COUNCIL
-President of ZAPU
-Party Commissar
-Secretary of Defense
-ZIPRA Commander
-Head of NSO also served as
War Council Secretary
-Different co-opted members
```

```
PARTY'S GENERAL MEMBERSIP
-Party workers & soldiers
```

```
CONGRESS OF MILITANTS
-Had limited powers
```

```
SECURITY AND INTELLIGENCE
DEPARTMENT (NSO)
-Research briefings crafted
-Strategies formulated
FOR PRESENTATION TO THE
WAR COUNCIL
```

```
THE HIGH COMMAND
-ZIPRA Commander & his Deputies
-Chief & Deputies of Department in
ZUPRA
Including; artillery, communications
Medical services, personnel, transpt.,
Reconnaissance, and training
-Front Commanders and Deputies
-NSO Department Heads & Deputies
```

```
ARMY
```

The Revolutionary Council functioned as de fecto National Exeutive Council, and the Congress for Militants as an ad hoc Party Congress. The members of the Council consisted of Joshua Nkomo, President of ZAPU, Samuel Munodawafa, Party Commissar, Lookout Masuku, ZIPRA Commander, Dumiso Dabengwa, Head of NSO & War Council secretary. The co-opted members were mostly other senior commanders who were asked to testify on one of the war.

RESOURCE: *Drawn from various documents and interviews with Nkomo, Edward Ndlovu, and other ZAPU commanders.*

To starve off these insidious machinations on the part of the imperialists, Moyo argued, ZAPU's strategy should be aimed at defeating this attempt to forestall "genuine independence." Moyo wrote:

> *The only way to ensure the independence of our country is to conquer state power...The objective is power to the people. This objective cannot be realized unless the liberation movement of Zimbabwe seizes state power.*[70]

With these preliminary cursory remarks, Moyo was ready to introduce a new course and direction of the war based on a new strategy. Evidently, at this point he was convinced that guerrilla warfare alone could not secure independence. Moyo then posited two strategic goals whose attainment could make it possible for the liberation movement to capture power. The first goal was to join with all movements that shared a mutual goal to eliminate colonialism. This goal was later realized when ZAPU joined hands with ZANU under the Patriotic Front umbrella. The second goal that the document identified was the stepping-up of the armed struggle with the aim of "seizing state power."[71]

The call for the seizure of state power, clearly, as has already been pointed out, needed more than guerrilla power, it called for the formation of regular forces. Inspired by this document, ZAPU decided to train some of its recruits in conventional warfare. Thus, conventional military training soon started in 1978[72] together with the movement of heavy weapons into the operational theater. The decision to create a regular army by ZAPU was, indeed, a groundbreaking venture in the history of guerrilla liberation movements in Africa. As Jeremy Brickhill observed:

> *For the first time in Africa, a liberation movement began to prepare military forces that actually had the potential to achieve its stated political objective: to seize political power.*[73]

Undoubtedly, ZAPU's decision to create a regular force which was capable of seizing and defending political power was influenced by what had happened with other political movements that succeeded in seizing power, and subsequently had to fight to survive in power. To ZAPU at the time of the conference, Angola featured prominently as an example of the disadvantage of not having a conventionally trained force at the eve of independence. MPLA was very close to losing the political power it had seized from the Portuguese when the Cuban regulars came in to its rescue.[74] ZAPU wanted to avoid this problem.

Simultaneously with the training of the regular army, ZAPU trained non-military personnel to provide basic services after independence. Short-term they provided services to ZAPU members where they lived, and to people inside Rhodesia in the liberated areas. ZAPU trained its recruits as administrators, doctors, nurses, custom officers, teachers, and nurses, *inter alia*.

Thus, Moyo's working document anticipated an intensification of guerrilla warfare and this time around, the deployment of anti-aircraft weapons, artillery units, and eventually regular infantry to back-up the guerrillas. In a very significant way, Moyo's plan included essential ingredients of the Zero Hour Plan that will be explained later in this chapter.

6.6 THE TURNING-POINT CONFERENCE, LUSAKA 1978

Beginning from August 1976, ZAPU engaged in a massive recruitment program of guerrilla trainees, especially among the AmaKalanga, AbeVenda, AbeSotho, and AmaNdebele people in Matebeleland. The Francistown ZAPU office carried out most of the recruitment, only fifteen miles from the Rhodesia border with Botswana. The exodus of young people, especially of those in Secondary and Teachers' Training schools was so great that ZAPU's chartered plane to ferry the recruits to Zambia had to fly twice a day.

The Manama Mission incident was the most dramatized one in that the Rhodesian government alleged students were taken at gunpoint and force-marched to Botswana. On January 30, 1977, ZIPRA visited Manama, a Lutheran Evangelical Mission. After addressing students and staffers they led a group of about 500 mostly students to Botswana en route to Zambia. It was also alleged that ZIPRA took $13,000 from the mission station.

The Smith regime protested, asserting the Manama Mission residents were kidnapped. Botswana government retorted and said the students, who were then in its country, left volitionally to escape oppression.[75] United Nations jumped in and asked ZAPU to allow the students' parents to talk to their children before they were flown from Francistown to Zambia for training so they could make a determination if they had left volitionally. ZAPU promised to cooperate, and the Rhodesian government arranged for a group of 140 parents to travel by bus to Francistown to persuade their children to come back home.

The government had paid for parents' travel in a convoy flanked by the military, but only fifty-five students out of about 500 students went back, and these were mostly girls. This was a big morale-booster for ZAPU, more so because its war strategy after its 1976 Conference demanded more personnel not only for army training but civic one as well. Literate people made it easier for ZAPU to achieve two of its major goals: first, the training of at least a functionally literate army capable of operating sophisticated weapons and prosecuting a very complex psychological warfare, and second, preparing people for civic duties. As a matter of fact, ZAPU had a sizeable number of literate people, affording it a core of easily trainable personnel.

About forty-five percent of ZIPRA's recruits were functionally literate, and more than eleven percent had at least ten years of education. More over, ZAPU cadres were mature people as it forbade the training of recruits under the age of eighteen years.[76]

6.7 The Backdrop of ZAPU's 1978 Change in Strategy

The situation on the ground in Rhodesia had irrecoverably deteriorated. The March 3, 1978 internal agreement, which put Bishop Abel Muzorewa into power in 1979, had failed to stop the war, which had, instead, escalated. The emigration of the white population, particularly of professionals, was on the increase. In fact since 1974 Rhodesia had been experiencing an increase in emigration and a negative growth rate in the economy as a result of sanctions and guerrilla warfare. If it were not for the South African government, which, since 1976 was paying half of the country's defense bill,[77] Rhodesia's economy would have suffered a collapse by 1977.

From a military vantage point, the situation had broken down as well. Between 1977 and 1978 ZAPU infiltrated about 2,000 guerrillas, and widened its operational theater.[78] By the last quarter of 1978 ZIPRA had a heavy presence in almost all of the country's provinces in the exception of Manicaland where its presence was still very light. Andrew Nyathi, who was the deputy political commissar in the Northern Front from late 1978 to the time of the cease-fire, tells of part of the areas he and his comrades covered in the Northern Front in his book:

> *It was...towards the end of 1978. It must have been midnight by the time I paddled across the Zambezi in a small boat at a point called Risitu or BL2. Our unit was to fight in an operational area which extended from Binga on the Zambezi River right through to Mount Darwin in the north-east. It included Harare and Chinhoyi....*[79]

Dabengwa mentioned a more extensive area:

> *By the end of 1978, ZAPU guerrillas were operating in a wide arc, from Sipolilo and Urungwe in the north, through Gokwe and Silobela in the center of the country, to Lupane, Nkai and Tsholotsho in the west. ZAPU forces had also crossed the Salisbury-Bulawayo rail line, south of Shangani, and opened their Southern Front towards Shabani, and further south towards Gwanda and Beit Bridge.*[80]

Thus, ZIPRA and some of its elements in ZIPA were now infiltrating from several fronts and maintaining their presence in numerous locations nationwide (see figure 6.2.)

This is contrary to most published accounts on ZAPU that leave one with the impression that ZAPU forces had a hard time operating among the AmaShona. ZIPRA, actually, massively operated in dominantly Shona lands with the active cooperation and support of local people. Nyathi succinctly summarized the good relationship between his ZIPRA forces and the Shona speaking people when he observed after war:

> *People will sometimes say to me today: 'Tell me comrade, during the war you ZIPRA guerrillas were fighting hundreds of Kilometers away from Matebeleland, and yet this is the area where ZAPU has most of its support.*

The Storm and Then Spears Turned into Plowshares

Figure 6.2: Areas Infiltrated by ZIPRA and ZIPA by the End of 1978.

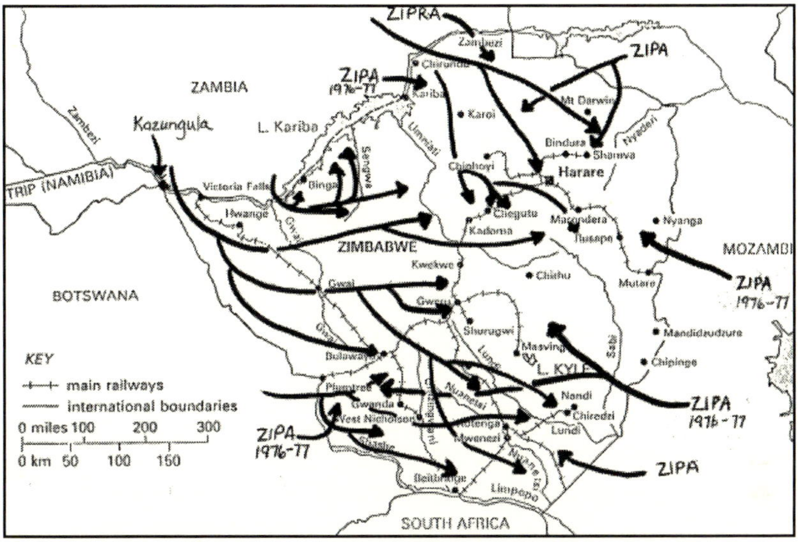

'How is this possible?' I have to laugh every time this question is put to me. For at that time the people of Zimbabwe were not worried about who belonged to which particular political grouping [or ethnic group]. People supported the guerrillas who came to fight with them in their particular and ongoing struggles against the colonial government.[81]

ZIPRA's presence almost everywhere in the country was testimony to the fact that the Rhodesians were losing the war, and losing it big. From 1974 on Rhodesians started incursions into neighboring states, Zambia and Botswana in 1974, and in 1975, and after its independence, Mozambique was added to the hit list.

Because the Rhodesians could not stem the tide of ZIPRA's infiltration from Zambia, Botswana, and ZANLA from Mozambique, they decided to take preemptive strikes. Even the top brass Rhodesian cadre, Lieutenant-Colonel R. F. Reidy-Daly, the founding leader of the Selous Scouts, and a Malayan war veteran had to make a very honest confession about the army's ignorance of Nkomo's Military war strategy, and admit they had lost most of the rural areas to guerrillas, and that most of their aircraft had been depleted. In 1977 Reidy-Daly admitted his army could no longer successfully stop the infiltration of insurgents:

The security forces in every operational area were feeling an increasing strain because insurgent reinforcements were now able to reach their target areas with little difficulty. Huge tracts of Tribal Trust land were closed within the grip of the insurgents and the tribesmen there began to know only too well who was controlling the whip hand. Unfortunately it was not us, but incredibly few people in government wished to admit it.[82]

According to Reid-Daly the RSFs were losing the war because of three basic reasons: disorganization within the RSF, lack of strategy, and ignorance of insurgents' structure, civilian network and *modus operandi*.[83] Uncharacteristic of a white Rhodesian trooper who almost invariably accused black guerrillas and their politicians of disorganization Reid-Daly observed:

> *Even worse, from a soldier's viewpoint, there was no laid-down military strategy applicable for the conduct of the war. Brigadiers were given their operational areas to command and thereafter each one did his own thing, as did the police, as did the Special Branch, as did the Internal Affairs, They blamed the politicians for the developing state of disastrous affairs and, needless to say, the politicians blamed them for not getting on the job.*[84]

The change of strategy on the part of ZIPRA as a result of the 1976 conference was beginning to bear fruits. The big weapons had improved their effectiveness. By mid-1977 the RSF had been driven into big garrisons, away from their multi-scattered satellite or shift camps among the rural population. However, despite this success in driving the RSF into garrisons ZIPRA could not effectively establish complete liberated areas. Rhodesians still could carry out devastating aircraft attacks against ZIPRA in their semi-liberated areas. Although artillery units had started infiltrating they were still small in numbers and the main strategy was still the use of mines and light weapons in ambushes and smaller skirmishes. Consequently, they could not attack big garrisons.

This was the assessment that ZIPRA front regional commanders made of the war, and reported to their leaders in Lusaka. They reported success in driving the Smith regime soldiers from the larger parts of the rural areas into bigger garrisons, and on the deficit side, their failure to protect themselves from the RSFs aircraft strikes and to attack the garrisons because of lack of necessary weapons. They then asked for more logistical support, better weapons and the deployment of their own regular forces. At this point the training of the regular infantry battalions had been going on for some time and was well advanced.

The authorities understood their commanders as saying that ZIPRA had established semi-liberated areas, and what they then needed were heavy weapons to defend their positions and to attack the RSFs garrisons in order to create more liberated zones. Having received reports and proposals from field commanders and different departments, the Conference concluded that the RSRs had lost most of the rural areas and that the time had arrived for them to implement what they called The Turning Point Strategy. Undoubtedly, the two fundamental principles of Mao Tse Tung's revolutionary war had been fulfilled. Mao stated that the first principle in a revolutionary war was that the guerrillas should have a safe place from which to operate, and to a certain extent Zambia met this criterion.

The second was that a revolutionary guerrilla should be able to merge with the local population. ZIPRA had met this second qualification, especially during the early 1970s. However, this did not remain true for the period beginning in 1977. For instance, in September 1977, the Zambezi/Wankie area, a ZIPRA commander started the operation with nine insurgents, and in five months the group had grown to 400 guerrillas. Another group of 200 guerrillas were

The Storm and Then Spears Turned into Plowshares

concentrated on the Northern side of the Khami River. Armed primarily with light weapons, they were easy targets for the Rhodesian forces of airborne "Fireforce" tactics. Hiding from the enemy troops was no longer an option. With this spectacular growth, organizational problems ensued. RSFS overall strategy was to concentrate around the more vital places of the country. These included critical lines of communication with South Africa, industrial areas and the most productive agricultural areas. As Alan Lindner, the Rhodesian Light Infantry commando second-in-command, in a resigned manner, remarked in his presentation at the ComOps, "the remainder of the country ... must be left to its own devices." He concluded by saying that the area should be occasionally visited by small units of Selous Scouts who would use the occasion to monitor guerrilla activities.[85]

At this 1976 Conference ZAPU concluded that the time to move to the next stage of the revolutionary war was upon it. Clearly, ZAPU was closely following the Maoist, Eastern paradigm of prosecuting the war. According to the Eastern paradigm, at the beginning of revolutions as Samuel Huntington observed, the government is strong, forcing opponents to:

> *[W]ithdraw from central, urban areas of the country, establish a base area of control in a remote section, struggle to win the support of the peasants through terror and propaganda, slowly expand the scope of their authority, and gradually escalate the level of their operations from individual terroristic attacks to guerrilla warfare to mobile warfare and regular warfare. Eventually they are able to defeat governmental troops in battle. The last phase of the revolutionary struggle is the occupation of the capital.*[86]

It is important to note that Huntington did not come up with a new paradigm but simply interpreted Mao.[87] According to Mao, guerrilla warfare went through four stages. At stage one, the insurgents infiltrate the community. Insurgents immediately mobilize, carry out some terroristic activities, agitate, spread propaganda, and basically carry out sabotage activities, in rural areas.

Warfare then moves to the second stage, where the guerrillas are ensconced in their base areas. At this point guerrillas are able to attract allegiance from an increasing number of the local population. Violence at this level is generalized into guerrilla warfare. At the third stage, the guerrilla's administrative scope continues to increase, and they at this point engage enemy troops conventionally. Insurgents establish more bases and liberated zones. This was the point at which ZIPRA was at the time of the 'Turning Point Strategy.'

In keeping with Mao's stage-theory, ZIPRA's revolution had started in the remote and marginal areas, moved into more economically active agricultural areas, small provincial towns and had succeeded in isolating bigger cities. In the last stage, which is stage four, peasant armies paralyze towns and cities, resulting in the collapse of government. Subsequently, guerrillas take over political power, and the revolution is nationally institutionalized.[88] The stage is the one that ZAPU was now preparing for.

NSO headed by Dumiso Dabengwa had the task of drawing-up the "Turning Point Strategy." Inherent in this document were cannons that heralded the beginning of the mobile warfare that the party had theorized about for many years. To arrive at the decision of a mobile war, ZAPU looked to Vietnam instead of to China or Russia its main supplier of weapons. To effect the elements of the 'Turning Point Strategy' the ZAPU War Council, in November 1978, prepared the following declaration:

All ZIPRA forces throughout the country are ordered to act as follows:

1) Openly engage and drive any remaining enemy or its agents out of controlled areas;
2) Protect all citizens within the liberated areas, irrespective of race, color or creed;
3) Organize and defend the masses of Zimbabwe; and
4) Advance with gallantry on all those areas still in enemy military, economic and strategic installations.

Members of the Revolutionary Council within the liberated and freed areas were expected to: organize administrative units; run agricultural, educational and health services; and harmonize the consolidation of the liberated and controlled areas.

However, these orders were not openly publicized until the following year in April 1979, many months after the High Command had received and, to a large degree, effected them. The specific orders given to the High Command, however, remained a guarded secret and what was publicized was only a summarized version that appeared in this short form:

1) New command structure to be established to enable better command and control of forces within the country;
2) The transfer of half the High Command into the battle field;
3) Communications equipment to be upgraded and moved into the country;
4) Guerrilla units to be organized into detachments and brigades;
5) Regional offensive plans to be drawn up by the High Command inside the country; and
6) Large quantities of war materials, including heavy weapons, to be moved into the country and cached.

The discussion of eastern revolutionary strategies in a serious manner was not undertaken for the first time at this 1978 Conference. It was first discussed at the 1976 Consultation Conference and had been a focus of discussions ever since. ZAPU got attracted to Vietnamese theories and practices of mobile warfare and studied them. Although Cuban and Russian advice was sought and followed, it was the Vietnamese who provided a fresh and effective experience of success in guerrilla tactics.

The Storm and Then Spears Turned into Plowshares

To Vietnamese Revolutionaries, guerrilla warfare was only a preparatory stage in the war of liberation, and this is how ZIPRA viewed its first activities against the regime up to 1970. Guerrilla warfare, they argued, must be developed beyond this preparatory stage into higher forms of warfare, not only to avoid stagnation but also to achieve strategic victories. According to one of their (Vietnamese) theorists and revolutionaries, Vo Nguyen Giap:

> To keep itself in life and develop, guerrilla warfare has necessarily to develop into mobile warfare. This is a general law.... If guerrilla warfare did not move to mobile warfare, not only the strategic task of annihilating the enemy manpower could not be carried out, but even guerrilla activities could not be maintained and extended.[89]

The Comintern revolutionaries, speaking as A. Neuberg[90] show the need of moving beyond guerrilla movement to higher forms of resistance when they assert:

> In the overall pattern of...struggle, guerrilla movements play the role of an auxiliary factor; they cannot of themselves achieve historic objectives, but can only contribute to the solution provided by another force.[91]

The key in the new strategy was the taking over of semi-liberated areas, defending the positions and eventually creating rear bases inside Rhodesia's liberated zones.

Following the Turning Point strategy, ZIPRA started caching heavy weapons around the country and also increasing its use of armor piercing missiles such as the Soviet RPG-7, a hand-held anti-tank rocket launcher surface-to-surface missile (SSM) able to penetrate 320mm of armor; Soviet SAM-7, a hand-held anti-aircraft missile; 76mm guns, heavy machine guns, Soviet B-10 recoilless rifles, and Mortar 82mm (in the course of the war ZIPRA would capture from the Rhodesian forces lighter mortars 51mm to 61mm which were ideal for guerrilla warfare). In 1978 and 1979, ZIPRA stepped up its attacks and proved to the Rhodesians its formidable capabilities.

6.8 THE MAKING OF ARMAGEDDON: ZAPU TAKES WAR TO THE PSYCHE OF THE WHITES, 1978-79[92]

On September 3, 1978, precisely six months after the signing of the Salisbury internal agreement of March 3, using a SAM-7 missile launcher (commonly know as a strela), ZIPRA downed a four-engined passenger aircraft. The Viscount Flight RH 825 that was on its return trip from Kariba to Salisbury had 58 people aboard, and only eighteen survived the crash. Of the eighteen, armed men, whose identity still remains a mystery, killed ten.

The Rhodesians claimed the armed men were ZIPRA forces, but Nkomo denied it, claiming that ZIPRA actually helped the survivors, whom they left alive,[93] thereby implying that the Rhodesia forces killed them. Nkomo may be correct in his suspicion because Rhodesian Selous Scouts used to carry out such actions as these in order to discredit their opponents.[94] For that matter, according to the Selous Scouts Commander, Lt. Col. R. F. Reidy-Daly, they had been operating in that area for a long time and had left the area a day before the incident.[95]

Given the Selous scouts' character, the massacre of the Viscount survivors cannot be put beyond them. Suspicion is further deepened by the fact that it took at least twelve hours for the Rhodesia troops to get to the scene of the accident, when they could, given their vast resources, easily secured the place in far less time. Before this incident, a firing mechanism, a part to a SAM-7 missile launcher was found at the Victoria Falls airport. Immediately thereafter, a second part was found. Both had been fired at the South African Airways but missed. According to Nkomo, his forces' attempt to down the South African airways was targeted at P. W. Botha, the South African Defense Minister "who was flying to Victoria Falls."

Nkomo further acknowledges that the missile malfunctioned and missed the aircraft. To Nkomo, as a Minister of Defense whose troops were involved in the war against ZIPRA, Botha was a legitimate target.[96] This first incident marked the first ZIPRA attempts of aggression against civilians suspected to be traveling with military personnel.

ZIPRA claimed it had shot down the aircraft because it had gotten intelligence it was transporting military personnel. Nkomo correctly alleged that "the Rhodesians used civil airliners equally for carrying passengers and for carrying troops." More over, the Rhodesian television, before attacks on ZANLA in Mozambique, had shown Viscounts ferrying paratroopers for the job. On that day, the shot down aircraft had been seen landing in Victoria Falls where ZIPRA intelligence knew there were paratroopers stationed there. Nkomo, however, regretted that civilians were killed as it was not the policy of his party to target civil airliners.[97] However, ZAPU's suspicion that the Rhodesians killed the ten survivors was not far-fetched as this was usually the case.[98]

The Rhodesians swiftly retaliated for the downing of the Viscount by attacking a refugee camp for boys, Freedom Camp, North of Lusaka, killing 351 boys and girls. The Red Cross and the UN High Commission for Refugees confirmed ZAPU's claim that Smith's forces struck at defenseless, civilian trainees, and not `armed terrorists' as Smith had alleged.[99] South Africa sensationalized the shooting down of this civilian plane incident by alleging that ZIPRA raped the white victims before shooting them dead. The white community got angry and demoralized. To the majority of the black community this was a question of chickens coming home to roost, the fulfillment of the biblical principle, "you reap what you sow."

Suffering in the hands of the regime soldiers had, indeed, hardened their hearts. In contrast a white South African based Friends of Rhodesia Society put some money on Nkomo's head, and promised to pay R100,000 to anyone who would either kill or bring Nkomo to Salisbury for trial.[100] Try as they may, they failed to capture the evasive and slippery Nkomo and no one collected the

The Storm and Then Spears Turned into Plowshares

money.[101] In Rhodesia, the Selous Scouts unit was ordered to kill Nkomo as soon as possible.[102] Nkomo was increasingly becoming a problem; worse still, his military strategy had become of grave concern to the RSF's officers because it was proving to be very effective against the regime. According to the Selous Scouts' commander, Nkomo's strategy remained "shrouded in mystery and we were left guessing what he intended to do."[103]

Plans to assassinate Nkomo ranged from transforming a Ford Escort car into a huge claymore mine with the intention of sending it off to Zambia to be positioned in Nkomo's way, to literally attacking his residence. Nkomo, the man who had gotten used to being hunted, and had by this time perfected the skill of evasiveness, proved as slippery as what his "Ilitshe" name meant: the Slippery Rock. As Reid-Daly the headhunter, said of his assassin, Lt. Anthony White, reminiscing about the war:

> But luck was not with him, and although he repositioned the car seven times, on two occasions right in the center of Lusaka, Joshua Nkomo used a different route each time. And Anthony, who had rapidly become a past master in the art of loitering, missed him every time. Anthony became desperate, and so did I....[104]

When the second plan failed, that of parking the mined car in the way of the vehicle carrying Nkomo and remotely activating a bomb as his car passed by, the ever resourceful Selous Scouts hatched the third assassination plot. This time the plan was to attack Nkomo's house in Zambia and assassinate him. The plan would, however, begin to unfold after Anthony got back to Rhodesia. Anthony had spent five weeks just before the end of January 1979 futilely trying to realize an assassination plan. The only thing he succeeded to do was to get himself beaten-up by the Zambian Youth Wing which caught him loitering around Nkomo's house after completing some surveillance on the latter's house. The youth broke his nose, and, after his five-week abortive assassination, he left Zambia for Rhodesia.[105]

This time, the Special Air Service unit was deployed to kill Nkomo and a Selous Scout team worked in tandem with it. Once they crossed the Zambezi River in the cover of early darkness, on April 14, 1979, the Rhodesians drove up in seven Sabre Land Rovers, each carrying between six to seven soldiers. The Land Rovers, as were the uniforms of their occupants, were re-painted in Zambian camouflage.[106] Expecting fierce resistance not so much from the Zambian soldiers as to that of the ZIPRA forces, the RSF were well gunned-up, with two machine guns and an RPG-7 per car. Each gun had 1,500 rounds in it.[107] In addition they were armed with FNs, AKs, 9mm pistols and hand grenades. In the early hours of April 15, the following day, they attacked Nkomo's house and were met by tenacious resistance from the guards.

Unfortunately for the Rhodesians, Nkomo had out-maneuvered them again. He had, according to Reid-Daly, "listened to the advice of his walking stick[108] and escaped death." The mission "failed again. Reflecting the resigned spirit of his soldiers Reid-Daly concluded, "this raid effectively ended all hopes of assassinating Nkomo in his Lusaka residence," as there "would never be another opportunity."[109]

Every attempt to assassinate Nkomo had come to nought. However, at times the Rhodesians were successful in either capturing or killing some of ZAPU's high-ranking officials. In fact from 1974 and on, the RSFs intentionally sought to capture alive or kill ZAPU War Council members. Among the notable figures captured during this period were Richard Sibanda, the Senior Intelligence Officer for ZIPRA's Security Operations, and Alexander Brisk Vusa, Deputy Head of Intelligence. However, these were not their first, second or even third prizes within the military structure.

The RSFs' most three prized targets were Dumiso Dabengwa, Head of ZIPRA NSO (that was located in the Vatican), Victor Mlambo, Assistant Director of Intelligence and Gordon Butshe, Assistant Director of Counter-intelligence. Try as they may, the RSFs failed to assassinate these three. However, the RSFs managed to assassinate Jason Moyo, Vice-President of ZAPU, and Alfred Nikita Mangena,[110] the General Commander of ZIPRA. One of the major reasons for these great losses was because the Zambia soldiers, unlike their counterparts the FRELIMO forces, made very little efforts to resist the RSFs. Not only did the FRELIMO forces provide military support to the ZANLA cadres, they also fought on their side right inside Rhodesia, providing military leadership and logistics, among other things.

ZIPRA enjoyed none of this support from the Zambian troops. Part of this indifference was because the Zambia Intelligence, and other military units, particularly the air force, had been heavily infiltrated by the Rhodesia's Intelligence and were therefore collaborating with them.[111] FRELIMO on the other hand, was still brimming with revolutionary zeal. The Rhodesians felt it was imperative that they killed Nkomo, not just because they wanted to avenge the death of the Viscounts occupants, but because they considered him, "the ZIPRA War machine"[112] and killing him they thought would effectively destroy the `fierce' ZIPRA forces.

However, ZAPU had already made a very significant point, especially to the white community that supported the supremacist regime. The message was, even traveling by plane was no longer safe. Up to this point the travel scare affected mostly blacks using buses because they were very vulnerable to being killed by land mines. Consequently, the white community morale plummeted significantly after the incident, and some started to vote with their feet. By this time, South African aircrafts had stopped flying into Victoria Falls, specifically after ZIPRA forces almost downed an aircraft on which Botha was traveling.

A little over three months after the Viscount incident, ZAPU dealt the Smith regime another terrifying blow when its forces fired rockets and tracers at the central oil storage depot in the capital city, Salisbury. More than 25 million gallons of scarce fuel were destroyed. The fuel tanks burned for six days, and were only put out with the help of South Africa. The fuel loss had a tremendous

The Storm and Then Spears Turned into Plowshares

impact on the prosecution of war by Rhodesians as it reduced the number of military trucks, aircrafts and supply trips they could make to their target areas and their army garrisons. Also, it had an adverse impact on the economy, especially on industries that were oil driven.

The loss of petrol also resulted in a sharp increase in petrol prices, and this hit the white community members most because it was they who largely depended on cars. Smith was terribly shaken by the event.[113] ZIPRA was clearly on the move, and it was proving to be unstoppable, picking its own targets and in most situations, taking the initiative, and thereby putting the Rhodesian army on the defensive. Subsequent to soliciting oil storage sabotage, ZIPRA fired some more SAM-7 missiles into fuel-storage tanks, this time in Bulawayo, the second biggest city. Officials reported that in the months of December 1978, and January 1979, twenty-six white farmers and fifty-eight members of the security forces were killed (most of the security forces killed by ZIPRA), White emigration shot to a net high of 2,771 over the month of December alone, and in a futile effort to boost increasingly plummeting morale on the part of its white community the regime extended martial law to over seventy percent of the country.

The situation was so serious and so bleak that even Smith's own Co-Minister of Internal Affairs, in charge of organizing the April elections, resigned because he saw the take-over of black liberation movements as inevitable.[114]

Because of its professionalism and high standard of training, ZIPRA was more difficult to find than ZANLA, despite the fact that the **West** was more sparsely populated. Its infiltrators traveled in small groups, and sometimes carried their own food, and that way sometimes covered great distances without attracting attention from the locals because they did not need to visit villages for food. Avoiding villages was sometimes advisable in order to avoid detection by Selous Scouts who sometimes managed to fool locals into believing they were part of the guerrilla forces.

These Selous Scouts would also pose as ZANLA, attack ZIPRA forces generating animosity between the two nationalist parties. The organization of such small groups depended on the kind of mission to be undertaken. For example the urban-based units would operate in two-man sticks or four-man stick depending on the kind of operation, logistics, size of the target and security.

However, such a stick would be answerable to a larger unit, such as a section of seven or nine guerrillas. In the rural areas, however, from 1977 and on, smaller groups were a thing of the past. Guerrillas were now operating in bigger sections and platoons, and towards the end of the war in battalions. For example the Northern Front had as many as 2,000 ZIPRA forces by the Cease-fire.[115]

In the rural area the Black population was becoming increasingly paramilitarized and defiant to the system. Two incidents attest to the defiance of the black population especially from 1977 on. In the Lupane region, an American mercenary who had fought in the Vietnam war inquired if the rural people would be frightened when they saw soldiers mounted on horses. An officer Hawkins, who had been operating in that area for a long time, responded:

Not to my knowledge...but remember, you're working here with Matabeles [sic]. These niggers [sic] aren't afraid of anything except bad spirits.[116]

In the Godlwayo area some villagers were even communicating their defiance against the system in paintings on their huts. Peter Godwin, an officer with PATU, remembers vividly how as he and his group patrolled in the Gondlwayo area, he came upon a hut on whose decorative patterns was written the words: 'Hate us and see if we mind,' and he interpreted that as "an audacious challenge" to the system.[117] With this public attitude of hostility against the regime soldiers, it became increasingly difficult for them to gather any information on the movement of the guerrillas. Instead, the rural folk either pointed out the RSFs' Observation Posts to the trained ZIPRA cadres so that they could lay land mines on them or did it themselves. Also as a para-militarized group the rural people became very aware of pseudo groups, whom they either attacked themselves or reported to ZIPRA.

As 1979 commenced, the Rhodesian regime was in dire straits. They badly needed something with which to boost their morale. However, to the further drop of their morale, ZIPRA forces, exactly five months, one week and two days after the downing of Hunyane, on February 12, 1979 shot down the second Viscount, Umniati, using a SAM-7 missile. This time there were no survivors as all the 59 people aboard the aircraft died.[118] Nkomo justified the shooting by claiming the target was General Peter Walls whom ZIPRA intelligence had indicated was on that plane. Walls actually traveled on the second Viscount a few minutes later. Guerrilla intelligence apparently missed his last minute change of flights. Although ZIPRA missed Walls, it got another big target, Lieutenant "Spike" Powell, one of the early leaders of the notorious Selous Scouts.[119]

The Smith regime swiftly retaliated by launching air strikes on a ZIPRA's training base at Luso, Angola as well as in Zambia. By this time Rhodesia was running out of ideas to stop the war and was losing the war dismally. The Smith Regime had tried every method from isolating the liberation forces from the African population, to the Africanization of its own army, to the forcibly removing populations into groups. Also they created pseudo groups who fought and gathered intelligence behind the lines. However, their effectiveness was soon curtailed.

Then came cross border air attacks, and guerrilla tactics in the insurgents' host countries. Unable to stop the advance of ZIPRA, Rhodesia resorted to vicious ways to undermine ZAPU's strength from inside. The assassinations of Jason Z. Moyo and Alfred Magena, were part of this policy. Rhodesia went further to try and force ZAPU's host country Zambia, to kick them out by attacking its economic infrastructure and bombing its villagers.

These were undoubtedly the last kicks of a dying regime that was totally desperate. The army confessed as early as the beginning of 1978 that they could not bring the securing situation under control. They were running short of helicopters, their kill rates had dropped drastically, "to almost zero, and the influence of insurgents had increased."[120]

The Storm and Then Spears Turned into Plowshares

6.9 THE ZERO-HOUR PLAN (ZHP)

By April of 1979, about eighteen months after their formation, the Patriotic Front forces had made enormous military gains. Bishop Abel Muzorewa who had ascended the premiership of what became known as Rhodesia-Zimbabwe had failed to bring the war to a stop despite his incessant appeals to the PF cadres to surrender, and frequent predictions by politicians that supported the internal agreement that the war would come to an end soon. Instead, to their chagrin, war escalated and the end seemed not to be in sight. In recognition of the deterioration of the situation, starting from the signing of the internal agreement in 1978, most of Rhodesia was put under martial law. By mid-1979, 85.90 per cent had come under martial law and defense expenditure had astronomically risen to R$1million.[121]

Another indication of the escalation of the war, particularly the gains that the guerrillas had achieved in the country was their increase in numbers. In March 1976, it was estimated that there were 700 guerrillas in the country. By mid-1979 the figure had grown to 13,000, and the number would rise to 15,000 in November,[122] a month before the cease-fire that marked the beginning of the process which led to independence. The escalation on the part of ZIPRA was a deliberate one, which also took advantage of the weakening of the RSF.

Smelling military victory, ZAPU started preparing for the last stage of the war, the major offensive involving a conventional army in collaboration with its guerrilla forces and the para-militarized black ZAPU members. The plan came to be known as *"The Zero-Hour Operation."* The operation was to ZAPU what an *Inxwala* theme song was to a traditional AmaNdebele, AmaSwazi, or Zulu nation; a guarded secret.

Nkomo, the leader of ZAPU, five years later, in the post-independence Zimbabwe, would remind his audience of the secrecy surrounding the Zero-Hour Plan:

> *Behind the scenes a time bomb was ticking away, and nobody but myself and senior ZAPU colleagues knew of its nature. A year previously, ZAPU and ZIPRA, in the closest secrecy, had decided that war must be ended, the agony could not be allowed to drag on. We had set in motion what we called the `turning point' strategy, for a transformation of the war from a guerrilla operation into a full-scale conflict in which we would match the Smith regime's armor and air cover of our own.*[123]

As if to remind some of the AmaNdebele fighters of their mostly forgotten historic festival, the Zero Hour Operation was to take place during the rainy season, and the period selected was summer of 1979-1980.

This is how the Zero Hour Plan was going to be carried out. The Plan involved the launching of a co-ordinated attack by the ZIPRA forces from several fronts at the same time. The offensive was to begin inside Rhodesia, and it was to be done by conventional forces, guerrillas already inside the country, and locally trained sympathizers. Since the late 1960's ZAPU started caching small weapons around the country, and also training young people from within the country to lay mines and to use weapons. The activity came to a 'trickle' during the leadership crisis in 1969 through the early part of 1970.

In 1974, as has been mentioned elsewhere in this chapter, the caching of mostly small weapons in the rural areas and in the cities increased, and after 1976, heavy weapons were added to the list of cached weapons. The recruiting increased since the plan depended on the presence of having as many people as possible under arms within the country itself. By mid-1976 most missionaries around the rural areas had moved into cities, leaving the running of rural churches to black pastors. This gave black pastors the opportunity to engage politics in their local churches. These churches provided free space for the recruitment of young people to enlist in what many black pastors saw as a just war. The number of young people in rural areas rose as a result of the closing down of schools around the country, and the shortage of jobs in the cities.

At this point, the role of the "Ibandla LeZintandane" had dwindled since most of the population could now use their own regular churches to organize for political activities. Thus, rural churches did not only provide sanctuary to the guerrillas but also aided and abated the spirit of insurgency. Pastors chaired cell, branch and district meetings. In Matebeleland South, the Brethren in Christ Church pastors,[124] for example were extensively involved in organizing for ZAPU and so did the Seventh Day Adventist, the African Episcopal Church, and the Lutheran Evangelical Church. The involvement of traditional churches in political organization for ZAPU provided the party with a ready-made audience where the issue of trust was not a question as the pastors were well known to their flock. Here they could weed out strange faces, and thereby minimizing the activities of pseudo gangs.

At about the same time five conventional battalions with heavy artillery support were to capture two bridgeheads, one, near Victoria Fall, and the second one in the Northern Front in the Chirundu/Kariba area. ZIPRA forces would then drive in large numbers of conventionally trained infantry in armored vehicles capable of pushing their way through any opposition. Their main objective would have been to seize and hold the strategic rear bases inside the country, along the border, from which to launch further offensives on the cities.

The forces were to seize the airfields at Kariba and Wankie. Once these airfields had been secured, they would then airlift more conventionally trained soldiers into the area, including ZIPRA's air force from Angola. Russian-made Mig Fighters manned by ZIPRA pilots would provide air support. According to Reid-Daly, aircraft parts arrived but were never uncrated as the situation never reached the point where an invasion was launched.[125]

The central offensives were to be carried out by the reinforced ZIPRA insurgents already within the country.

The Storm and Then Spears Turned into Plowshares

> *[Attacks were to be mounted] along simultaneous lines of advance. In the north they were to attack Karoi and Sinoia. In Midlands the guerrilla brigade based at Gokwe was to attack Que Que and Hartley, whilst the brigade based in Nkai was to assault Gwelo. The brigades based in Tsholotsho had the task of attacking Bulawayo. In the Southern Front there were three lines of advance: towards Plumtree, Kezi and Gwanda/Beitbridge.*[126]

As has already been pointed out, the locals played an integral role in the realization of the ZHP. Organized through local party branches and co-coordinated by ZIPRA commissars, the locally trained cadre were to pick up arms which had been cached around the country over a period of time and join in the fighting. The commissars were to be responsible for distributing about 50,000 AK and SKS rifles and ammunition. Some of the armed local 'militias' were to include those who would have received crash course training inside the country in preparation for the offensive.[127] Generally, by mid-1977 most young people in the rural area could operate AK rifles and professionally lay land mines. ZIPRA by then had done a good job in training them.

In the cities, commando and sabotage units, guerrilla units and specialized intelligence were to simultaneously launch a wave of ambushes and attacks behind enemy lines. Their targets inter alia, were military garrisons and air bases, and their goal to cut off lines of support to the RSFs engaged with the main offensive fronts. To crown it all, ZIPRA forces would then take over political power from the Smith regime.[128]

This was a well thought out Plan, and ZIPRA forces were ready for any eventuality. They had engineers, medics, and pontoons to throw across rivers in the event the enemy blew up bridges to prevent them from crossing. The Rhodesian regime, whose forces had gathered some information on the Zero Hour Plan from some ZIPRA forces they had captured, started to panic. ZIPRA became their main concern and their objective therefore became to cut off ZIPRA's lines of supply and reinforcement from inside Zambia.[129] Before discussing what came to be known as pre-emptive strikes by the RSFs, it would be helpful to discuss the misunderstandings that surrounded the ZHP. The main reason for explaining what the ZHP was and how it came to be understood by people outside of ZAPU is because it was, after independence, used as a basis by the ruling party, ZANU-PF, to try and eliminate ZAPU as a party.

Towards the end of the war, some scholars wrote on the Zero Plan, showing little but distorted knowledge of the plan. Almost invariably, each of the scholars, particularly the white Rhodesian or sympathizers of the Rhodesian regime, argued that the Plan's main objective was to eliminate ZANLA after the fall of the Rhodesian government. The Rhodesian CIO said ZAPU strategy was Soviet-inspired, and its promotion by ZAPU was calculated at internationalizing the country's conflict in hope of forcing the Western powers to intervene on behalf of the Rhodesian government.[130] The disinformation about the plan being a strategy calculated at eliminating ZANLA after Smith's defeat was aimed at fostering some conflict and division between ZAPU and ZANU.[131]

Since the ZHP was a top secret,[132] ZAPU did not attempt to challenge the disinformation, consequently, the misleading information was believed. What made it worse for ZAPU was that even respected scholars became active disseminators on misleading information on the Plan. For one, J. K. Cilliers, alleged that the ZHP was meant to forestall ZANU from taking over Zimbabwe, and that it was sponsored and crafted by the Soviet Union. He even went to the extent of claiming that the Soviets, early in 1979, flew into Lusaka to reorganize ZIPRA strategy.[133] Nkomo vehemently denied any direct role by the Soviets in the crafting of the ZHP Strategy. Dumiso similarly disputed the claim and even went to the extent of divulging that the Soviets military advisers expressed serious reservations about the strategy.[134]

In the post-independence era, the Mugabe government would use the same information to justify its ethnic cleansing of the AmaNdebele people.

Terrified at ZIPRA's plan for a conventional offensive the RSFs quickly changed their strategy and became more brutal. They used both biological and chemical weapons against guerrillas, and this affected the general population as well. For instance, in 1977, mostly in the Lupane region, the RSFs impregnated organophosphate poisons into clothing given to guerrillas. They also put thallium, a heavy metal and slow-acting nerve poison, into drinks, food, and medical products. The use of anthrax almost created serious division between the fighters and the locals because the former thought the latter bewitched them, especially after the unsuspecting locals distributed clothing treated with contact poison among the insurgents.[135] Radios distributed to guerrillas were booby-trapped.[136]

In areas where the RSFs or Selous Scouts still could reach, the locals were fined, beaten or killed for allegedly collaborating with guerrillas. By 1978, 300 villagers were being dislocated daily by the war, either through moving into town, becoming refugees or having their homes destroyed.[137] The Refugee population grew dramatically so that by end of May 1979 there were 19,800 Rhodesian refuges in Botswana alone,[138] located mostly in Silibe Pikwe, Pandamatenga, Dukwe and Francistown. Figures of Rhodesian refugees in Botswana vary according to sources. Another figure quoted were 28,000. In Zambia, there were 54,000 Rhodesian refugees, and in both countries the refugees were mostly ZAPU supporters.[139]

The increasing number of refugees terrified the Rhodesian government because all of a sudden the nationalist parties had a great reservoir of personnel from whom they could recruit fighters. To decrease such chances, the RSFs carried out pre-emptive strikes into Zambia and Mozambique. The reasons for these strikes were varied: one, to disrupt ZIPRA's preparation for the ZERO HOUR PLAN, by cutting-off its supply lines to the forward bases along the Zambezi River on the Zambian side. Two, to try and assassinate the ZAPU leadership. Good examples are the Entebbe-type assaults on Nkomo's house in Lusaka and the attack on the ZIPRA Head Quarters in Lusaka.

Third, it was to punish the host counties of the Rhodesian nationalists by destroying their economic infrastructure, and fourth, to punish ZAPU for its downing of the two Viscounts in 1978/79. Fifth, the RSFs also hoped to reduce considerably the infiltration of guerrillas into the country.[140]

The Cross border attacks on ZIPRA became ineffective as time went on, and the same can be said of attacks on ZANLA. However, in 1979, especially towards the end of that year, and in the course of the Lancaster House Talks in which both nationalist parties were involved, the RSFs concentrated their attacks on ZIPRA because of the "clear and present" danger they correctly perceived the latter posed. By this time ZIPRA had already won the attention of the RSFs as a fierce fighting force, and as a result, the Smith soldiers avoided attacking them directly most of the time.

For instance, in November/December 1978, the RSFs engaged in an operation against ZIPRA, code-named Operation Pygmy, decided not to attack ZIPRA's Mulungushi camp for fear of suffering heavy casualties. The camp housed conventionally trained ZIPRA forces,[141] and the RSF's Aerial photographic reconnaissance, and reconnaissance team of two soldiers provided information to the effect that the place had a very strong defensive system, with trenches, pit-holes to hide from gunfire and a bunker system surrounding the camp.[142]

Two more incidents effectively proved the strength of ZIPRA to the Smith regime, and both involved conventional warfare in the month of October 1979. The first incident was in early October 1979. Through photographic reconnaissance the RSFs learnt that ZIPRA had moved to Lusuto area, 13 miles northwest of Lake Kariba on the Zambian side. This was a half-strength ZIPRA regular battalion. Beginning from July/August, ZIPRA began moving its regular army into the rocky and rugged escarpment on the Zambian side of the Zambezi River. It moved enormous amounts of war materiel in readiness to move into Rhodesia to execute the ZHP in the early rainy season in October/November.

Hoping to stop the ZIPRA forces before they crossed the Zambezi River, the RSFs, consisting of the elite Rhodesian Light Infantry and the Special Air Service, attacked. ZIPRA responded, their artillery shells and rockets screaming into the Rhodesian positions, killing several according to a ZIPRA informant.[143]

A wave of Rhodesian aircraft came in first to soften the target in preparation for a ground troops assault, which never occurred Barbara Cole, whose book valorizes the RSFs, described the firing accuracy of ZIPRA this way: "it was accurate fire and quite worrying," and it showed right from the beginning that the Rhodesians were against "an opposition whose discipline and determination were outstanding."[144] The attack lasted for seventy-two hours, but the RSFs failed to winkle out well-entrenched ZIPRA forces that took advantage of their excellent trench-defensive system. The Rhodesian planes would return to base to refuel and rearm. But despite all these efforts, as Barbara Cole noted:

> *The mission had been bad news for the Rhodesians. They had grossly underestimated the enemy and had the living daylights shot out of them. They had been outgunned and outranged and had been unable to take the position.*[145]

The Rhodesian elite forces eventually unceremoniously hastily withdrew. And as Cole observed, the Rhodesians had been "stopped dead in their tracks."[146] Even the elite SAS members themselves, conceded "the enemy had undoubtedly won that round."[147]

These defeats were a setback for the RSFs who had set their strategy on wiping-out the insurgents in the forward bases and ending the advances. Combing the Lusuto camp subsequent to ZIPRA's tactical withdrawal, the RSFs learnt for the first time about how much the advancing troops were prepared for war. What the saw told them that the insurgents were well organized and determined to fight to the last man in defense of their positions.

As Cole accurately observed:

> *The security forces found endless kilometers of wire that linked the headquarters post in a corner of the pan to the positions all over the ridges. ZIPRA were so well organized that they had field telephones in every platoon headquarters. The Rhodesians were to take home the ZIPRA 14.5s, but the enemy had taken the precaution of removing the breach blocks. They were, therefore unusable. They found trenches with overhead cover, foxholes, and many positions contained steel helmets and gas masks.*[148]

However, their campaign to try and stop the ZIPRA build-up continued despite their defeat. Instead of attacking the nine ZIPRA bases by land, for fear of losing more men, the RSFs launched their fiercest and largest ever series, of concentrated air attacks of the war on the ZIPRA Chinyunyu Camp from towards the end of October into November, with 4,500 regulars in late October.[149] In fact the last time the RSFs deployed its regulars was during its early October 1979 attack on ZIPRA regulars in the Zambezi gorges. The major factor that discouraged the RSFs from deploying regulars was because it could no longer effectively or safely airdrop its forces. The RSFs drop-zones were either too close to be safe or too far to be effective.

Again in October 1979, they had learnt through their aerial photographic reconnaissance on ZIPRA's degree of readiness, sentry, guard system and general routine that the latter were more than ready so that ground attack would be suicidal. Thus, in this last conventional attack on the ZIPRA forces, the RSFs used eighteen warplanes. The attack lasted for more than an hour. In the Chinyunyu air raid, ZIPRA lost between fifteen and twenty of its men and the RSFs between five and eight of its aircraft.[150]

Finally concluding the obvious, that ZIPRA camps had become impenetrable, the RSF now turned to guerrilla warfare. Their main aim was to disrupt ZIPRA supply roads inside Zambia by mining the supply routes in

The Storm and Then Spears Turned into Plowshares

order to delay the implementation of the ZHP. However, this could not have delayed the plan because the essential ground preparations had already been largely completed by the time the Rhodesians attacked in early October. The offensive was actually held back by ZIPRA's air force readiness. Russia and East Germany governments sabotaged the offensive by keeping ZIPRA pilots who were supposed to form the large part of the air service men.[151]

Later, the diplomatic initiative dealt the ZHP a deathblow. But not until the ZHP gravely concerned the British government, which according to Nkomo, was fully aware of the inevitability of ZIPRA's attack in the event a diplomatic solution to the Rhodesian Crisis was not found soon enough. In the meantime ZANLA used the time when the RSFs concentrated on ZIPRA to prepare for its own version of ZAPU's ZHP code named *Gore reGukura hundi* [The Year of the Storm], literally meaning the torrential rains that sweep everything on its way, which it too had planned to launch during the early rainy season in 1979. ZANLA's plan too fell victim to the Lancaster House diplomatic initiative.

The ZHP posed one of the gravest threats to the RSFs, and had it occurred, it is possible it might have precipitated the downfall of the Rhodesian government. With ZAPU attacking the regime on such a large scale, it is most likely that ZANU[152] would have seized the opportunity to fulfill its goals for the "Gore reGukura hundi." The belief that the RSFs would have fallen had the ZHP succeeded, assuming that ZANU would have jumped into the fray and unleashed its forces on the regime, is based on the following reasons:

1) At this time, the RSFs military capabilities had been worn out considerably. From the beginning of 1978, the RSFs started to experience a helicopter shortage, a liability it could not afford since its edge in the war was based on its air firepower. This point was clearly put by Reid-Daly, the leader of the Selous Souts, when he said, "to fight insurgents effectively, whether internally or externally, we needed more air power, particularly helicopters."[153] Thus Rhodesia forces had lost control of the "internal situation."[154] Many of their helicopters had been lost through attrition for lack of spare parts, or shot down by the liberation forces.

2) Both havens for the liberation forces, ZAPU and ZANLA, especially the military bases, had become almost impenetrable both by ground or air troops by mid-1979. What had changed here is that both ZANLA and ZIPRA had acquired anti-air weapons and were putting them to effective use.[155] This provided the freedom fighters with their first real anti-air defense ability.[156]

3 Also the RSFs had lost morale, an ingredient vital for military success. Reid-Daly succinctly summed up the political, military and morale situation on the part of the regime when, in hindsight, he wrote:

> *The situation in Rhodesia is crumbling. It has been crumbling visibly for at least a year [1978]. The stink of political defeat, which pre-empts a military defeat,...*

had begun to seep like blood-poisoning into the veins of the security forces, and even more visibly, into the veins of Rhodesia itself.[157]

Reid-Daly further indicates that morale was "fast disappearing " among a community of 300,000 whites faced with opposition from seven million blacks. Numbers were against the regime.[158]

Since the ZHP was a ZAPU creature, a question could be asked if ZAPU, indeed, had the ability to carry it out. There is no doubt that ZIPRA had the capacity to effect this plan given the fact that it had already proven its competence in the field, by defending its positions, and taking the initiative in the attack. Also it had the necessary manpower, a well-trained conventional army as well as an efficient guerrilla force. The plan was contigent on four basic elements, the air force, ground troops, necessary weapons, and the militarized civilian population and all the variables had been well mobilized.

This study has shown that ZAPU had a well-trained army that had proven its ability to fight.[159] Remaining to be tested was its air force, which, after independence, we learnt was well trained. ZAPU also had given military training to the civilian population and armed them, especially the "imijimba." Also, ZAPU had the necessary weapons.[160]

However, even if the air force was still untested and by its own admission was less experienced than the Rhodesian one, they still had the necessary weapons to effectively protect themselves against the RSF's aircrafts, which by this time had been greatly reduced in number, and in its capacity to effectively attack the liberation forces.[161] With the confluence of all these factors, the liberation forces would have prevailed, had the ZHP been unleashed.

SPEARS TURNED INTO PLOUGHSHARES: ZAPU'S FIRST CHOICE WINS: A LONG PAINFUL ROAD, FROM 1960 TO 1979

There is a SiNdebele saying which goes thus, "umonakalo uqondiswa ngomlomo" [any wrong situation is corrected through speaking or negotiating]. The reason for this rationale was because, as goes another SiNdebele saying, "induku kayakhi muzi," [meaning physical fighting does not build a home]. The implication of the two sayings combined was that long lasting peace could only come through negotiations.

ZAPU believed in these sayings from the time it was formed. Its first preference as a means of finding a solution to the Rhodesian problem was through constitutional means. In the 1960's, the 1961 British proposed constitution became the last negotiations of which it was part. When it rejected the constitution, which denied them immediate majority rule, it became considered as irrelevant by both Britain and the Smith regime. Consequently the Smith regime initially had no interest in involving them in negotiations.

Smith declared independence, and Britain arrogated upon herself the responsibility of negotiating on the part of the blacks, and called for negotiations, which excluded the latter. Thus, negotiations on the Rhodesian

The Storm and Then Spears Turned into Plowshares

crisis from 1964 to 1971 were held between the rebellious Smith regime and the British government.

The Fearless and the Tigers talks are a classic example. When the Smith regime declared the UDI, the British Labor government vowed that it would not sit at a negotiation table with the regime that had rebelled against the Crown. Despite its solemn vow, on April 27, 1966, the British Prime Minister, Harold Wilson, told the House of Commons that talks would soon start between his government and the Smith regime.[162] Negotiations that started in London before transferring to Salisbury collapsed when Smith rejected British proposals.

The second round of talks between the two governments was aboard the HMS Tiger on the Mediterranean on December 2, 1966. According to its proposals Britain was prepared to grant independence to the white government as long as majority rule could be guaranteed in the future. Britain also proposed to expand the "B" roll franchise to include all blacks over the age of thirty and who met the citizenship and residence criteria. This involved cross voting for all seats.

To Smith, accepting the proposal meant giving over power to the majority blacks and so he rejected the British proposals. However, secret talks continued between the two governments, leading to the holding of talks on board HMS Fearless off Gibraltar on October 8, 1968.[163] The British proposals lacked any terror for the Smith regime, as it did not even require for the country to return to legality before it could receive independence.

This directly negated the position of ZAPU, whose position was that Rhodesia had to come under the Crown once again before power could be handed over to them. Despite the fact that the proposals posed no threat whatsoever to the status quo, Smith rejected them as an abject surrender to the blacks.[164] During this time ZAPU was beginning to experience its own internal convulsions, and perhaps this made it easier for Britain to believe it would accept whatever settlement came of ZAPU'S negotiations with the Smith regime.

When talks between Britain and Smith failed, ZAPU, as was its counterpart ZANU, was annoyed and surprised that Britain would not intervene militarily. It viewed Britain's refusal of use of force against Smith as a breach of her responsibility as the colonial power.[165] The only alternative became the armed conflict. As they would do after the failure of the 1976 Geneva talks,[166] ZAPU came to the conclusion that the only way to achieve power was fighting and defeating the regime.

As ZIPRA military incursions increased in the 1970s, Britain became anxious to find a solution that would rid it of the Rhodesian situation without necessarily immediately delivering majority rule to the blacks. Britain wanted the slightest of excuses to bow out of what had turned to be an internationally embarrassing situation to herself as one ultimately responsible for what was happening in Rhodesia.

Taking advantage of the Rhodesian homespun constitution, which allowed for ultimate parity in Parliament, the British government started negotiations with the white regime which ended, with 1979 in what blacks in Rhodesia considered a "white man's agreement." In the final analysis, the agreement, if blacks had signed on it, was capable of implementation only with regard to Smith's wishes. This was because its implementation depended on situations that were basically under the control of the white regime. For instance, the higher roll qualifications were depended on levels of education and income, and the whites controlled all these.

Worse still, nothing would have stopped the regime from reneging from its agreement once it had archived independence, international recognition, and had sanctions against it lifted.

On November 24, 1971 the Conservative government breathed a sigh of relief when its emissary, the Foreign and Commonwealth Secretary, Lord Douglas Home, signed a settlement proposal agreement with Smith. For once Britain thought they had struck a solution to what had become its international embarrassment. But the agreement had to meet the "test of acceptability" which was one of the six principles set as conditions to be met before independence could be granted. So it was that Britain appointed Lord Pearce, to lead a commission to Rhodesia to sound out black opinion on the proposed constitution.

The commission was important because this was the first time since 1961 that Britain involved blacks in deciding their future. Members of the Commission traveled throughout the rural areas, cities and towns holding fifty meetings, attended by 20,000 people, explaining the settlement proposals. From January 11, 1972 to March 11, the Pearce Commission received about 2,000 petitions, and more than 45,000 memoranda and letters.[167]

ZAPU directly participated in the organizing of opposition against the Home-Smith settlement proposals. Since ZAPU could not work openly because it was still a banned party, it proposed to its counterpart ZANU the formation of a provisional party inside the country to be led by a neutral person. According to Nkomo, it was he who chose Bishop Abel Muzorewa, an American-trained Methodist minister, to lead the newly formed party the African National Congress (ANC). The party was formed precisely to organize opposition the Home-Smith settlement proposals. All the ZAPU and ZANU leaders were in prison or exile. However, they managed to be represented by their seasoned politicians, ZANU by Michael Mawema, and ZAPU by Josiah Chinamano.

Despite its peaceful campaign and promise of protection by Lord Pearce, the ANC was met with violence from the Smith police force, resulting in the death of fifteen civilians and the arrest of 1,736 people. Clearly, blacks had made up their minds that nothing would separate them from their opposition to minority rule, not even death. Characteristically they massively voted down the proposals.

Subsequent to the failure of the Pearce Commission proposals, Smith vowed not to negotiate with Britain again, alleging that the latter "has lost the will to settle with us."[168] Instead he immediately tried to reach a settlement

The Storm and Then Spears Turned into Plowshares

with Muzorewa. To the Smith regime ZAPU and ZANU remained outlaws he despised, and therefore saw no need of negotiation with them. However, to Smith's chagrin, Muzorewa refused to accept any proposals that did not promise immediate majority rule. Despite Muzorewa's refusal to accept Smith's proposals, Britain and South Africa remained confident that he would finally give in, and flirted with the idea that such an agreement would put in power a moderate black government, which would deliver peace goods.

The intensification of the war from mid-1971 followed by the independence of Mozambique in 1974 squashed whatever little hope Britain and South Africa had that a political solution to the Rhodesian crisis could be found without the participation of ZAPU and ZANU.

Up to this time, to the east, Rhodesia had another strong allay in Mozambique, a white-led Portuguese colony situated along the African coast. Its harbors provided outlets for Rhodesian imports and exports. It was from these harbors that huge tankers carried the oil, among other things, which Rhodesia used, among other things, for its industries and the fueling of its military automobiles and planes. With the collapse of the Portuguese government in 1974, and its subsequent granting of independence to its African colonies, Mozambique became independent. That meant that a black government on its eastern border, which might close its border with it and cut off all trade relations, immediately confronted Rhodesia, right at the height of its civil war. Worse still, the new regime supported ZANU. After all, FRELIMO had started fighting against the RSFs long before independence.

In South Africa, the Vorster regime watched the events inside Mozambique with growing concern. The Prime Minister of South Africa undoubtedly recognized that white Rhodesia would now be surrounded by mostly black African states and could not survive too long. Vorster also realized that if he continued backing Smith his own country would soon find itself surrounded by black hostile governments, which might support the ANC against his regime. So Vorster started to put pressure on Smith to negotiate with his black opponents.

What followed was the playing out of an old saying that "politics makes strange allies," or "countries have no friends but interests." Both sayings mean avowed enemies occasionally work together if they share the same interests or want the same thing. Up to this time, Vorster and Kaunda were enemies but because both of them shared a common interest in their political survival, they co-operated in putting pressure on their clients to come to the negotiation table. Kaunda too wanted to end the crisis in Rhodesia as soon as possible because it was destroying his economy. Before Rhodesia declared independence in 1965, after which Kaunda closed his border, Rhodesia had always been one of Zambia's primary trading partners. Vorster's initiative promised to stop Kaunda's economic strangulations.

In time, secret meetings between the Vorster and Kaunda governments on how to start negotiations between the Smith regime and its black nationalists began. Kaunda promised to put pressure on ZAPU and ZANU, which he did. As a result of this agreement to negotiate a peaceful end to the Rhodesian conflict, Smith released the black liberation leaders from his prisons, including Nkomo the leader of ZAPU.

The release of the nationalists was followed by a conference held in Lusaka the Presidents of Zambia, Botswana, Tanzania and Mozambique as well as the leaders of four Rhodesian nationalist parties, ZAPU, ZANU, FROLIZI and ANC. The purpose of this conference was to try and unite the four nationalist organizations. On December 8, 1974, the four nationalist parties united under the umbrella of the ANC. The Lusaka talks came at the heels of failed negotiations between the RF and the ANC which had started on July 17, 1973, and which lasted for a year and ended in an impasse over the latter's demand for immediate majority rule. The ANC had gone into these talks divided, with some of its executive members doubting the efficacy of such talks.

Muzorewa isolated the doubting Thomases, and pressed for constitutional talks with Smith asserting that the need for the country to return to normalcy was "greater than the temporary suffering of our brothers," and therefore "we declare that we will press for constitutional talks."[169] Initially Muzorewa had the backing of Britain who erroneously thought that Muzorewa was a legitimate spokesperson for Africans. Little did Britain know that the bishop did not have any significant support base, especially in the rural areas where the war was raging.

Also, Britain was unaware that whatever little support Muzorewa had at that time, most of it was because of ZAPU and ZANU members on his executive.[170] As soon as twenty of these members were detained on August 1 1973, less than a month after the commencement of talks between Muzorewa and Smith, the former's popularity among Africans began to plunge precipitously. However, it can be correctly said that between 1971 and 1974 Muzorewa played a positive role in the nationalist politics in Rhodesia, and was insistent on his demand for majority rule now. Undoubtedly, his position at this time was largely influenced by the original ZAPU and ZANU organizers of the ANC.[171]

Between 1974 and 1980 Muzorewa's role was disastrous. He even commanded the bombing of ZAPU and ZANU external bases. The destructive part of his life, however, does not take away the fact that he, for the first four years of his leadership played a positive role as one of the black leaders who called for majority rule. His 1974 adamant position in favor of nothing short of majority rule in response to Smith's 1973 proposals is one good example of his positive role as a nationalist. This was despite the fact that Smith had offered an additional six seats in Parliament to the number of seats promised by the 1971 Home/Smith proposals over a given period of time.[172] These talks were again, led by Muzorewa, this time as leader of an expanded ANC. The expansion of the ANC was followed by the abortive white train talks that were held on August 25-26, 1975, on a train car provided by South Africa, and positioned on the Victoria Falls bridge.

The Storm and Then Spears Turned into Plowshares

Since this was no man's land, Smith could not arrest some nationalists to whom he had not given immunity. The talks failed because Smith would not accept the majority rule principle and also refused to give immunity to exiled ZAPU and ZANU nationalists who were banned in Rhodesia. The question of immunity was as crucial to them as that of achieving majority rule.[173]

There are, however, some scholars who believe that the Victoria Falls Talks collapsed because black nationalists disunity and rivalry among themselves.[174] While the observation about disunity and rivalry among the black nationalists is true, the argument that their disunity could have contributed to the collapse of the talks is very weak because they were at least united on the cardinal demands. All of them demanded majority rule now, and all of them wanted immunity for exiled nationalists.[175] Unity around these cardinal demands should certainly have convinced South Africa to break Smith's obduracy and pave the way for majority rule. The Victoria Falls Talks were important all the same because they were a product of regional efforts towards a peaceful negotiated settlement.

According to the 1974 Lusaka Agreement, ANC was supposed to hold a Congress to choose a national president to replace Muzorewa who was only an interim leader. At that point all the four parties, which were signatories to this agreement, were to merge into one party. However, Muzorewa, Sithole and Chikerema did not want one party, so they refused to comply with the Lusaka Agreement. Possibly, since they all wanted to be leaders, they were not sure they would win. ZAPU decided to stick by the letter of the agreement and held a congress on September 26-27, 1975.

Two important things transpired at this congress, namely: (a) since ZAPU was banned in the country ANC-Zimbabwe (ANC-Z) was formed to represent ZAPU internally; and (b) Nkomo was chosen its president.

The election of Nkomo as president of the ANC-Z was a formality since he did not have a challenger for the leadership. In essence, the Congress merely confirmed his leadership. However, for the sake of democracy it was important that the congress voted on the leadership at this meeting. This congress was held after Muzorewa expelled Nkomo and his four senior officials on September 11, 1975 for demanding a National Congress as required of the party by the Lusaka Agreement.

In the meantime, on the side of the Rhodesian government, Smith was troubled by the increasing number of guerrilla incursions and the dramatic change in the Southern African political landscape, with Mozambique becoming independent, and more importantly, being led by a government that was pro-black liberation. To the northwest of his country, Angola's independence was being retained with the involvement of the Russians and Cubans on the side of MPLA.[176] Smith feared the Russians and Cubans would soon be training ZAPU soldiers.

Smith's suspicion that Russians and Cubans would be training ZAPU cadres was not unfounded given that the two nations were its biggest supporters. The rumor-prone Rhodesian white population to which black leadership was synonymous with communism exacerbated the situation. Confronted with this bleak future Smith opted for the unthinkable, talks with Nkomo's ANC-Z. Smith knew very well, although he hardly confirmed it until things got bad, that Nkomo was a seasoned and pragmatic politician, with a strong army who if he had chosen to join the internal government would have made it hard for Mugabe to wage the war alone.

Besides, Nkomo had popular local, regional and international support. Also, Smith might have believed Nkomo as "a pragmatist" would be willing to protect white interests by accepting the shadow of power.[177] However Smith, like many other western and even some African leaders, underestimated the resolve of Nkomo to attain a fair and just settlement for his people. Nkomo accepted Smith's invitation for talks fully aware he was taking a risk to be labeled a sell-out by his counterpart, Mugabe, who had made it a career to be suspicious of anything Nkomo did without him or his patron Nyerere being in control. Talks might also slow the tempo of the liberation struggle.[178] To protect himself from being accused of selling-out by negotiating with Smith, Nkomo notified the FLPs who did not oppose his participation. Further, Nyerere stated that the talks would be a solid test for Smith's seriousness toward accepting majority rule. Vocalizing his full support for the talks between Nkomo and Smith, Nyerere said:

> *Tanzania has always supported peaceful means to achieve independence in Rhodesia. But we want our enemies and our friends to know that should peaceful negotiations fail, we have no alternative but to fight.*[179]

Nyerere then ended on an optimistic note:

> *Because if it is possible for this country [Zimbabwe] to achieve independence without shedding more blood, it is our duty to do it. We must do it.*[180]

Nyerere was here merely repeating what ZAPU had said over and over, that war became an option only when all peaceful means had been exhausted. However, it left the window open for peaceful talks at any time. Nyerere would further provide one of his advisors, Ronald Brown to join ZAPU's team of legal advisers. President Samora Machel of Mozambique was also equally unambiguous about his support for the talks:

> *[Addressing Smith, Machel said], Follow the course of negotiations while you still have time, before you are completely defeated by the winds of history.*[181]

In short, contrary to the popular belief that Nkomo's internal talks with Smith were private, these negotiations happened under a watchful eye of the FLPs.[182]

After ZAPU and the RF signed a declaration of intent to negotiate on December 1, 1975, the conference started in Salisbury on 11 December 1975. ZAPU came out demanding for majority rule now, and to allay whites' fear, it bent backwards to guarantee safeguards for them. The moving back and forth in the negotiation process is summarized by Nkomo in his book. He wrote:

> *From our side, we went to great lengths to offer conditions that the Rhodesian regime might find acceptable. We offered `safeguards' for white people, including some seats reserved for white people in parliament, which we detested. But Smith ... would not budge away from [his] position that white people, elected on a racially defined electoral rolls, should retain a majority in parliament. We advocated strictly non-racial criteria for electing the majority of MPs, and this Smith declined....*
>
> *I proposed that our ideas be put to a referendum in which all of the people of Southern Rhodesia would be free to choose their future constitution. Smith said no. He would not even agree to put it to vote. He said:'Nkomo, I represent white people. As a white man, I know your ideas are nonsense.*[183]

Talks between Nkomo and Smith finally hit an impasse over ZAPU's demands for majority rule, a non-racial electoral process, and the rejection of these demands by Smith and his colleagues. If anything, ZAPU's entering negotiations with Smith did two major things; one, it proved to the FLPs that Smith did not want to hand over power to the majority blacks, and two, and flowing from the first, it convinced the FLPs that the only way Smith could be ousted out of power was by an armed struggle, and they subsequently resumed their full support of it.

Another set of talks came in 1976 at Geneva after the formation of the Patriotic Front by ZAPU and ZANU. Attending this Conference were the Patriotic Front, led by Joshua Nkomo and Robert Mugabe,[184] the illegal regime led by Smith, the United African National Congress, led by Bishop Abel Muzorewa, and Rev Ndabaningi Sithole, who though rejected by ZANU, claimed to be representing it. The British Ambassador to the UN, Sir Ivor Richards, chaired the conference to the disappointment of the PF because it considered him an amateur, unsophisticated and incompetent.[185]

This was an Anglo-American initiative,[186] which also failed because its proposals virtually left power in the hands of the whites. What was unique with the Geneva Conference was that the U.S. was directly involved in the Southern Rhodesian situation for the first time in trying to find a peaceful settlement. Its previous vital involvement had been in passing the Byrd Amendment.[187] Harry Byrd of Virginia introduced the Amendment, which promoted U.S. imports of the Rhodesian chrome and other minerals in violation of the U.N. sanction resolutions of which the former was part.

Thus, the Byrd Amendment strengthened the Rhodesian white regime. Up to this time, the U.S. had followed the lead of Britain. The reason for not charting its own course might be because, for instance, when Rhodesia declared independence from Britain, the US was engaged in the Vietnam war, so that it was content with following Britain's lead in the Southern Rhodesian situation as long as it did not condemn its meddling in the Vietnamese situation.

With the fall of Mozambique and Angola into the hands of Marxist governments the US Secretary of State, Henry Kissinger, the man who viewed "national liberation movements and rebels as handmaidens of Moscow,"[188] talked his government into direct involvement in the Southern Rhodesia political crisis. His major involvement was to try and forestall the influence of Moscow in Southern Rhodesia specifically, and Africa in general.

Undoubtedly, Kissinger's concern was that after the Soviets' successes in Mozambique and Angola, they were now ready to extend their influence throughout the Continent. So he was worried if Southern Rhodesia fell through the use of arms it would naturally come under the influence of the Soviets since the nationalists according to him were Moscow's "handmaidens." In April 1976, Kissinger transformed American policy towards Africa to one whose basis was opposition to white governments and financial backing for new black nations.

To the surprise of the world, the man who believed in the might of arms started to talk about alliances based on common values, and in his speech to the U.N., Kissinger enjoined the world to seek a "just" new order based "not on the strength of arms but on the strength of the human spirit."[189]

After a thirteen-day tour which took him to Kenya, Tanzania, Zambia, Zaire, Liberia, and Senegal, Kissinger returned to his country only to immediately return to Africa, this time on a shuttle mission aimed at finding a peaceful political settlement for the Southern Rhodesian crisis. The only black Southern Rhodesian nationalist with whom Kissinger met on his shuttle was Nkomo. According to Nkomo, he and Kissinger met for only seven minutes, and Kissinger did not impress him.

Nkomo remarked:

I spent about seven minutes with Kissinger. He spoke in short sentences in a dull, flat voice, like a businessman doing a quick deal. It was more like talking to a robot than to a person. First he would say something, then withdraw it and say something else, then add a further point to that, so by the end I only knew that whatever he wanted it was not what I wanted. He struck me as clever, of course, but unpleasant and untrustworthy.[190]

After conferring with the heads of Angola, Botswana, Mozambique, South Africa, Tanzania and Zambia, Kissinger presented Smith with a five-point plan. These included majority rule within two years, the establishment of a multiracial Council of State with two whites and two blacks with a white chairperson, the creation of a Council of Ministers with a black majority and chairperson, an economic package, and an end to sanctions.[191] The plan also ambiguously envisaged whites being heads of the ministries of police and the military during the interim, a proposition that was bound to be vehemently opposed by the PF.

Strictly speaking, what came to be known as the Kissinger proposals were actually British proposals. As the conference was called a month after Smith signed for black majority rule, the Kissinger initiative had died. Since at this time the U.S. was one month from presidential election, the administration wanted to concentrate on its own internal affairs. Besides, the PF had strongly opposed the leading role of the US, arguing for dealing with Britain, directly.

The Storm and Then Spears Turned into Plowshares

However, Kissinger did achieve one 'feat' which was moving Smith through trickery, ambiguity or threat to accept the principle of majority rule. It is worthy noting though that the Kissinger's initiative, which indirectly led to the Geneva Conference, talks were a result of external interests rather than the interests of the Southern African parties involved in conflict. Thus, to Kissinger to bring the war in Rhodesia to a cessation was essentially meant to pre-empt Soviet advances in the region.[192]

Problems at this Geneva conference ranged from differences on the date of independence, the composition of the transitional leadership group, to the length of that transitional period. To agree on the independence date took a month, from the beginning of the Conference on October 28 to November 29, 1976. The PF was of the position that only twelve months were needed for the transition to majority rule, and therefore demanded that September 1, 1977 be accepted as the date for the independence of Rhodesia.

However, they were prepared to extend the date to December 1, 1977 if their first choice was unacceptable. They also demanded that the PF, as a liberation force representing the oppressed majority in Rhodesia should have at least four-fifths of the Council of Ministers and the Prime Minister.[193] Smith strongly objected arguing that independence could not be attained in less than twenty months, but in twenty-three months at the earliest. Clearly, the PF and Smith were on a different page, with Smith sticking to the Kissinger plan, which the PF had rejected, and did not respect. After receiving pressure from Nigeria and Tanzania to come up with a transitional date, Britain arbitrarily, albeit in a compromise, chose March 1, 1978.

Having gone past the setting of the date which the PF had demanded as *a prior proviso* for discussing the nature of government, the conference then turned to discussing transitional arrangements but did not get started on that topic as it adjoined in early December never to reconvene.

After the collapse of the 1976 talks, the Patriotic Front, of which ZAPU was part, vowed not to participate in any negotiations whose main object was not to immediately deliver majority rule. According to Nkomo, the PF put forward the following conditions for its participation in any future negotiations:

> *Now that the British Government intends calling another conference.... If the British government is interested in a conference on Rhodesia, then, it must be a new conference right from scratch, and certain things have got to be accepted right from the beginning. The first is that the Geneva Conference is dead, and the second is that the Rhodesian situation is a war situation. Third, those who take part in any conference must be those involved in the war. On our side it is the Patriotic Front, and on the British ... side it is the British Government with the Rhodesian regime as [its] extension. Fourth, that the agenda must have only one item and it should be the transfer of power from the minority to the majority. This means a constitution based on universal adult suffrage. Fifth, that this item should take four to five days. Sixth, that the rest of the time ... be spent on drafting the constitution.*[194]

When the Lancaster House Conference was convened towards the end of 1979, some of the PF's conditions were met; the discussion and drafting of the constitution on which Zimbabwe was ruled for the first five years of its independence and the transfer of power from the minority to the majority. However, the Rhodesian government attended as a separate entity, independent of the British government, to the chagrin of the PF.

The US was back playing a critical adjunct role to Britain[195] though, during the Jimmy Carter administration, which right from the outset showed itself to be different from its predecessor. The Carter Administration's involvement in Rhodesia though tertiary, had a deep impact because of its promotion of human rights as opposed to the Nixon policy, which had defined the conflict in Rhodesia in cold war terms.

With this kind of approach, the Carter administration quickly distanced itself from the South African government, and supported the principle of black majority rule as an expression of its commitment to human rights. It was in this spirit that Rev Andrew Young, the US Ambassador to the United Nations, and Cyrus Vance,[196] the US Secretary of State, were dispatched to Southern Rhodesia to play a supporting role to Dr. David Owen, the then British Foreign Secretary, who was trying to organize another conference with the parties to the conflict in Rhodesia.

Besides its conviction on human rights, the Carter Administration was under tremendous pressure from the African-American population who strongly supported black rule in Southern Rhodesia. As a critical constituency of the Democratic Party, the Carter administration could not ignore its critical members with impunity.

The Owen-Young-Vance initiative, what was at this time known as the Anglo-American initiative, led to a Conference in Malta on January 30 to February 1, 1978, known as Malta I. Present at this Conference were the PF, Andrew Young, Richard Moose, the US Assistant Secretary of State for African Affairs, General Prem Chand and the UN special representative for Rhodesia. Dr. David Owen chaired the talks.

The main goal of this meeting was to reconcile the PF's position with the Anglo-American proposals. The Anglo-American plan proposed a governing council to be set up to advise the resident governor, ten in number, and two from each of the five delegates to the Geneva Conference two years back. Also among the hot button issues was the demand that the black government that would come into power grant amnesty to the Rhodesian officials.

While grudgingly accepting amnesty for the Rhodesian operatives, ZAPU and ZANU rejected the composition of the governing council, demanding more power for their parties during the transitional period. They further demanded that all judges, magistrates and senior civil servants be removed during this time. Smith refused.

The Storm and Then Spears Turned into Plowshares

Malta II occurred in Dar es Salaam that same year, and at that time ZAPU and ZANU changed their position regarding the composition of the governing council. They demanded that the internal African leaders and Smith be considered as one entity and therefore should not be given separate representation. Smith and the internal black parties did not attend this conference, however, there is no question they were going to object to this demand. The Malta II initiative was overtaken by the initiative of the Commonwealth Meeting in Lusaka, Zambia, which led to the Lancaster House Conference, the third and last British Conference aimed at introducing a peaceful settlement in Rhodesia.

In the meantime, inside Rhodesia, and after the collapse of the Malta I initiative, the war escalated, and Smith turned inside for a solution. He invited the internal black parties for a conference on peace. On March 3, 1978, Smith, Muzorewa, Sithole and Chirau signed an Internal Peace Agreement, with one year's transition to majority rule. According to this arrangement, a Council of Ministers with a rotating chair position among the signatories to the agreement, replaced the cabinet. ZAPU scorned the agreement as a big farce and rallied the international community to denounce the settlement. Most British Conservative party members supported it, and so did South Africa. The following year in May 1979, national elections were held and Muzorewa won 51, Sithole 12, Chief Kayisa Ndiweni 9, and Chief Jeremiah Chirau nothing.[197] On the side of the whites, the RF won all the 28 blocking seats.

What Smith could not get from the Kissinger plan he got from his own internal settlement. According to the agreement, whites got twenty-eight reserved seats out of one hundred seats; a blocking number, and the ministries of police and defense, as well as secretary posts of all ministries remained in their hands. Muzorewa hoped against hope the world recognized his government, as a black government, which satisfied the requirements of majority rule and lifting sanctions. During the interim, he and Sithole had managed to woo some of the ZANLA cadres to return to Rhodesia and join them. As should have been expected most of the international world denounced the elections, with the FLPs leading the diplomatic fight.

No one could be fooled; this was a white government with blacks as window-dressers. At this point what was important to Smith was the lifting of sanctions and the ending of the war. Deep down in his heart of hearts he knew the chances were very slim for the internal nationalists to stop the war. That is why he had initially, earlier on, approached Nkomo wanting to surrender power to him.

According to Nkomo, Smith in the last quarter of 1978 approached him, ready to hand over power to him on a platter. They met in Lusaka at the State house where Kaunda hosted them. Nkomo said at this conference he found Smith "a tired man, a battered man. He told me he wanted to surrender power …I am convinced he knew the game was up…"[198] Nkomo held these face-to-face talks with Smith without the knowledge of his counterpart Mugabe. But when Smith offered to hand over power, Nkomo did what he did best, which was to indicate to Smith that he had to bring in his compatriot, Mugabe.

Mugabe, to the disillusionment of Nkomo, did what he did best, which was to reject anything of which he was not leader, even if it was a good deal. According to Nkomo, Mugabe rejected the deal because Nyerere who felt left out in this deal influenced him.[199]

As a "Messiah" of African liberations, Nyerere reasoned, he should lead all peace initiatives. It was unfortunate that for the sake of their selfish `egos' Nyerere and Mugabe, as Nkomo again observed, "condemned my country to three years of civil war."[200] The beleaguered Smith perhaps would have continued with his efforts to hand over power to Nkomo had the latter's army not shot down a civilian Viscount aircraft in early September. Whites, Smith's mainstay constituency, were incensed and his overtures to Nkomo went up in smoke.

With Muzorewa in power as of June 1, 1979, war escalated, and hope that he would stop it soon evaporated. By the middle of 1979 the PF had made enormous military gains. However, Muzorewa was still banking on Margaret Thatcher who had promised to back up the winner of the elections if the Tory Group of Observers declared them fair.[201] Unfortunately for Muzorewa, the observers did not, and consequently Thatcher withheld her support. More disappointment was in store for Muzorewa and his manipulator Smith.

In August 1979, a Commonwealth Heads of Governments met in Lusaka. At this Conference the heads of states exerted their final pressure on Margaret Thatcher to try and cut the Gordian Knot of the Rhodesia political stalemate by calling for a conference involving all parties to the problem.[202] They reiterated the position that Britain had the responsibility to grant independence to Rhodesia, a position which ZAPU had maintained since its founding. Thatcher had declared on her arrival in Lusaka on July 31 that Britain would not recognize Zimbabwe/Rhodesia if it was not recognized by the other Commonwealth states.[203] Sensing the intensifying tension around the Rhodesian political impasse, Thatcher and her Foreign Secretary, Lord Carrington, consented to convene an all-party constitutional conference that would include even Smith's blue-eyed boy, Muzorewa.

Before August was out, Thatcher had sent invitations to Muzorewa and the PF leaders. Along with invitational words, Thatcher called for a cease-fire. Nkomo accepted the invitation but refused to accept British plea for a cease-fire during the conference. Mugabe too accepted the invitation, but put as his condition for attending the total dismantlement of the Rhodesian army and its replacement by PF forces. Reluctance to participate in future negotiations on the part of the PF had a historical basis. Previous trials to attain a peaceful settlement had collapsed on mutual intransigencies largely around the modalities of the transitional process, more specifically relating to the modalities of a cease-fire. For instance, the 1977 initiative ran into trouble with the Rhodesian white regime because it envisioned a transitional force whose nucleus was composed of guerrilla forces. Equally unacceptable to the Smith regime as envisaged by the Anglo-American initiative, was the deployment of a force and

The Storm and Then Spears Turned into Plowshares

a UN representative with substantive oversight powers. On the other hand, PF nationalists found the Kissinger Initiative unacceptable because it gave whites veto power and also stipulated that the Ministry of Defense, among other key ministries remain in the hands of the whites.[204] So as all the Rhodesian parties prepared for the all-party conference, there was a spirit of skepticism as to its success based on previous failed conferences.

From September 10 to December 21 the parties to the Lancaster House Conference met to discuss a settlement that led to the independence of Southern Rhodesia, and the introduction of majority rule. These parties included Britain, the colonial power, who presided over the conference, PF delegates led by Nkomo and Mugabe respectively, Prime Minister Muzorewa whose delegation included Sithole and Smith. Right from the outset, the PF clearly expressed what they had come for. Nkomo spoke on behalf of the PF. His opening statements were in keeping with ZAPU's stated purpose when it attended the Geneva Conference.

Nkomo said in his opening statement:

We must at this conference, close and seal the chapter of British colonialism. We regard this conference as strictly between Zimbabweans of whatever color and race on the other hand, and the colonizers, the UK government. The simple straightforward issue before the conference is the transfer of power from the colonizer, the UK government to the people of Zimbabwe, through a process of decolonization.

Nkomo, at this conference in his opening statement on behalf of the PF raised very touchy questions to set the tone for the conference, questions that pretty much set by ZAPU's position about the conference. PF's position was the same as that stated by Nkomo: the transfer of power. Among the many issues Nkomo raised questions about whether the PF forces would be integrated into the enemy army, police, and civil service during the transition to ensure free and fair elections, whether the UN forces would be called upon to maintain law and order, and how the British government would exercise her power during the transitional period.

While Mugabe called for total disintegration of the enemy forces, Nkomo called for integration. If anything, although he did not get most of what he wanted, Nkomo at the Lancaster House talks showed his skills as a consummate negotiator. The biggest loser was Mugabe, who from time to time tried to take an independent stand to that of the PF, and at some point threatened to leave the conference for New York to argue his case before the UN. Mugabe demanded that the Muzorewa army to replaced by PF forces, he called for the elimination of the Rhodesian institutions, which had been constructed to protect key interests of the white regime, but none of these changes were made.

At the end of the conference, Mugabe literally had very little to show for his radical revolutionary rhetoric. However, his suspicion of the British was justifiable given its past dealings with black nationalists in Rhodesia. The only major problem with his mistrust is that it had developed into a destructive paranoia so that any negotiations with him were at this point almost impossible. Nkomo trusted the British no more than Mugabe did; however, it had been his policy, from the beginning of the struggle for independence, more so as leader of ZAPU, to force Britain's hand. The final settlement was disappointing to ZAPU too, but because they had not made untenable demands, their sense of defeat was not as great.

After fourteen weeks and forty-seven sessions of negotiation, with Nkomo playing a very influential role of keeping Mugabe in the negotiations, assisted in this situation by President Machel and ZANLA General Commander Josiah Tongongara, an agreement was reached on December 15, 1979. The PF had made very crippling concessions:

1) The 'one man, one vote' principle had been watered down to permit the 200,000 whites (3% of the population) to retain 20 out of 100 parliamentary seats;

2) According to the new Constitution not even the uncultivated white lands could be expropriated without compensation;

3) The new government would inherit a public debt of nearly $200 million;

4) Pensions would have to be paid to all the civil servants of the illegal regime, even those who immigrated; and

5) The Salisbury government troops would not be disbanded, but would form the core of the new state's defense.[205]

Even though Nkomo and Mugabe did not agree with these terms, they had to but sign because of pressure coming from their patrons, Kaunda and Machel. Earlier on, when Mugabe threatened to leave the Conference, Machel made it clearly known to him through his spokesperson in London that he would not be welcomed to prosecute war from his country, but would only be given a haven as a refugee. Machel told Mugabe to stop quibbling, and to sign the agreement. Kaunda put similar pressure on Nkomo so that his signing on the agreement, like that of Mugabe, was *fait accompli*. However, the PF too had its own victories, when Carrington agreed to put its forces and that of the regime under the authority of Governor Christopher Soames.

Among the unpalatable concessions, the one on land hit the Zimbabwean population the hardest because land was the central issue during the liberation. The expropriation of African land by white settlers guaranteed them economic domination, and for Africans poverty, during the colonial era. With the independence constitution promising no easy way of acquiring land by government for its general population, enduring structures of inequality between the whites and blacks were almost guaranteed. Thus, as far as the black general population was concerned, the land concession was its greatest loss.

In all, the conference produced arrangements for a transitional period before independence, during which time Britain assumed full colonial control

The Storm and Then Spears Turned into Plowshares

over Rhodesia. A constitution, which envisaged a legislature with one hundred lower house members, with twenty seats reserved for the whites, and a senate. This was a unitary state system as opposed to a federal kind, which could have served Zimbabwe very well, given its diverse ethnic composition. Unfortunately none of the parties involved in negotiations raised this issue, even Nkomo himself, when it was clear that ZANU was intent on using the tribal card in elections leading to majority rule.[206]

Also, it produced a cease-fire agreement, effective on December 28, 1979. According to the cease-fire terms, guerrillas were to assemble in sixteen Assembly Points (APs) by January 4, 1980.[207] ZAPU had a conservative count of about 12,000[208] armed cadres at the time of independence, and at least ninety percent of them went into Assembly points. However, the full ZIPRA force was believed to have been between 16,000 and 25,000 depending. During the transitional period, also repatriated were refugees who had fled the country, a task that was executed with the help of churches.

Since customs were under the Rhodesian regime, refugees had a hard time coming into the country; the processing went too slowly, with some being mistreated by customs officers. ZAPU complained about the harassment to Soames, the man representing the British government in the decolonization process.[209]

At the time of the signing of the agreement ZAPU's threat on the security of Rhodesia was real. So Nkomo gave his concession when he was still strong militarily. By the time of the cease-fire, ZIPRA forces had occupied as much geographical space as their counterpart, the ZANLA forces. In the cities highly trained but small ZIPRA expeditionary forces were already well positioned for the execution of the ZHP. The RSFs, however continued to attack and destroy the Zambian economic infrastructure, and this probably, was one of the major factors that pushed Kaunda to putting more pressure on Nkomo to sign the agreement. So, from a client's standpoint, Nkomo was at a disadvantage since Kaunda seemed more inclined to refuse him bases if he did not sign the settlement agreement.

Mugabe, according to his Deputy Commander General, who confided in one of the former regime's soldiers nineteen years after independence, was quickly losing his best trained men to the regime attacks and their replacement was too slow. ZANLA was at a desperate point. ZANLA's strength then owed largely to the presence of seasoned FRELIMO troops who were within its ranks.[210] With Machel threatening a withdrawal of his support, Mugabe was immediately confronted with essentially a problem of a weak military and no havens.

With the beginning of the Lancaster House Talks, things on the ground in Rhodesia were changing very rapidly. On December 7, the government of Britain appointed Christopher Soames as governor of Rhodesia during the transitional period, and with his arrival in Salisbury on December 12, Southern Rhodesia regained its legality and sanctions got lifted. Again, with the signing of the peace deal, Britain got out of the Rhodesian imbroglio. Over the last three days of February 1980, in what appeared to be an election inspired by ethnic loyalties, Mugabe was swept into power in a landslide victory. Of the eighty seats contested by blacks, Mugabe won fifty-seven seats, Nkomo twenty, and Muzorewa, despite his unlimited resources, got only three seats. ZANU, a dominantly Shona party, won more than eighty percent of votes in Mashonaland, and the dominantly Ndebele party, ZAPU, got the same percentage in Matebeleland.[211]

These elections were well covered, as they were 680 journalists and 281 observers. Also there were 1,300 solders from the Commonwealth countries who served as monitors of the cease-fire.[212] On the whole, the election results were a big victory for ZAPU and ZANU as the liberation movements, and of the Southern African struggle in general. On April 18, 1980 at midnight, the Union Jack went down as the new Zimbabwean flag went up, signaling the achievement of Zimbabwe's independence. The new government had four ZAPU cabinet ministers, with Nkomo heading the ministry of Home Affairs, and two white ministers.

6.10 SUMMARY AND CONCLUSION

This was an action filled period which saw political change in Rhodesia moving from failed attempts at peaceful negotiations, based on mutual intransigencies on the part of the parties involved, to an increased tempo of the war, resulting in a great loss of life and a great exodus of the Rhodesian black population to cities and to external countries.[213] ZAPU moved its military strategy to the second level during this period.

After having spent the first era, 1964 through part of 1970, politicizing the general population and creating war structures inside of Rhodesia, studying its war theater, training "imujibha" internally, as well as caching arms, ZAPU stepped into a full scale war against the RSFs. Starting with the Pierce Commission in 1971, ZAPU was involved for the first time since 1961, in deciding the fate of Rhodesia albeit by way of indirection, under the ANC, as it was still banned in the country.

In fact, throughout the 1970s ZAPU applied its two-pronged approach of fighting and negotiating. At the same time it seriously engaged in trying to form coalitions with other black liberation movements in the country, first with the ANC in the early 1970, and then under the PF with ZANU. Also it tried its hand at a military unity with ZANU, leading to the formation of ZIPA. ZIPA, as would later the PF, faltered largely because of ZANU's lack of interest in any kind of unity that did not put it in the leadership. Commenting after independence on the character of Mugabe and his inclination towards unity Wilfred Mhanda (a.k. Dzinashe Machingura) said, his leader was "arrogant, paranoid, secretive and only interested in power," and on Mugabe's desire for unity during the liberation struggle Mhanda noted, "he didn't want unity at all

The Storm and Then Spears Turned into Plowshares

since he was scared that Nkomo, as the senior African nationalist, would take over a united movement."[214]

However, as an African saying goes, that however long the darkness, the light will eventually come, coming it did in 1979. The era, which started with daggers-drawn, causing untold suffering and a death toll overall, including those who died in the 1960s, of at least 30,000 to 40,000,[215] ended with olive branches exchanged as an all-party conference delivered a peaceful settlement.

The ending of the war in such a manner, short of a complete military take-over was, perhaps, unsatisfying to some hawks within ZAPU who might have believed that revolutionary wars end in total surrender on the part of the opposing forces. If Jason Moyo, the late Vice-President of ZAPU, were alive then he would have shared in the same feeling of dissatisfaction.

In reality though, according to some scholars of revolutionary wars, revolutionary struggles can have more than one ending. Louise Pirouet presents four ways in which such wars end, putting some emphasis on their inconclusive nature. The first way of concluding a struggle is in a formal negotiated settlement of the conflict between the regime and the revolutionary leaders. Sudan provides a good example of this kind of ending.

The second type is an informal negotiated settlement, and the ending of the Mau Mau Uprising in Kenya is a good example. Third, a complete takeover by the revolutionary forces, and four, a defeat of the revolutionary combatants by the state, such as in Malaya where a military defeat of the regime was avoided.[216] Earlier, another scholar of revolutions, Ted Gurr, had reached similar conclusions based on his study of internal wars in 119 nations which began or ended between 1961 and 1965. Gurr observed:

> *There were forty-eight distinguishable guerrilla, civil and revolutionary wars, not counting coups, military rebellions, or isolated instances of armed resistance. By 1978 three were still major conflicts, while fragmentary accounts indicated that sporadic resistance continued in nine other instances; clear-cut revolutionary victories are uncommon.*
>
> *It is also evident that decisive outcomes are not as common in most internal wars as they have been in the best-known historical examples, for instance, France 1789 and 1848, the United States 1865, Russia 1917, China 1949, Greece 1949, Cuba 1959, Nigeria 1970 and Vietnam 1974. Dramatic victory and defeat have impressed these examples on political memory. The more numerous revolts that ended in compromise and mutual exhaustion are less often remembered....*[217]

Such disappointment on the part of the likes of Moyo was understandable in light of the fact that ZAPU was at the brink of militarily overrunning Rhodesia. Rightly, most of the ZIPRA cadres saw themselves as losing power and being robbed of 'sweet' military victory by accepting a negotiated settlement at a point when their military prowess and might was a threat to the RSF than never before.

All the same, ZAPU accepted the verdict of the peace settlement, and went home. It ran in the first independence elections and lost; however, ZAPU won all the seats in Matebeleland, and one in Mashonaland while the ruling party won not even a single seat in Matebeleland. A conclusion can be reasonably made that the results of the elections formed a basis for the ensuing conflict between the ruling party and ZAPU, leading to the dissolution of the latter.

This period also saw ZAPU shine on three different fronts,

1) In the execution of the war with considerably quantitative as well as qualitative contributions to the liberation struggle.

2) ZAPU also sought peace by pursuing a path of negotiations whenever opportunity availed, and thereby helping in the keeping of faith in negotiated settlement alive. And

3) Last, but not the least, ZAPU trained personnel for an independent Zimbabwe, a key contribution to the civil service after independence.

Endnotes

1. For sources providing a good overview of negotiations on Zimbabwe, see Joshua Nkomo, *The Story of My Life* (London: Methuen, 1984); Canaan S. Banana, *Turmoil and Tenacity: Zimbabwe 1890-1990*, Harare: The College Press, 1989; M. Tamarkin, *The Making of Zimbabwe: Decolonizing in Regional and International Politics* (London: Frank Cass, 1990); Stephen John Stedman, *Peacemaking in Civil War: International Mediation in Zimbabwe 1974-1980* (Boulder: Lynne Rienner, 1991).

2. According to the interview information I got from twelve responds representing Zimbabwe's eight provinces, ZIPRA was, already, living among the villagers in the rural areas. Their melting into the local population was made easier by the fact that ZAPU's political organization had organized structures in all the provinces by this time, albeit operating underground. Although it operated as a legal organization in Zimbabwe before it was banned, ZAPU membership was in all of the provinces, largely because it inherited most of its membership from its predecessors, SRANC and NDP. For the numerical growth of SRANC, NDP and ZAPU as well as their geographical spread, see Nathan Shamuyarira, *Crisis in Rhodesia*, New York: Transatlantic Arts, 1965; Ishmael Mlambo, *Rhodesia: The Struggle for a Birthright*, London: C. Hurst & Company, 1972; Nkomo, *The Story of My Life* (1984); Banana, *Turmoil and Tenacity* (1989). According to Black Moses, a former ZIPRA Commander and Commissar, to be well ensconced meant:

   1) To have been able to put a courier system for information dissemination and intelligence sharing in place.

   2) To have been in the operational theater for at least six months without being found-out.

   3) To have been able to establish a very trusting relationship and co-operation from a majority of the community.

   4) To have been able to identify ZAPU's underground structures, and established a co-operative working relationship with them.

The Storm and Then Spears Turned into Plowshares

    5) To have been able to familiarize one's self with the terrain, its access and escape paths.

    6) To have been able to convert the locals in the operational theater into providers, informants, transporters, in brief, a complement to its armed ZIPRA forces, (Black Moses, Interview with the author, July 24, 1990)..

3. Dumiso Dabengwa, "ZIPRA and ZIPA in the Zimbabwe War of National Liberation," a paper presented at the University of Zimbabwe, (July 8, 1991), p. 16.

4. *Ibid.*, pp. 15-16.

5. Elliot Sibanda, as the Senior Intelligence Officer, became the highly prized catch by the Rhodesian forces in the late 1970's. He created fear among the Rhodesians, and they nicknamed him `the Black Swine.'

6. Joshua Nkomo, Interview with the Author, 26 July 1995, Black Moses, interview by author, 24 August 1997.

7. Maxey, *The Fight fro Zimbabwe* (1975), pp. 98-131; Martin and Johnson, *The Struggle for Zimbabwe* (1981), pp. 73-91.

8. Dumiso Dabengwa, "ZIPRA and ZIPA in the Zimbabwe War of National Liberation," a paper presented at the University of Zimbabwe, July 8, 1991.

9. Sibiya Mpofu, interview by author, 15 September 1980.

10. Ngwabi Bhebe & Terence Ranger, *Soldiers in Zimbabwe's Liberation War* (London: James Currey, 1995), p. 12.

11. The word *ibhabhayila* (sweet potato), was fondly used by the guerrillas and their supporters in reference to land mines. Initially, it was used as a code word but in the course of time when the enemy had learnt what it meant, it was merely used as an affectionate term for land mines. This goes to show how wide spread the use of land mines was during this period under study. It was indeed the weapon of choice.

12. Peter Godwin and Ian Hancock, 'Rhodesians Never Die': The Impact of War and Political Change on White Rhodesia, c.1970-1980 (New York: Oxford University Press, 1993), Chapter III.

13. Allert, *The Rhodesian Front War* (1989). pp. 115-116.

14. A. R. Wilkinson, "From Rhodesia to Zimbabwe," in B. Davidson, J. Slovo and A. R. Wilkinson, *Southern Africa: The New Politics of Revolution* (London: Penguin Books, 1976), p. 258.

15. Peter Godwin & Ian Hancock, "The Rhodesians Never Die" (1993), pp. 88-89.

16. Basil Davidson, Joe Slovo and Anthony R. Wilkinson, *South Africa: The New Politics of Revolution* (New York: Penguin Books, 1976), p. 310.

17. Francis Sibanda, interview by author, 20 August 1980. Francis operated on several occasions from bases in Botswana and was part of the 3-2-3 scheme. His account finds collaboration from an unexpected source, the wife of a SAS man Barbara Cole in her book, *The Elite: The Story of the Rhodesian Special Air Service* (Amanzimtoti: The Three Knights, 1984), pp. 66-67.

18. *Ibid.*, p. 67.

19. Francis Sibanda, interview by author, 20 August 980.

The Zimbabwe African People's Union 1961-1987

20. Barbara Cole, *The Elite* (1984), p. 78.

21. Moorcroft & McLaughlin, *Chimurenga* (1982), pp. 167-168.

22. Paul Moorcraft, *African Nemesis: War and Revolution in Southern Africa_1945-2010* (London: Brussey's, 1990), p. 130.

23. Michael Raeburn, *We Are Everywhere: Narratives From Rhodesian Guerrillas* (New York: Random House, 1979), p. 200.

24. Michael Bratton, "Settler State, Guerrilla War, and Rural Underdevelopment in Rhodesia," *Issue*, Vol. 9, No.1/2 Spring/Summer (1979): 56-62.

25. Simon Nkala, interview by author, 25 December 1981.

26. *Ibid.*

27. *Ibid.*

28. Ernest van den Haag, *Political Violence and Civil Disobedience* (New York: Harper, 1972).

29. See James Scott, *Weapons of the Weak: Everyday Forms of Peasant Resistance* (New Haven: Yale University Press, 1985). Also see his *The Moral Economy of the Peasant* (New Haven: Yale University Press, 1976).

30. Barbara Cole observes that up to 1978, ZANLA's contact with the Rhodesian Security Forces invariably resulted in high kills on the part of ZANLA, and she says the reason of these disastrous results was because ZANLA was, up to 1978, largely using obsolete weapons, such as the World War II Thompson Machine Gun. But after 1978 on, once they acquired modern machine guns, ZANLA ferociously and successfully defended its position.

31. A specific number of ZANLA forces as compared with those of ZIPRA around this period still remained inconclusive. According to Sibiya Mpofu, who crossed over from ZIPRA to ZANLA in late 1971, when he joined ZANLA it had about two hundred cadres, about half of whom were former ZIPRA forces that had joined ZANLA in the course of 1971. Mpofu speculated that ZIPRA at that time had around nine hundred armed men after the defection (Sibiya Mpofu, Interview by Author, January 15, 1983). Fay Chung, a ZANU official stated that before the ZAPU leadership Crisis, ZIPRA had 800 soldiers and ZANLA had 12. After the split, ZIPRA had 600 and ZANLA 212, a gain of two hundred soldiers from ZIPRA. It is doubtful that two hundred cadre switched sides for ZANLA at this time. I believe Mpofu's figures constitute an acceptable approximation, seeing he was actively involved as a fighter in both groups. That said, the specifics in terms of numbers remains elusive, but one thing is clear; that ZAPU had more soldiers than ZANU.

32. However, most of the cadres correctly considered themselves better trained than Nhongo and Togongara both of whom had received training at the beginning of the war and did not have an opportunity of going for advanced training thereafter.

33. Sheba Gava, (whose real name is Vitalis Zvinavashe) who had a rank of Major General in the early 1990s and is a former ZANLA cadre, asserted that as late as 1967 ZANLA had serious recruitment problems to the extent that at one time it attacked ZAPU's recruiting Luthuli Camp to try and force the latter to join them. The strong drive to recruit, according to Gava was decided upon by his party because of the pressure from the OAU requiring them to demonstrate commitment to the armed struggle by having men under training or risk losing support. On the

other front, Nyerere was threatening to close down their virtually empty Intumbi training camp for the same reason.

34. Astrow, *Zimbabwe: The Revolution That Lost Its Way?* (London: Zed Press, 1983), p. 151. Nkomo was condemned by some scholars, such as Astrow, for deploying only about 2,000 trained troops when he had allegedly 10,000 trained soldiers in camps in Zambia, with 17,000 more in training. These were the same scholars who once condemned ZAPU for deploying large groups instead of small ones since this was guerrilla warfare. Nkomo had a very clear strategy, and that strategy involved strategically deploying his troops in such a way that he avoided mass slaughter on their part since they did not have heavy weapons to defend their positions yet, especially from military aircraft. For most of these scholars it just became a religious cult to condemn any political action Nkomo followed, and thereby becoming unwitting supporters of the division that existed between the Black Nationalist parties, and ultimately supporters of the regime. None of these scholars tried to understand ZAPU's position.

35. M. Tamarkin, *The Making of Zimbabwe: Decolonization in Regional and International Politics* (London, 1990). Deducing from Tarmakin's observation of the quantitative growth of nationalist forces in the north-east towards the end of December 1975, and the increase in fighting and its improved quality, it is clear that the presence of ZIPRA forces did not add numbers but also significantly improved the fighting. Undoubtedly, ex-ZIPRA forces contributed immensely to army discipline and professional war tactics given their extensive training.

36. Godwin, *et al, Rhodesians Never Die* (1993), pp.103-105.

37. *Noticias de Beira* (Beira) September 7, 1973.

38. *Moto*, Gwelo (July 28, 1973).

39. Godwin, *et al, Rhodesians Never Die* (1993), pp. 213 and 235.

40. The PVs were surrounded with mesh fence and barbed wire. Generally, each PV would have two entrances, which were guarded by African District Assistants armed with .303 rifles. Most of these Africans ended up being sympathetic to the cause of the insurgents. Africans could still go out and work their fields, which were at least five kilometers from the PVs and this allowed them more contact with incoming guerrilla groups, even chances of bringing them in into the PVs. Only the perimeters of the PVs were lit all night long, otherwise the villages themselves enjoyed the cover of darkness, and because there was no monitoring at night guerrillas used the night to organize the people.

41. Raeburn, *We are Everywhere* (1978), p. 12.

42. Kees Maxey, *The Fight for Zimbabwe: The Armed Conflict in Southern Rhodesia Since Independence* (London: Rex Collings Ltd, 1975), pp. 121-122.

43. The Francistown office was temporarily closed in 1974 when the Rhodesian operatives kidnapped its staffers.

44. Levi Luphahla, interview by author, December 17, 1996.

45. Barbara Cole, *The Elite: The Story of Rhodesian Special Air Forces* (Amanzimtoti: Three Knights Publishing, 1984), p. 231.

46. *Ibid.*

47. Dumiso Dabengwa, "ZIPRA in the Zimbabwe War of National Liberation," in *Soldiers in Zimbabwe's Liberation War*, edited by Ngwabi Bhebe and Terence Ranger (London: James Currey, 1995), p.33.
48. Anthony Lake, *The "Tar Baby" Option: American Policy Toward Southern Rhodesia* (New York: Columbia University Press, 1973), p. 24.
49. *Rhodesia Herald* (6 December, 1976).
50. *Ibid.*
51. Quoted in Andre Astrow, *Zimbabwe: A Revolution That Lost Its Way?* (London: Zed Books Ltd., 1983), pp. 96-97.
52. Colin Legum, *The Battlefront of Southern Africa* (London: Africana Publishing Company, 1988), p. 36.
53. Thomas Nhari's real name was Raphael Chinyanganya. Nhari was trained in Russia under ZAPU during which time he fell in love with Russian weaponry, and also ZIPRA's way of fighting as opposed to the purely Maoist one. In 1973, after he defected from ZAPU to ZANU, Chinyanganya was involved in press-ganging students from St. Albert, a Roman Catholic Mission school, and went via Mozambique into Zambia. However, when he got to Zambia only a handful of students remained as most of them had run away.
54. Dumiso Dabengwa, "ZIPRA in the Zimbabwe War of National Liberation," in *Soldiers in Zimbabwe's Liberation War*, edited by Ngwabi Bhebe and Terence Ranger (London: James Currey, 1995), p. 33.
55. The Joint High Command was formed in Maputo, Mozambique on November 12, 1975.
56. Blessing D. Maringapasi, "The Development of ZANLA Strategy of Guerrilla Warfare," B.A. dissertation, University of Zimbabwe (1983), p. 12.
57. Bhebe and Ranger, ed., *Soldiers in Zimbabwe's Liberation War* (1995), pp. 33-34.
58. *Ibid.*, pp. 73-86.
59. Alfred Nikita Mangena, who led the ZIPRA forces back to Zambia after the collapse of the unity pact between ZANU and ZAPU is said to have reported that there were some ex-ZANLA guerrillas who viewed ZIPA as an independent military and political entity, (C [harles] Utete, *The Road to Zimbabwe: The Political Economy Settler Colonialism, National Liberation and Foreign Intervention* (Washington: University Press of America, 1979), p. 117.
60. Once Mugabe realized he could no longer use ZIPA for his own personal interests, he turned around and denounced it. At one time Mugabe characterized ZIPA as "a negation of the negation (which) we must negate in turn ... as the negation of the negation," David Moore, "Struggles for Socialism and Democracy," unpublished manuscript, p. 26. Immediately after the Geneva Talks, ZANU leaders denounced ZIPA leaders as counter-revolutionaries. This was the beginning of the end of ZIPA.
61. *Ibid.*, p. 34.
62. *Ibid.*, p. 34.
63. 77 Cadres of the African National Council (Zimbabwe), "Memorandum to the OAU Liberation Committee," Morogoro Camp, 24 August 1976. The Morogoro

The Storm and Then Spears Turned into Plowshares

camp was predominately ZIPRA and Mgagao, ZANLA. However, they were both in Tanzania were ZANLA enjoyed the patronage of Nyerere, its President.

64. Astrow, *Zimbabwe*, 1983, 97.
65. David Moore, "The Zimbabwe People's Army: Strategic Innovation or More of the Same," in *Soldiers of Zimbabwe's Liberation War*, edited by Ngwabi Bhebe and Terence Ranger (London: James Currey, 1991), 86.
66. Robin Moore, *Major Mike and His Galloping Goffles*, New York: Charter, 1978), p.304. Robin Moore and Major L. H. "Mike" William were among the mercenaries that fought on the side of the white Rhodesians under a misconception there were fighting against communism. They joined some of their fellow American soldiers of fortune that called themselves the Crippled Eagles, in the 1970s. Major Mike was kicked out of Rhodesia because of his alleged atrocities, some of which fringed on sexual abuse of the locals in 1977.
67. Paul Moorcraft, *A Thousand Years: The End of Rhodesia's Rebellion* (Salisbury: Galaxie, 1979), p. 164.
68. ZAPU, *Our Path to Liberation* (Lusaka, 1977).
69. *Ibid.*, p. 3. The conference to which Moyo made reference in this document was the Geneva Conference of 1976.
70. *Ibid.*, p. 4.
71. *Ibid.*
72. Dabengwa, "ZIPRA and ZIPA in the Zimbabwe War" (1991), p. 28.
73. Jeremy Brickhill, "Daring to Storm the Heavens: The Military Strategy of ZAPU 1976 to 1979," in *Soldiers in Zimbabwe's Liberation War* (1995), p. 50. Jeremy Brickhill was an assistant to Dumiso Dabengwa in the Department of National Security and Order. One of his many functions was to analyze operations. Brickhill is a white Zimbabwean who decided to join ZIPRA and fight against the racist Rhodesian regime.
74. *Ibid.*
75. Stiff, *Selous Scout: A Pictorial Account* (Alberto, RSA: Galago, 1984), pp. 107-108.
76. Brickhill, "Daring to Storm the Heavens: The Military Strategy of ZAPU 1976-1979," in *Soldiers in Zimbabwe's Liberation War* (1995), p. 66.
77. *Financial Times*, (November 1, 1976). The financial times quoted an extract from Ted Sutton Pryce, the then Deputy Minister in the Prime Minister's Office, to a closed meeting, where he painted a very dire economic situation in Rhodesia.
78. Bhebe, ed. *et al, Soldiers in Zimbabwe's Liberation War* (1995), p. 51.
79. Andrew Nyathi with John Hoffman, *Tomorrow is Built Today: Experiences of War, Colonialism, and the Struggle for Collective Co-operatives in Zimbabwe* (Harare: Anvil Press, 1990), p. 31. The commander in this area was Richard Mataure (really last name Ngwenya), his deputy, James Savanhu. Nyathi was deputy commissar to his friend with whom they left Rhodesia together for training Ishmail Kabaira, who unlike Nyathi who received advanced training in East Germany (GDR) was trained in the Soviet Union.
80. Dumiso Dabengwa, Interview with Jeremy Brickhill, (21 October, 1988) cited in Jeremy Brickhill, "Daring to Storm the Heavens: the Military Strategy of ZAPU

(1976-79), a paper presented at a Conference on the History of the Zimbabwe's Liberation War, (University of Zimbabwe, 1991).

81. Nyati, *Tomorrow is Built Today* (1990), p. 36.

82. R.F. Reidy-Daly, *Pamwe Chete: The Legend of the Selous Scouts* (Weltevreden Park, South Africa: Covos-Day Books, 1999), p. 312.

83. *Ibid.*, pp. 314-315.

84. *Ibid.*, p. 313.

85. Reid-Daly, *Pamwe Chete* (1999), pp. 365-366.

86. Samuel P. Huntington, *Political Order in Changing Societies* (New Haven: Yale University Press, 1968), pp. 271-272.

87. Following the Second World War, several Western scholars who were interested in guerrilla Warfare studied the writings of Mao. Their interest in such revolutions was largely in learning about strategies. Notably, among the writers in this area were: Sir Robert Thompson, *Defeating Communist Insurgency: The Lessons of Malaya and Vietnam* (New York: Praeger, 1967); J. S. Pustay, *Counter-insurgency Warfare* (New York: Free Press, 1965); David Galula, *Counter-insurgency Warfare, Theory and Practice* (New York: Praeger, 1964); A. Campbell, *Guerrillas a History and Analysis* (London: Arther Baker, 1967); R.L. Rylander, "Mao as a Clausewitzian Strategist," in *Military Review* (August, 1981), pp. 13-21; Peter Paret and John Shy, *Guerrillas in the 1960s* (New York: Praeger, 1962); D. Wilson, *Mao the People's Emperor* (London: Futura Publications, 1980).

88. Mao himself did not come-up with this revolution stage theory in any clear and precise terms. The polishing up of the stage theory based on Mao's works and practice, has been done by different scholars, see John N. McCuen, *The Art of Counter-Revolutionary War* (London: Faber and Faber, 1966), pp. 50-73); M. Rejai, ed., *Mao Tse-Tung on Revolution and War* (Garden City, New York: Doubleday & Company, 1970); Mao Tse-tung, *Guerrilla Warfare*, translated by Samuel B. Griffith (New York: Praeger, 1961).

89. Vo Nguyen Giap, *People's War People's Army* (Hanoi, 1961), p. 107.

90. A. Neuberg was not an individual, but rather a pseudonym for a group of Comintern revolutionaries, which included Ho Chi Minh.

91. A. Neuberg, *Armed Insurrection* (London, 1970), p. 264. This book was published for the first time in Germany in 1928.

92. According to Christians' reading of Revelations 16:16, Armageddon is the last War that would be fought on this earth between the forces of good and evil, resulting in God's final overthrow of evil. Thus, how the war in Rhodesia was viewed by the blacks: a war between good (Blacks' cause) and evil (whites' interests).

93. Nkomo, *The Story of My Life* (1984), p. 167.

94. For accounts on Rhodesians posing as guerrillas to sow mistrust among the guerrillas and the people see Julie Frederikse, *None but Ourselves* (New York: Penguin Books, 1984), pp. 281-303; J.C. Cilliers, *Counter-Insurgency in Rhodesia* (London: Croom Helm, 1985), pp. 118-134; Bruce Moore-King, *White Man, Black War* (Harare: Baobab Books, 1989).

95. Reid-Daly with the benefit of hindsight regretted: "The saddest part of this whole episode (shooting down of the aircraft) was that a Selous Scouts group had been

The Storm and Then Spears Turned into Plowshares

operating in that part ... for some time. Because of lack of information, I had moved them the day before the aircraft had been shot down," Reid-Daly, *Pamwe Chete*, (1999), p. 386.

96. Nkomo, *The Story of My Life* (1984), pp. 167-168.
97. *Ibid.*, p. 166.
98. In the second Viscount there some soldiers aboard, and the third one that came immediately after the second one had been shot down, was carrying the General Commander of the Rhodesian Forces.
99. Nkomo, *Story of My Life* (1984), pp. 167 and 191.
100. Cole, *The Elite* (1984), p. 222.
101. Cole, *The Elite* (1984), p. 222.
102. Reid-Daly, *Pamwe Chete* (1999), p. 388.
103. *Ibid.*, p. 367.
104. Reid-Daly, *Pamwe Chete* (1999), p. 391. This was the second plan to assassinate Nkomo after the first plan, which involved the hire of a Zambia driver, who, on some pretext was made to drive the claymore mined Ford Escort close to the car carrying Nkomo, at which point, using remote control, Anthony would have initiated the detonation, had failed. Anthony abandoned the first plan because he had concluded, "it was too dangerous and also impractical to employ a Zambian driver to drive the car close to Nkomo" (*ibid.*).
105. *Ibid.*, pp. 392-394.
106. *Ibid.*, pp. 404-406.
107. Cole, *The Elite* (1984), pp. 284.
108. What Reid-Daly describes here, as Nkomo's walking stick was actually a short knob-kerrie, which he received from traditional leaders and was believed to have some mystic powers. It was by no means a walking stick.
109. Reid-Daly, *Pamwe Chete* (1999), pp. 406-407.
110. Mangena was killed by a land mine laid by the Selous Scouts in Zambia between Simani Mine, ZIPRA's staging post, and Kabanga Mission, a Zambian Army's Brigade Head Quarters. See Cole, *The Elite* (1984), pp. 215-216.
111. In the 1960's when Air Rhodesia was still flying into Lusaka, Ellert wrote that pilots were used as agents and couriers. After Zimbabwe became independent, again Ellert would repeat that during the war of liberation, agents were recruited within the Zambian army, Intelligence Service and Air Force, (Henrick Ellert, "The Rhodesian Security and Intelligence Community 1960-1980: A Brief Overview of the Structure and Operational Role of the Military, Civilian and Police Security and Intelligence Organizations Which Served the Rhodesian Government During the Zimbabwean Liberation War," in Ngwebi Bhebe and Terence Ranger, eds., *Soldiers in Zimbabwe's Liberation War* (London: James Currey,1995), p. 92.
112. Cole, *The Elite* (1984), p. 284.
113. H. Ellert, *The Rhodesian Front War: Counter-Insurgency and Guerrilla War in Rhodesia, 1962-1980* (Gweru: Mambo Press, 1993), p.77.
114. Godwin and Hancock, *"Rhodesians Never Die"* (1993), p. 238.

115. Levi Mayihlome, An Interview with the Author, December 17, 1996. Levi was a ZIPRA officer in the Northern Front. He is currently a high rank officer in the Zimbabwe National Army.

116. Moore, *Major Mike* (1981), p. 290.

117. Peter Godwin, *Mukiwa: A White Boy in Africa* (New York: the Atlantic Monthly, 1996), p. 303.

118. Lane Flint, *God's Miracles Versus Marxist Terrorists: The Epic True Story of Men and Victims Who Fought The Rhodesian and South West African WARS* (Ladybrand: Meesterplan Publishers, 1985), pp. 202-203.

119. Reid-Daly, *Pamwe Chete* (1999), p. 67.

120. Reid-Daly, *Pamwe Chete* (1999), p. 341.

121. *BBC Monitoring Service* (July 28, 1979).

122. A.R. Wilkinson, "The Impact of the War," in the *Journal of Commonwealth and Comparative Politics* (March 1980): 114.

123. Nkomo, *The Story of My Life* (1984), p. 196.

124. Rev. Jonathan Dlodlo, Brethren in Christ Overseer for the Gwaai District, in the late 1970's, was arrested with his wife, a teacher, for providing sanctuary to ZIPRA guerrillas, and also for aiding and abating the spirit of insurgency. Some lay pastors such as Mtshumayeli Sibanda, G. Mathuthu, Nyati, Deacon Timothy Mpofu, Mtshede Sibanda, Luka Sibanda, Matthew Ndlovu, just to mention a few became very active in organizing and recruiting for ZAPU, and also served the party as officers.

125. Reid-Daly, *Pamwe Chete* (1999), p. 406.

126. Bhebe and Ranger, *Soldiers in Zimbabwe's Liberation War* (1991) p.61. Contributed by Jeremy Brickhill who once served with the ZIPRA intelligence during the liberation war. Brickhill also discusses the ZERO HOUR PLAN in his paper, which he presented at a conference that was held at the University of Zimbabwe in July 12-18, 1991 entitled, "Daring to Storm the Heavens: The Military Strategy of ZAPU (1976-79), p. 18-33.

127. Brickhill, "Daring to Storm the Heavens: The Military Strategy of ZAPU (1976-79), p. 19.

128. The account on the Zero Hour Plan was constructed from many sources: interviews with Joshua Nkomo, ZIPRA Commanders, and Jeremy Brickhill, "Daring to Storm the Heavens: The Military Strategy of ZAPU 1976-1979," *Soldiers in Zimbabwe's Liberation War* (1995), pp. 48-86. Very few commanders knew of this Plan whose details up to this day are still kept as top secret. Because of this, most informants do not want to remain anonymous for fear of reprisals from what they see as "a paranoid Mugabe government."

129. Reid-Daly, *Pamwe Chete* (1999), pp. 376-466.

130. Brickhill "A Step Further: ZAPU Military Strategy" (1991), pp. 15-16); J.K. Cilliers, *Counter-Insurgency in Rhodesia* (London: Croom Helm, 1985), pp. 190-191. Also see Reid-Daly, *Pamwe Chete*, (1999), pp. 447-452; Martin and Johnson, *The Struggle for Zimbabwe* (1985); P. Stiff, *Selous Scouts: Rhodesian War-A Pictorial Account* (Alberton: Galago, 1984); R. Reid Daly and P. Stiff, *Selous Scouts: Top Secret War* (Alberton: Galago, 1982).

131. *Ibid.* Also, see Ken Flower, who in his book offers a deluding rendition on the Zero Hour Strategy. Flower presents the architects of the strategy as pro-white South Africa's 'Total War,' and thereby trying to move attention away from the role played by the organization he led at the time the Plan was crafted, the CIO, in the spreading of disinformation (*Serving Secretly*, 1987), p. 245.

132. Nkomo, *The Story of My Life* (1984), p. 196.

133. J.K. Cilliers, *Counter-Insurgency in Rhodesia* (London, 1985), pp. 190-191.

134. Dumiso Dabengwa, interview by Jeremy Brickhill, 21 October 1988.

135. Jeremy Brickhill did some extensive research on the use of both biological and chemical weapons against the liberation forces, especially ZIPRA during the war of liberation. For use of anthrax, chemical and biological weapons, see a feature on Zimbabwe in the *New African* (September 1992): 42.

136. Rhodesians in what the members of their Intelligence Corps called psychological or psyops, studied and used African belief in witchcraft against them Cillier, *Counter-Insurgency in Rhodesia* (1985), p. 185. Clearly poising clothes and giving them to the locals was one way of making guerrillas believe that they were being bewitched by the locals.

137. "The Current Situation in Zimbabwe," *Issue*, Vol. 9 (1979), p. 63. This article was based on the report given by three clergy from the Rhodesian Roman Catholic Commission for Justice and Peace who visited U.S.A. in late October and early November 1978. In Zambia, ZIPRA regulars were trained in Mulungushi and Solwezi.

138. T.J. Jokow, "The Effect of the War on the Rural Population of Zimbabwe," *Journal of Southern African Affairs* (April 1980): 123.

139. The figures exclude the number of refugees in Mozambique, who were mostly ZANU supporters and were estimated at 80,000. The figures are very conservative ones, as the counting of refugees did not include the unregistered ones. Besides, it was difficult to count refugees as the host countries depended mostly on Zimbabwean Nationalists leaders who because of a lack of resources resorted to counting only those residing on their camps. It is known that a good number of refugees decided to slip into the various communities and lived a life unannounced to their nationalist leaders.

140. See Reid-Daly, *Pamwe Chete* (1999); Cole, *The Elite* (1984); Nkomo, *The Story of My Life* (1984), chapter 16.

141. The first group of officer cadets, however, completed their training at Kohima, Zambia. From then on a number of trainees increased dramatically, with the availability of more trainers on the ground.

142. Reid-Daly, *Pamwe Chete* (1999).

143. Philip Kayisa, Interview with the Author, August 6, 1984.

144. Cole, *The Elite* (1984), p. 388.

145. Cole, *The Elite* (1984), p. 393.

146. *Ibid.*

147. *Ibid.*, p. 393.

148. Cole, *The Elite* (1984), pp. 392-393.

149. Bhebe and Ranger, Soldiers in Zimbabwe's Liberation War (1995), pp. 63-64.

150. Three of these planes were shot down during the October raid. The number of the dead is the total of all the ZIPRA cadres who died in all the RSFs attacks, which occurred in two series, each containing waves of attacks in late October, and in November 1979.

151. Nkomo confided in an interview that the Russians wanted Russians, East Germans or Cubans to fly planes for ZIPRA and when his Party refused they then sabotaged the plan by holding back pilots who they said had not completed their training. Nkomo went further to say he detected some racism from the Russians who did not want to see their own Caucasian group defeated by blacks. ZAPU, he said, refused to accept this offer by the Russians for two reasons, 1. They did not want to internationalize the war, 2. It was confident, after doing its own studies that it could win against the war-weary Rhodesians (Joshua Nkomo, An Interview by Author, August 1990).

152. According to Nkomo, there was no coordination between ZAPU and ZANU on the ZHP; however, the party "assumed " that when the attack began, ZANU would engage the RSFs at a larger scale as well. Nkomo, *The Story of my Life* (1984), p. 197.

153. Reid Daly, *Pamwe Chete*, (1999), p. 341.

154. *Ibid.*

155. See Cole, *The Elite* (1984); Reid-Daly, *Pamwe Chete* (1999); Bhebe and Ranger, *Soldiers in Zimbabwe's Liberation War* (1995), specifically the article contributed by Jeremy Brickhill, pp. 48-72.

156. According to Brickhill, large artillery weapons such as 105mm B10's, 82mm mortars, got used by ZIPRA for the first time during 1978 attacks on garrisons and the towns of Kariba and Chirundu. These heavy wepons helped increase the guerrilla offensive capacity. More capacity for effectiveness was further enhanced by the attachment of anti-craft units equipped with ZGU anti-aircraft guns and SAM missiles to the guerrilla units in the north of the country. Brickhill, "Daring to Storm the Heavens" (July 12-18, 1991), p. 7.

157. Reid-Daly, *Pamwe Chete*, (1999), p. 480.

158. *Ibid.*

159. Bhebe and Ranger, eds., *Soldiers in Zimbabwe's Liberation War* (1991), p. 110, Nkomo, interview by author, 18 June 1998.

160. Nkomo, *The Story of My Life* (1984), pp. 196-197.

161. Reid-Daly, *Pamwe Chete* (1999), p. 341.

162. Jericho Nkala, *The United Nations, International Law, and the Rhodesian Independence Crisis* (Oxford: Clarendon Press, 1985), pp. 16-19.

163. *Ibid.*

164. Robert C. Good, *U.D.I. The International Politics of the Rhodesian Rebellion* (Boston: Princeton University Press, 1973), pp. 257-286.

165. *Ibid.*, p. 55.

166. *The Zimbabwe Review* (May/June): 3.

167. *New York Times* (January 27, 1972).

168. *The New York Times* (June 7, 1972).

The Storm and Then Spears Turned into Plowshares

169. *Africa Contemporary Record Annual Survey Document (1973-1974)*, B489, Colin Legum.

170. Right from its inception on December 16, 1971, the ANC had largely depended on existing, albeit underground, ZAPU/PCC structures: cells, branches, districts and provinces throughout the country to build its membership. As late as September 1975, when Nkomo formed ANC-Zimbabwe, ANC still enjoyed support from ZAPU structures (*The Zimbabwe Review*, Vol. 6, No.7, July 1977, p. 7.

171. As has been mentioned elsewhere in this chapter, the original organizers of the ANC, when it was formed in 1971, were ZAPU and ZANU members. Despite the arrest of the twenty who questioned the validity of the 1973 ANC/RF talks, some remained who continued to influence Muzorewa's position.

172. M[asiphula] Sithole, *Zimbabwe Struggles Within the Struggle* (Salisbury: Rujeko Publishers Ltd., 1979), p. 104.

173. Nkomo, *The Story of My Life* (1984), pp. 154-156.

174. Martin Meredith, *The Past is Another Country* (London: Andre Deutsch Ltd.,1979), p. 194.

175. Nkomo, interview by author, 26 July 1995; M. Tamarkin, *The Making of Zimbabwe: Decolonization in Regional and International Politics* (London: Frank Cass, 1990), pp. 78-110; Joshua Nkomo, *The Story of My Life* (1984), Chapter 15.

176. Tamarkin, *The Making of Zimbabwe* (1990), pp. 10-11, 78.

177. *Ibid.*, pp. 85-87. Apparently, of the two nationalist leaders, Nkomo and Mugabe, Smith might have thought that the former would be more willing to compromise on some agreement that did not involve a complete hand-over of power to the majority.

178. Referring to the impact of his internal negotiations with Smith Nkomo commented: "In talking to Smith I took a big personal risk ... I am still criticized for trying to negotiate with Smith. I hated what the man stood for. I longed for majority rule in Zimbabwe, and justice for my people. I knew all too well that the fierce fighting would mean grave problems at the end of the war. The period of failed negotiations had a high price for the nationalist side. Smith's army and police took advantage of the lull [to strengthen their position]." Nkomo, *The Story of My Life* (1984), p. 158.

179. *The Zimbabwe Star*, Organ of the ANC (February 21, 1976), p. 4.

180. *Ibid.*

181. *Ibid.*

182. Nkomo, *The Story of My Life* (1984), pp. 156-157.

183. *Ibid.*, p. 157.

184. At this time ZANU was under the leadership of Mugabe who had staged a coup de grace against Sithole while they were both in prison.

185. Attributing the failure of the Geneva Conference in part to Ivor Richards, Nkomo described him as "a cold person, uneasy in private talks and formal meetings alike, and he made no useful contributions," Joshua Nkomo, *The Story of My Life* (1984), p. 172.

186. The deal as was agreed upon by Ian Smith as a result of the Vorster-Smith-Kissinger talks in South Africa, as announced by the former on September 24, 1976 offered the following:

1) Majority rule within two years even though Smith insisted on 'responsible majority rule.'

2) Rhodesian representatives had to meet nationalist leaders to work out an interim government to precede majority rule.

3) The interim government was to comprise: a Council of State, half of whom were to be black and the other half white, with a white chairman.

4) The UK was going to enact legislation enabling the transition to majority rule. In return for these concessions: (a) sanctions were to be lifted; (b) there was to be an injection of development capital into the country; (c) there was to be an end to armed struggle; and (d) the creation of an international trust fund to guarantee pension rights, investment and to assist in development.

187. Anthony Lake, *The "Tar Baby" Option: American Policy Toward Southern Rhodesia* (New York: Columbia University Press, 1976); Bruce Oudes, "Southern Africa Policy Watershed," *Africa Report 19* (November-December 1974): 46-50; Houser, *No One Can Stop the Rain*, pp. 234-235. The US would finally impose sanctions on Rhodesia at the request of Britain, closing its consulate in Salisbury early in 1970.

188. Walter Isaacson, *Kissinger: A Biography* (New York: Simon & Schuster, 1992), pp. 685-686.

189. *Ibid.*, p. 686.

190. Nkomo, *The Story of My Life* (1984), pp. 170-171.

191. See Elaine Windrich, "Rhodesia: The Road from Lusaka to Geneva," *World Today 33* (March 1977): 107-109; Isaacson, *Kissinger* (1992), p. 690.

192. See Nkomo, *The Story of My Life* (1984).

193. Canaan Banana, ed., *Turmoil and Tenacity: Zimbabwe 1890-1990* (Harare: The College Press, [Pvt] LTD, 1989), p. 174.

194. *The Zimbabwe Review* (May/June 1977): 3.

195. It is worthy mentioning here that this combined initiative by Britain and United States, received support from the Commonwealth Heads of government Summit that convened in London in June 1977.

196. Nkomo was apparently happy and content with the US representation. In his books he describes Andrew Young as "the black American ... whom was emotionally sympathetic to our cause," and about Vance, he said that he had "a strong public commitment to human rights," Nkomo, *The Story of My Life* (1984), p. 188. Young was responsible for the US policy towards Africa.

197. *Free and Fair? The 1979 Rhodesian Election: A Report by Observers on Behalf of the British Parliamentary Human Rights Group* (May 1979), Appendix VII.

198. Nkomo, *The Story of My Life* (1984), p. 189.

199. *Ibid.*, pp. 189-190.

200. *Ibid.*, p. 190.

201. *African Nemesis*, p. 141.

202. One of the countries that attacked Britain for its Rhodesian policy was Nigeria. On August 1, a day after Thatcher arrived in Zambia for the Conference, Nigeria

The Storm and Then Spears Turned into Plowshares

announced the nationalization of the British Petroleum (Tamarkin, *The Making of Zimbabwe* (1990), pp. 250-251).

203. *Ibid.*, p. 250.

204. Stephen John Stedman, *Peacemaking in Civil War: International Mediation in Zimbabwe 1974-1980* (Boulder: Lynne Rienner, 1991), p. 169.

205. Mai Palmberg, ed., *The Struggle for Africa* (London: Zed Press, 1983), pp. 199-200.

206. The scourge of tribalism, which had been a thorn in the flesh of the Southern Rhodesian nationalism from its inception, became accentuated with the formation of ZANU, and continued to raise its head from time to time during the liberation struggle. The birth of FROLIZI, the death of Chitepo, the demise of ZIPA and the death of numerous blacks in the hands of other black Zimbabweans, all could be traced to ethnic animosity. Nkomo, although he dismissed in public claims that some of the Zimbabwean nationalists worked from ethnic motives that were destructive of nation-building, was very much aware of this problem. It was therefore a big mistake that he did not influence his party to press for a federal system in the independent Zimbabwe in order to protect minority ethnic groups.

207. For full details see *Southern Rhodesia: Report of the Constitutional Conference, Cmnd.* 7802 (September-December 1979); *Time* (November 26, 1979: 62-64).

208. Colin Legum, *The Battlefronts of Southern Africa* (New York: Africana Publishing Company, 1988), p. 105. Approximately 3,500 ZIPRA forces remained in Zambia, and 2,000 ZANLA forces in Mozambique until after elections.

209. Governor Christopher Soames in a letter to Ambassador Rajeshwar Dayal of the Commonwealth Observer Group Secretariat, 23 February 1980. Soames was responding to Rajeshwar Dayal letters in which he raised concerns about delays in the repatriation process. According to Governor Soames, 23 February 1980 letter, repatriation of refugees was going to be suspended between February 25 and March 3. Ambassador Dayal's concern is understandable as elections were coming the last week of February. The ambassador wrote on the 18 February, just a week before the suspension of the repatriation process. Evidently, the Muzorewa regime thought that by considerably slowing down the repatriation of refugees, elections would be to his party's advantage.

210. The informant was a Major General in the Rhodesian Army. For his safety he chose to remain anonymous. The ZANU-PF commander he was referring to was Lt. Gen. Solomon Mujuru. There is no reason for this writer to disbelieve this source as he currently is in good books with the government, and is well trusted by the authorities.

211. *Southern Rhodesia Elections, February, 1980. The Report of the Commonwealth Observer Group on Elections Leading to Independent Zimbabwe* (1980), pp. 325-351.

212. For commonwealth deployment of troops see, Barry Schutz & Douglas Scott, "Natives and Settlers: A Comparative Analysis of the Politics of Opposition and Mobilization in Northern Ireland and Rhodesia," Monograph 12, 2, Denver University (1974).

213. Richard Sibanda, interview with the author, 26 August 1996.

214. Wilfred Mhanda, interview in *Focus* (HSF), December 2000.

215. While the official estimates of the war dead were 30,000, a revised unofficial one stands at 40,000 (*Africa Confidential*, 19 August 1987).

216. Louise Pirouet, "Armed Resistance and Counter-Insurgency: Reflections in the Anya Anya and Mau Mau Experiences," in Ali Mazrui, ed., *The Warrior Tradition in Modern Africa* (Leiden: E. J. Brill, 1977), pp. 205-210.

217. Gurr, "On Outcomes of Violent Conflict," in Ted Gurr, ed., *Handbook of Political Conflict* (New York: The Free Press, 1980), pp. 238-294.

Chapter 7
THE BEST AND THE WORST OF TIMES: ZAPU POST-INDEPENDENCE TO THE TIME OF ITS DEMISE, 1980-87

ZAPU accepted the 1980 election results with mixed feelings and deep suspicion. There was a sense in which this was the best of times for ZAPU, and this was to the extent that it celebrated the end of war and the winning of elections by their sister liberation movement, ZANU-PF. Together they had carried out a liberation struggle that had ushered in a dispensation of independence and majority rule in Zimbabwe. Nkomo actually had wanted he and Mugabe to run for elections on the same ticket, under the Umbrella name, PF.

This did not appeal to some of ZANU's stalwart supporters and senior officials. They advised Mugabe to refuse running on the same ticket with ZAPU because, they asserted, Nkomo's role in the history of the struggle made him a liability. The two basic reasons advanced by these opponents were well represented by Enos Nkala, a founding member of ZANU. Nkala said Nkomo's party was tribally based, and that he had in the past involved himself in questionable negotiations with the whites. As such, Nkala argued, if Nkomo ran on the same ticket as ZANU, the latter would lose the elections.

It is, however, difficult to believe that Mugabe was influenced by his people to oppose Nkomo's suggestion that ZANU and ZAPU run on the same ticket. Officious a person that Mugabe was, even without this kind of influence from the likes of Enos Nkala, he would not have accepted Nkomo's suggestion as long as he was not guaranteed the leadership of the umbrella party.[1] It seems with the ethnic variable factored into the equation, Mugabe did his mathematics homework, got convinced he could win the elections without ZAPU as a running partner, and so he chose for ZANU to run independently of ZAPU, even in light of the fact that their political platforms were essentially the same.

The silver lining for ZAPU in all this was that its sister party had won elections, a victory for all the liberation movements of Zimbabwe. It was from this point of view that ZAPU shared the general feeling of the country. The country was in a moment of efflorescence. The tensions of the revolution had mellowed into exhilarating optimism. Populist styles and themes were on the rise. The previously banned designations such as "comrade" and "povo" became part of the daily language. But this feeling was mixed with a feeling of disillusionment at the loss of elections, not because ZAPU thought it lost a free and fair election but because it felt cheated by its compatriots in ZANU.

ZAPU felt it lost elections because of two basic reasons: one, because ZANU intimidated blacks, mostly in the rural areas to vote for it, and two, ZANU also used tribalism to its advantage. To a certain extent there was a basis for this claim. In Mashonaland, ZANU made it a point that ZAPU could not campaign freely. It did this by keeping some of its cadres out of the Assembly Points so that they could intimidate ZAPU campaigners and the villagers in those areas.

According to one source, an estimate of as many as forty percent of ZANLA forces (about 9,000 to 10,000 guerrillas) are believed to have stayed out of the Assembly Points in Rhodesia during most of the time between the cease-fire and election time.[2] Also it was reported that more than 3,000 ZANLA cadres infiltrated the Rhodesian eastern border from Mozambique between December 22 and January 6, in contravention of the cease-fire agreement, and that all of them did not report to any of the Assembly Points in the country.[3]

According to the final Cease-fire Commission Communiqué, these were the total numbers of actual breaches and incitement to breach committed between the time of the cease-fire and the 1980 elections: ZANLA 99, 35; ZIPRA 24, 12; and RSFs 2, 12.[4] Most of these breaches were related to trying to influence the rural black population to vote for parties represented by these forces, and ZANLA was responsible for most of the election-related intimidation. Conversely, ZIPRA had an estimate of only one percent of its troops outside the APs during the same period.[5] However, no evidence was ever presented to the Commonwealth elections team of an attempt to force the blacks to vote one way or another. It seems most of the ZIPRA troops stayed out of the APs because they did not trust the Rhodesian forces.

Could Britain through her resident Governor Soames have prevented such acts of intimidation? Of course not. The neutral force, the Commonwealth Monitoring Force that monitored the cease-fire under Soames' authority, was far too small, and its role was strictly limited. The force was 1,319 strong,[6] with a responsibility over an estimated 35,000 guerrillas, seventy-five percent of whom were thought to be ZANLA[7] and 65,000 Rhodesian personnel under arms.[8]

Moreover, the Commonwealth was armed with light weapons, only for self-protection. Also their strict role was to monitor and not to enforce. In the event of its being attacked, the force was under orders to protect itself and leave the country. Thus, the force depended mostly on the discipline and self-policing of the monitored forces. Of the guerrilla forces ZIPRA proved itself to be well disciplined and professional. ZANU members did not show respect even to their compatriots in ZAPU. It ordered its forces to keep out ZAPU from campaigning in areas under its rule.

The Best and the Worst of Times

The question as to whether ZAPU would have won elections without this kind of intimidation by mostly ZANU's armed forces remains a subject of speculation. What is clear though, given the national popularity of ZAPU at the time of independence is that if such intimidation had not obtained, it would have won some seats in a majority of constituencies in the Mashonaland regions. Thus, a belief in that ZAPU could have won the elections was not beyond reality, so that ZAPU's complaint of being robbed of a victory was reasonable.

The second basis of ZAPU members' suspicion of their being robbed was Mugabe's trip to Mozambique where he is believed to have met with top-level South African and Rhodesian officials on the first day of polling. Commenting on ZANU president's visit to Maputo on this first day of voting, Nicholas Fenn, British Governor's spokesperson said, "we are surprised to learn of Mr. Mugabe's sudden departure.... The future of Zimbabwe is going to be decided here, not elsewhere."[9]

ZAPU saw the trip as something that was done with the knowledge of Britain, and therefore did not believe Fenn's remarks. Four days before Mugabe's arrival in Maputo, the Rhodesian Lt.-General Peter Walls, Commander of the Rhodesian Forces and Kenneth Flower, Head of Rhodesia's Intelligence Agency, held secret talks with the Mozambican Foreign Minister, Joaquim Chissano and the Army Commander, Sebastia Mabote.[10] From South Africa the Mozambican officials met with a delegation led by P.K. Botha, South Africa's Foreign Minister.

Mugabe denied he had talks with the Rhodesian or the South African delegation. Given the different times that these three groups visited Maputo it is reasonable to believe that these meetings with the Mozambican officials were bilateral, however, there is every reason to believe they were about elections, and the future of Zimbabwe. ZAPU therefore saw these secret meetings of which ZANU was part as an attempt to influence election results.

Third, some ZAPU members blamed the party's loss of elections on primordial history. Willie Musarurwa, ZAPU's Publicity Secretary claimed that the "Shonas wanted to vote for Shonas and the Ndebele wanted to vote for Ndebeles."[11] Professor Stanlake Samkange, one of the leading Zimbabwean intellectuals and a prolific writer, who at that time was member of the Zimbabwe Democratic Party (ZDP), viewed the results as "clear tribalism, there is no other way to explain it."

The Mashonaland people will never have Nkomo and Matabeleland will never have a Shona."[12] Although the use of the 'never' is too strong here, it should be pointed out that Samkange, put his finger on the monster that had and still bedeviled black Zimbabweans from time immemorial; tribalism. In the previous chapter this writer tried to demonstrate why tribalism (ethnicity) should be understood as one of Zimbabwe's worst problems.

The writer concluded by saying that those who consider ethnicity as epiphenomenal are imitating the ostrich by burying their heads in the sand in an attempt to avoid dealing with the problem they think only belongs to the uneducated. Thus, their logic went, tribalism and education are incompatible.

Undoubtedly, tribalism was still real, even immediately after independence. As already has been pointed out, ZAPU tried by all means to rid itself of this menace. Nkomo had a long history of fighting against tribalism, and he made it known in his speeches and interviews.

As far back as 1970, Nkomo had sent a message from restriction pleading with both parties to end the "history of disunity among the Zimbabwean people."[13] He further remarked, "this has further created an international atmosphere that is not favorable to our cause, especially since the rival groups are in reality fighting for the same cause."[14]

Tribalism was a perennial fear for Nkomo, a scourge that concerned him for the rest of his political career. What he had feared for all along was about to become a reality in the post-independent Zimbabwe with the reality of disunity between his party and that of Mugabe. What bore more eloquent evidence to Nkomo's insistence on a non-tribal party was the composition of his national executive. At the time of independence, eight of his ten top men were actually Shona.

In fact, over the years of the liberation struggle in Zimbabwe, ZAPU officials, across ethnic lines, used every opportunity to speak against the "cancer of tribalism." Addressing a group of AmaNdebele in Wenlock, on a meet-the-people tour, Joseph Msika, ANC-Z Secretary General, attacked tribalists as the worst enemies of Zimbabwe. At a separate gathering held at an A.M.E. church, Mrs. Ruth Chinamano, ANC-Z's Secretary for Women's Affairs, castigated tribalism as a "terrible disease" that had to be fought to the bitterest end. She said tribalism was a cancer, and ended by reminding her mostly female audience, since this was a Women's meeting, that it was their duty to fight against it.[15]

One of the strongest condemnation of tribalism came from an editorial in the Party's publication inside Rhodesia, *The Zimbabwe Star*. The editorial even went further to give the etiology of tribalism in Rhodesia, and the consequences its perpetrators had reaped as a result. The editorial ran:

> *It CAN be logically and properly said that the Rev. Ndabaningi Sithole introduced the politics of tribalism in our country when he, because of his power-ambition, divided the nationalist struggle in 1963 [by founding a splinter group ZANU]. Before the regrettable advent of Sithole on the nationalist scene, division, let alone tribalistic division, was taboo and unthinkable among the people of Zimbabwe. Now it is common fodder.*
>
> *Today Sithole is weeping because the division and the tribalism that he started has got[ten] out of control. The people whom he taught the gospel of tribalism, are now using [it] against their master.*[16]

The Best and the Worst of Times

This was in sharp contrast to Mugabe's Shona-dominated, and therefore tribal and regional oriented party. In ZANU popular consciousness was fraught with tribal generalizations and judgments on the essential nature of AmaNdebele and AmaShona. Statements such as "AmaNdebele are sell-outs," "they are strangers in Zimbabwe as much as Whites are," or "AmaNdebele used to plunder our forebears' land,"[17] although carrying inconsequential social insight, did have considerable social weight.

This was expressed strongly by ZANU when it became a government and, now with the state power apparatus, promoted ethnic differences as a basic tenet of governance. For instance, immediately after independence, of the twenty-eight ministers and deputy-ministers, only one, Enos Nkala, who was the Finance minister, was an iNdebele.[18]

The same situation obtained in the thirty-strong central committee where there were only two AmaNdebele.[19] With the unfavorable situation of voting along ethnic lines, created at the elections time, Nkomo's party, like Mugabe's has ever been, was sadly reduced to a tribal one. This bifurcation of parties along ethnic lines at independence, after a brief season of a marriage of convenience under the PF umbrella, further deepened the suspicion and ethnic tension between these two liberation parties.

After licking their political wounds of defeat, 250 PF-ZAPU members of the National Executive, Central Committee, National Assembly, Revolutionary Council and local election committees convened to discuss the future of their party. The meeting endorsed the party leadership's decision, which was to participate in government, but vigorously condemned any attempt to move the country towards a one party state.[20] The meeting also resolved that the party should restructure itself in accordance with changed circumstances now that it no longer was a liberation movement, and also pledged to retain its ZAPU identity. It was after this meeting that ZAPU accepted the cabinet posts Mugabe offered it.

7.1 A Marriage of Convenience: ZAPU Accepts Cabinet Posts, 1980

Following his landslide victory, and forced by circumstances of not having a truly national mandate to rule the country,[21] Mugabe grudgingly invited Nkomo to become a titular President.[22] Nkomo, in keeping with the resolution his party had made to retain its self-identity, turned the offer down. However, he and a couple of his Lieutenants accepted Mugabe's cabinet offer. Mugabe, however, did not give ZAPU any support in its run for the Senate where it ended up having only one representative.

Given that Mugabe did not want to run on the same ticket as ZAPU in the elections that led to independence, a question about why he decided to invite them after the elections is in order here. Two reasons can be offered for Mugabe's gesture. One, the results of the elections forced him to invite Nkomo.

Although Mugabe won an overwhelming majority of seats, they were all in Mashonaland, and that reduced him to a regional and not a national leader as Nkomo had won all the seats in Matebeleland.

This division of the electorate did not please Mugabe whose over-consuming desire was to introduce a One-Party State in Zimbabwe. Of course, he was aware for the next seven years a one-party system was impossible given the entrenched twenty seats for the whites. However, he figured an early beginning was not bad. Mugabe was going to do this by making ZAPU, by whatever means, to join his party, or at least support his decision on a one-party system of government. Also, he wanted to enlist and ensure ZAPU's allegiance since it had one of the best-trained military forces in Southern Africa. By enlisting ZAPU's cooperation, Mugabe could then and only then, see himself as a national rather than a regional or tribal leader.

This image of tribal representation had characterized his ZANU-PF party from its formation in the 1960's, and this time he wanted to part with it. Thus, Mugabe invited ZAPU to join his government after winning the 1980 elections because he wanted to be seen as a national leader, thereby win the mandate to lead the people of Matebeleland. In the Midlands, ZAPU had won four of the twelve contested seats. Without widespread intimidation by ZANU-PF, ZAPU contended that it would have won more seats than it did. A vast majority of blacks that had supported the liberation struggle was happy with the results, which overwhelmingly precluded black puppet parties.[23]

Still they were concerned about the results, which had the major liberation movements reduced to regional rather than national representation. Thus, as has been already mentioned, although Mugabe's party won nearly three times as many seats in parliament as Nkomo's, the voting divided almost entirely along ethnic lines. The 1985 election results, despite massive intimidation, imprisonment, torture and killings, among other repressive ways, had the same outcome in which voting followed ethnic lines, so that although Mugabe won ninety percent votes in Mashonaland, his own ethnic group, he barely got more than ten percent in Ndebele precincts of Matebeland.[24] Ethnicity was again one of the decisive factors that determined the results of the elections.

The second reason has already been alluded to, which was so that he could introduce his one-party state after the expiration of seven years at which time the twenty seats reserved for the whites would be legally eliminated. Mugabe himself made his desire to introduce a one-party state known to the world after being elected the Prime Minister of Zimbabwe. However, he pointed out that this was his party's ultimate goal rather than an immediate one and that its introduction would occur with the co-operation and consent of other parties.[25] ZANU said it wanted to introduce a one-party state in order to attain its economic and social goals, and this message was consistent with its message before independence. For that matter, a one-party state was consistent with Mugabe's autocratic leadership tendencies.

The Best and the Worst of Times

Mugabe was an individual obsessed with personal power who would not stop at anything on his way to achieving power. Ten years later, decrying tendencies of dictatorship among African leaders, A. H.M. Kirk-Greene would say this about Mugabe's approach to leadership: "whether Nkomo likes it or not, Mugabe is Zimbabwe, and Zimbabwe is first, foremost and forever, Mugabe."[26] So there was a personal interest on the part of ZANU-PF leadership, which was the desire of naked power for its own sake, with no reference to the welfare of the country. Given the results of the elections, and the entrenched seats, Mugabe became painfully aware that the road to a one-party state was going to be a rugged and difficult one, for which he was going to pay an exorbitant price.

To ZAPU, as we have already seen, a one-party state was a non-starter. Having ZAPU as part of his government, Mugabe hoped that would give him sufficient exposure so as to win some seats in Matebeleland in 1985 when the next elections are held. What Mugabe and his party stalwart underestimated was the resolve of ZAPU and its membership to retain the party's self-identity, and also to fight for power in order to implement its own vision which it thought was superior to that of ZANU.

7.2 Though I Walk in the Shadow of Death I Shall Fear No Evil: ZAPU's Resolve for a Democratic Zimbabwe Tested, 1980-1987--Zimbabwe's Darkest Hour in History_The Matebeleland Crisis

The crisis in Matebeleland started in the army. At independence, in 1980, it was agreed that ZANU and ZAPU soldiers would be integrated into one army, which actually meant integrating the two liberation guerrillas groups into the RSFs which, according to the Lancaster Constitution, was to form the nucleus of the army. After the integration, then paring down the army into affordable sizes was to follow. The process of integration started at the time of election under the supervision of the British military personnel.

Just before elections, and as the Commonwealth army prepared to leave between the end of elections and the announcement of its results, Operation Merger formally begun, in fact as voters started going to the polls, 1,200 guerrillas, half of whom were ZIPRA, commenced joint training with units from the Rhodesian army. ZIPRA forces were from a base at Essexvale (Esigodini), and ZANLA, from Rathgar. However the joint command would not be formed until April 15, 1981.[27] All the same the integration of forces, especially with some of the Rhodesian troops came as a relief to both ZIPRA and ZANLA who were in constant fear of being attacked by the former's air force.

By October of that year, nine mixed ZIPRA-ZANLA battalions had been trained or were still in the process of being trained, and it was hoped that by the end of the year, four brigades, each with consisting of three battalions, totaling altogether 12,000 men should be ready.[28] The army was to be an essentially ZIPRA-ZANLA force, carefully balanced numerically.

Despite the relatively smooth process of integration at the outset, there was deep mistrust even between the two national liberation forces, and indiscipline among their cadres. However, ex-ZIPRA combatants still could be counted upon to listen to their able leaders, Lameck Lookout[29] Mafela Masuku, who was assisted by Javen Maseko. Masuku had a strong grip on his well-disciplined ZIPRA forces, and that made his job easier.

However, as ZIPRA's cadres increasingly witnessed what it thought were unfair ways of choosing soldiers for further training in foreign countries, practices that favored former ZANLA forces, they started to complain openly.[30] The former ZIPRA forces also complained that a disproportionate number of its cadres was being demobilized, and yet they too had fought for the country. The situation of demobilized cadres in some cases was exacerbated by the fact that some of these de-mobilized ex-guerrillas had no education and few marketable skills, which meant that they had no job after they were demobilized.

Thus, ZIPRA members felt discriminated against by the army, and they believed the government was intentionally keeping them out of the national army because it wanted to eliminate its party, ZAPU. Those who were demobilized and had few marketable skills had to depend on their meager demobilization pay. For Mugabe, the aim of forming a single army was so that he could introduce a one-party system because without a single army it would not be feasible to introduce a one-party state.

Mugabe should have known that pushing the country towards the introduction of a one-party state would stir suspicion and anxiety on the part of ZAPU and its forces. It seems it was difficult for him, and some of his stalwart supporters, to envisage a multi-party election in 1985.[31] As Mugabe engaged in integrating the forces, he hoped to build a force out of ZIPRA and ZANLA that would be loyal to the state, and for the former, the ZIPRA cadres, he hoped by being loyal to the state they would cease to support Nkomo. Without the support of the former ZIPRA forces for Nkomo, Mugabe figured he could easily eliminate ZAPU.

At the same time he did not trust ZIPRA, and hence by 1983 the army was integrated 2:1 in favor of ZANLA. So the complaint by ZIPRA of discrimination had a basis. ZIPRA forces were so disillusioned that they gave the impression they were spoiling for war. ZAPU members' echoed ZIPRA's disgruntlement, the majority of whom were AmaNdebele who were daily subjected to negative messages belittling their role and that of their forces, ZIPRA, in fighting for the liberation of Zimbabwe.

As such, there is a sense in which there was legitimacy in the discontent of the grassroots of ZAPU and their army over how they were being treated by the ruling party. Their conclusion was, which seems to be accurate given what was occurring on the ground, that there was no genuine coalition at government level, so that the government was exclusively ZANU-PF with only four ZAPU ministers, Nkomo inclusive, who had no part whatsoever to the decision-

The Best and the Worst of Times

making process of how the country was run. Again, at this point, by ZANU-PF's definition, the word Ndebele had become synonymous with ZAPU-PF.

What particularly angered an average Ndebele, even those who did not support ZAPU, was the way Nkomo was being undermined by the government. The government did this by criticizing the police force, which was seen, particularly by ZAPU members and the AmaNdebele, as an indirect way of criticizing Nkomo who was then the Minister of Home Affairs. Indeed, Mugabe wanted to undermine Nkomo so that he could lose credibility even in the eyes of his own ZIPRA forces, which, in reality, was wishful thinking on his part.

In November clashes between ZIPRA and ZANLA erupted in the Assembly Points and also in three mixed battalions. The one that presented the government with the most serious threat was the one that broke out at eNtumbane[32], a Bulawayo township. Although clashes at eNtumbane poised the most serious threat to the government, "the overwhelming majority of guerrillas, however, had nothing to do with the fighting."[33] ZIPRA and ZANLA camps at Entumbane were hardly half a mile from each other.

As fighting progressed at eNtumbane, fighting broke out in mixed battalions, at Connemara and Silalabuhwa. For three days the two major roads, one between Bulawayo and Harare, and the other from South Africa to Harare by way of the Birchenough Bridge, were almost totally sealed off, with ZIPRA forces forward-falling into train cars with open windows, to move from one point to another. Soon, Mugabe sensing some real 'clear and present' danger, deployed a mixed army unit, mostly consisting of former RAR, and led by a white former Rhodesian trooper, to try and contain the situation at eNtumbane. Nothing had changed much, only the person leading the country, otherwise the apparatus of power were still in the hands of the former white regime, an observation that angered the ex-ZIPRA forces.[34]

To add insult to injury on their part, a former American mercenary who had continued in the army post independence commanded a platoon of black solders against them.[35] In the meantime Nkomo was begging Mugabe to allow him to talk to his former forces. Because Mugabe wanted to achieve a clear victory once and for all over the former ZIPRA forces, he initially turned down Nkomo's offer. Mugabe probably believed the largely ex-RAR unit was going to easily overcome the Ex-ZIPRA forces.

Learning about the involvement of the RAR forces against their comrades, ZIPRA forces from two key ZIPRA camps, Gwaai River, which was located about 200 kilometers to the northwest of Bulawayo and Essexvale (Esigodini), 50 kilometers to the southeast, started advancing towards Bulawayo to support the eNtumbane ZIPRA forces.[36] Three ZIPRA motorized columns left Gwaai, and four columns headed menacingly from Essexvaal towards Bulawayo. The leading vehicles in the ZIPRA's motorized column from Essexvaal were destroyed as they approached Bulawayo by the former Rhodesian armored car unit, but more were still coming.

At this point, when the danger of a general conflagration was increasingly becoming real, Mugabe grudgingly allowed Nkomo to be involved. It is true that in conventional military terms, Mugabe with the support of the former Rhodesian units, had logistical and air support, which given the balance of things, made ZIPRA totally helpless. However, this was a different guerrilla group, a significant number of them were well trained along conventional lines. It had bigger and better weapons than ZANLA, better training, and actually gave the former RSFs a run for their money.

Despite the destruction of the lead cars from the ZIPRA camp at Essexvaal, and the threat by the former Rhodesian air-force, ZIPRA was still pushing towards Bulawayo, and the eNtumbane forces were becoming increasingly ferocious, now with heavier weapons, most of which had been captured from the dead or fleeing ZANLA forces. Those who had gone on passes had come back to fight along side with their comrades. Ex-ZIPRA combatants once again, after the Lusuto military engagement in October 1978, displayed their discipline and masterful skills in fighting as they completely outfought their opponent, ZANLA. ZANLA was losing the fight, and losing it big and fast.[37]. The accuracy of ex-ZIPRA fighters' fire was not lost to Alan Cowell, one of the journalists who covered the fighting on the field. Cowell describes ZIPRA's fire accuracy this way:

> *One of the black soldiers ... beckoned to me to come join him as he crouched behind an armored vehicle, aiming his rifle at a tree in an open field. Behind the tree was a guerrilla from Nkomo's army ... Max [Lt Max, a National Army trooper] loosed off fire that chipped bark from the tree. The response came in a blast of unnerving accurate AK-47 fire that pinged off the steel plating of our cover.[38]*

Nkomo with his two top military personnel, Lookout Masuku and Dumiso Dabengwa, took to the air in a helicopter, and they pleaded with their former forces to stop fighting as they flew above the troubled areas. Undoubtedly, the Rhodesians came as Mugabe's ultimate saviors in this situation, although it is debatable that they alone, could have restored the situation without the intervention of Nkomo, his army commander Masuku and his chief commissar Dumiso Dabengwa. As the Africa Confidential[39] accurately noted:

> *Indeed, it was largely due to the efforts of Nkomo, his guerrilla leader Lameck Lookout Mafela Masuku and his chief commissar Dumiso Dabengwa that the ZIPRA fire was damped down.[40]*

An argument can be rightly made that the former Rhodesian forces played a very crucial, although not decisive, role in keeping Mugabe in power, although it does not appear that the intent by the ZIPRA forces was to take over state power. According to some ZIPRA cadres who were involved in the eNtumbane conflict, the clash was started by the ZANLA forces, which actually were better armed since they had heavier weapons. They say there was a plot to eliminate them, which was basically hatched by the ruling ZANU party.

The Best and the Worst of Times

According to these accounts, ZIPRA was lightly armed, with AK's mostly.[41] One of the cadres, Kayisa, informed that when ZIPRA was attacked by ZANLA, a good number of their comrades had gone on passes to visit with family and friends. Also their former Commander-in-Chief, Nkomo, supported the position of the ex-ZIPRA combatants that ZANLA started the fighting.

In February 1981 fighting between ZIPRA and ZANLA broke out again. There had been trouble at National Army camp near Bulawayo, at Ntabazinduna:

> *the ex-ZIPRA soldiers were given leave, and in their absence the ex-ZANLA elements took over the armory. The hostility at once spread to Entumbane, the site of the previous fighting.... Full-scale fighting broke out ... also at Connemara Barracks, near Gweru, where the National Army was split into ex-ZIPRA and ex-ZANLA elements.*[42]

There was also independent collaboration of Nkomo and his men's stories that ZANLA started the fighting, which makes that story more believable. For instance, ZAPU's position was supported by Joseph Lelyveld, who in turn based his conclusion on the unpublished Dumbutshena's Commission which investigated the causes of the conflict. If these accounts by both ZAPU and independent sources are true, as they appear to be, then the conflict from ZIPRA's point was purely defensive, and had nothing to do with trying to wrest state power from Mugabe. To date, no evidence exists to suggest that there was a concerted ZIPRA-Ndebele plot to overthrow the government.

The Entumbane clashes were a watershed in the military history of Zimbabwe in many ways. First, they gave rise to the first large-scale defection of forces from the national army[43] by ex-ZIPRA, who added to the number of the already existing dissidents. ZIPRA members who deserted and went back to the bush went with their guns.[44] The desertion would increase later when the government allegedly 'discovered' arms caches on ZAPU owned properties.

Another result, and to the advantage of Mugabe, was that the conflict accelerated the general disarming of the armed guerrillas, including those under Mugabe himself. Following the second eNtumbane clashes which eventually spread to the other groups awaiting integration, in February 1981 (the initial having taken place in November 1980, and lasted for a few days); Mugabe confiscated ZIPRA's heavy weaponry, which included Russian armored personnel carriers (BTR-152s), and tanks.

Technically, all weapons came under the auspices of the national army; however, ZIPRA still considered these weapons its possession, although the force knew the weapons would be eventually taken by the government at the time of either their integration into the national army or demobilization. The confiscation affected mostly the Gwaai River Mine and Essexvaale camps. This disarming process was generally met with passive disobedience on the part of some former ZIPRA forces.

To forestall any danger posed by the forces near the capital, Salisbury (Harare), Mugabe moved ZIPRA guerrillas from a camp that was located very close to a ZANLA one, at Chitungweza, just on the outskirts of Salisbury. Also moved were the eNtumbane, ZIPRA and ZANLA camps respectively. The ZIPRA forces were moved to a place 25 kilometers South of Bulawayo, and farther away from the Gwaai River Mine Assembly Point, to discourage them from moving up to join the Gwaai River Mine camp.

Because some ZIPRA troops already questioned the intentions of the Mugabe government they engaged in hectic siphoning of arms into caches. The generality of ZAPU membership, also, did not take kindly to the disarming of their former cadres because they believed Mugabe took away weapons from ZIPRA as a bad faith gesture. Thus, instead of winning over to his party the ZAPU grassroots membership, most of whom were AmaNdebele, by this disarmament process, and the relocation of ZIPRA forces from Bulawayo and the outskirts of Salisbury, Mugabe succeeded in further alienating them.

This pushed Mugabe into employing more desperate and vicious means of trying to win ZAPU members to his party. In Matebeleland, neither the authority of the whites nor of the government was unquestionably recognized. This was a region of fervent Nkomo support. Mugabe wanted people to consider him the sole leader of Zimbabwe. From 1980 through 1981, however, Mugabe's strategy against ZAPU was to isolate its leader Nkomo, minimize the role played by his forces in the liberation of Zimbabwe, while trying to court the support of the AmaNdebele and ZAPU members. For instance, in early January 1981, before the second eNtumbane clashes between former ZIPRA and ZANLA forces, Mugabe demoted Nkomo from the position of Minister of Home Affairs, where he had oversight of the police force to what Nkomo himself characterized as "politically meaningless post" job of Minister of Public Services, in charge of bureaucracy.[45]

Nkomo complained about the new post, and warned that this might cause unrest among his former ZIPRA forces who might correctly interpret his new post as demeaning. Mugabe responded by giving Nkomo another "meaningless" post, the Minister Without Portfolio.[46]

Early in 1982 things came to a head when arms caches were uncovered on property either controlled or owned by ZAPU. The collection included AK rifles, anti-aircraft, machine guns, mortar bombs, grenades, rocket launchers, land mines, pistols and binoculars. According to Emmerson D. Munangagwa, the main locations on which these weapons were discovered were Ascot Estates in Nyamayendlovu, Ngwenya Siding between Kadoma and Kwekwe, Woolendale in Matopo, Dandi River about 10Km east of Dande, Dande Communal land, Hampton Farm in Gweru, Silalabuhwa, Godhlwayo Communal Lands, Mashumbi Pools and Gwaai River Mine Camp.

In fact, the discovery of ZAPU arms by the government begun in 1981 and ended in 1982.[47] With the announcement by government of the discovery

The Best and the Worst of Times

of arms in ZAPU-owned property, more ZIPRA forces deserted the army in fear of reprisals from the government, some of whom melted into the forest and joined the burgeoning dissident ranks. Mugabe's government was obsessed, and demanded an explanation from Nkomo, although in actuality Mugabe had concluded since most of the known deserters were from former ZIPRA forces, ZAPU was responsible.

Thus, the government assumed that ZAPU cached weapons in preparation for war. Three main theories exist relative to the discovery of arms, which led to the punishment of ZAPU leadership.

1) The discovery genuinely surprised and outraged Mugabe and his ZANU-PF leadership, undermining whatever trust they may have had in Nkomo. The caches were interpreted as proof that Nkomo's [party] ... was bent on launching a coup some time in the future.

2) The exercise of arms caches-particularly in Ndebele territory, ZAPU's main area, but probably also in ZANU-PF country further east-had been widely supposed within known ZANU leadership ever since independence in 1980. But Mugabe and his colleagues simply decided that the time was ripe for Nkomo to be thrown out of government in order to consolidate ZANU (PF) power and to force the pace of ZANU-isation throughout Zimbabwe, leading eventually to a de facto one-party state.[48]

The first theory obviously represented the position of ZANU-PF and the second one that of ZAPU. For his part, Nkomo, the main target of most of government accusation, denied and dismissed the charges that his party was plotting to overthrow the Mugabe government with the assistance of South Africa as "ridiculous," and the discovery of arms as "exaggerated."[49] Nkomo charged:

> The charges were ridiculous, and soon became even more exaggerated.... In all, the government announced a total of thirty-five alleged finds of arms on properties owned by ZAPU, by myself, or by my political associates. Most of them were pure invention. One find was said to include enough electronic equipment to jam the communications of the entire Zimbabwe security forces. It turned out to consist of camera parts and the complete fittings (including X-ray equipment) for a dental surgery.... The armored personnel carriers turned out to be ordinary trucks.[50]

Nkomo, however, admits that two "dumps of arms" were found, which he claims their numbers were "swollen" by the arms smuggled in by government investigators. The two dumps of arms to which Nkomo admits were uncovered at two sites: Ascot Farm near Bulawayo and Hampton Ranch in the Midlands close to Gweru. Nitram, a private company Nkomo had founded for resettling ex-ZIPRA soldiers, owned both places. According to Nkomo, Mugabe was aware of the fact that both of the guerrilla movements, including Mugabe's ZANLA, had cached weapons before they were disbanded. He stated as a matter of fact:

> *It was not lawful, but by common knowledge both ZANLA and ZIPRA ex-combatants had held unto arms after their entitlement to do so had ceased. [And adds] This recognized problem should have been solved by recognized procedures. Instead, the discovery was exaggerated by the government, and then exploited as a means of discrediting my party, ZAPU, and expelling me from the government.*[51]

However, Mugabe responded to the discovery of arms with a battery of punitive actions against ZAPU. On February 17, 1982, Nkomo, and three of his senior colleagues, Josiah Chinamano, Joseph Msika, and Jini Ntuta, were expelled from the cabinet. Clement Muchachi resigned in protest of the expulsion of his comrades. To present to the public a facade of unity between the two liberation movements Mugabe left some of ZAPU's officials, Cephas Msipha and John Nkomo in government. To try and disrupt ZAPU, and in hopes that these ZAPU members might gradually draw fellow ZAPU members into at least accommodation, and eventual merger, with his ruling party, Mugabe appointed Jane Ngwenya to the deputy ministry of manpower planning and development, and Dr. Callistus Ndlovu to the ministry of construction.

Without even first consulting their party Ndlovu and Ngwenya accepted the posts, after all the two had already made up their minds to sell "their souls to ZANU-PF for thirty pieces of silver."[52] Ndlovu had just addressed a huge number of ex-ZIPRA cadres at the Makalanga Beer Hall. Because of the huge crowds he attracted from that time on, he thought ZAPU members respected him independent of his belonging to the party.[53] Worse still, he thought he could win a popularity contest against Nkomo. ZANU too misread the whole situation, and figured Nkomo was then much weaker than before when his former army was disarmed.

A rude awakening was surely awaiting Ndlovu, Ngwenya and the ruling party, as they would eventually discover that ZAPU grassroots and most of its leadership stood foursquare behind Nkomo. Nkomo also won overwhelming sympathy among the residents of Matebeleland and Midlands, as well as among his supporters in all the provinces across the country.[54] The 150-strong ZAPU central committee immediately convened a meeting to discuss how to respond to the expulsions, and on whether on not to permit John Nkomo, Cephas Msipha and Daniel Ngwenya to remain in government.

Also to be decided was a response to the new appointments, which Mugabe had just made after the expulsion of the four ZAPU ministers.[55] Grudgingly, the central committee resolved to allow the three, Nkomo, Msipha and Daniel Ngwenya to remain in government, while bitterly upbraiding Callistus Ndlovu and Jane Ngwenya for having accepted Mugabe's appointment, without even asking their party.[56] Predictably, the central committee refused to second the two to their appointments. By refusing to allow the party members who Mugabe had appointed to serve in his government, the central committee showed its party would fall down fighting, they were not about to roll-over and play "dead."[57]

The Best and the Worst of Times

ZAPU's grassroots was equally defiant. As far as a majority of them were concerned, they wanted a total pullout of all their members from government. Undoubtedly, Mugabe's action pushed the AmaNdebele people in Matebeleland, and most of those in Midlands, including those spread across the other provinces of Zimbabwe, further away from a conciliatory stance.[58] What Mugabe and his supporters did not realize was that so long as Nkomo remained publicly embarrassed by his ZANU followers, reconciliation with ZAPU was a far-fetched dream. Not only was the grassroots displeased with how its leaders were treated by the government, but also they were terribly disgruntled with how its former fighters continued to be treated in the army.

ZAPU members, like their former army, felt that their ZIPRA forces were being discriminated against in the army, and that they were being disproportionally demobilized. They could not understand why their ex-forces, having fought for the country for at least fifteen years, could be so unfairly treated, and their contributions to the liberation of the country minimized. They therefore protested the minimal combat role in the national army given to their former guerrillas.

With senior ZAPU military officers in prison, notably Dabengwa, Swazini Ndlovu, Lt. Gen. Masuku, and two Lt. Colonels, along with about fifty ex-ZIPRA regulars in the national army, any hopes of reconciliation further faded on the part of ZAPU, as an increasing number became hostile to the ruling party. To try and appease them, Mugabe promoted Major General Jevan Maseko to Lt. General in replacement of the imprisoned Masuku; however, he continued to appoint well-qualified ex-ZIPRA commanders to marginal roles in the national army.

Other ex-ZIPRA senior officers that remained in the army were Brigadier Ben Mathe 'Nyela', who came under an ex-RSFs Major-General Thompson in the administration section, and senior commander Brigadier Charles Grey (formerly known as Mike Reynolds) who served as commander of the 4th Brigade at Nyanda. Otherwise most other crucial positions went to the Mugabe's former guerrilla group.

At the height of its best representation, in the early 1980s ZIPRA had appointed to the national army roles, one Lt. General, three brigadiers and seven colonels. Thus, not only did Mugabe promote a disproportionate low number of ex-ZIPRA cadre into senior positions in the national army, but he also ensured that most of the key positions in the top went to his ex-ZANLA forces, most of whom were far less qualified than their ex-ZIPRA counterparts.[59]

For his part, Mugabe continued his attempt at the political realignment waltz by selectively farming out Nkomo and those who were his staunch executive members, while trying to court the favor of some whom he thought could bring with them a windfall of ZAPU members to his party. Because Mugabe wanted to be understood by the general ZAPU membership he explained why the four were expelled. Mugabe said he dismissed Nkomo and his colleagues because they supported dissidents, and were also involved in the caching of arms so that they could topple his government. He made sure at this point that he did not blame the dissident and arms crisis on the ZAPU grassroots and all its officials because he still believed he could isolate Nkomo and win the allegiance of his followers.

However, the journalist William Spring put his finger on what is probably the real cause for Nkomo's expulsion. Spring insightfully commented:

By his dismissal of Nkomo Mugabe showed his true colors: that he was intent on one party rule, which usually means in the tangled skein of African politics, one tribal rule.[60]

Nothing could stop him now, Mugabe figured, ZIPRA had been largely disarmed, and now he felt he could dispense with ZAPU easily without risking any civil war. Mugabe needed Nkomo's cooperation only in the disarming of his forces, which he himself was afraid to do, and Nkomo himself was aware of it.[61] Nkomo had personally addressed his men to disband, knowing too well they had no future. Nkomo however had to go along with government plan because he wanted to see stability in the country.

What hurt him most though in this whole process of disarming and disbanding his troops was the scene he witnessed after he persuaded more than 3000 ex-ZIPRA combatants to quietly disband at the Gwaai River Camp where one of the most feared, and well trained of his forces were assembled. In a moving way Nkomo, who had again turned out to be the 'man of sorrows', described his experience thus:

At Christmas 1981 the final dispersal of the men took place. The National Army brigadier at Gwaai River telephoned me on my holiday, asking for my help in persuading the 3000 men under his charge to leave quietly. I drove down from Bulawayo, over 150 Kilometers to the camp. I told the soldiers that the nation was grateful for their services, but their time in the forces was now over. There was no alternative: they must return peacefully to their homes, settle down, get married and find jobs.

The men accepted the demobilization. I went off to have a meal in a local hotel. When I drove back past the crossroads to the camp I saw these young soldiers lined up at the roadside, literally taking off their uniforms in the open air and putting on their civilian clothes before climbing into trucks to be driven home. It was humiliating: I felt humiliated just watching…That is how the army treated some of the men who had volunteered to serve their country.[62]

By this time Mugabe knew very well that the former RSF's were on his side, and therefore presented no threat to him. The RSFs had shown their allegiance when he set them against the ex-ZIPRA forces during the Ntumbane conflict between his ex-ZANlA forces and ex-ZIPRA fighters. They had obligingly followed his orders, and fought against his hitherto comrades.

The Best and the Worst of Times

This left him with ex-ZIPRA soldiers as the only group that Mugabe feared and was intent on eliminating. However, before the RSFs demonstrated their support of Mugabe's regime, he lived in fear that the former Rhodesian forces might join up with ZIPRA and overthrow him.[63] This position obviously seriously misinterpreted Nkomo whose actions at many occasions did much to contradict the accusations that he was a middle-class African nationalist, assimilated into the Western model, and ready to sacrifice the stability of Zimbabwe.

Even his avowed enemies knew too well that to Nkomo Zimbabwe came first, and under no circumstances would he sacrifice the goals of freedom he cherished for his country and his people. Speaking at his funeral, one of Nkomo's once comrade in arms, and later founder of ZANU and hater of Nkomo, made this remark which specifically spoke to the love and dedication Nkomo had for his country and people, a love and dedication, by extension, shared by his party ZAPU:

> *Nkomo was a warm and charming person who was personally liked by many a leader. [he was a pragmatist]. In his pragmatism, Nkomo never sacrificed cherished nationalist principles, even in his quest for the leadership of the country. There were circumstances during the course of the struggle when he was offered this and that by the settler government and the British, but when personal ambition meant sacrificing cherished nationalist principles he chose the latter. To Nkomo, Zimbabwe came first, second, and always.*[64]

However, it took Nkomo's death to have his sworn enemies step forward and praise him. Some of these chose to swallow their pride and give Nkomo the honor he deserved largely to resuscitate their ailing popularity, and others were genuine. In the absence of any evidence pointing to the fact that Nkomo in all of his previous negotiations ever compromised the cause of the struggle, the basis of Mugabe's attacks on Nkomo begins to form in conformity to the above citation from Spring.

Thus, Mugabe's main concern at independence, arguably, was the African power agenda. In his pursuit of raw power, as will be later shown, he did not have as his priority, as leader of Zimbabwe, the wider social justice agenda for its citizenry. Characteristically ZANU-PF continued to emasculate the only meaningful opposition in the country, and used as its vicious weapon, tribalism.

The second most important punitive step Mugabe took was to sequestrate the assets of eleven of ZAPU's companies on which land Mugabe's government alleged arms had been discovered. ZAPU owned a lot of property around the country, and most of it was gainfully utilized to the envy of the government whose resettlement policies were a national disaster. A lengthy citation on what ZAPU owned is worthwhile in order for the reader to appreciate the repercussions attendant to the expropriation of these institution without compensation, followed by the expulsion of personnel who inhabited the properties. These were what came to be known as African enterprises, and they consisted of:

> *A thousand-hectare vegetable farm on the outskirts of Bulawayo, growing mostly tomatoes, onions and carrots, with maize as the break crop. There was a small ranch with two hundred cattle just outside Gweru, a motel and entertainment complex (including a snake-park, a big tourist attraction) outside Harare, a garage in the town, and a clothing factory with its own retail outlet. There was a chicken farm, a pig-breeding establishment and a farm set up as an experimental women's cooperative.*
>
> *We had started a secretarial college and established the first of what was intended to be a chain of rural health clinics. We had bought some urban housing with the intention of selling it by installments to its occupiers. The whole idea was to give people a stake of their own country, to free them from dependence on the state or the municipalities by encouraging home ownership and cooperative enterprises. A main source of funds was the allowances of $150 a month paid to ex-combatants, who set aside a fixed proportion of that for investment in the cooperatives.*[65]

Arguably, the amount of property ZAPU owned suggests that the party had no reason to disturb the country. It clearly bespeaks of a people who had a stake in stability and peace. Nkomo, himself was immensely involved in the African enterprises. He raised most of the money for establishing these business concerns, which showed him as nothing short of a social-capitalist. So, the human-cost factor due to the expropriation of ZAPU's properties and those owned by its cadres was great.

For instance, Nitram Company, which consisted of four farms and four businesses had more than 4,000 ex-ZIPRA fighters involved in it, and each one contributed $50 a month from their service pension towards its maintenance. Its confiscation by the government therefore ultimately meant that more than 4,000 ex-ZIPRA fighters and their dependents lost their livelihood.

This was followed by a crackdown on Nkomo's former military officers and leaders of companies owned by ZAPU members. The first seven post-independence ZAPU activists tried for treason were Dumiso Dabengwa, Lamech Lookout Masuku, Nicholas Nkomo, Tshaka Moyo, Masala Sibanda, Misheck Velaphi and a director of a ZIPRA/ZAPU owned company, Dr. Isaac Nyathi. These senior ZIPRA officers were arrested on suspicion of plotting a *coup d'etat* against the Mugabe regime. ZAPU and Matcbeleland people reacted with disgust and anger at the arrest, four thousand former ZIPRA troops deserted the National Army on account of the arrests and also alleged discrimination against ZIPRA forces. All the deserters went with their weapons. In truth, most cadres, across party affiliation, cached weapons in case things went wrong.

After twenty-eight days of trial, which included fifty-five witnesses, on April 27, 1983, Judge Hillary Squires made his three-hour judgment, and all seven were found innocent of treason. However, Misheck Velapi, a junior ZAPU official, was found guilty of possession of weapons of war and sentenced to three years in prison. The state had lost, but they still had some powerful weapon, the State of Emergency Powers. To the chagrin of their supporters, after their liberty documents was signed, they were rearrested. The defendants were to spend another four years in detention despite several appeals.[66]

To the anger of many ZAPU supporters, and the AmaNdebele, who considered themselves as having lost a hero-son, General Masuku was released only to die at 46 years of age, on March 6, 1996.[67] Thus Mugabe accomplished both the confiscation of ZAPU property, and the arrest and subsequent detention of ex-ZIPRA officers by invoking the powers of the infamous Unlawful Organizations Act, widely utilized by the previous regime of Smith.

According to Joseph Hanlon, it was believed that the so called ex-ZIPRA officer who cached arms was actually a police agent who did it under the orders of Matt Calloway, the head of CIO in Hwange. Calloway later escaped to South Africa where he organized support of dissidents.[68]

Despite all the revolutionary rhetoric, after independence Mugabe not only kept the amnesty agreement but also went far beyond the Lancaster House Agreement by choosing not to investigate past human rights violations by the outgoing Smith regime. Consequently, serious human rights violators like Ken Flower, former head of the Central Intelligence Organization, Lt. Gen. Peter Walls, army chief of staff, kept their high positions. Ian Smith himself and the former cabinet Minister P.K. van der Byl remained active in politics.

Thus, the former Smith security personnel remained in their crucial positions after independence and their behavior remained essentially unchanged. Mugabe retained the state of emergency, which had been in place since 1965, and would continue for thirteen more years. This allowed Mugabe to detain his opponents, and he seems to have used the state of emergency more than any other regime before him. Mugabe would also retain the 1975 Indemnity and Compensation Act, an act that indemnified security force members for actions undertaken in "good faith." All these punitive pieces of law Mugabe would use against ZAPU. One may legitimately ask why Mugabe failed to investigate the violation of human rights, an undertaking he had promised his people throughout the struggle. Was it because he was so keen to retain Smith's officers? If that was the case, then why was he so keen to keep Smith's military operatives when he knew too well it was they who literally butchered his people? Was this part of the reconciliation which the Mugabe government extended only to the whites after independence?[69]

One of Mugabe's most trusted ZANU officers Emmerson Munangangwa, when asked why his government chose to retain Smith's operatives gave a two-fold reason. One, Munangagwa claimed that the well being of the army depended on the Smith regime security machine. Even on purely pragmatic grounds such logic is highly problematic, let alone that it was absolutely antithetical to what Mugabe had spent all of his liberation years arguing. Political enemies do not just convert overnight, and the Mugabe government soon learned this truth.

In 1988, Mugabe's government announced that it had uncovered a spy-ring, and that Kevin Woods, who until not long ago had been a CIO official, was involved. This spy-ring was blamed for several acts of sabotage and deaths. It makes sense to believe that this group of spies received help from those who had access to Zimbabwe's intelligence, and were most likely the former Smith regime security operatives.[70]

The second reason was that the government extended its hand of reconciliation to the white community for economic reasons.[71] Cognizant of the fact that the white community was crucial for economic progress, the Mugabe government chose to overlook the egregious past human rights violations on their part. The government had seen what happened to the black regimes that had immediately victimized the white community upon taking over the reins of power.

Apparently, the examples of Mozambique and Angola were still fresh in their minds. What stands out as an indictment to the Mugabe regime is not that it kept its indemnity agreement on the part of the whites, but rather that it left these people in positions where they continued to abuse their power as before.

This was in no way defensible. As a result of this approach, two drawbacks resulted. One, the white military officers, as we have seen on the case of Calloway, fomented the differences between and among black liberation parties, which made it virtually impossible for these parties to work together for the progress of Zimbabwe. Taking advantage of Mugabe's poor intelligence, white officers created problems, which eventually were attributed to ZIPRA, and each time that happened, Mugabe came down hard on the latter.

The second legacy of Mugabe's ill-fated reconciliation was that it made it difficult for Mugabe to redistribute land to the landless, an important economic base crucial for the welfare of the black population.

A series of events, following the dismissal of Nkomo and his army officers led to the deployment of the army in Matebeleland and Midlands. First, on June 23, 1982, there was an attempt to assassinate the Prime Minister Mugabe allegedly by ex-ZIPRA army mutineers. The government quickly pointed its finger at Nkomo and his party. The relationship between the two parties further deteriorated.

What actually broke the camel's back was the abduction, and subsequent murder of six tourists. On July 23, a tourist bus owned by the Encounter Overland, a London company concerned with adventure tours was stopped by a group of heavily armed people, as it was headed South-bound from Victoria Falls towards Bulawayo. Passengers were ordered to alight the bus and force-marched into the bush. One man, and the women, and children were released, leaving behind six male tourists, including two Australians, two Americans and two Britons.

Before leaving the bus, the armed men gave a ransom letter to a New Zealander, the only man released, and ordered him to deliver it to the Zimbabwean government. The letter demanded the return of ZAPU farms that had been confiscated by the government after it uncovered arms.[72] The note ended with a threat to execute the tourists if the government did not comply with the demands.

The Best and the Worst of Times

Despite extensive search by the security forces, and promise of $20,000 by government for any information leading to the discovery of the tourists, they were never found alive. The government blamed what it called ZAPU-led dissidents for the abduction, and beefed-up its military presence in Matebeland North. The first soldiers had been sent to this part of the country early 1982 to eliminate dissidents who were reported to be operating in this region, killing white farmers. The unit was known as the Task Force, and former RSF Lieutenant-Colonel Lionel Dyke led it.

Dyke used the vicious tactics used by the Rhodesian regime. Reports of torture and detention of villagers started making rounds as soon as the Force hit the area. Dyke and his men wanted the villagers to show them the dissidents. One eyewitness informant from Tsholotsho described the atrocious activities of the white-led force this way:

The soldiers beat and hit us and threatened us in a terrible way. They accused us of feeding dissidents. They hit one old woman and said that she was a mother of dissidents. Then the White soldier picked one boy and asked him what he was going to say. He said he knew nothing about the dissidents. The white soldier took his gun from his belt and just shot the boy in the head. Just in front of us.[73]

Farmers whom the Task Force had set out to protect continued being killed, and hope for finding the abducted tourists quickly fading. It is true that some dissidents who were former ZIPRA forces were in the bush in that area, after having deserted from the army. Whether or not these dissidents were responsible for the abduction of the tourists and the deaths of the farmers in that area still remains an unresolved question. There are too many things that make the whole event smack of "pseudo-gangs" of the National Army.

The tactic of impersonating guerrillas while committing atrocities was extensively used by the RSFs during the war of independence. A repeat situation by essentially the same people [army] here was not beyond possibility. What was more frustrating to the Task Force, more than not being able to protect farmers and to find the tourists, was its total failure to capture, or kill a single former ZIPRA army deserter. Of course these were thoroughly trained people who were very conversant with the area, as they had operated there during the war of liberation. Failing to show any results for their efforts the Task Force turned on villagers.

The Task Force proved useless to Mugabe because it did not do what he wanted: converting the villagers into ZANU-ISM. As early as 1981 Mugabe had put together a four-man commission to pave the way for a ZANU-ZAPU merger. Enos Nkala and Eddison Zvobgo represented ZANU, while George Silundika and Joseph Msika, ZAPU.[74] The commission did not make any headway at all as ZANU would not agree to the terms put forward by ZAPU. Nkomo made it clear to Mugabe that a merger, meaning ZAPU being dissolved in ZANU, was out of question and then went further to demand higher representation in government, the civil service and media as well as better jobs for his supporters.

This was too costly a price for Mugabe to pay. ZAPU's refusal to dismantle and join his party was not acceptable to him, and he was determined to make sure it happened. Former Rhodesian troops could not deliver this. He needed a political army, which would not only torture, maim and kill but one that would pressure ZAPU people into ZANU.

In January 1983, Mugabe sent his politically trained 5th Brigade to Matebeland North to replace the Task Force. The Brigade, which was trained by North Korean Military advisers, came directly under the control of the Prime Minister's office, and as such was outside the normal command structure of the army.

The composition of the 5th Brigade was almost exclusively Shona-speaking former ZANLA cadres. There were about 300 to 400 Ndebeles in the whole brigade, and given their small representation, their presence was insignificant. Essentially, this was a Brigade founded on tribalism, whose main mission was to eliminate any Ndebele person who did not want to join ZANU-PF. Ostensibly, the 5th Brigade was after dissidents, and those who had abducted the tourists. In reality, this was a bunch of rapists, murderers, who developed a reputation for "surliness, indiscipline and occasional drunkenness."[75] The deployment of the Fifth Brigade in Matebeleland began the darkest period in post-independence Zimbabwean history. Within days of the 5th Brigade's operation, reports were heard from rural mission stations, and from rural people who had escaped into cities, of massive abuses against innocent villagers. According to these reports the Fifth Brigade was busy butchering, maiming, raping, torturing innocent civilians and looting their property. Many rural Ndebeles fled their homes and commercial farms in areas surrounding Lupane, Nkayi and Tsholotsho, north of Bulawayo.

According to one rural mission doctor in the Lupane district, as many as seventy people were brought to his hospital in a single day.[76] Within the first three months of its deployment in 1983, the 5th Brigade killed hundreds of innocent civilians. Interesting enough, most of the Fifth Brigade targets were ZAPU officers. It came with names on its lists and thus, in no way was this a haphazard operation.

Typically, the Fifth Brigade soldiers would arrive in a village heavily armed with shoulder-fired rocket launchers and automatic weapons. They carried with them lists of army deserters--referred to as "death lists" by some Ndebeles--and demanded information about the deserters or about the presence of dissidents generally. They showed readiness to beat the villagers for the information, using sticks, clubs, rifle butts and bayonets.[77]

The methods of torture and killing used by the 5th were the same as those used by the Smith regime during the colonial war of independence. Phrases such as "killed in a cross-fire" in explaining the death of innocent civilians, once used widely during the Smith regime period regained currency, as did dusk-to-dawn curfews in the affected areas to control the free movement of people.[78]

The Best and the Worst of Times

On January 26, 1983 appalled by the savage massacre of his people, which he correctly saw as ethnic cleansing, Sydney Malunga, a ZAPU MP became the first among ZAPU legislators to protest in Parliament. Malunga reported that ninety-five people had been killed. On the February 1, Nkomo weighed in at a Press Conference, which he held in Harare, and accused the government of engaging in "mass murder." Nkomo told the Newsweek's journalist, Holger Jensen, that the government's 5th Brigade had killed more than five hundred villagers.[79] The following day, Nkomo would repeat his condemnation of the security forces in the House of Assembly, specifically accusing the 5th Brigade for going on a killing spree not just murder but mass murder."[80]

On its part the government denied that its forces were indiscriminately targeting innocent civilians. Mugabe's cabinet Minister, Sydney Sekeramayi for instance, responding to Malunga's report of massacres in Matebeleland in Parliament on January 26, matter-of-factly pointed out that in a conflict situation innocent people get hurt.[81] Mugabe, his chief, was more blunt. In a speech to a rural Ndebele group in Nkayi, one of the areas where the 5th Brigade extensively carried out its atrocities, Mugabe spelt out the strategy behind his government's response:

Where men and women provide food for the dissidents, when we get there we eradicate them. We don't differentiate when we fight, because we can't tell who is a dissident and who is not.[82]

As time wore on, Mugabe, stepped up his vitriolic attacks on ZAPU, especially on the person of Nkomo. He likened ZAPU to a cobra and said the only way to effectively deal with a snake is to strike and destroy its head. The head of the cobra was here a clear reference to Nkomo specifically and ZAPU leadership in general. Mugabe was no doubt inciting violence against the leadership of ZAPU. Over the course of the following year, Mugabe made good his threats, as ten ZAPU leaders close to Nkomo were killed by what was believed to be government agents, and later six ZAPU councilors were killed under similar circumstances.[83]

Even seven years later, in 1989, after the merger of ZANU-PF and PF-ZAPU, Mugabe still blamed the latter for the Matebeleland holocaust. Writing about the significance of the Unity Accord between the two main parties and specifically addressing the issue of dissidents Mugabe reflected:

It should be pointed out that while Joshua Nkomo and the other top leadership of PF ZAPU disclaimed the bandits and publicly denounced them, the dissidents claimed allegiance to Joshua Nkomo and PF ZAPU, and in fact carried upon their bodies PF ZAPU membership cards and the portraits of Joshua Nkomo. In addition dissidents pursued an opposition political program very similar to that of PF ZAPU. The ZANU government found it difficult to accept PF ZAPU's disclamation and denunciations of dissidents and saw an affinity of interests between the two.[84]

Thus, the government never admitted its soldiers were killing civilians, and it invariably responded to such reports of abuse by attacking the reporters be they Catholic Bishops, or foreign journalists.[85] The government further alleged that a more radical faction of dissidents was operating in Matebeleland North, specifically in Lupane and Tsholotsho. Further, it claimed that these dissidents were led by Dabengwa and loyal to ZAPU although the link between Dabengwa and ZAPU was never proven.

The most damning legal evidence the government presented to prove the connection between the dissidents and ZAPU was evidence provided by Gilbert Ngwenya, an ex-ZIPRA, at his trial in 1985 for the 1982 kidnapping and subsequent killing of the six tourist. Ngwenya alleged that he killed the six tourists on the orders of Nkomo.[86] Any support of ZAPU was equated with the support of dissidents.

The government therefore increasingly used anti-ZAPU rhetoric, and because an overwhelming number of AmaNdebele supported ZAPU, anti-AmaNdebele rhetoric. Otherwise the evidence was weak and circumstantial, based on the demands of some dissidents, who seemed to be pro-ZAPU. These came in a written form and they were as follows:

1) The return of the properties confiscated after the discovery of ZAPU arms caches in early 1982.

2) The release of ZAPU's chief guerrilla commissar, Dumiso Dabengwa, and its former guerrilla commander, Lt-Gen. Lookout Masuku, both detained since 1981 after their acquittal on charges of attempting a coup. And

3) That the harassment of Nkomo should cease.[87]

Dissidents further added more demands such as amnesty for hundreds of ZAPU supporters detained without trial, including ZAPU's tough grassroots organizer and Nkomo's closest comrade, Vote Moyo. Also they demanded that the government inject development funds to Matebeleland and Midlands, including the construction of a University.[88] Dissidents' demands became clearer between 1981-1985.

However, what is in question here is not whether or not dissidents existed but who their sponsor(s) was/were. According to the government ZAPU was responsible; however, ZAPU steadfastly denied any links with dissidents, and maintained that it did not take ZAPU to tell people "things were going wrong in Zimbabwe."[89] But, according to convicted Ngwenya, an ex-ZIPRA combatant and his colleagues, ZAPU was responsible. However, several of ex-ZIPRA army deserters interviewed consistently denied that they were encouraged and sponsored by ZAPU. They asserted that their persecution by government and not the political rift, was the determinant factor for their desertion. They felt they were left with no option but to leave with their weapons in order to protect themselves. Invariably, those interviewed said nothing that showed any clear direction or goal, let alone sponsorship by ZAPU. After their amnesty dissidents spoke openly about why they took to the bush with their weapons. One said,

The Best and the Worst of Times

In the 1980s war, no one was recruited; we were forced by the situation. All of us met in the bush. Each person left on his own, running from death.[90]

The sense of self-preservation as a motivating factor for dissidents was actually confirmed by several army deserters in these interviews, some of whom respectively claimed: "We wanted to defend ourselves personally. Our lives were threatened. Apart from defending ourselves there is very little we wanted to achieve. We were threatened. That is why I decided to desert."[91] Thus, ZAPU army deserters clearly contradicted government's claims that they were organized and sponsored by ZAPU. At the same time giving the government a pretext to blame ZAPU for their existence, they remained loyal to ZAPU and ZIPRA. It is possible, rather probable, that the government was well aware of the fact that ZAPU was not directly involved with its former ZIPRA combatants, but found the argument helpful in furthering its course of forcing ZAPU into ZANU.

Dissidents were of different kinds with a variety and sometimes-contradictory goals and motives. Motives for deserting included disaffection with the slow process of change in Zimbabwe after independence, hunger for land and political power.[92] Those who were after power and destabilization were believed to be sponsored by South Africa, and responsible for the death of many civilians and the destruction of property. The government referred to this group as "Super ZAPU." In actuality Super ZAPU was a group of former RSFs black soldiers who either had allegiance to Smith, Muzorewa, or Sithole, and South Africa used them to try accentuate the already existing division between ZAPU and ZANU,[93] and to a certain extent succeeded.

However, not all dissidents were, like Super ZAPU, hoodlums dressed in Machiavellian garb. There were some who had legitimate reasons for deserting and also had clear political goals. Such were dissidents that were indirectly connected to ZAPU through their membership. These deserted the army because they either thought the government was not making economic changes for the betterment of the black population fast enough, and was discriminating against ex-ZIPRA combatants in the Zimbabwe National Army, or persecuted Nkomo and his ZAPU leaders. Not only did the ex-ZIPRA combatants feel persecuted by the Mugabe regime, but also they felt 'ganged-up' against by the former RSFs and ex-ZANLA. The suspicion seems to be validated further by the exclusion of their Air force and Intelligence Units from the National army. When ZAPU came back from war, it had a highly trained Air Force Unit and a tight Intelligence cadre. The ZANU-PF government considered both of these units ineligible for integration, and subsequently forced them to disband.[94]

By 1985, the dissidents who were still loyal to ZAPU, were operating in three different zones. Each region had its own commander and a handful of platoons of 15 to 30 men, with sections of about five. The operational Zones were divided thus: The area stretching from the Victoria Falls railway line to Plumtree railway line (Western Region), was under a deserter known as Tulane, from the Victoria Falls Bulawayo railway line east to Silobela (the Northern region), these areas were under three successive deserters, first Gilbert Sitshela, then Mdawini, and finally Masikisela. The third region ran from the Plumtree railway line east to Mberengwa. This region was under the command of a man called "Brown" in 1987.

Because of the presence of Super ZAPU, deserters in this region did not organize themselves into a structure until 1987. The 5th Brigade found it difficult to track down the ex-ZIPRA deserters because of the latter's training. The ex-ZIPRA themselves did not fear the Fifth Brigade, a unit they considered to be ill-trained, and whose training was only for the elimination of unarmed, innocent civilians. To a certain extent, their claim was true seeing that the 5th Brigade never killed nor captured any genuine ex-ZIPRA deserter despite its claims.[95]

Before the 5th Brigade was withdrawn from Matebeleland North, thousands of innocent civilians had been cold-bloodedly massacred.[96] The exact count of civilians killed varies depending on the source. According to Nkomo, the 5th Brigade killed more than 3,000 AmaNdebele civilians during the early months of 1983.[97] Catholic sources confirm that most of the killing occurred during the first six weeks of the Fifth Brigade deployment in Matebeleland North, which coincided with a severe curfew in the area. During that time the 5th Brigade, torched people's huts, destroyed property, committed thousands of atrocities against the civilian population, ranging from physical abuse to murder. However, the Catholic sources significantly scale down the death of civilians to 900+ although they quickly point out that the figure is a conservative one.[98] Church officials in general put the figure to 1,500 civilian deaths for the period between 1982 and March 1983 and they too state the estimate is a conservative one. Although the number of those killed during this time is very difficult to independently verify, it is reasonable to believe the real number of those killed by the notorious Fifth Brigade lay somewhere between Nkomo's more than 3,000 figure and 10,000.[99]

Although the 5th Brigade extensive military campaign lasted about a year, the aftermath of its operation was untold suffering on the part of the AmaNdebele people. It killed, maimed, raped, abducted, imprisoned and drove thousands into neighboring states, especially Botswana, where they lived as refugees. Abductions occurred under the cover of darkness in such areas as Gwaai, Lupane, Silobela and Tsholotsho, and to a lesser extent in small towns in Matebeleland North.[100] On March 5, 1983, the Fifth Brigade moved into Bulawayo and began a house to house search, ostensibly for weapons after having cordoned-off all the black township. Their main target was Nkomo himself because the government had concluded it was best at that point to strike the shepherd and scatter the sheep. Accordingly, Nkomo's house was searched and ransacked. Living up to his name, the 'Slippery Rock,' and like Lobengula, the King of AmaNdebele, who vanished into thin air once Bulawayo was besieged by colonial forces in 1894, Nkomo beat the military dragnet, and fled to Britain via Botswana on March 9, 1983.[101]

The Best and the Worst of Times

The same day, Sydney Malunga, ZAPU's member of parliament had been the first to speak about army atrocities in Matebeleland, was arrested. Already most of ZAPU's leadership was either in detention or exile. Notable among these were Vote Moyo, a ZAPU MP and long-term detainee under the Smith regime, and George Marange, a member of ZAPU's central committee who had served in detention under Smith for fifteen years.[102] At this time it was clear Mugabe's strategy was to disrupt ZAPU's organizational structure in preparation for the up-coming 1985 general elections, and as others pointed-out, the kidnappings were meant to simply frighten the grassroots supporters by eliminating their leaders, so that they would join ZANU-PF.[103]

Mugabe's strategy failed in all fronts. Ostensibly, the 5th Brigade had been deployed to find the missing tourists and their kidnappers, and also to eliminate dissidents in that region. By the time the bulk of the 5th Brigade was pulled out of Matebeleland North, the fate of the tourists was still unknown and the dissident situation remained unabated. Neither was Mugabe any closer to fulfilling his political goal of using the 5th Brigade to achieve his political aim of eliminating ZAPU and forcibly absorbing its membership into his party. Instead, the residents became more hostile to the government and more army desertions by ex-ZIPRA combatants continued. On February 3, 1984 the 5th Brigade was deployed in Matebeland South. The government said it was deploying soldiers to eliminate a menace posed by the South African sponsored dissidents in the area. The curfew would last three months, leaving thousands of innocent people dead in the hands of the Fifth Brigade. During this time, stores were closed, villagers prohibited from moving one hundred-fifty feet from their houses at night, traffic stopped, and an all-round the clock curfew imposed. For the first, time since independence, food was used as a political weapon. To make sure no information left the area, journalists were prohibited from the area.[104]

The way the 5th Brigade conducted itself in this region was significantly different than it had in Matebeleland North in 1983. For instance cold-blooded civilian killings became less likely to happen in the village. However, mass beatings remained the mainstay. New methods of mass physical torture with sadistic refinements were introduced. Occasionally people were forced to lie on thorns before they were beaten, roll in and out of water while receiving a threshing and made to push government vehicles with their heads only and were then punished for bleeding on government vehicles.

Men's testicles were tied with rubber strips and then beaten with truncheons, and women had sharp sticks forced up their vaginas, and invariably they were forced up trees and to open their legs so that the Fifth Brigade members "could insult their genitals, while at the same time beating them." These sadistic refinements were less known in Matebeleland North. Most of these beatings and killings took place at Bhalagwe and Sun Yet Sen in Matebeleland South.[105] Indeed, this was barbarism at its apex, from a government whose conscience seems to have been completely seared. No one captured the terror of the government-sponsored military campaign against the people of Matebeleland South as did Peter Gordwin, a white Rhodesia lawyer by training turned journalist. In an article which he wrote for *The Sunday Times*, (April 15, 1985), entitled "Stench of Death Everywhere in Mugabe's Siege of Matabeleland," Gordwin graphically described the sight of killed AmaNdebele at Antelope Mine.

From that article, the world began to appreciate the enormity of the killing of innocent people by troops in that region. Gordwin's article angered the government, and for it he was expelled from Zimbabwe. Eleven years later, *Moto* would recount what it termed the "tales of Gestapo-style torture" in the Tuli valley in the Sitezi area of Gwanda under a very telling title "Death Valley Revisited."[106]

Indeed, these were the worst of times for the people in Matebeleland and Midlands. However, detentions were not restricted to people in these areas only, some people in some parts of Manicaland, especially those who belonged to ZANU-Ndonga and ZAPU were arrested and brought down to Bhalangwe and Sun Yet Sen in Matebeleland South.[107]

Standing on the ashes of his childhood hut and of nearly everything he had acquired in his lifetime, Mkhululi, a ZAPU supporter, remarked, "Only death can be worse than this." Spending nearly three months in the curfew area Mkhululi saw babies and the elderly die from starvation, and also witnessed mass killings of his family and community members. According to Mkhululi, several people after these murderous three months, slipped out of their hiding to reclaim the little the 5th Brigade had left behind.[108] Indeed, Mkhululi in that short sentence provided a chilling example of what people discovered after three months in which the world gained only a few glimpses into the Matebeleland and Midlands areas, and to a lesser degree, Manicaland. Indeed, the full enormity of atrocities committed by troops in Matebeleland will never be known in full. As the Comment writer in the *Moto* observed:

> *Ultimately, the Matabeleland story shall be told in full. Perhaps if it is told in manageable doses, we will learn to cope with the dark. Truth crudely buried in shallow graves, mine shafts and mass graves in that part of Zimbabwe.*[109]

Simultaneously with the cracking down on what was perceived to be ZAPU's general membership the ZANU-PF government persecuted the former's leadership. Again, here the idea was to neutralize the ZAPU leadership and forcibly absorb its members into ZANU-PF, and ultimately declare a one-party system of government. Evidently, Mugabe wanted to accomplish the first of these objectives before the 1985 elections. Thus by March 16, 1984 four out of twenty ZAPU MPs were in detention or exile, apart from Nkomo and Akim Ndlovu, a member of ZAPU intelligence, who were already in exile. Some of the Party's most capable officials had been absorbed by sectors that had no direct connection to active party politics.

For instance, George Kahari was back serving as a Professor at the local University, Willie Musarurwa, serving as editor of the *Sunday Mail* and Ariston Chambati, who had been an ambassador to Bonn, was then head of the august

The Best and the Worst of Times

TA Holdings. Other great party members who ZAPU could have used at this time when ZANU-PF was trying by all means to disrupt the latter's organizational structures had joined the diplomatic services: Arthur Chadzingwa, a former ZAPU representative based in London, had been given a senior diplomatic post, and Suman Mehta had been assigned as the new High Commissioner to Canada. Thus in very subtle ways, ZANU-PF at this point, theoretically had neutralized ZAPU's leadership. However, the strategy was still not yielding any results: the dissidents crisis continued to increased, and the general AmaNdebele population was increasingly becoming openly hostile to the ZANU government, and notwithstanding their being slaughtered, the AmaNdebele, and by extension, ZAPU, were consistently standing firm against a one-party state.

With all the ZAPU leadership either in jail, exile, or on assignments away from their supporters, Mugabe's political dilemma still remained how to integrate the AmaNdebele and ZAPU People into a national consensus. Mugabe was well aware that ZAPU was a genuinely national party, which had a far wider ethnic representation, at least, at the leadership level, than did his party ZANU-PF. So as part of his disruptive strategy against ZAPU, he forced most of its Ndebele leadership into exile, imprisoned, or killed some of them. This strategy backfired when Mugabe once again wanted to revive unity talks between his party and ZAPU.

The only leading ZAPU figures inside Zimbabwe and out of jail, were Josiah Chinamano, its Vice President, Joseph Msika, it Secretary-General, the ailing Samuel Munodawafa, very ill at this time, ZAPU's Chairman, Daniel Madzimbamuto and Clement Muchachi, who resigned from Mugabe's cabinet when the first ZAPU ministers were fired. All the five were respected ZAPU leaders, and with a long and rich history of fighting for the liberation of Zimbabwe.

However, in the sensitive tribal politics of Zimbabwe where stability seemed to depend on a tribal balancing act, these five had one big disadvantage; they were all Shona. Mugabe's farfetched hope was that Chinamano would adopt a moderate stance, disregard the resentful AmaNdebele and ZAPU followers, and influence ZAPU to join ZANU-PF. Clearly, Mugabe was seriously underestimating the resolve of the AmaNdebele people and ZAPU followers. The only person to whom they were ready to listen was Nkomo, and he was still in exile. Although it is true that ZAPU's formal organization at his time had been effectively emasculated,[110] the informal organization was still alive and vibrant, and the upcoming elections were about to just prove that. To the leadership of ZANU-PF, Nkomo represented the worst-case scenario in their political calculations.[111] The government was not about to invite him back to politics. Once Mugabe failed to woo Chinamano to his side, he tried Callistus Ndlovu.

At this time other ZANU senior members were openly calling for the banning of ZAPU before the 1985 elections. To them, all means of eliminating ZAPU short of banning had failed. One of the leaders on this crusade was Enos Nkala, the man whose personal vendetta with Nkomo went as far back as the 1960s, and who was at the time Minister of Home Affairs. Indeed, on June 17, 1984, Nkala's dream was partially fulfilled when the government, through his offices as Minister of Home Affairs, banned ZAPU meetings in the Midlands Province, alleging ZAPU had killed eight ZANU officials in May. ZANU mobs responded by stoning and ransacking ZAPU and UANC office in Katoma, and further burning ZAPU offices in Gweru and Kwe Kwe, resulting in five deaths and 150 injuries[112] of mostly ZAPU members.

In what appeared to be ZAPU cadres' revenge for violence against their party, on November 9, 1984 a high-ranking ZANU-PF official, Moven Ndlovu, was killed. ZANU-PF was swift to respond to what appeared to be ZAPU's murder of its senior official. Three days after the assassination of Ndlovu, Mugabe expelled the two remaining ZAPU members, Cephas Msipa and John Nkomo.[113] Later, on November 25, in what appeared to be a reprisal by ZANU, a ZAPU Member of Parliament, Njini Ntuta, was shot dead after his attackers chased him for more than a mile.

As the time for voting drew closer, the government intensified its harassment of the aMaNdebele people. As it had at the onset of the 5th Brigade military campaign, the government once again unleashed all of its notorious military and paramilitary apparatus on ZAPU members and AmaNdebele in Matebeleland and Midlands. This ZANU-PF machinery included the Zimbabwe Republic Police (ZRP), Police Internal Security and Intelligence (P.I.S.I.), a special intelligence police unit, the Criminal Investigation Unit, the Central Intelligence Organization(CIO), and the Support Unit and Special Constabulary. Besides the paramilitary forces and irregular units, Mugabe used ZANU-PF Youth Brigade, a brigade that was modeled after the Chinese Red Guard, and the People's Militia, an essentially military wing of the ZANU-PF Youth Brigade. All the units force ZAPU members and the AmaNdebele to buy ZANU-PF cards, and to attend its rallies. In addition, the People's Militia guarded development projects and accompanied development workers in areas believed to have dissidents.[114] Their boss, the ZANU-PF government, provided them with a very simple formula by which to identify and eliminate their targets, which was: if one was Ndebele he was ZAPU, therefore a "dissident" and supporter of Joshua Nkomo.

With this freedom and license to terrorize the Ndebele population, these government operatives stepped up their violence. Above all, they refused to let families bury their loved ones. Thus, the first four months of 1985 were fraught with reports of violence against people of Matebeleland and Midlands by the ZANU-PF government, using mostly the 5th Brigade and the CIO. For instance, during the run-up to the June-July 1985 elections, within the first four months, at least eight ZAPU officials and ex-ZIPRA members were abducted and subsequently disappeared. Scores of homes, most of ZAPU members, were looted and destroyed, leaving 2,000 people homeless.[115]

Because of international pressure, and certainly because of defiance by the people of Matebeleland South, Mugabe withdrew his notorious, ill-disciplined,

The Best and the Worst of Times

murderous troops.[116] More credit should go to the people of Matebeleland South who showed tremendous resilience throughout the curfew period. When the curfew was imposed, Matebeleland South had had three consecutive years of severe drought, resulting in its residents depending largely on relief aid, some of which was distributed by the government through local stores. With the beginning of the curfew in the first weeks of February, all of these stores were closed, transportation bringing food into this area was stopped, and people in towns were prevented from sending food to their loved ones.

Before long, and after the depletion of what little reserves people had, rural Ndebele began to starve. It is said that one health official reported that people in the curfew area were eating less than twenty percent of the amount of food they needed, and that the starving situation was critical for children and the elderly. However, according to local doctors interviewed by Bill Berkely, a representative of the lawyers' committee, a small number of people in this area died from starvation-related diseases.[117]

The reason the government gave for suspending food supplies at a time of severe need on the part of the AmaNdebele was to starve dissidents, so that without this kind of support they would be flushed out of the area. This strategy where food was used as a political weapon was not a new one to the rural people in Zimbabwe. During the Smith regime, under the code-named Operation Turkey, the RSFs had destroyed crops belonging to rural people in the name of flushing out 'terrorists.' By employing the same tactics as the hated Smith regime, Mugabe further alienated the people he wanted to bring over to his party. However, that was not how ZANU-PF saw it, it saw force and fear as appropriate instruments of winning the up-coming elections. Thus ZANU-PF wanted to make sure that when the elections came it won seats in Matebeleland. This would make it a national party instead of a tribal and regional one. The use of force by the ruling party against AmaNdebele backfired big time as evidenced by the June/July 1985 elections results. The voting occurred over five days, and was peaceful, a sharp contrast to the pre-elections days. Mugabe's party won again. In fact, it increased its seats from the 1980 fifty-seven to sixty-three in the new parliament, out of a total of eighty common-roll seats. ZAPU slipped from twenty seats in 1980 to fifteen in 1985 but still took all seats in Matebeleland. Of the total votes cast, ZANU won only ten percent of the votes in Matebeleland. Undoubtedly Mugabe had underestimated the determination of the AmaNdebele people to exercise their freedom of choice and expression.[118] Thus, by the end of the day, and after conducting a sadistic military campaign in Matebeleland, the 1985 elections did very little to change the political scene in the country as Mugabe, once again, failed to win one seat in Matebeleland, and also failed to force ZAPU to merge with his party.

But the ruling party's loss in Matebeleland would not go unpunished. The government detained, without charge, two hundred high-ranking ZAPU officials and ex-ZIPRA combatants in the last week of July. Among those detained were five ZAPU members of parliament: Kembo Mohadi, MP for Beitbridge, Edward Ndlovu, MP for Gwanda, Stephen Nkomo, MP for Kezi and Joshua Nkomo's young brother, Welshman, Mabhena, MP for Nkayi and Sydney Malunga, MP for Mpopoma, in Bulawayo, and ZAPU's Parliamentary chief whip.[119] Eight ex-ZIPRA high-ranking officers and all ZAPU Bulawayo Council members, including the Mayor and the Town Clerk were thrown into prison.[120] Government operatives searched Nkomo's home on August 10, and seized a private collection of licensed guns, and arrested several of his personal aides and bodyguards.

However, Nkomo himself was not arrested, but humiliated. Instead of fleeing to Botswana, this time Nkomo fled to the capital where he denounced the actions of the government at a press conference. Bulawayo was, indeed, under siege, the Barbarians were not at the gate but in the city. However, people sworn not to allow themselves to be brought under a one-party system of government stopped ZANU-PF's self-delusion politics of violence, which it romanticized as realpolitik, cold.

The account of Mugabe's reign of terror in Matebeleland from 1982-1987 cannot be complete without a mention of the dissidents' activities, the group which, this government used as a pretext for unleashing unfettered terror on Nkomo, ZAPU and AmaNdebele. According to government sources dissidents caused considerable damage in Matebeleland and the Midlands from 1982 through 1987. For instance, from 1983 to the early part of 1984, it was reported that dissidents killed forty farmers or members of their families. Evidently, farmers were killed for the sake of publicity since they played a great role in producing food for the population and export.[121] Matebeleland was affected most. During the first part of 1984, fearful white farmers who either fled into cities or fled the country abandoned about 500,000 acres of commercial farmland.[122]

In 1983 alone, the government reported that dissidents had killed one hundred-twenty people, raped forty-seven, and mutilated twenty-five. In 1984, the government reported a lower number of casualties; thirty-two killed and among these were twelve ZANU-PF officials. In 1985, the number of those killed rose again, and the dramatic increase came after elections in July with one hundred eighty-two killed. In January 1986 the minister of Home Affairs, Enos Nkala, told parliament that during the second half of 1985, dissidents killed one hundred-and-three people, raped fifty-seven women, destroyed property worth millions of dollars, clinics and government centers, and committed one hundred sixty-three armed robberies. Similarly worrisome numbers were reported in 1986 and 1987.[123]

The accuracy of these numbers given as representing dissidents' destruction is difficult to independently prove. It is doubtful that most of these brutalities were committed by 'genuine' ex-ZIPRA army defectors who had taken to the bush. Blame for these deaths was largely apportioned on two groups: the pseudo-gangs of the government army, and Super ZAPU operatives. For instance, in

The Best and the Worst of Times

November 1985, Luke Bhizeni Khumalo, a headmaster at a British Methodist High School, Thegwane, in Matebeleland South and his white wife Jean was killed by what was suspected to have been pseudo-gangs of the security forces. The government version though was that dissidents committed the atrocities. However, there is ample evidence pointing to the government as the killer of the Khumalo family.[124] Also, people interviewed in the affected areas informed that most of the people who claimed to be dissidents and were committing atrocities could hardly speak correct SiNdebele as they were Shona speakers. According to these sources, dissidents were fluent SiNdebele speakers.[125]

Super ZAPU shared in the committing of the most heinous of crimes. It is believed Super-ZAPU dissidents were responsible for the brutal death of missionaries around Esigodini,[126] and the death of many farmers in Matebeleland. The purpose for Super ZAPU's activities was two-fold, one, by killing missionaries, to increase the hostility between the government on one hand, and ZAPU and AmaNdebele, on another, and two, to drive away white farmers in order to undermine the country's economy. Both of these goals were in conformity with their sponsor, South Africa's goal of destabilizing Zimbabwe. South Africa, still suspecting that Matebeleland provided succor to the MK, might have figured out that if it destabilized the region, it would force the government to pour its troops into the region, and by its presence reduce the chances of South African guerrillas infiltrating into the northern part of Transvaal.[127]

Journalists like Jensen and Godwin covered these atrocities largely with little or no support from the publications they represented. The primary protesters of these atrocities were the AmaNdebele people themselves, ZAPU people and some churches in the country. ZAPU politicians, however, were the first to raise their voices against what turned out to be ethnic cleansing by the Mugabe government. The clergy later joined the politicians. On March 26, the Catholic Commission for Justice and Peace, an organization with a history of standing for human rights when the country was known as Rhodesia, broke its silence on the government inspired atrocities occurring in Matebeleland.

In their press statement, the Bishops stated that it was "clear that human rights in (Matebeleland) are being severely violated." On March 28, its representatives met with Mugabe and presented him with a confidential dossier of its evidence. On March 29, the Commission issued a pastoral statement, bitterly critical of the Mugabe government's military campaign in Matebeleland. Because the statement gives a more comprehensive picture of what people in Matebeleland and Midlands felt about Mugabe's campaign among them, it is worthy citing in full. The statement read thus:

> *We entirely support the duty of the government to maintain law and order, even by military means. What we view with dismay are the methods that have been adopted for doing so. Methods, which should be firm and just have degenerated into brutality and atrocity.... Violent reaction against dissident activity has, to our certain knowledge, brought about the maiming and death of hundreds and*

hundreds of innocent people who are neither dissidents [n]or collaborators...The facts point to a reign of terror caused by wanton killings, woundings, beatings, burnings, and rapings. Many houses have been burned down. People in the rural areas are starving, not only because of the drought, but because in some cases supplies of food have been deliberately cut off and in other cases access to food has been restricted or stopped.[128]

While condemning the government, the Catholic bishops rightly pointed out that the government had a legitimate right and duty to protect its citizens from unruly elements in the society. Nobody criticized the government for sending troops into Matebeleland and Midlands to control the crisis caused by the South African sponsored Super ZAPU dissidents.

The Roman Catholic Church remained vocal throughout ZANU-PF's military campaign in Matebeleland. One of the heated arguments between the government and the Roman Catholic clergy was started by Fr. John Gough's sermon. Fr. Gough was born in Lancashire, Britain, and came to Rhodesia in 1958. On April 1, Fr. Gough launched a blistering attack on the government for its atrocities in Matebeleland. Detailing atrocities done by the 5th Brigade in that region he warned his audience that they would hear of things that would make them wish they were dead: "babies thrown into boiling water [and] people buried up to their necks and shot."[129]

Essentially Fr. Gough accused the Mugabe government of genocide and trying to physically eliminate AmaNdebele. At the end of his sermon, which was delivered at the capital of Zimbabwe, Fr. Gough invited those who wanted to hear more details on the atrocities to stay behind after the sermon.

On April 2, a day after Fr. Gough's sermon, Henry Karlen joined by several fellow priests, presented a four page report to the Minister of Information, Nathan Shamiyarira, repeating the same complaints against atrocities the Catholic Church had made the previous year, "a campaign of starvation, beatings, torture, rape and murder."[130] The Catholic Justice and Peace Commission weighed in by presenting its own thirteen-page dossier to Mugabe, alleging similar atrocities by the 5th Brigade.[131]

Interviewed about Karlen's criticisms, Mugabe came out unglued and charging. Characteristically, he accused Karlen of "worshipping Nkomo instead of God," and further said Karlen and his priests were ZAPU supporters. Mugabe continued to accuse all Zimbabwean's Catholic Bishops of being in league with ZAPU. Sydney Sekeramayi, a government minister, and Mugabe's second 'blue-eyed' boy (the first being Munangagwa) did what Mary's little lamb did best, which was to follow his master. He accused Karlen of spreading "filthy lies about the government...in league with Satan, Joshua Nkomo and other evil forces."[132]

However, much the government tried, it could not silence the fearless Nkomo, who since the beginning of atrocities attacked the Mugabe government for engaging in ethnic cleansing for the sake of a one-party ideology. On March 11, 1984 Nkomo accused the government of practicing tribalism, racism and

The Best and the Worst of Times

regionalism, and of starving AmaNdebele, ending with a reminder that the AmaNdebele too had a right to life. Nkomo went on at a separate setting to charge that "the ruling party appears... bent on defeating the people they rule by force of arms," and then charged that "Mugabe's government was led by fascists, not even comparable to Herr Hitler."[133]

Slowly and belatedly, the world joined the voice of reason and conscience and started condemning the Mugabe government for its criminal acts of ethnic cleansing, albeit with little effect. By then the government had realized its tactics were not working, and that it risked starting a civil war, whose end result it could not predict. In mid-April 1984, the government lifted up the food embargo in Matebeleland South. While the belated international protests were symbolically important, it was the work of the AmaNdebele and ZAPU people themselves who must be given credit for enduring such unconscionable brutality from their own government. Basically, it was the non-violent resistance of the people of Matebeleland and Midlands, coupled with publicity by the Catholics that brought government holocaust against the people of Matebeleland to a stop.[134]

Thus in 1985, the government finally came to its senses and coaxed Nkomo to come back from his self-exile in Britain. Only Nkomo, and not any amount of force, could bring the AmaNdebele into national political consensus, which to Mugabe and his party meant into a one-party state. This kind of ZANU-PF logic of thinking would be later well stated in a 1989 editorial in the Catholic *Moto*:

> *Of late it has increasingly seemed as if unity is synonymous with the one-party state in Zimbabwe, and that those who might want to form another political party are against national unity. That is unfortunate, particularly when people get emotionally charged about these issues.*[135]

Nkomo had made, earlier in his book, a similar observation about African leadership in general not being able to tolerate differences of opinion. While in exile in Britain in 1984, and reflecting on the dictatorial behavior of the Mugabe government, Nkomo wrote:

> *The new African rulers who came to power at independence have all too often claimed the same unquestionable authority as their traditional and colonial predecessors. Instead of welcoming debate as the necessary means of improving government, they have confused opposition to particular policies with disloyalty. Constructive criticism is brushed aside, and suggested improvements are described as attempts to undermine the state ... they confuse self-preservation with national security.*[136]

Thus, when Nkomo was invited to come back to Zimbabwe he knew the government wanted for him to come and influence his party to merge with ZANU-PF, on ZANU-PF terms. Moreover, this was not the first time that Mugabe's government had extended an invitation to him to come home. Before he left for Britain, while he was in Botswana, Simon Muzenda, the Deputy Prime Minister, and Munangagwa, the Minister of State, invited Nkomo to come back home. They even went to the extent of asking if he would receive a high-powered delegation consisting of Munangagwa, Solomon Mujuru, the General Commander, and other senior officials. Mugabe was in India attending a meeting then.

For some reason the delegation called off their meeting with Nkomo.[137] When contact was made between Nkomo and Munangagwa, and Nkomo and Muzenda, Nkomo would ask each one of them of the government's commitment to genuine reconciliation and a guarantee of his personal safety. Nkomo got no satisfactory answer to both of these questions. Even at this time, nothing satisfying was promised Nkomo in terms of power sharing, although his safety was guaranteed, a promise he hardly believed. In fact, when Nkomo went to exile in London, it appeared he might never come back to Zimbabwe. But return he did when it appeared he might be able to stop the killing of his people by a 'maniac' government, although the cost of surrendering his party to Mugabe.

Once Nkomo was back in the country in October 1985, meetings began between ZANU-PF and ZAPU with a view to merging the two parties. Nkomo refused to play ball, and in April 1987 the talks collapsed. The real bone of contention in these talks was Nkomo's refusal to have his party merge with ZANU-PF, instead, he wanted a coalition government. He went back to his initial demands of more cabinet posts for his party and jobs in the civil service among other things. ZANU-PF senior leaders, led by Mugabe and Nkala, got angry with ZAPU for refusing to accept a merger with their party. They then determined force would bring ZAPU into their fold. Consequently, Nkala, the Minister of Home Affairs, banned ZAPU's public meetings, closed its offices nation-wide and dissolved six of ZAPU dominated local governments in Matebeleland North.[138] Mugabe vowed not to extend a hand of reconciliation to Nkomo and his party again. When Nkala banned ZAPU from holding public meetings and dissolved some of its local authorities he claimed he did it because ZAPU was supporting dissidents,[139] and yet in reality it was because the latter had refused to merge with his party.

With talks of reconciliation at a standstill, the government increased its harassment, arresting without charges and killing the AmaNdebele, particularly the AmaNdebele who were ZAPU members. While all this turmoil was occurring, churches were working behind the scenes trying to get both parties to resume unity talks. Members of the Catholic Justice and Peace Commission and the Heads of Denominations were secretly talking with both parties to restart the talks. Finally the Heads of Denominations approached President Canaan Banana, himself a minister of religion, and asked him to mediate.

Nkomo, too, was interested in talks being resumed if only to save his people the AmaNdebele, and his party members from extermination by what had turned out to be a murderous government. He knew the government considered him the primary target. At one point after he returned from his self-imposed exile in London it was rumored that in 1986 he considered going to permanent exile if that would save his people, the AmaNdebele and his ZAPU

The Best and the Worst of Times

supporters. It is reported Banana dissuaded him against leaving,[140] telling him his presence was crucial for the realization of peace in Zimbabwe.

It is important to note that this was not the first time that these church organizations had approached both parties asking them to resume talks. Again as he did earlier when things were not going well between him and Mugabe, Nkomo approached Banana and asked him to mediate. Banana in turn impressed on Mugabe that "History must include Joshua Nkomo. He started well, let him end well."[141]

Before the year was out, talks resumed with the mediation of Banana. After representatives from both parties grappled with issues from the name of the new party to the structure of the party after the merger, the parties agreed to a merger, and signed the Unity Accord Agreement on December 22, 1987.[142] By this unity accord, it was agreed that there was an irrevocable commitment under the name of ZANU-PF with Mugabe as the merged parties' first Secretary and President. More importantly for the stability of the country, it was also agreed that "both parties shall…take immediate vigorous steps to eliminate and end the insecurity and violence…in Matebeleland."[143] The parties also agreed to hold joint meetings across Matebeleland explaining and selling the agreement to the people of Matebeleland, after which they would hold separate party congresses to rectify the Unity Accord. Nkomo subsequently held several joint meetings with Enos Nkala of ZANU-PF explaining and selling the Unity agreement to a beleaguered people, AmaNdebele.

Reactions to the Unity Accord were mixed and varied. Mugabe, perhaps the happiest person at that moment, and at the signing of the Accord said, "the nation must feel jubilant this moment-that this great act has occurred which will bring them together."[144] Mugabe had all the reason to be excited about the agreement. Since his party broke away from ZAPU in 1963, he had worked towards the leadership of a national liberation movement of Zimbabwe. Talks on unity between the two parties had invariably collapsed because Mugabe would not agree to a unity of which he was not the leader.

Hard feelings between the AmaNdebele and AmaShona went as far back as the time when the founder of the AmaNdebele came into Zimbabwe from KwaZulu, South Africa, in the latter half of the 1800s. Some people in Matebeleland quickly made that connection between the 1980s years of tension between the AmaShona and AmaNdebele and the tension there was between the AmaNdebele and AmaShona in the late Nineteenth Century:

> *They [AmaNdebele] have had to pay dearly for the raids into Mashonaland by Mzilikazi and Lobengula and for Lobengula's defeat by the settlers in 1893. However much we may try to disguise the fact, it still remains that the people of Matebeleland are tolerated but not wanted.*[145]

Thus, over years, as Terence Ranger, a Zimbabwean historian, noted, the AmaShona and AmaNdebele reacted to the entrenchment of settler rule by scape-goating old memories. For instance, Ranger noted:

At the end of the 1920s Shona farmers were still recalling the Ndebele raids of the nineteenth century and using these memories to justify suspicions of Bulawayo politicians. The chiefs and headmen of Gwelo district were frightened out of the Native Welfare Association when the Bulawayo progressives began to come into it. In Bulawayo itself Ndebele town dwellers responded to increasing pressures of life in the towns by making Shona workers the scapegoats of urban violence and demanding separate Ndebele villages.[146]

The white settlers developed a version of AmaShona and AmaNdebele pre-colonial relationship that created tension between the two as long as they believed the white version of how their forefathers related. In part because of this version on who was found in Zimbabwe and by whom, some AmaShona people came to believe it was they, and not the AmaNdebele who were the rightful heirs to Zimbabwe. Based on this logic some AmaShona people resisted the leadership of AmaNdebele who they considered Colonialists. Mugabe and his party effectively used this version inherited from white settlers for their political benefit. Earlier, Mugabe and his colleagues had broken away from Nkomo in the early 1960s to found a rival movement "with strong tribal appeal."[147] There is no question Mugabe wanted to settle the question of state power, nation and political authority.

Elections had proved to him he had the consensus of the AmaShona, but not of the sizeable AmaNdebele minority. The nation was still as divided as ever, now seven years into his leadership. Mugabe was suddenly confronted by only one option, either to change the state and nation to suit the likes of the two diametrically different nations the AmaNdebele and the whites. To the whites he offered reconciliation, which basically meant whites staying where there were without loss of their identity and privilege. To ZAPU and the AmaNdebele, Mugabe used brute force to join up the ends of the triangle of nation, state and political authority. So by Nkomo signing on this agreement agreeing for his party to merge with ZANU-PF on unfavorable terms, Mugabe must have felt a sense of self-vindication or the vindication of his tribe, which he believed was once brutalized by the AmaNdebele people. Thus, Mugabe was excited because the result of the signing of the Unity Accord was a one-party state, and the cementing of his authority.[148]

Nkomo's response was rather guarded and subdued. He remarked:

The significance of this occasion will run through the whole fabric of our nation. It is the beginning of unity, for unity is not just the signing of documents, unity is what follows.[149]

By this cautious statement Nkomo undoubtedly had the development of Matebeleland in mind. Clearly Zimbabwe made significant achievements in the first five years of independence. It had improved health care, cut down the country's infant mortality rate by half, and built hundreds of schools for thousands of children who had very slim chances of getting an education under a white settler government. These in no way were minor achievements.

The Best and the Worst of Times

However, most of these developments were taking place in Mashonaland so that Matebeleland was left behind in development. AmaNdebele, attributed this to favoritism based on tribalism. The government, however, was partly true in its pointing to the cause of non-development in Matebeleland as being a result of dissidents' presence as the latter did destroy government projects in the area.

Nkomo, a nationalist, had a broader vision of a developed Zimbabwe as a whole. By and large, by the time the Unity Accord was signed, Zimbabwe had not undergone any significant systemic changes, whites still owned most of the means of production and the choicest land. This troubled Nkomo and hence his concerns, which are best summarized by his concluding paragraph of his article on the significance of the Unity Accord. He wrote:

> *The unity was not just between PF ZAPU and ZANU (PF), but is a basis for wider unity of all the people of Zimbabwe irrespective of color creed, religious affiliation or tribal background...[The Unity Accord] should address the issues of land reform, unemployment, housing, education, health, rehabilitation, social security, cultural development, community, development, crime prevention, corruption, women's rights, etc.*[150]

Nkomo was painfully aware that this Accord was strictly between ZAPU and ZANU-PF, and that troubled him greatly because the approach was not nation-building as it excluded a lot of Zimbabweans. For Mugabe, divide-and-rule tactics were what he wanted, and this was evidenced by the fact that he had never attempted to build a Zimbabwean nation on any basis other than on tribalism and brute force. Nkomo and his party were also concerned about Mugabe's Marxist-Leninist principles, and his obsession with a one-party system of government, and they let Mugabe know about it. In response Mugabe put the issue of a legislated one-party system of government to a vote at a politburo meeting and it was overwhelmingly shot down.[151]

Nkomo would later concede the obvious, that he signed the accord in order to save the lives of his people, the AmaNdebele, and his party members from government terror.[152] In other words, the Unity Accord was literally extorted out of the blood of the people of Matebeleland and ZAPU membership. Nkomo, in the words of Patricia Cheney, had been asked to make "the ultimate sacrifice and had made it, showing that old Father Zimbabwe...was...a patriot who put the interest of his country first," and at the time of the merger with ZANU-PF the rightly subdued Nkomo said "now, rather than saving my face, I am saving the face of my country."[153] Indeed, Nkomo had made an ultimate decision the greatest of which was to abandon his party's determination to maintain its self-identity, which thing would not have happened in a coalition. Here ZAPU had literally been absorbed by ZANU-PF, which refused to change its name.

The AmaNdebele's and the generality of ZAPU members' responses were mixed as well, with most of them not excited at all about the agreement. For the ZAPU people, they could not imagine their organization merging with a party they thought was inept and had failed to address national issues. For the

AmaNdebele the wounds from the government-sponsored terror were still open and hurting.

Consequently, they did not want to have anything to do with Mugabe and his party.[154] Arguably, their grudging acceptance of the unity agreement was in honor of the man who they respected and knew had their interests at heart. Otherwise, strictly speaking the agreement was between the leaders themselves and the general party membership remained unreconciled. ZAPU members and the people of Matebeleland and Midlands would not forgive Mugabe and his party for the atrocities whose redress was never addressed by this unity document. Richard Carver accurately captured the general feeling of the AmaNdebele people and ZAPU members in his comment on the accord when he said:

> *The government and even some ZAPU leaders may be inclined to forget such cases as being past history, but for the families of the "disappeared," who have lost loved ones and often breadwinners, the absence is no less acute because the party leaders have signed a unity accord. The government should investigate the "disappearances" fully and bring to justice those officials found responsible for prolonged unlawful detention, torture or killing of prisoners.*[155]

Some outsiders totally failed to appreciate this general feeling of hatred against the unity accord by most AmaNdebele and ZAPU members. Professor Ranger was among those who misread the mood of the AmaNdebele people when he visited Matopo for his research after the signing of the Accord. Expressing delight at what he saw Ranger wrote:

> *Paradoxically, perhaps, Matabeleland is the most optimistic region in the whole of Zimbabwe at the moment. The ready access to the field, the eagerness of the people to talk, their optimism is, of course, the fruits of the unity agreement....*[156]

Ranger's comments were nothing short of an outrage to most of the AmaNdebele who still wanted to see people like Mugabe, Munangagwa, Sekeremai and Perence Shiri, the commander of the 5th Brigade, tried for the role in the mass murder of the AmaNdebele people and ZAPU members. It is possible Ranger was blinded by his long and unquestioning support of the ZANU-PF.

However, despite the varied responses of euphoria, disgust, and a sense of betrayal, some tangible results came out of the agreement. One of the dramatic results of the signing of the peace accord was an immediate cessation of dissident related activities, bringing peace to Matebeleland and Midlands. Complete normalcy in these areas was returned six months from the signing of the accord when Mugabe granted amnesty to all dissidents who gave themselves up on or before March 31, 1988, and probably all did. For ZAPU members, peace dividends came at the cost of sacrificing their party to Mugabe.

The stopping of dissident activities after the signing of the accord proved Mugabe's position that the Matebeleland crisis needed a military rather than a political solution wrong. Rather it confirmed ZAPU's position that the

The Best and the Worst of Times

Matebeleland disturbances needed a political solution. Even Moven Mahachi, a senior ZANU official and a newly appointed Minister of Home Affairs at the time confessed, "the solution of the problem of dissidents was political."[157] To present a façade of unity, Nkomo was appointed the Senior Minister of Development and the second Secretary of ZANU (PF) and some ZAPU officials were assigned diplomatic duties. It was hoped that this would cement the accord between the two parties.

With ZAPU now merged with his party, Mugabe moved on to clear up some remaining hurdles to his objective of achieving a one-party state. The year of the signing of the accord, Mugabe abolished the twenty entrenched white seats and created a unicameral body, with an enlarged membership to one hundred-fifty. After his party merged with ZAPU, Mugabe moved on to have himself chosen an Executive President with very sweeping powers.[158]

In the 1990 General Elections, the new ZANU (PF) party scored a decisive victory sweeping one hundred-sixteen seats out of one hundred-nineteen seats contested. Later, it would win one more seat, bringing up its representation to one hundred-eighteen. Now Mugabe was feeling more relaxed and in total control, so he appointed five former ZAPU members to ministerial positions, with Nkomo given first a Senior Minister's post in the Office of the President, and later made a second Vice-President of Zimbabwe.[159] The most significant appointment was that of Dumiso Dabengwa, who was appointed the Deputy Minister of Home Affairs. This appointment was significant because since Nkomo was forced to leave the position of Home Affairs, no one from ZAPU had been appointed to a high-level security job where he or she could participate in making decisions at such a higher ministerial level. The appointments, however, did not change AmaNdebele's attitudes towards Mugabe and his former ZANU-PF colleagues whom they considered murderers and who now had capriciously co-opted their leaders.

With the signing of this agreement, subsequently approved by 3,000 ZAPU delegates,[160] ZAPU gave its last sigh of breath after twenty-five years of existence. Also, with its demise went the hope of the practice of democracy in the country. However, the spirit of its insurgency, whose seeds it had planted, would continue beyond the death of the organization itself. ZAPU continued its existence on intellectual and cultural levels, expressed through theater.

No sooner had it forcibly been merged with ZANU than its former membership and new recruits revived and continued ZAPU's rich, democracy propagating traditional theater. What ZAPU was responding to with its theater during 1982-1988,[161] was the historical predominance of force by the ruling party as a foundation of hegemony. Although denied its potent weapon of communicating discontent during the six years of genocide the opposition did not totally forget this potent strategy of drama on the part of its membership. Dramatizing the social terrain, drama was to be later used by the radical opposition cultural groups to fight for democracy, responsible and transparent governance and a non-racial nation. These groups used cultural symbols to convey their grievances to the government because of their potential to give meaning to their individual experiences.

Historically, ZAPU had used theater to negate the State's myths about Zimbabwe. It appealed to culture and traditional religion in mobilizing the civilian population inside Rhodesia during the open nationalist era, and later after its proscription, in the educational and socializing work at refugee and military camps in exile. In exile drama was encouraged for two basic reasons, one, as a form of entertainment and second, as a means of fostering a sense of responsible government and a unified nation. In the ZAPU camps, members were encouraged to be proficient in all three of the Zimbabwean major languages, Shona, SiNdebele and English, particularly those in theater.[162] Cultural performances from different areas and in different languages were collected and promoted in an effort to foster a sense of unity and a homogeneous nation among heterogeneous groups.

School children in camps also played a critical part in theater. They dramatized the lives of Mzilikazi and Lobengula, showering them with praise and criticism, by exploiting the dual nature of praise-poetry which, combined eulogy with criticism of authoritarianism. However the immediate focus of this humor and the ambiguous utterances were unpopular camp leaders and teachers. Later in the late 1970s, it was Nkomo, whose image as 'Father Zimbabwe' was being promoted at the time.[163] It should be pointed out that these cultural values and symbols were not uncritically adhered to. There were modernists who argued for the subjection of tradition to criticism to expose feudal or bourgeois mystification which, needed to be replaced by socialist, equalitarian, and scientific ideology. Cognizant of the dynamic nature of tradition ZAPU incorporated some elements of these views in what was now their 'refurbished' traditional theater. Arguably, theater is the most dynamic and social of the African cultural forms. Where there are areas of conflict and tension in world-view, tension between the rulers and the ruled, theater often serves to illuminate self-understanding and to express prevailing precise aspirations, grievances and needs.

Nkomo and some of the ZAPU leaders moderated sessions where marriage between tradition and modernist ideologies of governance and nation building were effected. Such issues as the power-sharing mechanism between men and women were hammered-out and conveyed through theater, as were some other conflict-ridden areas of power-sharing, checks and balances and even limitations on leadership, which had been non-existent in the traditional royal leadership.

What was of great significance to the crafting of most of these plays was that they were made through the collaborative process of "workshop," theater, a process analogous to the emergence of revolutionary action based on a mass-democratic movement in Zimbabwe politics first led by Nkomo himself. Themes were chosen during brainstorming sessions where a wide variety of topics were

The Best and the Worst of Times

considered. Thus, the creation of plays was in and of itself a work in democracy in that they were products of a process of collective discussion and decision-making. Participation in decision-making gave both spectators and drama practitioners a sense of ownership of the product and its intended implications.[164]

The practice was not new. It was a throwback to the times of Mzilikazi and Lobengula at the turn of the nineteenth century, when all roles of drama were collapsed into one person, the *imbongi* (Praise-critic). On appointed annual national gatherings, the *imbongi* was invited to give eulogies and to deliver a critique of the King's governance on behalf of the nation. The *imbongi* spent much of their time gathering what the nation thought about the King and his rule, and those around him, *inkundla*. Other forms of praise and critique were dance and song. Thus the utility of these forms of praise and critic were judged by their taking advantage of a broadly shared set of values that were in consonance with popular consciousness. Failure to accurately convey the feelings of the populace invited immediate disqualification.[165]

In summary, by theater, ZAPU hoped to promote the following indispensable values to a democratic environment: a vigilant electorate, transparent governance, a government responsive to its citizen's needs, equality between men and women and a non-ethnic and non-racial nation. There was however, an immediate drawback to the utility of drama as a tool by which to instill all these values. During their years of exile the theater players did not have immediate access to their primary audience: the people of Zimbabwe. The immediate inheritors of ZAPU's tradition of standing for democracy, critiquing and non-transparent policies of governance, tribalism and gender inequality, were two groups: *Iluba Elimnyama* (Black Flower) and *AmaKhosi*.

Amakhosi was led by Cont Mhlanga who later was part of a group that tried to resurrect ZAPU. In fact, community based theater of a political nature and of cultural expression became prevalent from 1980 on. By the mid-1980s there were more than ten such groups in Bulawayo alone, and by 1990 there were thirty-four groups, operating in the city's high-density suburbs. These groups specifically performed plays whose main focus reflected the main concerns of workers, students, women and a desire for national unity.[166]

The two groups mentioned above received more publicity than the rest of the groups, perhaps because they drew bigger audiences and had play-themes that were more troubling to the government. The *Iluba Elimnyama* which operated as the first theater Collective was composed of six members, three men and three women, a gender mix that emphasized the theme of its first full length production, which challenged gender inequality, a brave attempt given the patriarchal nature of the Zimbabwean society. *Impilo-le* (Oh, this life) questioned the notions of gender and equality and in a post-independence period that still had to grapple with patriarchal attitudes. According to one of the observers of these groups, such plays as *Impilo-le* helped to draw the attention of government and the public to the need for a strict legislation to protect women from being abused by men who abandoned them, leaving them to struggle with the raising of their children.[167]

On a political level, the *Iluba Elimnyama*, having as its backdrop the charged tribalistic atmosphere in Zimbabwe, largely promoted by the ruling party, drew attention to Zimbabwe's fractured society. In March 1987, it produced yet another indictment of the Zimbabwean society. It produced a play entitled 'Blood Brothers,' which specifically addressed the evils of tribalism in the work place, schools and other every-day life places. Integrating modern modalities of conflict-resolution into a mostly traditional way of solving problems the play ends by having groups reconcile at the *Elitsheni Le Njelele* (Njelele Shrine) as if to remind people of the place where traditionally intractable problems of a national nature were solved.[168]

A similar frankness in attacking the ills of the society was characteristic of the AmaKhosi Theater Productions led by Cont Mhlanga, an ex-ZIPRA combatant. From 1985, this group produced a flurry of plays that while infuriating the government, energized the general populace to focus of the issues of democracy, transparent governance, corruption, and tribalism. The group that started in 1978 had metamorphosed into a vibrant political and cultural critic.

Its first breakthrough came in 1985 when the group produced a play entitled *Nansi lendoda*. This play addressed issues of nepotism, youth unemployment and attitudes that demeaned women in the society. *Nansi lendoda* catapulted the popularity of AmaKhosi beyond their little Bulawayo Township, Makokoba, as it performed in schools and beer halls around Matebeleland. Like *Iluba Elimnyama*, its performances were in three languages, SiNdebele, Shona and English.

This significance of the use of these three languages in both instances was to emphasize the equality of all Zimbabweans irrespective of ethnicity or race. A year later, in 1986, the group produced one of its most controversial productions which brought it fame with the general population and infamy with the government as it saw its ugly face mirrored in this play.[169] "Workshop Negative," is a play about a tool-making workshop in the post-independence Zimbabwe, where a revolutionary war has changed things dramatically. The owner of the workshop, himself a former guerrilla, has, however, turned out to be an exploiter who was worse than the leaders before independence. Themes of reconciliation are presented in this play as well, but the chief leader in this workshop does not want reconciliation because he profits from a situation in which workers are estranged from each other.[170]

The government viewed the play as a direct indictment of its leadership, and confronted the groups in passive aggressive ways, such as refusing to endorse a tour of its performances to Botswana and Zambia. A spokesperson of the Ministry of Youth, Sport and Culture could not hold his fire; he publicly criticized the group in a way that bordered on censorship.[171]

The Best and the Worst of Times

The significance of this group's play was that it got the nation to looking into how it was ruled, uses of tribalism, governance and corruption in higher places. As one writer observed:

Performances of Workshop Negative brought about a liveliness of discussions and controversy over culture and politics in Zimbabwe that had not been experienced before. The reason for this was partly the popularity of the play and its unusual efficiency and outspokenness, but also the fact that the authorities responded to it rather obstructively by refusing to sanction a tour of performances in Botswana and Zambia.[172]

One keen observer of these groups of the post-ZAPU practitioners well captured their significant role in the creation of a democratic Zimbabwe, and their embodiment of a historical legacy of democracy when he wrote:

And the development in the over-all political situation of Zimbabwe has meant that democracy a promotion of channels for articulating frustration and criticism now figure much more prominently on the political agenda than ever before since independence. The Unity Agreement between ZANU (PF) and PF-ZAPU in December 1987, the amnesty offered to the 'dissidents' of Matabeleland in May 1988, the student demonstrations in Harare in September-October 1988, and the Bulawayo Chronicle's corruption and later the Sandura Commission's public exposure of nepotism in high political circles have provided the basis for a new type of realistic rather than rhetorical debate of social and political issues.

There can hardly be any doubt that the tradition of a grassroots based democracy theater of discussion going back to the liberation war, and the activities of the Zimbabwean drama groups have helped considerably to bring about the new political climate. Not only were the issues of corruption and nepotism that were at the center of the political campaigns by students and the press in 1988 first articulated openly by drama, but also the confrontation between drama groups like AmaKhosi and the authorities in 1987 helped to clarify and increase understanding of different political philosophies of culture.[173]

Above all, the groups "stimulated self-respect and a culture of participation among the 'little people'--the workers, peasants and unemployed men and women of the country."[174] Another picture that emerges from this account on ZAPU theater is the kind of government and nation that ZAPU was trying to create: a democratic, multiparty system, with a diverse citizenry whose differences in culture and ethnicity were not only encouraged but affirmed. This put ZAPU's vision of the kind of government it wanted to introduce to Zimbabwe, and its nation in the same camp as Senghor and to the opposite camp of that of Nyerere and Kenyatta.

In all, no sooner had ZAPU celebrated the beating of spears into plowshares following the independence of Zimbabwe than it became, once again, the hunted, and this time by its own compatriots. A short season of optimism and high hopes for the new independent Zimbabwe was enjoyed by many a ZAPU member after independence with the promise of the two major parties working together in government, albeit with unfair distribution of power from the outset. Mugabe extended a hand of reconciliation to the whites who eagerly accepted it because essentially they lost nothing in terms of property and privilege after independence, while ostracizing a major section of the population that supported rivalry parties like UANC and ZANU-Ndonga.

On the bright side though, initial demobilization of the army was successfully completed, and so was the creation of a national army out of the three fighting forces. A hand of friendship was extended to ZAPU primarily, because besides being a national party, it represented a significant minority population, the AmaNdebele who as an ethnic nation gave almost an undivided allegiance to it. Arguably, an alliance between the majority ZANU and the minority ZAPU in one sense meant an alliance between the majority Shona and minority AmaNdebele, an indispensable ingredient to the stability of Zimbabwe.

The intentions of Mugabe's invitation of ZAPU to participate in government were very clear; so that he could become a national leader and prepare a process to introduce a one-party state. Consequently in less than two years of independence, the fragile tribal alliance between the two major ethnic groups collapsed. First, Mugabe offered Nkomo the chance to become the first black president of an independent Zimbabwe, and when the latter turned the offer down, the former invited ZAPU to become a junior partner in government, an arrangement to which ZAPU agreed.[175] In the meantime, ZANU was farming out well-trained ex-ZIPRA fighters from the army, and also engaging in demobilizing most of them. ZAPU's air force and intelligence suffered the biggest blow as they were cleverly excluded from the army.[176] Later Mugabe would attempt to separate Nkomo from his followers in an attempt to destroy his party.

Soon it became very clear to ZAPU that Mugabe was involved in a misconceived political game, and it made it very clear to him, through the committee he had set up to try and work-out some modality of cooperation between the two parties, that it was not interested in a merger but only a government of national unity.[177]

When persuasion failed Mugabe resorted to brute force, and ZAPU was on the receiving end, and so were the AmaNdebele people as a whole, in the whole, resulting in thousands of deaths.[178] Mugabe denounced ZAPU leader Nkomo who also was a de facto leader of the AmaNdebele as a "cobra in the house," in hopes of ostracizing both ZAPU and AmaNdebele from him and forcing them to support him. White doomsayers watched on, possibly with a sense of self-satisfying vindication as former comrades in arms during the liberation struggle went against each other.

Undoubtedly the level of barbarity of ethnic cleansing in Matebeleland, and to a lesser extent in Midlands from 1982-1988, was a result of ZANU-PF's resolve to force a one-party state on the country without the blessing of the minority groups. All the authoritarian tendencies, resulting in the persecution of ZAPU by ZANU could be traced back to 1980 when the latter ascended the throne. ZANU had gotten into power by mainly appealing to the Shona ethnic majority, and to some degree through use of intimidation so that it knew it would have a very difficult time retaining unchallenged political power if it were to hold free and fair elections. To keep itself in power ZANU resorted to the use of tribalism combined with authoritarian tendencies.

The failure of ZANU-PF leadership to rise above tribal politics during the transition from a settler regime virtually increased the possibility of ethnic conflict of this nature. Rather than accept ethnic diversity, and multi-party-ism, and work towards accommodative politics, Mugabe and the ZANU-PF leaders stooped low to play the card of tribalism, and in the process undermined democracy, the freedom of press, association, assembly and indeed the rule of law, leading to its committing ethnic cleansing.

ZAPU saw the military campaign by the ruling party against it as a war against democracy and multiparty-ism, and it determined to defend these ideals, and so did the people of Matebeleland as well as those in the affected parts of Midlands. They totally refused to succumb to Mugabe's military campaign against them, which they viewed as no exercise in democracy. Also ZAPU totally repudiated accusations ZANU placed on it. To ZAPU they were the lamb and ZANU was the wolf in Aesop's fable of the wolf and the lamb; innocent victims of a bloodthirsty regime, intent on imposing a one-party rule at all costs.[179]

Finally, a bogus Unity Accord was agreed upon between the two parties whose main result was the cessation of atrocities by both the army and dissidents and the creation of false peace in the land. False peace because the loss suffered by ZAPU, and the people of Matebeleland and some parts of Midlands remained un-addressed. Also the agreement brought to an end one of the best-organized and well-disciplined party Zimbabwe had ever seen.

7.3 SUMMARY AND CONCLUSION

Effective from the mid-1960s to the time of the cease-fire in 1979, ZAPU maintained a military presence in the operational theater in Rhodesia in varying numbers, fighting, teaching and training. In the 1970s it engaged in many talks in an attempt to achieve a peaceful solution to the seemingly intractable political crisis in Rhodesia. This study has shown that despite little publicity, and belittling disinformation, ZAPU made priceless contributions towards the liberation of Zimbabwe, and subsequently, to the stabilization of the country.

One of ZAPU's primary contributions was in prosecuting the armed struggle for the liberation of Zimbabwe. As Daniel Kepton correctly stated, Nkomo led the "best armed revolutionary organization in Zimbabwe."[180] ZAPU's armed struggle had very humble beginnings, starting with stones, home made bombs and purposive violence against government and white settler property. In fact these methods of struggle were inherited from the NDP. With the founding of ZAPU, a first consignment of weapons was brought into the country by none other than its leader, Nkomo. This was after the party's leadership in the early 1960's made clear its commitment to the armed struggle and pledged itself to bringing weapons into Rhodesia for sabotage, and thereby becoming the first party to embark on armed struggle in Rhodesia against settler oppression. Soon thereafter, in February 1963, Bobylock Manyonga was tried in Bulawayo for the possession of weapons of war.[181]

In essence, ZAPU had already started the armed struggle when ZANU was formed in 1963, which makes laughable the suggestion by some scholars and ZANU itself that the latter was the first to engage in armed struggle. The beginnings were humble and the number of trained cadres small. ZAPU was aware it was fighting against a formidable force. Also, it knew that since the settler government was set on its own ways, it could achieve majority rule only through fighting and that the war was going to be a protracted one. Of course this observation, which was made by Chikerema as he reflected on the gains and losses of the armed struggle, is in conformity with how liberation theorists view guerrilla warfare.

For these theorists, liberation movements get from their oppressors at the negotiation table what they have already earned in the battlefield, and liberation war is protracted. Frantz Fanon was one such theorist. Reminding the colonized of the importance of an armed struggle in the securing of concessions from a negotiated settlement Fanon said:

The native must realize that colonialism never gives anything away for nothing. Whatever the native may gain through political or armed struggle is not the result of the kindness or good will of the settler, it simply shows that he cannot put off granting concessions any longer. More over, the native ought to realize that it is not colonialism that grants concessions, but he himself that extorts them.[182]

In Zimbabwe, as this study has shown, it was the protracted war that finally led to the signing of the Lancaster House Agreement. Just like Fanon observed:

War is not a single battle, but rather a series of local engagements; and to tell the truth, none of these are decisive.... Colonialism has greater and wealthier resources than the native. The war goes on; the enemy holds his own; the final settling of accounts will not be today, nor yet tomorrow, for the truth is that the settlement was begun on the very first day of the war, and it would be ended not because there are no more enemies left to kill, but quite simply because the enemy for various reasons, will come to realize that his interest lies in ending the struggle and in recognizing the sovereignty of the colonized people.[183]

Thus according to Fanon, each battle fought for liberation is important and contributes to the struggle and its final outcome. Often scholars and observers have condemned ZAPU as a party that was ineffective because it did not score decisive victories against the settler government, and on that basis have minimized

The Best and the Worst of Times

its contributions in these areas. Fanon's observation changes the way armed struggle contributions are to be evaluated, and according to the schema, ZAPU indeed, through what some scholars and observers saw as non-decisive battles, contributed to the achievement of majority rule. That is true even if we believe that ZAPU's attacks on the regime forces throughout the war were ineffective.

All this to say the argument that ZANU was the first to wage an effective attack on the regime cannot be sustained for the following reasons: Because of ZAPU's pressure, the regime started to engage mercenaries as early as the last half of the 1960s and also to expand its army before ZANU's army could pose any serious challenge to the regime's soldiers.

Additionally, ZANU's guerrillas were poorly armed and their offenses not as effective as those of ZAPU. So it can be argued that although ZAPU's battles during this time were non-decisive, they were effective enough to undermine the morale of the army and win the hearts of villagers.

In the prosecution of war itself ZAPU also made many qualitative contributions that significantly contributed to the lowering of the morale of the white community, the incapacitation of the Smith's war machinery, and the crippling of the economy. Two of the events that seriously undermined white morale were the downing of the two civilian Viscounts, one in September 1978 and the second one in February 1979, both of which were brought down by ZIPRA.

The first Viscount had few survivors, and the second one had none. Undoubtedly the death of so many whites in such a terrible manner, with the two incidents happening within six months of each other, came as a greatest shock to the settler.[184] ZIPRA also attacked Rhodesian aircraft and contributed immensely to its incapacitation and attrition. Nkomo asserted that ZIPRA shot down nearly thirty Rhodesian planes and helicopters the first time his troops used the Soviet surface-to-air missiles,[185] which was in 1977.

A month after the downing of the first Viscount in 1978 Nkomo again claimed his troops had shot down seven planes and in November of that same year ZAPU reported that five more Rhodesian warplanes had been shot down. The RSFs responded in desperation to the attrition of their war-planes, their best and most effective weapon against guerrillas.[186] Among other sources of revenue, Rhodesia depended immensely on tourism, and the Elephant Hills Hotel was one of those geese that laid the golden eggs. Aware of its importance to the white settler economy, ZIPRA rocketed the famous hotel and considerably damaged it.

Equally devastating to the morale of the white community and the economy of Rhodesia was the shelling of the central oil storage place in the capital in December 1978. Oil was a priceless commodity in Rhodesia, and the oil embargo had made it to be even more precious. The accumulative impact on the main sources of income, tourism, industry and farming was horrendous, and this was a qualitative contribution to the destruction of the Rhodesia economy.

With military attacks, ZIPRA simultaneously mounted a successful psychological warfare against the Rhodesia Troops. This element of ZAPU's contribution is generally disregarded, denied or downplayed by most extant literature on the liberation of Zimbabwe.[187] This is because of the 'false' distinction made by some observers between ZIPRA's and ZANLA's military strategies.

Most war analysts/observers have invariably associated ZIPRA with its later conventional strategy,[188] and therefore characterized it as less radical and far removed from the people among whom it operated, than its counterpart the more politicized ZANLA.[189] Through Brickhill's research and that of other ex-ZIPRA combatants, as well as information from the rural people themselves among whom ZIPRA operated, the theory of an inactive ZIPRA has been proven nothing but a myth.

Throughout its struggle, ZIPRA used both quasi-conventional to conventional and guerrilla military tactics. The defense of its forward base in the Zambezi gorges at Lusuto and of its Chinyunyu base, are two good examples of ZIPRA's conventional style of self-defense. In a small way, ZIPRA, operating jointly with the MK, applied the same tactics in defense of its position in the first serious battles in the last half of the 1960s. Thus, it mostly used small expeditionary, heavily armed groups, groups of four, six, seven and eight.

As the groups moved among the population they organized people politically where ZAPU structures were not in existence; for instance, the areas around Urungwe, and Mt. Darwin, the areas mostly in the Northeast and Northwest of Rhodesia, which had not had ZAPU structures created during the open political organization era or had the structures that were once in place disintegrated by the time when the first ZIPRA forces operated in the early 1960's. Dabengwa, one of the first freedom fighters in ZIPRA remembers when how little people were prepared for the struggle in these areas during their first infiltrations.[190]

Andrew Nyathi, who was the political commissar in that area from 1978 to 1979, was able to remark that this area was highly politicized towards the end of the war,[191] which goes to show the good work his predecessors in ZIPRA did to politically conscientize the rural population in that area. The conscientization process included the Nyati group as well. Nyati tells of how ZIPRA held meetings to try and resolve problems with which the locals were confronted rather than to merely denounce Smith all the time.

These problems, however, were not regarding petty conflicts between the locals; ZIPRA largely left these to the locals themselves to resolve. That way it avoided situations where it killed people for petty issues, as did its counter part ZANLA. In fact ZIPRA rarely killed civilians unless they interfered with its military operations.

Thus, contrary to what many war observers have made us to believe, ZAPU contributed both qualitatively and quantitatively towards the liberation of

The Best and the Worst of Times

Zimbabwe despite its deployment of fewer forces than its compatriot ZANU. It destroyed very key centers of the economy and the Rhodesian war machine, and by the end of the war, together with some remaining elements of ZIPA, "posed the Rhodesian Security Forces a serious military challenge."[192] Thus, by carefully selecting its targets and fighting a smart war, ZAPU made dramatic contributions to the escalation of war in Zimbabwe, resulting in the collapse of the white regime.

The second of the invaluable ZAPU contributions was keeping the option of a peaceful settlement open by participating in negotiations. ZAPU was always ready to negotiate for peace with anyone who counted in the peace process. However, its willingness to negotiate was always misinterpreted as a sign of weakness. The willingness to negotiate for peace was, in fact, in line with the character of its leader, Nkomo, who was a pragmatic pacifist at heart. Nkomo the most part of his political career was guided by a pragmatic principle based on his simple observation that:

If granted two paths, one violent and the other peaceful, but both leading to the same destination [majority rule], every normal person will choose the peaceful one.[193]

When ZAPU engaged in armed struggle, it was accused of being anti-peaceful in its negotiations. As has been observed before in this study, ZAPU viewed participation in the armed struggle and negotiations as compatible.[194]

Thus, according to ZAPU and scholars of similar views, the bifurcation of armed struggle and negotiations, implying that the latter is an alternative to violence, in a fight for liberation, is analytically misleading because it suggests there is no relationship between the two except as discrete and oppositional options. Historically, few liberation struggles have ended in total surrender of one side.

Most wars, especially liberation wars, have culminated in peaceful settlements. Thus, as ZAPU saw it, the armed struggle paved a way for negotiations. The logic is when the armed struggle takes its toll, thereby inflicting heavy costs on the part of its opponent, that side becomes more inclined to talk peace. Such logic did not escape Clausewitz, who once made what is today considered a seminal observation when he said, "War is peace by other means." Thus, by engaging in peaceful negotiations ZAPU was actually involved in the struggle for the liberation of Zimbabwe, and its willingness to talk peace should not be interpreted to mean it was a moderate organization, and therefore, not revolutionary.

ZAPU's third contribution was the internationalization of grievances of the Zimbabweans and their desire for majority rule. Throughout the 1960s, ZAPU officials crisscrossed the international world (OAU, UN, Asian Countries, Socialist countries, the Communist Bloc, Arab Countries) presenting their people's economic, social and political grievances as well as canvassing for support. Nkomo did most of the traveling and speaking in different fora at a time when the world knew very little about Southern Rhodesia, much less about the plight of its black population.[195]

Many observers, even its critics agree that ZAPU through Nkomo contributed immensely in making the world know the Southern Rhodesia's needs for a system of undifferentiated majoritarianism. After his arrest and subsequent restriction, his senior officials based outside the country continued with Nkomo's mission to the world. Eventually, ZAPU's crusade for international support paid in form of weapons, humanitarian support and sanctions. Thus, the international community, while offering ZAPU, and later ZANU as well, diplomatic material and moral support, denied Rhodesia vital economic resources, e.g., oil, and also withheld financial and training resources.

A few countries, however openly supported Rhodesia namely South Africa, Portugal and its white settler colonies, Mozambique and Angola, as well as West Germany before it was admitted to the U.N. member.

The fourth contribution ZAPU made to the struggle for Zimbabwe was raising national consciousness so that every Zimbabwean felt proud to be Zimbabwean. Thus, right from the outset ZAPU, by word and example propagated the notion of a non-racial nation. Its executive was well representative of the general population of Zimbabwe and so was its membership, Ndebele, Shona, Indian and white.

ZAPU tried to create a sense of a non-racial and non-tribal nation through a variety of ways. One, by attacking the notion of tribalism and letting people know that out of the heterogeneous ethnic and racial groups that constituted the population of Zimbabwe, a homogeneous nation could be created. To make this project possible ZAPU had to deal with the scourge of tribalism and racism.

To deal with tribalism, ZAPU practiced what it preached, even at various committee levels, it made sure there was representation of Zimbabwe's various ethnic groups. Nkomo, its leader, keenly aware of the destructiveness of tribalism used every occasion he could find to attack its practice. As late as 1976 in a message to the population of Zimbabwe he said:

> *My heart bleeds when I see the extent to which tribalism has corroded the hearts and minds of many Zimbabweans. It is the God-given duty of all true sons and daughters of Zimbabwe to fight tribalism with might.... Very few of our people realize fully the death for Zimbabwe that is contained in tribalism. Let us learn from the holocaust in Nigeria, in the Congo, in Burundi and now in Angola. How does anyone with his full senses think that we can escape what happened to these countries, if we play with tribalism.*[196]

Nkomo's hatred for tribalism was one of the reasons he admired the South African Anton Lembede. Lembede emphasized the importance of Africans across ethnic barriers uniting to form a nation, although most of the time Lembede spoke of unity in a pan-Africanist sense which ZAPU also espoused. Lembede said what should unite Africans "irrespective of tribal connections, social status and educational attainments or class" was "the feeling of being

African." For Lembede as it would become for Nkomo, unity of various ethnic groups into a nation was a *sine qua non* for liberation and progress.[197]

Like one of his heroes, Lembede, Nkomo used culture to build and foster a sense of a homogeneous nation among the black population in Zimbabwe. As we have already seen, Nkomo provided the necessary indigenous foundations on which an independent non-racial and non-tribal Zimbabwe could be constructed out of African traditional culture.

Clearly, Nkomo's practice in emphasizing indigenous African culture and its values as early as the 1950s represented a sharp disjuncture with the white oriented perspectives which had preoccupied the thinking of most African intellectuals up to that period, and this approach made him the national leader that he was. The proof of Nkomo's role as a nation builder became more evident after his death as people of different ethnic affiliations poured their hearts in praise of his efforts to build a Zimbabwean nation.

Raymond Mumanyi described Nkomo as "a true dedicated and illustrious son of the soil," who was "fair, courageous, truthful and unbiased."[198] Hudson Taivo said this of Nkomo:

Nkomo was a man of great political appeal, [cadre] who fought tirelessly for unity and freedom of all Zimbabweans irregardless [sic] of their tribal affiliation.[199]

For Lupi Mushayakarara, Nkomo was "by far the best nation-builder." In an article entitled "Nkomo A Savior and A Servant" the Daily News of July 2, 1999, hours after Nkomo passed away, represented the majority of the Zimbabweans when it described him this way:

Under Nkomo's leadership, all black people in this country [Zimbabwe] became politically conscious. Without in any way trying to trivialize other nationalists or nationalist leaders past, present and future, it can be said in all sincerity and honesty that he was the first and probably the last leader of a political party in this country that had the support of the entire nation from the remote villages of Buhera to the bright-lit townships of Bulawayo. That speaks volumes of the man's leadership qualities.

By the use of the phrase *umntane nhlabathi* or *mwana wevu* (son or daughter of the soil), in reference to one another, Zimbabweans under the guidance of ZAPU, transcended ethnicity, created and consolidated the sense of themselves as one nation. An argument can be made that tribal fighting especially among the general membership of AmaNdebele and AmaShona was avoided in the 1980s because most Zimbabweans saw themselves as one nation irrespective of their ethnic differences.

The fifth contribution that ZAPU made to the country, after independence, was stability. It did this in two ways: one, by providing Zimbabwe with well disciplined and highly trained military cadres to constitute the National Army. Of the two main liberation groups, ZAPU had a better-trained and disciplined army, and a more literate one.

The Zimbabwe African People's Union 1961-1987

We have already pointed out that ZANU mostly had very young combatants most of whom were functionally illiterate, poorly trained, ideologically poisoned with a tribal orientation and ill disciplined. ZIPRA's training even became the envy of the BMATT. Although most of its troops were not given positions they deserved, they formed the basis of a professional army. Their discipline was seen more in what they did not do more than in what they did.

During the time that Mugabe harassed them and their people, ex-ZIPRA forces could have easily melted in the bush in toto and caused Mugabe more grief than Savimbi was giving Dos Santos in Angola. However, because of their training as soldiers that emphasized the defending of the constitution and the government of the day, ZIPRA forces did not. Their party ZAPU showed the same discipline. Despite all the maltreatment, the party restrained itself and did not encourage the insurrection of its military, which it could have easily done.

ZAPU's behavior in this fashion had the effect of avoiding a very vicious civil war that would have mostly likely led to the disintegration of the Zimbabwean black nation. Thus, ZAPU contributed to promotion of the sense of nationhood at a very critical time after independence, and at a time when all rational thinking dictated otherwise. More praise during this period is given to Nkomo for signing the 'infamous' unity accord that merged both ZAPU and ZANU. The document was important not because it materially improved the lives of the generality of the Zimbabwean population, much less, the AmaNdebele. It was important because it stopped the carnage by the government.

It was against this background that we saw Nkomo's probably most cherished and enduring legacy after independence. The signing of the Unity Accord that brought an end to a six-year fratricidal conflict that had denied his people the AmaNdebele and his party members peace. Again, this action by Nkomo, like that of his troops earlier, immediately after independence, was seen as important in keeping the nation from disintegrating.

The last contribution, but not the least, and this one also in terms of a legacy that ZAPU bequeathed to all the people of Zimbabwe, was standing for democracy, human rights and a unified nation. Throughout the years of military campaign by which the ruling party tried to force ZAPU to merge with it so that the former could introduce a one-party rule, the latter stood steadfast on the principles of democracy, respect for human rights and a non-racial nation. It condemned decadency, corruption and patronage in ZANU-PF.

Although ZAPU's theater survived for a short season after independence, it did not last long enough to have an immediate impact on the general population of Zimbabwe. Had ZAPU won elections, and at least been allowed to play a significant role in the social reconstruction of the Zimbabwean society, probably its theater values would have been realized in the crucible of a wider life experience.

Like the people of old say, *"udiwo oluhle kaluphekeli,"* literally meaning that a good earthen pot does not get the opportunity to realize its full usefulness to the

The Best and the Worst of Times

society, ZAPU fell prey to the implications of this expression of conventional wisdom. Like *udiwo oluhle olungaphekeliyo* breaks before it meets its full potential to benefit of the household members, ZAPU was forced to disband before it reached the acme of its usefulness to the nation of Zimbabwe.

However, in light of its significant contributions to the liberation of Zimbabwe and its newly born nation, it may as well join Paul of the Bible in saying, "I have fought a good fight, I have finished a good race, I have kept the faith," and now there is a crown of victory in store for me."200 Also, those who longed for the advent of a Zimbabwe where color, ethnicity, religion, creed, gender or economic standing is of no consequence at all should join in this recitation.

ENDNOTES

1. Mugabe was known to be opposed to elections for fear of losing. For instance, when Nkomo suggested that they have elections immediately after the Geneva Conference in the event that a settlement was reached, Mugabe strongly opposed the idea. Mugabe's position was that the PF should take over without election by virtue of their having fought a war of liberation. After all, his leadership of ZANU did not come by way of national elections among his party's membership. Earlier, in 1975, Mugabe was among those who opposed the holding of elections in compliance with the Lusaka agreement..

2. Susan Rice, "The Commonwealth Initiative in Zimbabwe, 1979-1980: Implications for International Peacekeeping," D. Phil thesis, New College, Oxford University, 1990, p. 161.

3. D. Smith and C. Simpson, *Mugabe* (London: Sphere Books 1981), p. 180.

4. *The Herald* (February 23, 1980).

5. Different and conflicting numbers have been given by various writers as to the number of ZIPRA forces that reported to the Assembly Points, with some even claiming that ZAPU left some of its forces in Zambia. For instance, without providing any evidence to that effect, Colin Legum claimed that ZAPU kept a substantial portion of his troops in Zambia (Colin Legum, "Southern Africa: The Road to and from Lancaster House," *Africa Contemporary Record*, An Annual Survey and Documents, 1979-80 (London: Africana Publishing Company, 1981), p. A20.

6. At the initial stage of planning, around the middle of November, Britain toyed with deploying only three hundred peacekeeping forces (Brig. J. H. Learmont, "Reflections from Rhodesia" *RUSI: Journal of the Royal United Services Institute for Defense Studies*, Vol. 125, No. 4 (December 1980): 47), and it was at the insistence of the PF that the number was increased. Even with the final number, which was a little over a thousand, the Commonwealth Monitoring Force was still far too small to effectively monitor the cease-fire, and hence it was greeted with a great deal of pessimism at its arrival. Financial logic determined the number of CMFs, and not effectiveness. Thus, the number of the CMFs finally deployed in Rhodesia was pathetic and not even symbolically important to parties concerned, especially to the PF whose idea of a CMF was that of an army forming a buffer between them and the RSFs. Hence privately it was agreed that a number of CMFs approximating

7. It is believed that ZANU included *mujibha* (courier guys) as part of its trained guerrilla groups, and sent them along to the Assembly Points to inflate its cadre numbers. This was evidenced by the fact that when integration occurred a good number of ZANLA cadres could not handle their weapons well, let alone strip and assemble them. Clearly, these were the *mujibhas* who had not benefited from a crash-course in military art.

8. The breakdown of the RSFs was as follows: regular forces = 15,000 plus; white-led territorial = 20,000; the infamous and controversial auxiliaries: 20-30,000 ("Zimbabwe Survey," *Financial Times*, April 22, 1980).

9. *The Herald* (February 28, 1980).

10. *African Confidential* (February 27, 1980).

11. Willie Musarurwa cited in Tony Rich, "Legacies of the Past? The Results of the 1980 Election in Midlands Province, Zimbabwe," *Past and Present in Zimbabwe*, edited by J. D. Y. Peel and T. O. Ranger (Manchester: Manchester University Press, 1983), p. 43.

12. *Ibid.*, pp. 43-44.

13. Patricia Cheney, *The Land and the People of Zimbabwe* (New York: J. B. Lippincort, 1990), p. 135.

14. *Ibid.*

15. *The Zimbabwe Star*, (February 21, 1976), p. 3. In the mid-1970s when ZAPU pulled away from ANC-Muzorewa, since the name ZAPU was banned in the country it went by ANC-Z (African National Congress-Zimbabwe).

16. *Ibid.* (June 19, 1976). The editorialist, when he reminded Sithole that he was reaping the results of the tribalism he had sown, undoubtedly, had in the back of his mind the fierce struggle that was going on within ZANU for the leadership of the party. Shonas who constituted a majority of the party felt that they could not be led by Sithole, basically because he was not Shona but Shangane, the same logic of reasoning Sithole and his colleagues had used to fight against Nkomo's leadership in 1963.

17. Nkomo, interview by author, July 26, 1995.

18. See *Parliamentary Debates* (July 1980); Banana, *Turmoil and Tenacity* (1989), p. 230.

19. The names of the 1980 ZANU central committee members were in one of the many pamphlets ZANU party circulated among its membership, and this author is in possession of one.

20. *Moto* (April 5 1980).

21. Mugabe lacked a national mandate in that his party did not win not even a single vote among the AmaNdebele people who constituted twenty percent of the nation.

22. Dumiso Dabengwa disclosed after Nkomo's death that he and Lt. Gen. Masuku tried to persuade Nkomo to accept the position of President but he refused (*Financial Gazatte*, July 8, 1999), p. 3.

The Best and the Worst of Times

23. In the run-up for elections there was a general feeling that the division between ZAPU and ZANU, coupled with the potential manipulation of elections by, possibly the Muzorewa puppet government with the assistance of Britain and South Africa was going to help install a Muzorewa's puppet government. This was no idle thinking as Muzorewa, just the previous year, had won fifty-one out of seventy-two seats reserved for blacks under the Internal Settlement constitution which had excluded the Patriotic Front. Among the stipulations agreed upon in the agreement was a new one-hundred-seat Parliament, of which twenty-eight seats were reserved for whites for a period of ten years. A year latter Muzorewa won only three seats out of one hundred.

24. Lawyers Committee for Human Rights, *Zimbabwe: Wages of War: A Report on Human Rights* (New York: Lawyers Committee for Human Rights, 1986), p. 126.

25. *Financial Times* (April 22, 1980).

26. A. H. M. Kirk-Greene, "His Eternity, His Eccentricity, or His Eccentricity, or His Exemplarity?: A Further Contribution to the Study of H. E. The Head of State," *African Affairs* (1991): 168.

27. By end of June 1981, significant progress had been made in the integration of the armed forces. On the Joint High Command (JHC), representing the RSFs was Gen. Sandy MacLean. Serving with him were ZIPRA and ZANLA commanders Lameck Lookout Mafela Masuku and Rex Nhongo (real name Solomon Mujuru), who had just been promoted Lieutenant Generals. The rests of the members were white, and like MacLean, former members of the RSFs. These were the JHC's Chief of Staff, Major General Leon Jacobs and the four brigade commanders. Part of the reason the integration was going too slowly could be attributed to the fact that Mugabe had entrusted the process to the British. The 150-member strong British Training and Advisory Team, under the command of Maj. Gen. Patrick Palmer, was by and large, responsible for the training and advising on the integration. Because the British believed in the competence of the whites, in contradistinction to that of the former guerrillas, they wanted to make sure that white officers were not quickly phased out before giving training to the in-coming black commanders. However, this slow process resulted in large numbers of guerrillas languishing in the Assembly Points with little to do, and thereby posing a danger of these freedom fighters expressing their boredom by engaging in violence. At this point, an estimate of 7,400 ZIPRA and about 12,500 troops under other leaders, were still in seven Assembly Points, increasingly seething with anger from frustration and boredom because they did not have any meaningful engagement with which to concern themselves.

28. *Africa Confidential*, Vol. 21/No 22 (October 1980), p. 3.

29. "Lookout" was Masuku's *nom de guerre* or his war name. Several of guerrilla war veterans kept their 'war' names after returning home as a badge of honor for having fought for the liberation of their country.

30. ZIPRA took umbrage at, for instance, the selection of One hundred ZANLA cadres who were sent to Nigeria because none was chosen from their group. Next the government picked thirty former ZANLA men for training in Yugoslav, and only five former ZIPRA cadres, and this also angered the latter.

31. *Ibid.*, p. 4.

32. Foreign media not surprisingly, covered the eNtumbane military conflict between former ZIPRA and former ZANLA forces. The printed medium covered events at this Bulawayo suburb under a variety of graphic headings, as follows: Battle Town in Zimbabwe was called 'Powder Keg,' *International Herald Tribune* (November 13, 1980); "Factional Fighting Leave Zimbabwe Uneasy," The *New York Times* (December 22, 1980); "Perils for Mugabe from the Warring Armies," *The Financial Times* (London, February 19, 1981).

33. *Africa Confidential*, Vol. 22, No. 5 (February 25, 1981), p. 1.

34. To ex-ZIPRA combatants, it was ironical that the new government would deploy a mostly old Rhodesian unit against its liberation compatriots. The deployment but only helped to accentuate their mistrust of the government, and also their strong belief that Mugabe was not revolutionary at all, only a nationalist after naked power and fame with no regard to the social change for the benefit of the had been oppressed Zimbabweans.

35. Cowell, *Killing the Wizards* (1992), p. 79.

36. On February 12 the three columns that set off from the Gwaai River Mine at dawn each was composed of 15 to 20 vehicles and between 100 and 150 ZIPRA troops. The Gwaai River Mine cadres largely consisted of conventionally trained, and hard-core guerrilla ZIPRA cadre. Most of ZIPRA's military hardware was here. Consequently, it was the most defended of all the ZIPRA Assembly Points. For instance, its anti-aircraft gun emplacements gave the camp protection from air attacks.

37. Cowell, *Killing the Wizards* (1992), p. 79.

38. *Ibid.*, pp. 79-80.

39. *Africa Confidential*, Vol. 22, No. 5 (February 25, 1981), p. 1.

40. *Ibid*. During these conflicts between the nationalists' forces it is believed that Dabengwa, Maseko and Masuku worked in tandem with Mugabe's personal intelligence and security minister, Emmerson Munangagwa, who was then serving as a *de facto* chairperson of the JHC, ZANLA commander Rex Nhongo and his deputy Josiah Tungamirai. For a break down of JHC figures along party/state affiliation see *Africa Confidential*, Vol. 21/No. 22 (February, 1981).

41. Khayisa, Black Moses, Mpenhlo, interview by author, 20 August 1982. These informants blamed ex-ZANLA cadres for starting fights at both instances at Ntumbane, one in 1980, and the other at the beginning of 1981.

42. Nkomo, *The Story of My Life* (1984), p. 221. The capitalization of ZIPRA and ZANLA is mine. Nkomo here is referring to the second outbreak of the Entumbane clashes, and that completes the story that on both occasions the fighting was started by ZANLA.

43. Lawyers Committee for Human Rights, Zimbabwe Wages of War: A Report on Human Rights (New York: Lawyers Committee for Human Rights, 1986), p. 20.

44. The Africa Watch Committee, Zimbabwe: A Break With the Past: An Africa Watch Report (New York: The Africa Watch Committee, October 1989), p. 15.

45. Nkomo, *The Story of My Life* (1984), p. 220.

46. *Ibid*.

The Best and the Worst of Times

47. Emmerson D. Mnangagwa, "Post-Independence Zimbabwe: 1980-1987," in *Turmoil and Tenacity* (1989), p. 237. What is interesting with Munangagwa's listings of locations where weapons were supposedly found is his lack of precise knowledge on the exact locations of the places he mentioned. For instance, Ngwenya Siding is not between Kadoma and KweKwe, it is very close to Bulawayo, what he called Woolendale farms in Matopo were, in fact, Woodvile farms near Bulawayo, Hampton Ranch was closer to Connemara Barracks than Gweru, just to give a few examples. This misplacement of locations makes Munangangwa's allegations about the discovery of weapons in these areas very questionable.

48. *Africa Confidential*, Vol. 23, No. 5 (March 3, 1982), p. 1.

49. Nkomo, *The Story of My Life* (1984), p. 224.

50. *Ibid.*, p. 225.

51. *Ibid.*, p. 226.

52. Nkomo, interview by author, 26 July 1995.

53. Joshua Mzila Moyo, interview by author, 28 August 1994; Thenjiwe Lesabe, interview by author, 24 January 1998.

54. Once Dr. Callistus Ndlovu changed parties to ZANU, he joined Enos Nkala in being the hated politicians in Matebeleland, see (Africa Confidential, Vol. 26, No. 7 (27 March 1985), p. 7.

55. After the 1980 general elections, Mugabe gave ZAPU four ministerial posts and two deputy ministries. The ministers were Joshua Nkomo, George Silundika, Joseph Msika and Clement Muchachi and the deputies were Jini Ntuta and Cephas Msika. At the time of the expulsion of Nkomo and his comrades, Silundika was already dead, as he had passed away in 1981.

56. Nkomo, interview by author, 26 July 1995.

57. *Ibid.*

58. Thenjiwe Lisabe, interview by author, 24 January 1998, Mtshumayeli Sibanda, interview by author, 10 January 1994.

59. White officers helping with the training of the national army argued that the government was lowering the army's standards by appointing far less qualified ex-ZANLA troops to key positions when ZIPRA had more senior officers of high military quality in terms of conventional training. For details of military integration and composition, see Africa Confidential Vol. 23, No. 5 and Vol. 22, No. 13.

60. William Spring, *The Long Fields: Zimbabwe Since Independence* (Hants: Pickering and Inglis, 1986), p. 80.

61. Nkomo, *The Story of My Life* (1984), p. 223. Afterwards Nkomo would remark, "Once Zipra was disbanded, my usefulness to Robert Mugabe was at an end. My office became more than ever a backwater. Cabinet documents arrived too late for me to consider them. I was not consulted on security matters. I was not even told about appointments to the civilian public service. The Zanu central committee had taken over the functions of the cabinet and of parliament," *ibid.*

62. *Ibid.*, p. 222.

63. Mugabe had reason to be suspicious of the former Rhodesian Security Forces at independence because, even by the account of the leader and founder of the

Selous Scouts, R. F. Reid-Daly, the Rhodesian Security forces wanted to prevent the new African government of Mugabe from taking the reins of power by taking over power and installing, possibly, Muzorewa. When the elections results were announced, they the RSFs had taken position at strategic points with the intention to forestall the incoming government if the elected party was any of the two major liberation groups. It took the persuasion of General Peter Wall to dissuade them against the plan (Reid-Daly, *Pamwe Chete*, 1999. Immediately after independence it is believed that some former Rhodesian military higher-ups including General Walls, as well as some prominent white politicians approached ZAPU and said they could help its forces dethrone the Mugabe government and install Nkomo as President if he agreed to safeguard the interests the whites. ZAPU refused, and according to this group of ZAPU political and military officials, thus why, once Mugabe proved to be harmless to white interests, their former troops were eager to punish ZIPRA during the Entumbane ZIPRA/ZANLA conflict (interview by author of nine ex-ZIPRA military officers and four senior ZAPU officials, 1994-7.) Thus, the shift of allegiance to Mugabe came very quickly after independence, when the former white security forces saw Mugabe as supporting the status-quo; white interests.

64. *Zimbabwe Independent* (July 9, 1999), p. 2.

65. Nkomo, *The Story of My Life* (1984), p. 227.

66. Peter Godwin, *Mukiwa: A white Boy in Africa* (New York: The Atlantic Monthly Press, 1996), pp. 336-338. Godwin was one of the Lawyers who defended the seven ZIPRA treason trialists. This was paradoxical in light of the fact that just a few years back, in 1976/77 Godwin had actually led his Rhodesian men against ZIPRA forces in Filabuso that were led by one of the treason trialists (*ibid.*, pp. 332-333).

67. Lawyers Committee for Human Rights, *Zimbabwe: Wages of War* (New York: Lawyers Committee for Human Rights, 1986), p. 88.

68. Calloway's role in the caching of arms and the subsequent destabilization of Zimbabwe is outlined in Joseph Hanlon, "Destabilization and the Battle to Reduce Dependence," in *Zimbabwe's Prospects*, Colin Stoneman, ed. (London: 1988 Clearly Nkomo had such people as Collaway when he said some government operatives planted arms in order to implicate ZIPRA or to make the situation worse than it was.

69. Mugabe received wide international praise for his reconciliation policy after independence. What the international world chose to ignore was that Mugabe's reconciliation did not include his own people such as the former Prime Minister Bishop Abel Muzorewa and the founding president of his party Ndabaningi Sithole. ZAPU also was not included in this reconciliation policy; the only thing Mugabe wanted of his fellow black parties was complete surrender to his leadership.

70. Joseph Lelyveld, *Move Your Shadow: South Africa Black and White* (New York: 1985), p. 213.

71. *Ibid.*

72. Spring, *The Long Fields* (1986), p. 88.

73. "Rhodesian Troops Prop Up Mugabe," *Africa Now* (July 1984).

74. *Africa Confidential*, Vol. 23, No. 5 (March 3, 1982), pp. 1, 4.

75. Lawyers Committee for Human Rights, *Zimbabwe Wages of War* (1986), p. 33.

76. *Ibid.*, pp. 34-35.

The Best and the Worst of Times

77. *Ibid.*, p. 34.
78. For repressive tactics adopted by the Mugabe regime from the Ian Smith government see, Lawyers Committee, *Zimbabwe Wages of War* (1986); William Spring, *The Long Fields* (1986); Richard Carver, *Zimbabwe: A Breaking with the Past?* (1989); Catholic Commission for Justice and Peace in Zimbabwe, *Report on the 1980s Disturbances in Matabeleland and the Midlands* (March 1997).
79. Holger Jensen was then a Jo'burg based Newsweek correspondent. Following Nkomo's allegation of mass murder in his press conference, Jensen slipped into the affected and prohibited area in Phumula to verify Nkomo's allegations. In Jensen's report entitled "Mugabe's Rein of Terror", he substantiated many of Nkomo's allegations. In an interview with this author in 1996, Jensen would again confirm that Mugabe was fighting a tribal and self-seeking war.
80. Spring, *The Long Fields* (1986), pp. 116-117.
81. *Ibid.*
82. Steve Taylor, *Times* (London, April 27, 1983).
83. Nkomo, *The Story of My Life* (1984), p. 229.
84. Robert Mugabe, "The Unity Accord: Its Promise for the Future," in *Turmoil and Tenacity*, Banana, ed. (1989), p. 343.
85. "Mugabe Assails Media Atrocity Reports," *Washington Post* (March 13, 1983).
86. The government maintained that its most crucial legal evidence of the link between ZAPU and the dissidents was the testimony of Gilbert Ngwenya (also known as Eskimo Wasi) an ex-ZIPRA combatant, who was convicted in April 1985 of the 1982 kidnapping and murder of the six foreign tourists because in his criminal trial he implicated ZAPU. Ngwenya alleged that he and his co-defendants kidnapped the six tourists on specific orders from Nkomo. However, Ngwenya's credibility as a witness was very questionable as he gave sharply contradictory statements at various times during the course of his incarceration. In his appearance on the Zimbabwe Television, and interviewed by Eddison Zvobgo, the then Zimbabwe's Minister of Justice, Ngwenya claimed Nkomo knew about the kidnapping and subsequent killing of the tourists. However, this assertion conflicted with his statement during his trial where he informed that the tourists were still alive and and that they were living in a camp at Zambia (*State v. Gilbert Ngwenya and Others*, 1985). Nwenya and his co-defendant, Austin Mpofu, along with three other convicted murderers were hanged on April 7, 1986, (*New York Times*, April 8, 1986).
87. *Africa Confidential*, Vol. 25, No. 7 (March 27, 1985) p. 5.
88. *Ibid.*, Vol. 25, No. 8 (1985).
89. Christine Sylvester, *Zimbabwe: The Terrain of Contradictory Development* (London: Dartmouth, 1991), p. 76.
90. Catholic Commission for Justice and Peace in Zimbabwe, *Report on the 1980s Disturbances in Mateleleland and the Midlands* (March 1997).
91. *Ibid.*
92. Lawyers Committee, *Zimbabwe: Wages of War* (1986), p. 20.

93. Joseph Hanlon, "Destabilization and the Battle to Reduce Dependence," *Zimbabwe's Prospects: Issues of Race, Class, State, and Capital in Southern Africa*, Colin Stoneman, ed. (London: Macmillan Publishers, 1988), p. 38.

94. Sigawugawu, by Author, May 13, 1995. Some observers believe Mugabe was so genuinely afraid of ZAPU that despite the fact that he would have gained much in terms of saving money in training ex-guerrillas who joined the air force and intelligence units. Also in avoiding bad intelligence such as the dissident crisis of the 1980s,which was largely manufactured by hostile intelligence groups in the service of the country, which led to the destruction of the country. The problem the had was that he measured the well disciplined ZIPRA cadres by his own poorly trained cadres, most of whom has very little functional education, (Former US Ambassador to Zambia, an Interview by Author, April 10, 1994.

95. Catholic Commission for Justice and Peace in Zimbabwe, *Report on the 1980s Disturbances in Matebeleland and the Midlands*, March 1997.

96. The Fifth Brigade in Matebeleland North was deployed in three stages. The first stage was when it was deployed in January 1983, then withdrawn for a month before the year was out, only to be redeployed again. In 1984, when most of the Fifth Brigade troops were deployed in Matebeleland South, a platoon of its forces was deployed in Matebeleland North.

97. Spring, *The Long Fields* (1986), p. 116.

98. Catholic Commission, *Report on the 1980s Disturbances in Matebeleland and the Midlands* (March 1977).

99. The figure 10,000 was cited by Lawyer's Committee, *Zimbabwe: Wages of War* (1986). Because journalists were, for a long time banned during the violent campaign of the Fifth Brigade in Matebeleland North banned, researchers into this unit's atrocities were forced to rely mostly on church officials, missionaries, especially missionary doctors in rural areas, commercial farmers, international aid workers, and some journalists like Holger Jensen of *Newsweek* who succeeded in sneaking behind the lines of the military campaign. These could be said to be independent sources. However, it should be noted that these sources had very limited resources of gathering information, more so because of severe curfew restrictions so that whatever estimates they came up with, were in the main conservative and difficult to verify. Notwithstanding these limitations, these were very important independent sources of the atrocities of this period.

100. Nkomo and some ZAPU officials have alleged that between 200-250 of their supporters were abducted in these areas during this time, however, ZAPU was able to produce a detailed list of only fifty-six of these (copy with the author).

101. For detailed information on circumstances surround Nkomo's flight to Britain and his actual flight see his autobiography, *The Story of My Life* (1984).

102. Moyo was arrested in June 1982 and held under Ministerial Order until March 1986 in connection with the 1982 attack on the Prime Minister's residence. Marange was arrested later in 1984 and released in February 1986.

103. Lawyers Committee, *Zimbabwe: Wages of War* (1986), p. 62.

104. *Ibid.*, p. 135.

The Best and the Worst of Times

105. Catholic Commission, *Report on the 1980s Disturbances in Matabeleland and Midlands* (March 1997).

106. *Moto* (March 1995): 5-7. This article tells of human bones of people who were killed by the 5th Brigade at the Sitezi Rest A1 Rest Camp. In a very graphic way it tells of the sadistic torture, beatings, castrations and murders that went on in this area. Also, it carries interviews of people who lived in Sitezi covering incidents that involved people living in their neighboring areas like Gwakwe, Makwe, Mtsheleli, Lushongwe, Gongwe Dam, Talila, Donkwe Donkwe, and Sibula, inter alia. The author also captures the anger of AmaNdebele people, most of whom were ZAPU members who were once detained at this Sitezi A1 Rest Camp by quoting the charcoal graffiti on the wall, which the inmates wrote. Scrolled on the cells by inmates "as parting shots" were heard, were: "Liqeda abantu mazimu ... libadla ng [e] xa yo keto" (lit. you are finishing people you savages/beasts, all because of elections), and "zinja, hambani emashoneni" (dogs, go to Mashonaland). According to the author these words were written before the 1985 general elections. Intentions of the 5th Brigade to have locals in their theater of operation were made known by their behavior of trying to force them to purchase ZANU-PF cards.

107. ZANU-Ndonga's supporters(led by Ndabaningi Sithole) were arrested for ostensibly supporting the Mozambique Resistance Movement (RENAMO), a group formed with the help of Ken Flowers to destabilize the Mozambican black government which the Mugabe supported.

108. Mkhululi, interview by author, 28 August 1987.

109. *Moto* (March 1995): 1.

110. According to Nkomo by mid-March, nine of the 120-strong central committee members had already been murdered by government troops around this time, and a huge majority in prison or exile (Nkomo, Interview with author, August 15, 1991).

111. Despite the fact that Mugabe and his ZANU-PF had won the 1980 elections, Nkomo's image still overshadowed Mugabe. People would fondly refer to Nkomo as "Josh" and honorifically as "Father Zimbabwe", and this did not sit well with Mugabe who wanted the charisma and honor for himself. So, for Mugabe it became a lifetime mission to establish himself as a "charismatic" leader over and above Nkomo. For information on Mugabe's feeling threatened by Nkomo's charisma see (Patricia Cheney, *The Land and the People of Zimbabwe*, 1990, p. 134). Emmerson Munangagwa betrayed this quest for leadership on popularity when he cited as one of the main reasons why ZANU-PF chose not to run for elections together with ZAPU under the Patriotic Front. This reason, he said, was the question of leadership (Munangagwa, "Post-Independence Zimbabwe: 1980-1987" in *Turmoil and Tenacity* (1989), p. 227.

112. Spring, *The Long Fields* (1986), p. 183.

113. *Ibid.*, p. 184.

114. It should be noted that Mugabe co-opted state law enforcement agencies for reasons of promoting partisan interests, an egregious abuse of power, and also used State funds to promote his own Youth Brigade and its Military wing the People's Militia, whose job was to force people to purchase ZANU-PF cards. The people's militia, a poorly trained rag-tag para-army, was armed with G-3's and SK's (a modified version of the AK with fixed bayonets).

115. Lawyers Committee, *Zimbabwe: Wages of War* (1986), p. 121.
116. International protests against Mugabe's carnage of the innocent AmaNdebele, a holocaust by definition, came late, and was generally feeble. Otherwise most of the time, the international world stood-by like it did when Hitler slaughtered Jews. The reasons for its inaction were purely political and economic. Mugabe served their economic interests and was by and large compliant with its politics, especially economic interests of the Western countries, despite his rhetoric. Because of its late and feeble protests, its contribution to the withdrawal of the troops by Mugabe is problematic.
117. *Ibid.*, pp. 136-137.
118. See Chapter II for AmaNdebele's participation in decision-making on affairs related to their living.
119. For constituencies represented by each of the ZAPU parliamentarians see the *Zimbabwe Parliamentary Debates_House of Assembly* (1985-1986).
120. *Chronicle*, August 20, 1985. Council members were arrested on August 16, 1985. The arrest of eight officers brought to ten the number of ex-ZIPRA High-ranking fighters detained in the last half of 1985.
121. Zimbabwe's 4,500 farmers accounted at that time accounted for three-quarters of the country's staple food production, and also their commercial produce was responsible for half of the country's foreign exchange earnings.
122. Lawyers' Committee, *Zimbabwe Wages of War* (1986), p. 27.
123. *Parliamentary Debates* (1982-1987); *Amnesty International News Release* AFR/46/06/86. The primary source of most destruction involving dissidents was the government itself as independent journalists were not allowed into the curfew areas.
124. For evidence pointing to the government's pseudo gangs as the killers, see Africa Watch Report, *Zimbabwe: A Break with the Past* (1989), p. 17. Luke Khumalo came from an area, Mayezane, know for its staunch support of ZAPU, and even his school was located in a ZAPU dominated area. Being a strong ZAPU supporter himself, it made sense that the government would kill him as it did most of the ZAPU leadership. His wife got killed probably, since she was white, for the sake of publicity. The government knew pretty well that when a white person was involved among the killed there would be wide publicity. So the government wanted the world to know that dissidents were bad and cold murderers.
125. *Ibid.*, p. 18.
126. In November 1987, sixteen members of a Protestant mission at Esigodini, "including babies and small children," were killed by the South African sponsored dissidents (*ibid.*, p. 17).
127. The strategy by South Africa of keeping MK out of Matebeleland by destabilizing the region and forcing the Mugabe government to send its troops was a well calculated one on the part of the former. The white South Africa knew pretty well that the relationship between Mugabe's party and the ANC was not a good one. Mugabe and his party supported PAC, and South Africa correctly figured he would not want to help ANC in any way. As a matter of fact, it is believed that some of the clashes that occurred in Matebeleland during the curfew time between the Zimbabwean soldiers and armed groups involved the MK. Whether the MK

The Best and the Worst of Times

was mistaken for dissidents or their attempted elimination was part of Mugabe's government's policy is something that might remain unknown for ever. Both are however probable.

128. Bishops Pastoral Statement (March 27, 1985).
129. Spring, *Long Fields* (1986), p. 172.
130. *Ibid.*, p. 173.
131. *Ibid.*
132. *Ibid.*, p. 175. ZANU seemed to have lost its bearings here by condemning a group, the Catholic Church that was outspoken throughout the struggle on behalf of blacks in Zimbabwe. Of course it did not come as anything new to this government when the Catholic clergy came out in defense of human rights. The government could only hope against hope that they could silence this voice of reason.
133. *Ibid.*, pp. 173, 186.
134. Those who believe the international world played a great role in the stopping of a government sponsored-carnage against the AmaNdebele and ZAPU people both in Matebeleland and the Midlands or city as the basis of their position the fact that the government started distributing food when the United States insisted it would sign an aid agreement with the government to provide 30,000 tons of maize for drought relief only if the government agreed to equitably distribute it. The problem with this position is that the government needed that food for Matebeleland anyway, which happened to be the area that had suffered the severest from the drought. People in Mugabe's area could have done well with the little they had. So the reason for the stoppage of the carnage was for other reasons other than this one, possible the ones cited in this chapter.
135. *Moto*, No. 77 (June 1989).
136. Nkomo, *The Story of My Life* (1984), pp. 245-246.
137. It is believed that the trip by the government delegation to meet Nkomo was canceled by Mugabe's instructions. Mugabe was once again involved in a misconceived political game. Apparently he thought that without Nkomo in the country his followers and the AmaNdebele people would be cowed into joining his party. He would soon prove himself wrong.
138. John Hatchard, *Individual Freedoms & State Security In the African Context: The Case of Zimbabwe* (Harare: Baobab, 1993), p. 20.
139. *Ibid.*
140. Tendayi Kumbula, "A Mandate for Mugabe," in *Africa Report* (September-October, 1986): 71.
141. Victor De Waal, *The Politics of Reconciliation: Zimbabwe's First Decade* (Trenton, New Jersey: Africa World Press, Inc., 1990), p. 96.
142. For detailed information on the proceedings of various deliberation on the unity talks between ZANU-PF and ZAPU leading to the signing of the Unity Accord, list of committee members, and responses to the signing of the Accord, see Banana, ed., *Turmoil and Tenacity* (1989), pp. 242-359.

143. See Article 8 of the Agreement Accord. The participation of ZANU-PF in the bringing the situation in Matebeleland to normalcy is implied; otherwise the explicit reading of the article puts the onus on the existing ZAPU leadership.

144. Banana, *Turmoil and Tenacity* (1989), p. 288

145. B. Sodindwa, "The People and Their Wounds," *Moto* (January 1993): 6.

146. T. O. Ranger, *The African Voice in Southern Rhodesia, 1898-1930* (Evanston: Northwestern University Press, 1970), p. 10.

147. Allan Cowell, *Killing the Wizards: Wars of Power and Freedom from Zaire to South Africa* (Simon & Schuster, 1992), p. 78.

148. Refer to the Unity Accord to see how the articles sought to entrench Mugabe's leadership. It is rather ironic note that the question of leadership is what kept ZANU from merging with ZAPU during the liberation war because its leaders, Mugabe included, who insisted they could only unite with ZAPU if the question of leadership was left open. Here the question of leadership was decided way ahead of time; Mugabe was going to be the leader, no elections.

149. Banana, *Turmoil and Tenacity* (1989), p. 288.

150. *Ibid.*, p. 304.

151. It is said more than twenty out of less than twenty-five politburo members voted against a legislated one-party system, and with a majority of former ZANU (PF) members joining their ZAPU colleagues in voting against. Also Nkomo informed that most of the politburo members who were formerly ZANU (PF) again joined their former ZAPU colleagues in speaking disparagingly of running the country on Marxist-Leninist principles. Shamuyarira, Kantugure, and Mugabe were the only ones said to have voted for both notions (Nkomo, interview by author, 15 August 1994).

152. *Ibid.*

153. Cheney, *The Land and the People of Zimbabwe* (1990), p. 134.

154. In an interview with Nkomo, he told the author that he was receiving "an overwhelming disapproval of the merger of ZAPU with ZANU. For more reactions to unity see, Banana, *Turmoil and Tenacity* (1989), pp. 294-296.

155. Africa Watch, *Zimbabwe: A Break with the Past* (1989), p. 30.

156. Terence Ranger, "Matabeleland Since the Amnesty," in *African Affairs*, Vol. 88, No. 351 (April 1989): 161.

157. *The Herald* (June 1988).

158. The first time Mugabe was chosen President it was not in a national election. A College of all members of the House of Assembly and the Senate both of which were overwhelmingly dominated by ZANU (PF) elected him. This gave him six years to work for a national election as presidential elections occurred once every six years. Thus, Mugabe as was characteristic of him and his ZANU (PF) arrogated himself to the Presidency without the blessings of the nation by being imposed by a clique of those who worshipped him regardless.

159. Nkomo in an interview by author characterized his new post as non-position, meaning it did not carry with it any meaningful decision-making power. For an interesting reading on the Nkomo's positions see (W. Shaidi, *The Old Brick Lives* (Gweru: Mambo Press, 1988), pp. 76-77.

The Best and the Worst of Times

160. Mtshumayeli Sibanda, interview by author, 10 January 1994.
161. For information on black theater in the colonial Rhodesia, during the liberation war of independence in both Zambia and Mozambique and post-colonial Zimbabwe, see Preben Kaarsholm, "Mental Colonization or Catharsis? Theater, Democracy and Cultural Struggle from Rhodesia to Zimbabwe," in the *Journal of Southern African Studies*, Vol. 16, No. 2, (1990): 246-275. Kaarsholm concentrates mostly on theater by ZAPU. Also see Stephen Chifunyise, "Trends in Zimbabwean Theater Since 1980," *ibid.*: 276-289.
162. John Mpofu, interview by author, 26 August 1987.
163. For detailed information on praise poetry, see Leroy Vail & Landeg White, "The Art of Being Ruled. Ndebele Praise Poetry, 1835-1971," in Landeg White and Tim Couzens (eds), *Literature and Society in South Africa* (London, 1984), pp. 41-59.
164. Dingilizwe Dewa, interview by author, 24 December 1996.
165. Zimangele Mpofu, interview by author, 24 August 1995.
166. Melwa Ntini, interview by author, 24 July 1996. Ntini, who has been following the cultural groups since the colonial period was speaking from his unpublished manuscript on "Democracy through Theater: Zimbabwe as a Case Study."
167. *Ibid.*
168. *Ibid.*
169. *Ibid.*
170. Cont Mhlanga, *Workshop Negative: A Play* (Mzilikazi, 1986).
171. Melwa Ntini, interview by author, 1996.
172. Preben Kaarsholm, "Mental Colonization or Catharsis? Theater, Democracy and Cultural Struggle from Rhodesia to Zimbabwe," in *Journal of Southern African Studies*, vol. 16, no. 2 (June 1990): 273.
173. *Ibid.*, p. 274.
174. *Ibid.*
175. Banana, *Turmoil and Tenacity* (1989), pp. 228-229, 291.
176. Bhebe and Ranger, eds., *Soldiers in Zimbabwe's Liberation War* (1995), p. 110.
177. Nkomo, interview by author, 16 July 1996.
178. Spring, *The Long Fields* (1986).
179. The bloodthirsty wolf in this fable is remembered for its aggressive unprovoked actions towards the lamb. According to the fable, the wolf was standing upstream as the lamb was drinking water downstream. Suddenly, and for no cause, the wolf angrily accused the lamb of muddying his water. The lamb quickly reminded the 'thick' wolf that the stream was flowing from his side to it. Instead of acknowledging the flaw in his logic the wolf then charged that the previous year the lamb had verbally abused his father at the market place. This time the lamb reminded the wolf that he could not have done it because at that time he had not been born. To this the wolf responded by saying if it was not the lamb then it was his father at which point the wolf pounced on the lamb, an innocent victim.
180. Kepton, p. 136.
181. Mlambo, *Rhodesia: The Struggle for a Birthright* (1972), p. 214.

182. Franz Fanon, *The Wretched of the Earth*, Translated by Constance Farrington (New York: Grove Press, 1963), pp. 142-143.

183. *Ibid.*, p. 141.

184. Tanarkin, *The Making of Zimbabwe* (1990), p. 229.

185. Nkomo, *The Story of My Life* (1984), pp. 165-166. As has already been pointed out, the Selous Scout Commander confessed that by the beginning of 1978 the RSFs had lost control of military situation partly because of shortage of planes. Most of the war planes possibly had been shot down by the ZIPRA forces since it was they who at the time had anti-air missiles, and had their camps attacked first and more often by the RSFs. However, the Rhodesian government would not in public agree to this. It is known that the RSFs either, in the course of time, avoided attacking ZIPRA camps or flew their planes too high to be effective as the latter perfected its use of anti-air missiles.

186. *The Zimbabwe Review* (October-November, 1978).

187. Martin and Johnson, *The Struggle for Zimbabwe* (1981).

188. Christine Sylvester, *Zimbabwe: The Terrain of Contradictory Development* (Boulder and San Francisco, 1991), p. 50.

189. Kriger, *Zimbabwe's Guerrilla War* (1992); Cliffe, Mpofu, Munslow, "Zimbabwe Nationalist Politics," *The Review of African Political Economy* (1981). Cliffe, Mpofu, and Munslow, while their information about ZANU's penetration into Matebeleland is to a certain extent accurate, they seem to exaggerate it though. They also seem oblivious of the role played by pseudo-gangs who posed as either ZIPRA or ZANLA. After the war, it has now become clear that contrary to what these scholars say, ZIPRA mobilized the masses and operated extensively in Mashonaland (Andrew Nyathi, *Tomorrow is Built Today* (1990).

190. Bhebe and Ranger, *Soldiers in Zimbabwe's Liberation War* (1995), pp. 24-35.

191. Nyati, *Tomorrow is Built Today* (1990).

192. *The Making of Zimbabwe* (1990), p. 231.

193. Nkomo, "Majority Rule is [the] Only Medicine," *The Zimbabwe Star* (Saturday, February 14, 1976), pp. 3-4.

194. *Ibid.*, p. 4.

195. Mlambo, *Rhodesia: The Struggle for a Birthright* (1972), pp. 165-187.

196. Nkomo, *The Zimbabwe Star* (February 14, 1976), p. 3.

197. Lembede, Policy of the Congress Youth League," in Thomas G. Karis and Gwendolen M. Carter, eds., *From Protest to Challenge: A Documentary History of African Politics in South Africa 1882-1964*, Vol. 2 (Stanford: Hoover Institute Press, 1973. For a detailed account on what Lembede called a philosophy of Africanism see, Lembede, "Some Basic Principles of African Nationalism," Ibid. Also A Lembede, "National Unity Among African Tribes," *Inkundla ya Bantu*, October 2nd fortnight, 1945.

198. Raymond Mumanyi, in a letter to the editor, *The Daily News*, Zimbabwe (14 July 1999).

199. Hudson Yemen Taivo, in a letter to the editor, *The Daily News* (12 July 1999).

200. 2 Timothy 4:7.

GLOSSARY

Ibandla leZintandane – The Church of Orphans. Its message was fundamentally of that of liberation Theology.

Ibhabhayila – (Literally meaning, sweet potato) a word fondly used by guerrillas and their supporters to denote landmine.

Ilitshe – Shrine, a sacred mountain to the AmaNdebele, which they believed was inhabited by God. What mount Sinai was to the Israelites or the church to the Christians, was the Ilitshe to the AmaNdebele Amatshe is the plural.

Imbongi – Praise-critic

Impi YoMvukela – War of Rising referring to the the rising of the AmaNdebele against the colonial power between 1896-1897, which ended in Indaba (negotiations) between the AmaNdebele and Cecil Rhodes

Indaba – Talks as in Negotiations. Initially the word was used in reference to the Talks that ended the war between the AmaNdebele and the Colonialists in 1897.

Iwosana – Rainmaker

Lobola – Understood among the AmaNdebelethe word implies a very complex relational concept that is often mistakenly defined as Bride Price. Lobola was mainly given in cattle, and was meant to redeem the name of the husband so that the offsprings born into that marriage were called by the husband's last name.

Udiwo – Earth pot

Umfecane – Essentially a process of nation–building among the Southern African peoples involving war, scattering and re-gathering in the 1800s.

Umkhonto WeSizwe – The Spear of the Nation, The South African National African Congress' military wing.

Umjibha – Courier between supporters and the guerrillas. Intelligence and counter–intelligence agents. Umijibha is plural. Most of the Imijibha eventually were trained fighters.

Appendix 1
THE ZANU (PF) AND PF ZAPU AGREEMENT

1. The Zanu (PF) and PF Zapu have irrevocably committed themselves to unite under one political party;
2. That the unity of the two political parties shall be achieved under the name Zimbabwe African National Union (Patriotic Front), in short Zanu (PF);
3. That Comrade Robert Gabriel Mugabe shall be the First Secretary and President of Zanu (PF);
4. That Zanu (PF) shall have two Second Secretaries and Vice Presidents who shall be appointed by the First Secretary and President of the party;
5. That Zanu (PF) shall seek to establish a socialist society in Zimbabwe on the guidance of Marxist-Leninist principles;
6. That Zanu (PF) shall seek to establish a one-party state in Zimbabwe;
7. That the leadership of Zanu (PF) shall abide by the Leadership Code;
8. That the present leadership of PF Zapu shall take immediate vigorous steps to help eliminate and end the insecurity and violence prevalent in Matabeleland;
9. That Zanu (PF) and PF Zapu shall convene their respective Congresses to give effect to this Agreement within the shortest possible time;
10. That, in the interim, Comrade Robert Gabriel Mugabe is vested with full powers to prepare for the implementation of this Agreement and to act in the name and authority of Zanu (PF).

Signed at...........this...........day of.............1987.

JOSHUA MQABUKO NKOMO
President, PF Zapu

ROBERT GABRIEL MUGABE
First Secretary and President of Zanu (PF)

Appendix 2
ZIMBABWE DECLARATION OF UNITY

Made at Lusaka, Republic of Zambia, on December 7, 1974

1. ZANU, ZAPU, FROLIZI, and ANC hereby agree to unite in the ANC.
2. The parties recognize the ANC as the unifying force of the people of Zimbabwe.
3. (a) They agree to consolidate the leadership of the ANC by the inclusion into it of the Presidents of ZANU, ZAPU and FROLIZI under the Chairmanship of the President of the ANC.

   (b) ZAPU, ZANU, and FROLIZI shall each appoint three other persons to join the enlarged ANC Executive.
4. The enlarged ANC Executive shall have the following functions:

   (a) To prepare for any Conference for the transfer of power to the majority that might be called.

   (b) To prepare for the holding of a Congress within four months at which:

   (i) A revised ANC Constitution shall be adopted;

   (ii) The leadership of the united people of Zimbabwe shall be elected;

   (iii) A statement of policy for the ANC will be considered.

   (c) To organize the people for such conference and congress.
5. The leaders of the ZAPU, ZANU, and FROLIZI call upon their supporters and all Zimbabweans to rally behind the ANC under its enlarged Executive.
6. ZAPU, ZANU, and FROLIZI will take steps to merge their respective organs and structures into the ANC before the Congress to be held within four months.
7. The leaders recognize the inevitability of continued armed struggle and all other forms of struggle until the total liberation of Zimbabwe.

Abel Tandeyaki Muzorewa
PRESIDENT OF ANC

Ndabaningi Sithole
PRESIDENT OF ANC

Joshua Mqabuko Nkomo
PRESIDENT OF ZAPU

James Robert Dambaza Chikerema
PRESIDENT OF FROLIZI

Appendix 3
DECLARATION OF INTENTION TO NEGOTIATE A SETTLEMENT

1. The prime minister and other cabinet ministers of the Rhodesian government and the president and other representatives of the African National Council met at Victoria Falls on 25 August 1975, and subsequently in Salisbury on 31 October 1975, and thereafter.
2. Both parties took this opportunity of expressing their genuine desire to negotiate a constitutional settlement.
3. Both parties publicly expressed their commitment to work out immediately a constitutional settlement which will be acceptable to all the people of our country.
4. In pursuance of this objective, the negotiating teams from both representatives chosen respectively by the government of Rhodesia and the ANC. At this meeting detailed discussions of all aspects of the constitutional issue will commence and, where appropriate, sub-committees will be established to consider and report to the plenary meeting on particular aspects.
5.1. Representatives of the ANC at any meeting or meetings in Rhodesia whether formal or informal and including both plenary and committee or sub-committee meetings, held in terms of Clause 4 hereof shall have full freedom and/or diplomatic immunity in respect of the following.

(a) From preventive detention or restriction for any act or omission in or outside Rhodesia; and

(b) To enter and depart freely from Rhodesia; and

(c) subject to the confidentiality of the discussions agreed Claus 8 hereof, to exercise freedom of expression and speech at any meeting or meetings in Rhodesia as described hereinbefore in the clause and to communicate freely with any person inside or outside Rhodesia; and

(d) Not be subjected to any observation, harassment or recording by film, tape, other mechanical device, or other means not expressly authorized by themselves.

2. For the purposes of subclause (1) of this Clause-

(i) Any reference to 'Representatives of the ANC' shall be construed as a reference to all persons nominated by the ANC to attend any meeting or meeting in Rhodesia as described hereinbefore in subclause (1) in any capacity whatsoever, whether as delegates, advisers, aides or in any other capacity;

(ii) The freedom and immunities referred to in subclause (1) shall apply and be enjoyed as aforesaid not only at and/or during any of the meetings mentioned hereinbefore, but at all times from and including 31 October 1973, until the conclusion of the Constitutional Conference referred to in Clause 7 hereof;

(iii) Any reference to 'preventive detention' shall be constructed as a reference to detention in terms of any regulations made under the Emergency Powers Act [Chapter 33]

6. Because of the urgent need to end the present uncertainty it was agreed that every effort should be made to expedite the proceedings.

7. When agreement has been reached on the form and content of the Constitutional Settlement, a final Constitutional Conference will be arranged at a mutually agreed venue, which shall be outside Rhodesia. The purpose of this Conference will be to ratify formally the terms of the Constitutional document giving effect to the agreement reached.

8. All those present agreed on the important of preserving the confidentiality of the Constitutional discussions and undertook not to reveal any details to the press and other media.

Signed:

Joshua Mqabuko Nkomo
THE ANC PRESIDENT

Ian Douglas Smith
THE RHODESIAN
PRIME MINISTER

Witnessed:

Witnessed:

Salisbury, 1 December 1975

Appendix 4
THE AGREEMENT

1. The Zanu (PF) and PF Zapu have irrevocably committed themselves to unite under one political party;
2. That the unity of the two political parties shall be achieved under the name Zimbabwe African National Union (Patriotic Front), in short Zanu (PF);
3. That Comrade Robert Gabriel Mugabe shall be the First Secretary and President of Zanu (PF);
4. That Zanu (PF) shall have two Second Secretaries and Vice Presidents who shall be appointed by the First Secretary and President of the Party;
5. That Zanu (PF) shall seek to establish a socialist society in Zimbabwe on the guidance of Marxist-Leninist principles;
6. That Zanu (PF) shall seek to establish a one-party state in Zimbabwe;
7. That the leadership of Zanu (PF) shall abide by the leadership Code;
8. That the present leadership of PF Zapu shall take immediate vigorous steps to help eliminate and end insecurity and violence prevalent in Matebeleland;
9. That Zanu (PF) and PF Zapu shall convene their respective Congresses to give effect to this Agreement within the shortest possible time;
10. That in the interim, Comrade Robert Gabriel Mugabe is vested with full powers to prepare for the implementation of this agreement and to act in the in the name and authority of Zanu (PF).

Signed at............this ....day of......................................1987

JOSHUA MQABUKO NKOMO
President, PF Zapu

Appendix 5
PF Assembly and Rendezvous Points

Assembly Place	Associated Rendezvous Position
1. Hoya	Bukassa store
	Modombwe Mission
2. Magadze	Masemibura School
3. Marymount	
4. Dendera	Muchintiki School
5. Elim Mission	
6. Dzapasi	St. Michaels School
	Mahuzekwa
	St. Annes
	St. Barbara's School
7. Mutandawhe	Pumushana Mission
	Rusitu Mission
	Chikore Mission
8. Makambe	Lower Gwelo
	Hanke Mission
	Chibi
9. Zezani	Mtshabezi Mission
	Masase Mission
	Kafuse School
10. Brunapeg	

Appendix 5

Assembly Place	Associated Rendezvous Positions
11. Madhlambuzi	
12. St. Pauls	Bethesda Mission
	Lubimbi
	Jombe
	Kambo Store
13. Siabuwa	
14. Ruhomechi	Morororo
	Shamrock Mine
15. Magurekure School	

Where the associated rendezvous points were not shown, PF forces (ZIPRA and ZANLA) went directly to their designated Assembly Places.

Index

Accra 49, 50, 52
Adams College 80
Addis Ababa 75
Africa 1, 3, 5, 11-13, 16-20, 22, 26, 34, 35, 45, 46, 49, 50, 54, 55, 59, 73, 75-77, 79-81, 84, 85, 87, 89, 106, 107, 111, 122, 126-130, 134, 162, 167, 174, 176, 177, 180, 184, 189, 192, 194, 207-209, 212, 215, 239, 242, 245, 246, 249, 255, 261, 269, 273, 288
African Episcopal Church
African National Congress 2, 34, 80, 162, 211
African Youth League 34
AK rifle 106, 199, 246, 248
Aldeamentos 171, 172
All African People's Conference 46, 49, 87
Amakhosi Theater Production 280
ANC-Zimbabwe (ANC-Z) 209, 240
Anglo-American Initiative 211, 214, 216
Angola 2, 128, 129, 175, 176, 198, 212, 288, 290
Arrighi 124
Ascot farm 248, 249
Assembly Points 219, 238, 245

Bango 83
Bella, President Ahmed Ben 129
Birchenough Bridge 245
Bonn 264

Botha 192, 194, 239
Botswana 11, 16, 80, 106, 127, 166, 174-176, 185, 187, 200, 208, 212, 262, 268, 271, 280, 281
Brethren in Christ Church 83
British Methodist Church 80
Brown, Ronald 210
Brown, Stuart 91
Bulawayo 13, 14, 16, 22, 23, 35, 54, 55, 59, 60, 80, 81, 83, 89, 90, 175, 186, 195, 199, 245-249, 252, 254, 256, 258, 261, 262, 268, 274, 279-281, 284, 289
Butshe, Gordon 194
Byrd Amendment 211
Byrd, Harry 211

Carrington, Lord 216, 218
Carver, Richard 276
Catholic Bishops 260, 270
Catholic Commission for Justice and Peace 269
Central Intelligence Organization 255
Chadzingwa, Arthur 265
Chambati, Dr. Ariston 264
Chand, General Prem 214
Chikerema, James D. 34, 36-38, 52, 53, 72, 91, 94, 96, 98, 99, 107, 125, 142-148, 150, 162, 209, 284, 308
Chimurenga Day 104
China 1, 50, 96, 105, 122, 163, 190, 221
Chinamano, Josiah 206, 250

The Zimbabwe African People's Union 1961-1987

Chinamano, Ruth 240
Chinyunyu base 286
Chipoera, Parker 180
Chirau, Chief Jeremiah 215
Chirundu 198
Chisiza, Dundizye 34
Chissano, Joaquim 239
Chitepo, Herbert 58, 72, 81, 92, 146, 148, 164, 178
Church of Orphans 102, 108, 127, 168, 169, 305
City Youth League 34
Cold Comfort Farm 93, 147
Comintern 191
Commonwealth Heads of Governments 216
Commonwealth Meeting in Lusaka 215
Conference 41, 46, 49, 50, 52, 53, 56-59, 72, 75, 81, 86, 87, 91, 93, 104, 146-148, 162, 164, 182, 184, 185, 188-190, 208, 210-218, 221, 259, 268, 308, 310
Connemara 245, 247
Conradie, John 124
Consultation Conference, 1976
Council of State 212
Councils 168-170
Criminal Investigation Unit 266
Cuba 96, 122, 167, 221
Cyrene Mission 175

Dande communal land
Dar es Salaam 215
Dare 146, 178
Democratic Party 33, 34, 52, 214, 239
Dengezi
Dube, John 179
Dukwe 200
Dula 9, 83, 136
Dumbutshena, Enock 53, 80, 81, 140
Dyke, Lieutenant Colonel Lionel 257
Dzinashe, Machingura 179, 220

East Germany 203
Eastern Bloc 98
Egypt 52, 97, 98, 110
Entumbane 84, 245-248
Esigodini 60, 89, 243, 245, 269
Essexvale 243, 245
Ethiopia 75
Evangelical Mission 185
Fanonian Apocalypse 96
Fenn, Nicholas 239
Field, Winston 77
Fifth Brigade 258, 262, 263
Fireforce 189
Flower, Kenneth 239
FLPs 177, 180, 181, 210, 211, 215
Ford Escort 193
Formosa 105
Francistown 174, 175, 185, 200
Freedom camp 192
FRELIMO 2, 111, 149, 162-164, 171-174, 176, 194, 207, 219
Friends of Rhodesia Society 192
FROLIZI 145, 148, 150, 208, 308
Front-line Presidents 177
Fuyane, Johanna 81

General Elections 263, 277
Geneva Conference 217
Ghana 49, 76, 96
Giap, Vo Nguyen 191
Ginyilitshe 84
Gordwin, Peter 264
Gore reGukura hundi 203
Gough, Fr. John 270
Grey, Charles 251
Group of Observers 216
Guevara, Che (Ernesto) 131
Guinea Bissau 122
Gumbo, Mhariwa B. 94
Gwaai Gorge 106
Gwaai River Camp 252
Gwaai River Mine Camp 248
Gwanda 89, 186, 199, 264, 268

Index

Gwauya, Webster 179
Gweru 247-249, 254, 266

Hadebe, Mlingo 79
Hampton farm 248
Hani, Chris 126, 127
Heads of Government Meetings 216
High Command 178, 179, 183, 190
HMS Fearless Talks 205
HMS Tiger Talks 205
Home, Lord Douglas 206
Home-Smith Settlement 206
Hondo, Elias 179
Hoskin, Mrs Julia 80
Houser, Rev. George 38, 49
Hove, Mike 81
Huggins, Prime Minister 44, 45, 48, 49, 81

Ibandla Lezintandane 102, 168-170, 305
Ilitshe 9, 10, 82, 83, 136, 305
Iluba Elimnyama 279, 280
Imbongi 84, 279, 305
Imijibha 161, 170, 305
Impi YoMvukela 10, 23-25, 42, 54, 59, 305
Impilo-le 279
Internal Peace Agreement International Commission 215
Inxwala 197

Jan Hofmeyr School 80
Joint High Command 179
Joint Military Command 162

Kagure, Edmund 179
Kahari, Prof. George 264
Kariba 105, 191, 198, 201
Kaunda, President Kenneth 104, 128, 145, 148, 174, 177, 207, 208, 215, 218, 219
Kazungula 106
Khama, President Sir Seretse 80, 177

Khami River 189
Khumalo, Luke 269
King Jr., Martin Luther 41
Kissinger, Henry 211, 212

Lancaster House Conference 214, 215
Lancaster House Talks 201, 217, 219
Land Husbandry Act 42, 43
Law and Order Maintenance Act 134
Lembede, Anton 288, 289
Lesabe, Thenjiwe 82
London 18, 37, 52, 53, 56, 80, 81, 83, 98, 205, 218, 256, 265, 272
London Missionary Society 18, 80, 83
Lusaka 105, 107, 123, 130, 132, 148, 164, 168, 178, 185, 188, 192-194, 200, 201, 208, 209, 215, 216, 308
Lusaka Agreement 209
Lusaka Negotiations 168
Luso, Angola 196
Lusuto Base 201, 202, 246, 286
Lutheran Evangelical Church 198
Lutheran Evangelical Mission 185
Luthuli Detachment 127

Mabhena 268
Machel 176-178, 180, 181, 210, 218, 219
Mahachi, Moven 277
Makarati, William J. 94
Malianga, Morton 72, 91-94, 139
Malta I 214, 215
Malta II 215
Malunga 259, 263, 268
Mana Pools Game Reserve 165
Manama Mission 175, 185
Mandela, Nelson 80
Mangena 162, 179, 181, 194
Manyika 13, 26, 163, 164, 170
Manyonga 97, 284
Mao 122, 188, 189
Maputo 239
Marange, George 94, 263
March 11 Movement 147, 148

Maripe, Knight T. T. 35
Maseko, Major General Javen 179, 244, 251
Mashumbi Pools 248
Masuku, Lamech Lookout 162, 183, 244, 246, 251, 254, 255, 260
Mathe, Brigadier Ben 251
Matopo 16, 59, 83, 84, 89, 175, 248, 276
Matopo Mission 83
Matopo Reserve 83, 84
Mau Mau Uprising 221
Mawema, Machael 53, 60, 206
Mbita, Col. Hashim 177
Mehta, Suman 265
Mgagao Camp 181
Mhanda, Wilfred (a.k. Dzinashe Mashingura) 220
Mhlanga, Cont 279, 280
Midlands 111, 162, 199, 242, 249-251, 256, 260, 264, 266, 268-271, 276, 282, 283
Mig-Fighters
Military Intelligence 99, 183
Milner, Aaron 147
MK 127-130, 162, 269, 286
Mkushi camp 175
Mlambo, Victor 86, 194
Mlilo, Dingani 180
Mohadi, Kembo 268
Monckton Commission 56, 58
Moose, Richard 214
Morogoro camp 170
Moyana, David 179
Moyo, Jason Z. 72, 92, 94, 148, 179, 196
Moyo, Tshaka 254
Moyo, Vote 260, 263
Mozambique 2, 11, 122, 128, 129, 164, 171-174, 179, 181, 187, 192, 200, 207-212, 238, 239, 256, 288
Mpadeni 175
MPLA 2, 167, 184, 209
Mpoko, Report 179
Mpopoma 268

Msika, Joseph 36, 72, 92, 94, 98, 139, 240, 250, 257, 265
Mthimkhulu, Mr. 147, 148
Mtshabezi Mission 175
Mtshabezi Teachers Training College 175
Mubako, Dr. Simbi 104
Muchachi, Clement. 72, 92, 94, 250, 265
Mudzingwa, Dr. Augustus 180
Mugabe, President Robert G. 3, 58, 72, 86-88, 91-94, 109, 140, 146, 167, 177, 180, 181, 200, 210, 211, 215-220, 237, 239-259, 261, 263-267, 269-277, 282, 283, 290, 307, 311
Mulungushi Camp 201
Munangagwa, Emmerson 248, 255, 270-272, 276
Munodawafa, Samuel 94, 183, 265
Munyanyi, Gordon 179
Musarurwa, Willie D. 94, 239, 264
Mutinhiri, Ambrose 180
Muzenda, Simon 179, 271, 272
Muzorewa, Bishop Abel 186, 197, 206-209, 211, 215-217, 220, 261, 308

Native Land Husbandry Act 42
Nazi Germany 111
Ncube, Dan 72
Ndiweni, Chief Khayisa 215
Ndlovu, Akim 96, 162
Ndlovu, Edward S. 35, 142, 144, 147, 183, 268
Ndlovu, Moven 266
Ndlovu, Swazini 251
Nehwati, Francis 35
Neto, Agastino 177
New York 73, 74, 217
Ngwenya, Gilbert 260
Ngwenya, Jane 72, 94, 250
Nhari, Thomas 170, 179
Nhongo, Rex 163, 179
Nigeria 76, 213, 221, 288
Nitram, a private company 249, 254
Njelele 82, 280

Index

Nkala, Enos 54, 72, 91, 92, 140, 237, 241, 257, 265, 273
Nkala, Simon 169
Nkomo, John 250
Nkomo, Joshua 9, 10, 33-38, 41-46, 49-53, 57, 59-63, 71, 72, 74-76, 79-95, 97, 98, 100-103, 110, 133, 136, 138-141, 143, 145-147, 167, 177, 179-181, 183, 191-194, 196, 197, 200, 203, 206, 208-213, 215-221, 237, 239-254, 256, 257, 259-262, 264-266, 268, 270-275, 277, 278, 282-285, 287-290, 307, 308, 310, 311
Nkomo, Nicholas 254
Nkomo, Stephen 268
Nkomo, Thomas Nyongolo 79
Nkrumah, Kwame 49
NSO 183, 190, 194
Ntini, Melwa 33, 40, 54, 86, 91
Ntumbane 14, 252
Ntuta, Jini 250
Nyanda 251
Nyandoro, George B. 34, 36, 38, 45, 52, 53, 72, 94, 143-145
Nyasaland 27, 34, 39, 43, 50, 51, 75, 76, 81
Nyathi, Andrew 186, 254, 286
Nyathi, Isaac 254
Nyikadzinashe, James. 179

OAU 110, 146, 147, 149, 162, 163, 177, 180, 287
OAU Liberation Committee 162, 177, 180
OP Cauldron 108
Operation Hurricane 173
Operation Polo 167
Operation Pygmy 201
Operation Turkey 267
Owen 143, 214

PAIGC 122
Pan-African Freedom Movement 75
Pan-Africanism 55, 73

Parirenyatwa, Dr. Samuel 72
Path to Liberation Document 182
Patriotic Front 177, 181, 184, 211, 213, 307, 311
PATU 106, 196
Pearce Commission 206
Pearce, Lord 206
People's Caretaker Council 94
People's Militia 266
Pfepferere, Tendai 180
Police Internal Security and Intelligence 266
Portugal 107, 128, 288
PV's 171-173

RAR 245
Red Cross 192
Reed, John 124
Refugees 192, 200, 262
Reidy-Daly, Colonel R. F.187
Revolutionary Army 87
Rhodesia Front 27, 77, 128
Rhodesia Light Infantry 108, 134
Richards, Sir Ivor, 211
RLI 165
Roman Catholic Church 270
RSFs 163-165, 168, 173, 174, 187-189, 194, 199-203, 207, 219, 220, 238, 243, 246, 251-253, 257, 261, 267, 285
Rudd Concession 20, 26, 61
Russia 1, 96, 97, 142, 146, 170, 190, 203, 221

Sadza, Saul 180
Salisbury 26, 34-37, 54, 61, 89, 93, 104, 108, 124, 128, 146, 176, 186, 191, 192, 194, 205, 210, 218, 219, 248, 309, 310
SAM-7 Missile
Samkange, Prof. Stanlake 45, 54, 239
Savanhu, Godrey 148
Sekeramayi, Dr Sydney, (or Sekeramai), 259, 270
Selous Scouts 134, 173, 187, 189, 191-193, 195, 196, 200

Semokwe 79-81, 84
Seventh Day Adventists
Shamuyarira, Dr. Nathan 47, 49, 53, 92, 146
Shiri, Perence 276
Sibanda, Masala 254
Sibanda, Mtshumayeli 169
Sibanda, Richard. 85, 169, 194
Silalabuhwa 245, 248
Silundika, George T. 54, 58, 72, 94, 101, 106, 107, 144, 145, 257
Sithole, Edson 45
Sithole, Ndabaningi 58, 72, 91, 92, 138, 211, 240, 308
Siwela, Shelton 148
Smith, Prime Minister Ian, 27, 98, 102-105, 110, 111, 131, 137, 140, 148, 165, 196, 201, 205, 206, 208, 210-213, 215-217, 255, 261, 263, 310
Soames, Christopher 218, 219, 238
Sofasihamba, Association 83, 84
Sofasonke, Association 83, 84
South Africa 1, 11, 13, 16, 18, 19, 22, 26, 34, 35, 80, 81, 87, 89, 106, 107, 111, 127-130, 134, 162, 167, 174, 176, 177, 189, 192, 194, 207-209, 215, 239, 245, 261, 269, 273, 288
Southern Rhodesia 1-4, 6, 24, 27, 33, 34, 36-41, 43, 44, 47, 49-52, 54-57, 59, 60, 62, 63, 73-76, 78-83, 88, 90, 91, 93-96, 98, 100, 103, 107, 109, 110, 128, 138, 139, 211, 212, 214, 217, 288
Southern Rhodesia Railways African Employees' Association 37
Soviet RPG-7
Soviet TM-47
Soviet Union 50, 96, 141, 145, 149, 163, 167, 200
Special Air Service 134, 193
Special Constabulary 266
Squires, Judge Hillary 254
Super ZAPU 261, 262, 268-270
Support Unit 266

Takawira, Leopold 45, 53, 60, 72, 90-94
Tambo, Oliver 107
Tanzania 90, 97, 98, 130, 162, 170, 181, 208, 210, 212, 213
Task Force 257, 258
Tete Corridor 163, 164
Thatcher, Margaret 216
The Turning Point Strategy 188, 191
Todd, Prime Minister Garfield 46, 51, 78
Tongogara, Josiah 179
Tory Group of Observers
Tribal representation 242
Tsangano, Enoch 179
Tshabangu, Owen 143
Tshuma, Nqabe 83
Turning Point Conference 185

UANC 3, 266, 282
UDI 27, 78, 103, 104, 110, 126, 205
Umjibha 131, 132, 166, 305
Umvukela 124
UN High Commission for Refugees 192
Unholy Alliance 128
Unilateral Declaration of Independence (UDI) 27, 61, 76, 78, 95
Union Jack 220
UNITA 167
United African National Congress 211
United College (Teachers') 175
United Federal Party 77, 78, 81
United Nations 27, 72-74, 76, 87, 88, 128, 185, 214
Unity Accord 259, 273-276, 283, 290
University of South Africa 81
Unlawful Organization Act 52, 89
US Civil Rights Movement 38

Vance, Cyrus 214
Vatican (NSO Headquarters) 194
Velapi, Misheck 254
Victoria Falls Bridge 208
Victoria Falls Talks 209
Vietnam 190, 191, 195, 211, 221

Index

Viscount Aircraft 216
Viscount, Flight RH 825
Vorster, President J. 127, 130, 167, 168, 207
Vusa, Alexander Brisk 194

Wallace, George 41
Walls, Lt. General Peter 196, 239, 255
Wampoa College 170
Wanezi Mission 175
Wankie 106, 108, 127, 188, 198
Wankie Game Rerseve 106, 108
War Council 143, 183, 190, 194
Welensky, Prime Minister Sir Roy 51, 128
Wenlock 60, 83, 84, 89, 127, 240
White Train Talks 208
White, Anthony 193
Whitehead, Prime Minister Sir Edgar 51-54, 56, 61, 75-78, 88, 89, 100, 134
Wilson, Prime Minister Sir Harold 56, 103, 205
Wingwiri, Alois Z. 94
Women's Brigade 175
Woods, Kevin 255
Woolendale 248

Yamba, Dauti (David) 48
Young, Andrew 214

Zambezi River 14, 107, 163, 164, 166, 179, 201
Zambia 11, 14, 27, 81, 87, 89, 93, 98, 104, 105, 107, 110, 123, 127, 129, 130, 138, 142, 145, 147, 149, 163, 164, 167, 174-176, 178, 179, 181, 185, 187, 188, 193, 194, 196, 199, 200, 202, 208, 212, 215, 280, 281, 308
Zambia Youth Wing
ZANLA 104, 122, 131, 133, 162-165, 167, 168, 170-174, 176, 177, 179-182, 187, 192, 194, 195, 199-201, 203, 215, 218, 219, 238, 243-252, 258, 261, 286
ZANU-Ndonga 264, 282

ZANU-PF 1-3, 72, 81, 90, 91, 93-97, 101, 102, 104, 109, 110, 125, 127, 131, 136-142, 145, 146, 148, 162-164, 167, 168, 170, 171, 176-181, 184, 199, 200, 203, 205-209, 211, 214, 215, 219, 220, 237-244, 246, 249-251, 253, 255, 257-259, 261, 263-268, 270-277, 281-285, 287, 288, 290, 307, 308, 311
ZAPU 1-5, 9, 10, 33, 34, 62, 63, 71-77, 79-81, 83, 85-111, 121-130, 132, 133, 135-151, 161-171, 174-186, 189-191, 194, 197-201, 203-211, 213-216, 218-222, 237-245, 247-279, 281-291, 307, 308, 311
ZAPU Organizational Structure, 1960's
Zero Hour Plan 197
Zimbabwe Democratic Party 239
Zimbabwe National Army 261
Zimbabwe People's 87
Zimbabwe Republic Police 266
ZIPA 170, 171, 176, 179-182, 186, 187, 220, 287
ZIPRA 87, 106, 108, 109, 111, 123-125, 127-136, 141-143, 145, 146, 149, 150, 161-168, 170-172, 174-177, 179-183, 185-205, 219, 221, 238, 243-257, 260-263, 266-268, 280, 282, 285, 286, 290
Zvobgo, Eddison 91, 257